Acclaim for Peter Ackroyd's

VENICE

"Captures Venice's bewitching effect on the artists, writers and musicians who flocked there over the centuries."
—*The New York Times Book Review*

"Thoughtful, thorough and insightful. . . . Ackroyd is at least as much interpreter as historian. He brings this iconic city to vivid life."
—*Pittsburgh Post-Gazette*

"Ackroyd covers an immense amount of ground with verve and elegance."
—*The Independent* (London)

"Engaging. . . . Peter Ackroyd understands Venice, perhaps even better than modern Venetians. . . . A grand biography of a subject that is as complicated and labyrinthine as Venice's tiny alleyways. . . . Ackroyd might have been the best person to write such an insightful book."
—*The Star-Ledger* (Newark, NJ)

"[Ackroyd] pulls the reader through the city's winding *calli* on a vivid, frenzied journey of discovery. It's an ever-shifting scenery of stern-faced Dogi, secretive statesmen, canny merchants, thieves, whores, artists, geniuses: all jostling for favor in Ackroyd's city of intrigue. . . . Highly evocative. . . . He writes beautifully and succinctly."
—*The Times* (London)

"As close as one can come to possessing or repossessing this magical city. . . . An insider's account of Venice. In an effortless style, he seamlessly stitches the storied city's crazy quilt of past and present. . . . Rendered with a historian's curiosity and a novelist's feel for plot."
—*The Free Lance-Star* (Fredericksburg, VA)

"Fully explores the past and present of this undeniably glorious canal city. . . . Ackroyd's marvelous book certainly adds to the allure of this magical metropolis."
—*Minneapolis Star Tribune*

"Ackroyd has reinvented the art of writing history, at once putting his subject into a myriad of perspectives while infusing his books with a riveting storytelling narrative style."   —*Asbury Park Press*

"Astonishing. . . . Ackroyd is hugely intelligent and formidably industrious; there can be few people, Venetian or foreign, who know Venice better than he."   —*The Daily Telegraph* (London)

"Lovely. . . . Ackroyd's book has everything: romance, death, art, splendor, treachery, espionage, Byzantine architecture, Byzantine politics, Byzantine art filched from the Byzantines themselves."
                                                            —*The Philadelphia Inquirer*

PETER ACKROYD

VENICE

Peter Ackroyd is the author of *Thames: The Biography*, *London: The Biography*, *Albion: The Origins of the English Imagination*, and *Shakespeare: The Biography*; acclaimed biographies of T. S. Eliot, Dickens, Blake, and Sir Thomas More; several successful novels, and the series Ackroyd's Brief Lives. He has won the Whitbread Book Award for Biography, the Royal Society of Literature's William Heinemann Award, the James Tait Black Memorial Prize, the Guardian Fiction Prize, the Somerset Maugham Award, and the South Bank Award for Literature.

VENICE

Pure City

PETER ACKROYD

ANCHOR BOOKS

A DIVISION OF RANDOM HOUSE, INC.

NEW YORK

For
Alison Samuel

FIRST ANCHOR BOOKS EDITION, NOVEMBER 2011

Copyright © 2009 by Peter Ackroyd

The Library of Congress has cataloged the Nan A. Talese/Doubleday edition as follows:
Ackroyd, Peter, 1949–
Venice: pure city / Peter Ackroyd.—1st ed. in the United States of America.
p.   cm.
"Originally published in Great Britain by Chatto & Windus, London, in 2009"—T.p. verso.
Includes bibliographical references and index.
1. Venice (Italy)—History.   2. Venice (Italy)—Social conditions.   3. Venice (Italy)—
Social life and customs.   4. Venice (Italy)—Civilization.   I. Title.
DG672.2.A25 2009b
945'.311—dc22
2010010350

Anchor ISBN: 978-0-307-47379-0

www.anchorbooks.com

Printed in the United States of America
10   9   8   7   6   5   4   3   2   1

Contents

List of Illustrations

Jan van Grevenbroeck, *Venetian Bellmaker's Shop*, 18c. Museo Correr/Bridgeman

Venetian glass in the Pauly showrooms, Milan, 1910. Alinari/Rex Features

Lace workers on Burano, 19c. Collezione Naya-Bohm, Venice/Bridgeman

Ferdinando Ongania, *A Venetian Courtyard*, c. 1880. Museo di Storia della Fotografia Fratelli Alinari, Florence/Bridgeman

A funeral gondola, 1880–1920. Collezione Naya-Bohm, Venice/Bridgeman

Giovanni Pividor, The railway bridge across the lagoon, from *Views of Principal Monuments in Venice*, 1850. Bridgeman

The remains of the Campanile, *La Domenica del Corriere*, 27 July 1902. Cameraphoto Arte Venezia Corriere /Bridgeman

"Windows of the Early Gothic Palaces," from John Ruskin, *The Stones of Venice*, 1851–3

Section Three

Giovanni Bellini, *Leonardo Loredan, Doge of Venice*, c.1501. National Gallery, London/Bridgeman

Joseph Heintz, *Audience with the Doge in the College of the Ducal Palace*, early 17c. Museo Correr/Bridgeman

Pietro Uberti, *Portrait of three lawyers, Orazio Bembo, Orazio Angarano and Melchior Gabriel*, 1730. Palazzo Ducale/Cameraphoto/Bridgeman

Jacobello del Fiore, *Justice and the Archangels*, 1421. Galleria dell'Accademia/Cameraphoto/Bridgeman

The lion's mouth. Palazzo Ducale/Bridgeman

The Pozzi prison, from *Vedute delle Prigioni*, 18c. Museo Correr/Bridgeman

Vittore Carpaccio, *Dream of Saint Ursula*, 1495, Galleria dell'Accademia/Cameraphoto/Bridgeman

Pietro Longhi, *The Tailor*, 1742–3. Galleria dell'Accademia/Cameraphoto/Bridgeman

Pietro Longhi, *The Geography Lesson*, c.1750–2. Galleria Querini-Stampalia/Bridgeman

Pietro Longhi, *The Perfume Seller*, c.1750. Ca'Rezzonico, Museo del Settecento/Alinari/Bridgeman

Madonna of Mercy, 16c. Museo Correr/Alinari/Bridgeman

Paolo Veneziano, *Madonna and Child Enthroned with Two Devout People*, 14c. Galleria dell'Accademia/Cameraphoto/Bridgeman

Giovanni Battista Cima da Conegliano, *The Coronation of the Virgin*, late 15c. Santi Giovanni e Paolo, Venice/Cameraphoto/Bridgeman

Giorgione (Giorgio da Castelfranco), *The Tempest*, c.1506–8. Galleria dell'Accademia/Cameraphoto/Bridgeman

Giovanni Bellini, *Young Woman at Her Toilet*, 1515. Kunsthistorisches Museum, Vienna/akg-images/Erich Lessing

Titian (Tizian Vecellio), *Venus of Urbino* (detail), before 1538. Galleria degli Uffizi, Florence/Bridgeman

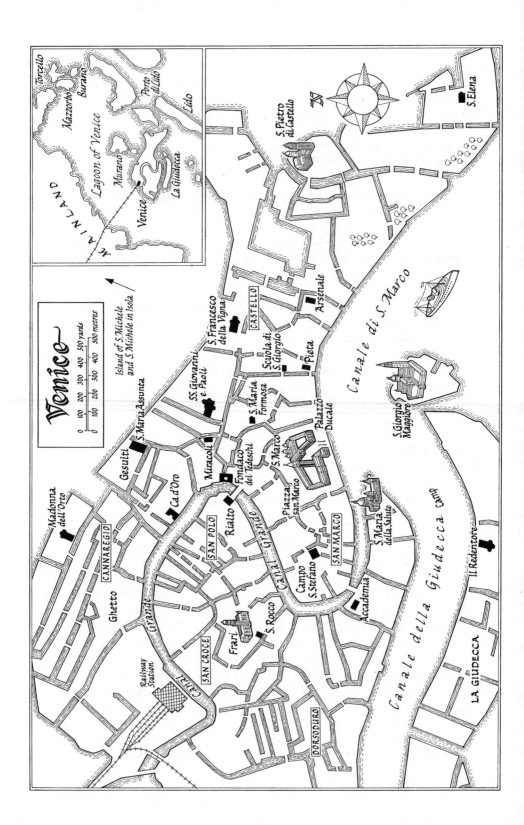

I

City from the Sea

I

Origins

They voyaged into the remote and secluded waters. They came in flat-bottomed boats, moving over the shallows. They were exiles, far from their own cities or farms, fleeing from the marauding tribes of the North and the East. And they had come to this wild place, a wide and flat lagoon in which fresh water from the rivers on the mainland and salt water from the Adriatic mingled. At low tide there were mud-flats all around, cut through with streams and rivulets and small channels; at high tide there were small islands of silt and marsh-grass. There were shoals covered with reeds and wild grasses, rising just a little way above the waters. There were patches of land that were generally submerged but, at certain low tides, rose above the water. There were desolate marshes that the water only rarely covered. The salt marshes and the shore seemed from a distance to make up the same wide expanse, marked with ponds and islets. There were swamps here, too, as dark and uninviting as the waters that the tide did not reach. A line of islands, made up of sand and river debris, helped to protect the lagoon from the sea; these were covered with pine woods.

Although the lagoon was not far from the once great centres of Roman civilisation, it was remote and secluded. This was a solitary place, its silence broken only by the calls of the seabirds and the crash of the billows of the sea and the sound of the wind soughing in the rushes. At night it was the setting of a vast darkness, except in those patches where the moon illumined the restless waters. Yet in the daylight of the exiles' approach the silver sea stretched out into a line of mist, and the cloudy sky seemed to reflect the silvery motions of the water. They were drawn into a womb of light. They found an island. And a voice, like the sound of many waters, told them to build a church on the ground they had found. This is one of the stories of origin that the Venetians told.

The lagoon itself is an ambiguous area that is neither land nor sea. It is approximately thirty-five miles (56 km) in length and seven miles (11 km) in width, taking a crescent shape along part of the coast of north-eastern Italy. It was created some six thousand years ago, emerging from the mud and silt and debris that came down into the Adriatic from seven rivers. The principal among them—the rivers Brenta, Sile and Piave—carried material from the Alps and the Apennines; a city of stone would one day rise on the minute debris of mountains. The swamps and marshes and mud-flats are protected from the sea by a long and narrow bank of sand, divided into islands by several channels; the longest of those islands is now known as the Lido. The channels make openings in the barrier, entrances known as *porti*, through which the sea rushes into the lagoon. There are now three such *porti* at the Lido, at Malamocco and at Chioggia. These tides breathe life into Venice.

It is a continually various and unsettled scene, part mud and part sand and part clay; it is changed by tides, always shifting and unstable. There is a current in the Adriatic that flows up and down from the Mediterranean, and each of the *porti* creates its own distinct basin or force of water. That is why the appearance of the lagoon has altered over the centuries. There is one theory that, as late as the sixth and seventh centuries, the lagoon was essentially a marsh covered by water at high tide. In the nineteenth century, according to John Ruskin, there were times at low tide when it seemed that Venice was marooned on a vast plain of dark green seaweed. The whole lagoon in fact would have become dry land five hundred years ago, were it not for the intervention of the Venetians themselves. The lagoon is now simply another part of Venice, another quarter that happens to be neither land nor sea. But it is slowly returning to the sea. The waters are growing deeper, and more salty. It is a precarious place. Saint Christopher, carrying the infant Christ across the water, was once a popular saint of the city.

There have always been inhabitants of the lagoon. The wilderness could, after all, be fruitful. From the earliest times there were small pockets of people—fishermen and fowlers ready to take advantage of the abundance of wildfowl and marine life as well as the autumnal migration of the fish from the rivers to the sea. The marshes are also a natural place for the harvesting of salt. Salt was a valuable commodity. The Venetians were always known as a mercantile people, but the first stirrings of trade in this area began even before their ancestors had arrived.

The earliest tribes are lost in the darkness of prehistory. But the first recognisable ancestors of the Venetians inhabited the region surrounding the lagoon from the eighth century BC. These were the people who dwelled in the north-eastern part of Italy as well as along the coasts of what are now Slovenia and Croatia. They were known as the Veneti or the Venetkens; Homer refers to them as the "Enetoi," because there is no "v" sound in classical Greek. They were primarily merchants, as the Venetians would become, trading in amber and wax, honey and cheese. They set up great markets, like those which the Venetians eventually established. They traded with Greece, just as Venice would one day trade with Byzantium and the East. They specialised in the extraction of salt from coastal areas, in a way that anticipates the Venetian monopoly of salt production.

They dressed in black, which became the colour characteristically worn by patrician Venetian males. Hercules was the tribal hero of the Veneti, and became a legendary protector of Venice; he is the demigod who acquires by labour what others claim by right. The Veneti traced their descent from Antenor, who led them from the ruined city of Troy. They were well known for their skill in seamanship, and were essentially a maritime people. They submitted, in marital and familial matters, to the authority of the state. These were the people who inhabited cities such as Padua and Altino, Aquileia and Grado. These were the exiles who came for safety to the waters of the lagoon.

Before the time of flight, the Veneti were thoroughly Romanised. By the second century AD they had made a pact with the powers of Rome. In the reign of Augustus the area of the lagoon was part of the Tenth District of Italy and then in the fourth century it became part of the eastern Roman Empire, the Byzantine Empire. The lagoon was already partly settled. On one of the islands, S. Francesco del Deserto, have been found the remains of a Roman port with pottery from the first century and wall plaster of the third century.

The port was no doubt used by those vessels sailing between Aquileia and Ravenna, bearing grain from Pannonia as well as goods and supplies from more distant shores. Amphorae have been discovered here, for the carriage of wine and olive oil that had come from the eastern Mediterranean. The larger ships would dock on the island, their goods then transported to smaller ships for the shallows of the lagoon. There must have been local pilots, therefore, to guide the craft through these exiguous waters. A walkway, dating to the second century AD, has been found beneath the nave of the basilica of S. Maria Assunta on the island of Torcello. Roman remains have been found at a great depth on the island of S. Giorgio Maggiore, and material from the first and second centuries has been discovered on smaller islands. Other finds, on other islands, can be dated from the fourth to the seventh centuries. It has been suggested that the outer islands of the lagoon could have been used as a station for the Roman fleet; it is conceivable, to say no more, that villas were constructed here.

Yet there was a fundamental change in the nature of the lagoon when the exiles from the mainland began to arrive in larger and larger numbers. There was no central exodus, but rather successive waves of migration that culminated in the late sixth century. The Veneti were escaping from invaders. In 403 Alaric the Visigoth descended upon the province of Venetia; in the words of Claudian, the historian of Rome, "fame proclaimed the march of the barbarian, and filled the land with terror." Aquileia and Verona fell, with many of their inhabitants fleeing to the safety of the islands. When the threat of Alaric had passed, some returned home. But others stayed, making a new life in the lagoon. In 446 Attila gained Roman provinces from the Danube to the Balkans and then, six years later, took Aquileia; Altino and Padua were also sacked. Once more the refugees from these disasters fled to the lagoon.

There was a pattern to their movement. The people of Altino migrated to Torcello and Burano, for example, while those from Treviso went to Rialto and Malamocco. The inhabitants of Padua sailed to Chioggia. The citizens of Aquileia moved to Grado, which was itself protected by marshes. They came with craftsmen and builders, with farmers and labourers, with patricians and plebeians; they came with the sacred vessels from their churches, and even with the stones of their public buildings so that they might build anew. But how could they build on such shifting ground? How could they build upon mud and water? It was possible, however, for wooden poles of from ten to a dozen feet in length to be sunk into the mud before reaching a layer of harder clay and dense sand that acted as a firm foundation. This was the "boundary" at the bottom of the lagoon. So there sprang up small houses known as *casoni* made from the wood of poles and boards, with pitched roofs of wattle and reed.

New towns, such as Heraclea and Equilio (Jesolo), were founded by the edge of the lagoon. On the islands were established village communities, with leaders consulting assemblies of the people. The Veneti may also have set up fortified encampments, in the event that the Huns or Goths decided to move against them. But the islanders were fractious and competitive; there was no unity in the lagoons. So in 466, just twenty years after the appearance of Attila, a meeting of all the Veneti of the lagoon was held at Grado. It was decided that each island would be represented by a tribune, and that the tribunes would then work together for the common good. They were, after all, facing the same dangers and difficulties—not least from the depredations of the sea. This was the first sign of the public and communal spirit that would one day manifest itself so clearly in Venice itself.

The Veneti were by the sixth century a defined presence in the region. They were paid to ferry people and goods between the ports and harbours of the mainland. They transported the soldiers of Byzantium from Grado to the river Brenta. They carried officials and merchants to Byzantium itself. Already they were known for their maritime skills. Their boats travelled up the rivers of northern Italy, trading salt and fish to the cities and villages en route.

The first description of these island people comes in a letter sent in 523 to their tribunes by a legate from the Ostrogoth kingdom then prevailing in northern Italy. Cassiodorus was asking them to transport wine and oil across the waters to Ravenna. "For you live like seabirds," he wrote, "with your homes dispersed, like the Cyclades, across the surface of the water. The solidity of the earth on which they rest is secured only by osier and wattle; yet you do not hesitate to oppose so frail a bulwark to the wildness of the sea." He was not quite accurate in his description; there were already some houses constructed from the stone and brick of the mainland. He went on to say that the Veneti "have one great wealth—the fish which suffices for you all. Among you there is no difference between rich and poor; your food is the same, your houses are all alike." Again, this was not quite true. Extant testimonials suggest that, even at an early stage in the development of the lagoon, there were rich as well as poor families. Cassiodorus then added that "your energies are spent on your salt fields; in them indeed lies your prosperity." In this, at least, he was right. And he added the significant detail of "your boats—which like horses you keep tied up at the doors of your dwellings." By good fortune one of these boats has emerged from the mud of the lagoon. Part of a rib of oak, and a hull of lime, have been found on the island of S. Francesco del Deserto; the boat itself dates to the fifth century. It was lying at a level that, in this period, would have been submerged except at times of low tide.

Yet Venice itself was not yet born. It is not shown in a fourth-century map of the region, in which the lagoon is depicted as a sea route without people. Venetian historians claimed, however, that the city was established at midday on 25 March 421, by a poor fisherman known as Giovanni Bono or John the Good. There are advantages to this theory, since the same date has been given to the vernal equinox, the Annunciation and the supposed date of the foundation of Rome. The triple coincidence, as well as the provident arrival of John the Good, is too good to be true; but it is part of the extraordinary Venetian ability to supplant history with myth. As the German poet, Rilke, said on a visit to the city in 1920, "as with mirrors one grasps nothing but is only drawn into the secret of its elusiveness. One is filled with images all day long, but could not substantiate a single one of them. Venice is a matter of faith."

In fact Venice emerged over a century later, after a series of invasions by the Lombards in the late 560s and early 570s. Once more the province of Venetia was overcome by alien tribes. Unlike the Huns, however, they did not wish to plunder and depart. They intended to stay and to settle. They overran what is now called in their name the region of Lombardy. Their arrival prompted a mass exodus of the Veneti. The bishop of Aquileia moved his see to the edge of the lagoon at Grado. The bishop of Padua removed himself to Malamocco, and the bishop of Oderzo sailed to Heraclea. These men were secular as well as religious leaders; they took citizens as well as congregations, ready to create new communities on the water. Burano and Murano were extensively settled, as well as smaller islands such as Ammiana and Constanziaca; these last two disappeared beneath the waves in the thirteenth century, swallowed up by the main enemy of the island people. They have never rested in their battle against the sea.

Venice was born in this flight from the Lombards. The most recent archaeological investigations have dated the first signs of human habitation to the second half of the sixth century and to the seventh century; these remains were situated in the neighbourhood of Castello, in the east of the city, and beneath Saint Mark's Square. There is evidence, too, that in these early years work had already begun on raising the surface of the land and reclaiming earth from water. The settlers fenced the soil with planks and poles; they drained the water; they laid down building rubble, or sediment, or sand from the dunes; they erected wooden palisades to resist the sea. It is the beginning of the city.

The exiles had decided to settle on a favoured group of islands, midway in the lagoon, known collectively as the Rivoalto or the high bank. This eventually became the Rialto, the pre-eminent market-place and emporium of the city. The islands were interspersed with rivulets and water-courses but there was one larger river, a tributary of the Brenta known as the Rivoaltus; this became in time the Grand Canal. Two more solid hills or islands—their description depends entirely upon how you judge the nature of the territory—faced each other along the course of this river. This is where Venice was created. This was land where the exiles could build. It was not easy work. In 589 there are reports of catastrophic flooding throughout the entire region, the force of which was so great that the course of certain rivers was altered. The calamity would have changed the hydraulic structure of the lagoon, but its effects upon the emerging Venice are not known.

Venice did not immediately become the most important city of the lagoon. Grado was the seat of the patriarch; Torcello was the great emporium or market of the region. The ducal seat, as it became known, moved from Eraclea to Malamocco. In the period when Venice was first being settled, there were elaborate building works elsewhere. The basilica of S. Maria Assunta was then being built on Torcello; an inscription on that site is dated 639, and confirms that the church was erected within the context of Byzantine ritual and worship.

The connection with Byzantium is important. The historiographers of Venice insisted that from the beginning the Venetians asserted their independence. There is a famous legend of their leaders telling a representative from Byzantium that God Himself "has preserved us that we may live in these watery marshes, in our huts of wood and wattle. For this new Venice which we have raised in the lagoons has become a mighty habitation for us." They could not be touched by the kings and princes of the world "unless they come by sea, where lies our strength." This is pure myth-making. The Venetians were at the beginning a subject people. The language of the early Venetians had an admixture of Greek, for example, and as late as the last century there were still Graeco-Roman elements in the dialect of the islanders of Burano.

There is some disagreement about the date when the first military commander of the lagoon, or *dux*, was appointed by the Byzantines; it is most likely to have been in the early eighth century. The Venetians came to believe that he had been chosen by the island people themselves, but there is no doubt that this duke or doge reported to the emperor in Byzantium. The appointment of a military commander did not in itself bring any harmony to the lagoon; the early centuries were filled with internecine strife, between island and island or family and family; there are reports throughout the eighth century of civil war, of battles in the forests surrounding the lagoon, of doges being blinded or murdered or sent into exile. But the political institution survived the early crises; a doge reigned in Venice for more than a thousand years, 120 doges in unbroken succession.

Venice is made up of 117 separate islands that were with effort and labour eventually conjoined. There were at first scattered island parishes, some of them dominated by monastic foundations and others by small communities such as fishermen or salt producers. There would have been islands of boat-builders, too. These insular communities were grouped around a church and *campanile* or bell tower; the green or square in front of the church was (and is still) known as the *campo* or field. In the *campo* was a well or cistern of fresh water collected from the frequent rain. The houses were characteristically of reed and wattle construction, although the houses of the more prominent citizens may already have been constructed out of brick and tile. Some islands were dominated by powerful families, exiled from the mainland, who kept their retainers around them to cultivate their gardens or vineyards; the Orio and Gradenigo families, for example, controlled the island of S. Giovanni di Rialto. Each island had its own patron saint.

The island parishes were separated from each other by marsh or water, but waterways had been established to connect them. There was already a pattern of habitation that grew steadily more intensive and determined. The drive towards cohesion was advanced by another invader. In 810 Pepin, the son of Charlemagne, brought his forces to the lagoon in order to claim it for the Frankish Empire. He attempted to storm the ducal seat of Malamocco, and the doge fled to the islands of the Rivoalto for protection. It is said that Pepin followed in pursuit, but that his fleet became enmired in the marshes and receding waters; that he despatched rafts made of timber and brushwood, but that Venetian sailors destroyed them; and that an old woman directed them across the treacherous shallows with the old Venetian instruction, *sempre diritto*—just go on in the same direction. There are unmistakeable intimations here of the army of the pharaoh being overwhelmed by the Red Sea, an analogy upon which future Venetian painters would dwell. Whatever the true circumstances of the defeat, Pepin was forced to abandon his mission. So the place of ducal refuge, Venice, was proved to be the place of safety. It was inviolable, sheltered among the marshes. It was protected by the *lidi* from the sea, and separated from the mainland by water. After the invasion of the Franks, Venice became the ducal seat. It became the centre of the lagoon. It had begun its great career.

It prospered, too, from its secluded position. In a treaty of 814, it was agreed that Venice would remain a province under Byzantine rule but that it would also pay an annual tribute to the Frankish king whose seat was now in Italy. This may sound like a double obligation, but in fact it freed Venice from single domination. It now stood between Franks and Byzantines, between West and East, between Catholic and Orthodox; its central position allowed Venice to steer a somewhat uncertain course, sometimes leaning to one side and sometimes to the other. It also provoked many disagreements among the ruling families of the lagoon, which had different allegiances and loyalties among the parties of the mainland and of the Eastern Empire. Nevertheless the position of Venice effectively secured its independence. One of the clauses of the treaty of 814 allowed Venetian merchant ships to sail freely to and from Italian ports. The Venetians, in other words, were able to trade. They could move between East and West. Venice became, predominantly, a city of merchants.

And it grew very rapidly. Many of the inhabitants of the lagoon soon migrated to the small islands around the Rivoalto. By the end of the ninth century there were some thirty island parishes, and by the close of the millennium there were more than fifty; the effects of a fire in 976, when three hundred houses were destroyed, is a testimony to the dense population. Those parishes grouped closest to the Rivoalto became connected by bridges or canals. The ramparts were erected, the marshes drained, the dykes constructed; the swamps were reclaimed, and the ground made fertile. Some of the major streets, surviving still, were then first laid out as footpaths. Stages and landing stairs were built, some public and some private. Dams were created to prevent the silt from the rivers washing into the lagoon. A service of ferry boats was instituted. Venice became an urban mass, hot and energetic, fixed upon the mud and water. It represented a vast human and communal effort, urged on by necessity and practicality. The goal of common existence was always there. There was a desire to make or to reclaim land, to conquer the water, to unify and to protect the common soil.

Venice in the ninth and tenth centuries was a medieval city, where pigs roamed about the streets and where pastures and gardens interrupted the vista of houses and churches. There were districts with the epithet "In the Marsh" or "In the Wilderness" or "In the Seaweed." The citizens travelled on horseback along the main street, the Merceria, and tethered their animals to the great elder trees which flourished in what is now the Piazza S. Marco or Saint Mark's Square (otherwise simply known as the Piazza). There were flat wooden bridges, without steps, connecting the islands. There were trees along the banks of the canals. On the surrounding islands there were meadows where cattle and sheep grazed; there were vineyards and orchards; there were ponds and small lakes. On the central islands, which gradually coalesced, there were courtyards and narrow alleys that bequeathed to the *calli* of modern Venice their unique circuitry. In front of the houses of stone, or even of the poorer houses of wood and reeds, were short stretches of land; these became the *fondamenta* of the mature city, the streets running along the canals.

By the end of the first quarter of the ninth century the area around what is now Saint Mark's Square had been completed. There was a ducal palace or castle here, together with a large ducal chapel dedicated to the Byzantine Saint Theodore. The more important families also built residences here, to be close to the centre of power. Eventually the fields were cleared to make way for a piazza; a large pool or fishing-pond was filled in, thus forming the piazzetta or little piazza in front of the ducal palace. This duopoly of sacred and secular authority held its place on the site for more than a thousand years.

It was not called Venezia until the thirteenth century. But the region of the lagoon was known as Veneto or Venetia. The Latin term for Venice was always Venetiae, thus registering its origin as a federation of islands or cities. It has nineteen different appellations, ranging from Venegia to Veniexia, thus affirming its multiple identity. It might be construed a portmanteau word, containing Venus and ice.

Venice had no single or distinct origin. The cities of the Italian mainland had been settled through prehistory, their territory defined by their burial grounds and defended by a circumambient wall. They had grown in organic fashion from a ritual centre to an expanding periphery. The reverence for the city is linked to the reverence for place and reverence for the dead who lie interred there. The earliest cities are primeval in origin. From the beginning Venice had no perimeter. It had no outline. It coalesced from a hundred different points. Venice, in a literal sense, had no roots. It had a fluid origin indeed, one written in water. It is insecurely placed in the world. That is why it has always been subject to anxiety, as in the present "Venice in Peril" campaign.

Venice has therefore sought to define itself. It has sought for origins. It has felt obliged to uncover some hidden, or reveal some absent, origin. Machiavelli wrote that "the beginnings of religions and of republics and of kingdoms must possess some goodness by means of which they gain their first reputation and their first growth." This was the problem facing the Venetians. They had, in that sense, no "goodness."

So they invented stories of origin, all of them involving some kind of divine dispensation—not least in the apparently "historical" fact that the Venetians were Christian exiles fleeing from pagan invaders. On the pavement of S. Maria della Salute, in Venice, is carved the inscription *"unde origo inde salus"* or salvation springs from origin. Thus there grew up certain exquisite and elaborate legends of the beginning. They are not to be dismissed. Legends represent the earliest form of poetry.

Venice is the place of legends, particularly of religious legends, just as it has always been a city of miracles.

The people of Altino were in doubt where to flee from the pagans, until they heard a voice from the heavens declaring "Go up into the tower and look towards the stars." When they climbed the tower, the reflections of the stars in the water made a path toward the islands of the lagoon. In another version of this story all the birds of the region were seen, with their young in their beaks, flying towards the islands. The voice out of the bright cloud, calling the exiles in their boats, has been heard at the beginning of this chapter. Eight of the earliest churches of Venice were established by divine decree. Saint Magnus was told in a vision to build a church where he first saw a flock of sheep; this was in Castello. The Virgin Mary appeared in a bright cloud, heralding the rise of S. Maria Formosa. A great assembly of birds chose the site of the church of S. Raphael. A red cloud hovered above the site of S. Salvatore near the Rialto bridge. There were other more secular legends that the Venetians had as their ancestors the Romans or even the Trojans but they, too, can be discounted. These legends, like Venice itself, have no foundation.

The city was built upon water by celestial decree. It was a miracle, in itself, to build upon the sea. Thus it became a city of miracles. It was a predestined spot, a providential site. Everywhere in the Venetian chronicles there is a great and shining image of the city. Venice became part of the history of human redemption. Its divine origin was attested by its perfect constitution, enduring for a thousand years, and even by its mercantile supremacy. In paintings by Venetian artists God the Father and the Holy Spirit preside over Saint Mark's Square. On the Rialto bridge are carved the figures of Gabriel and the Virgin Mary at the moment of the Annunciation. Venice was idealised beyond any recalcitrant historical fact or inglorious episode.

Yet the real origins of Venice, scattered or random as they are, vouchsafe a great truth about the city. They convey certain character-istics, or certain qualities, to the nature of life there. Every organic thing wishes to give form and expression to its own nature; and so, by obscure presentiment and by the steady aggregate of communal desires, Venice took shape. The statue is latent in the marble. The Venetians had no arable land of their own, so they were obliged to earn their living by trade and industry. The city which was half land and half water devised a quintessentially "mixed" constitution in which the various forces of the state were balanced. There was a constant preoccupation, among all sections of the community, with stability and continuity. Where are those qualities more necessary than in a place shifting and uncertain? A city created by exiles became, over the centuries, a home for many and various refugees. Its empire overseas, and its incursions into mainland Italy, were all based upon the necessity for self-preservation. It always perceived itself to be a city under threat. Venice did not emerge from the union of rural peasantry. It was always urban. Venice was not, in its infancy, a feudal society. By the tenth century it was already known as "la civitas Rivoalti," civitas implying a citizen state.

The great and enduring fact, however, was the fight against the sea. Out of this arose the need for common purpose and community of effort. There was no antagonism between the individual and the collective or, rather, the Venetian individual through the centuries subsumed himself or herself within the organism as a whole. It is an organism that, like the human organism, can be seen as a unity. It obeys its own laws of growth and change. It has an internal dynamism. It is more than the sum of its parts. Each aspect of Venetian culture and society reflects the whole.

From the ninth century three Venetian commissioners were appointed to administer and oversee the defence and reclamation of the land. An entire bureaucracy eventually emerged to control the depredations of the sea. From the beginning Venice was a state of intervention. The earliest sea-defences consisted of wooden stakes interwoven with wickerwork; at a later date rivers were diverted, and great walls of stone built against the water.

Land could not be reclaimed, nor islands joined, without the co-operation of neighbour with neighbour and community with community. Dams could not be built without the unity derived from common interest. So from the beginning Venetians were possessed by the idea of communal life. They created the first communal palace, and the first civic square, in Italy. Venice was perhaps also the first city in Europe to benefit from what has been called city-planning, with the deliberate "zoning" of industries and activities along the peripheries of the city. All this was part of the search for the common good. The battle against natural obstacles is the battle for human culture and improvement. It requires immense cohesion, and a social discipline that is best reinforced by religious observance. So emerges the concept of the state as divinely inspired.

Yet we must not discount the character and temperament of these early settlers. Their work was hard and continual, and could not have been carried on successfully without large measures of energy and optimism. These are, or were, the distinctive qualities of the Venetian people. They are, or were, proud of their city. It was one of the characteristics noted by travellers. Yet nature sometimes retaliates against those who attempt to curb it. Certain islands of the lagoon were submerged by the encroaching sea; settlements disappeared or were abandoned. There was always, somewhere in the Venetian soul, the threat of punishment and disaster.

2

Water, Water Everywhere

Venice was, until the building of a railway bridge in the middle of the nineteenth century, a small island, or collection of islands. Venetians were islanders, with all the benefits and burdens that accrue to that especial status. To be insular is to be independent; but it is also to be alone. It secures a measure of safety, but it also attracts attention from those on the larger mainland. It exemplifies vulnerability, even when outward circumstances seem favourable. Yet as an island city Venice survived all the wars and invasions that have beset Italy since the eleventh century; it successfully defied both pope and emperor, French invasion and Spanish incursion, and the continual forays of the other city-states of Italy. If it had not been surrounded by water, it would have been destroyed many centuries ago.

But that separation from the mainland, from Italy and the world, has taken its own toll. Although Venice has been part of Italy since 1866, Italy has largely ignored it. It is considered as somehow extraneous. The Italians do not really think of Venice at all; it belongs to some other realm of fancy or of artifice. On the part of the Venetians the tradition of liberty, and of freedom from the fear of invasion, bred a certain insouciance. The island guaranteed the citizens their self-sufficiency, perhaps, but it also encouraged a certain self-enclosed or self-referential attitude towards the rest of the world. It is still easy, in Venice, to grow indifferent to what is happening elsewhere. Venetians themselves are not particularly concerned with the affairs of what might be called the wider community. From the remoteness, and isolation, can also spring melancholy. Venice is no longer an island, but the island temperament remains.

And of course the islanders must always look out to sea. It is their context. It is their horizon. Where would they be without the sea? The city rests on the silt at the bottom of the sea. It is as much a part of the sea as the tides and the waves. The sea flows between the wooden piles that sustain it. The sea flushes beneath it. There is something innately unsettling about living in Venice. There is salt in the air, and the atmosphere is rendered hazy by evaporation. The haze easily becomes sea mist or sea fog. The air seems to melt above the buildings. The salt and damp leave silvery traces on the whitened walls, as if they were made out of mother-of-pearl. The birds flying above them are the seagulls. And there is seaweed floating along the canals beside them.

So there are images of the sea throughout Venice. The floor of the basilica of Saint Mark gently undulates, as if the congregation were walking upon waves. The area of marble slabs, on the floor of the central crossing of that church, was known in the sixteenth century as *il mare*. The marble columns of Saint Mark's are veined or striated like the waves. In the other churches of the city we might note the popularity of "dolphin capitals" and the motif of the shell. Ruskin described the imposing houses along the Grand Canal as "sea-palaces." In maps of Venice, particularly those from the seventeenth and eighteenth centuries, the shape of the city is reminiscent of a fish or dolphin. The islands and sand-ridges, out of which Venice was made, seemed to the first settlers like the backs or *dorsi* of slumbering whales; one area of modern Venice is still called Dorsoduro or hard back. On top of one of the two presiding pillars in the piazzetta, Saint Theodore is astride a crocodile. There are crabs and dolphins on the capitals of the ducal palace. It would not be wonderful to meet a leviathan, or what in *Moby-Dick* Herman Melville calls "strange shapes of the unwarped primal world," swimming at times of *acqua alta* in Saint Mark's Square. It would not be wonderful to see a great polyp or medusa wallowing in the Grand Canal. It is a sea city.

The first impression of Venice may also be one of the sea. Goethe saw the sea for the first time in his life when he came to the city in the autumn of 1786; he glimpsed the Adriatic from the arched window of the campanile in Saint Mark's Square. Ruskin arrived in Venice some fifty-five years later and, in his autobiography, he writes that "the beginning of everything was in seeing the gondola-beak come actually inside the door at [the hotel] Danieli's, when the tide was up, and the water two feet deep at the foot of the stairs." To find the waves of the Adriatic lapping within the city—to find the sea changing the nature of the stone buildings all around him—that was the great enchantment.

The moon rules Venice. It is built on ocean shells and ocean ground; it has the aspect of infinity. It is the floating world.

The sea embodies all that is changing and variable and accidental. It is the restless and wilful element. It emerges in endless variations of colour and surface pattern. The paintings of Titian and Tintoretto have been said to manifest a "sea" of light, in which shape is fluid and ambiguous; the Venetian school of painting has been characterised as one of flowing colour rather than of form and outline, a curvilinear impulse that creates its own weight and volume. All is in flux. You glimpse the movement of the sea in Venetian statuary as well as Venetian painting. The mosaics of the city favour the depiction of the various biblical legends of the sea. Thus in the basilica of Saint Mark's can be found "The Miraculous Draught of Fishes," "His Walking on the Water" and "The Stilling of the Tempest." There are certain churches that might have risen out of Neptune's kingdom. The church of the Gesuiti, or S. Maria Assunta, has a baroque interior in which great cascades of grey and green and white marble are supposed to imitate wall hangings. But they more closely resemble waves, waves flowing and crashing down the sides of the church until arrested in a moment of silence and stillness. The floor of green marble might have furnished some cave beneath the ocean, as rays of light penetrate the marine gloom of the interior.

The rhythmic intelligence of the Venetians has informed much of the architecture of the city. The oncoming sea changes the perception of structure along the Venetian canals, where the buildings seem more delicate and attenuated. The façades of the churches undulate, weight-less and unstable, against the surface of the water like shells at the bottom of a rock pool on the seashore. The architecture of Venice is horizontal in mass, like the sea. From a distance, across the lagoon, the impression of the city is of flatness along the horizon. It is perpetually in motion. It is baroque and mannerist rather than classical; it shimmers, as if seen through water; it is encrusted with ornament like a coral reef.

Venetian craftsmen were well known for their work in satin, where the gleamings and shimmerings of a particular fabric were known as "watered silk." To work in silk was known in Venice as *dar'onda all'amuer*, or to make waves on the sea. There is an especial type of Venetian risotto, more liquid than elsewhere, that is known as *all'onda* or with waves. A sponge found in the Aegean is known as *enetikos* or the Venetian. In the last century you could buy in the tourist shops of Venice small ornaments made from the pearl shells found in the Lido, known as *fiori di mare* or the flowers of the sea. They are the only flowers indigenous to Venice.

There are other deep correlations between place and spirit. Venetian society has been described as fluid and ever-changing. Of Venetian politics Sir Henry Wotton, the English ambassador to Venice in the early seventeenth century, said that it "fluctuated, like the element of which the city was built." That is the reason why Venetian historiographers were intent upon emphasising the continuity and stability of their society. They were always aware of the motion and restlessness of the sea within Venetian polity. At the heart of *la Serenissima* was a horror of transience, like the Venetian sailor's dread of the sea. As the Venetian poet of the late sixteenth century, Veronica Franco, put it, "the sea itself yearns towards this city." This may be considered a compliment, as long as the sea does not come too close.

It has been said also that the character of the Venetian people is like the tide, six hours up and six hours down according to the proverb. In fact there is a dialect phrase that the Venetians use to describe them-selves—*andara alla deriva,* to be adrift. The mobility and lightness of the Venetian temperament are well known. The Venetians themselves have songs and proverbs about the sea. *Coltivar el mare e lasser star la terra*—cultivate the sea and leave the land to itself. There were once many popular songs that opened with the same phrase, *in mezo al mar.* In the middle of the sea is—what? Not familiar things. Not beautiful things. In the middle of the sea, according to the songs, are strange presentiments and terrifying apparitions. Here is a smoking chimney coming out of the waves. Here is an image of a dead lover. There is no celebration of the charm or poignancy of the sea, but rather a recital of its perils and its strangeness.

There are many legends and superstitions of the sea within popular Venetian lore. It is a shifting city, between sea and land, and thus it becomes the home for liminal fantasies of death and rebirth. According to the English traveller, Fynes Morisson, there was a statue of the Virgin in Venice which was always saluted by passing ships; it was surrounded by wax candles, burning perpetually in gratitude for her saving lives at sea. It is said that the sharp prow of the Venetian gondola was a replica of the shining blade of one of the soldier saints, Saint Theodore. On the approach of a storm Venetian sailors would take up swords and place one against the other in the shape of a cross. It was also recommended that the sailor take out a knife with a black handle and cut the air in the face of the coming storm.

Yet the sea is an intimation of impermanence. All things come from, and dissolve into, the water. It is enveloping. There is no evidence that the Venetians ever really loved the sea. It was essentially the enemy. Byron declared that the Venetians did not know how to swim and were possessed by the fear "of deep or even of shallow water." The Venetians always prided themselves on having "dominion" over the sea, but that mastery was provisional and fearful. There was a constant fear of inundation. Of course it was the path to wealth, but the consequence was that the preponderance of their trade and power was at the mercy of the sea. The sea represented evil and chaos. It was cruel, and it was also divisive. The terror of complete submersion could also be seen in part as a nervous apprehension of divine anger. That is why there were ceremonies designed to propitiate the god or gods of the water. They may have been nominally directed towards the Christian God, but there was an element of awe and fear within the Venetian state that derived from much older creeds.

The city guarded the water, too. In the ducal palace the seat of the *Magistrato alle Acque*, or Master of the Waters, was adorned by an inscription stating that "The city of Venice benefiting from divine Providence was founded in water surrounded by water with water for walls. Thus, whoever might dare in whatever way to bring injury to these waters must be judged enemy of his country . . ." It ended with the declaration that "this law has been reckoned eternal."

Each spring, on Ascension Day, there was a ritual that became known as "the marriage to the sea"; the spouse was the doge of Venice taking for his bride the turbulent waters. After mass in Saint Mark's the doge and his retinue rowed into the lagoon in the doge's own boat, the *Bucintoro*, followed by the nobles and guilds of the city. The doge halted at the part of the Lido where the waters of the Adriatic and the lagoon meet. The patriarch of Venice then emptied a large flask of holy water into the mingling currents. The waters of the earth and the waters of the spirit became indivisible. The *Bucintoro* was described by Goethe as "a true monstrance," which means the receptacle where the holy eucharist may be displayed. So it becomes a holy grail tossing upon the waters, spreading benediction with a ritual of healing.

On the prow of the ship the doge took a marriage ring of gold and threw it into the water with the words "We espouse thee, O sea, as a sign of true and perpetual dominion." Yet what true dominion could there be in such a union? One of the attributes of the ring is fertility, so the festival can be construed as one of the oldest of all ceremonies. It might also have been an act of supplication, designed to placate the storm-tossed and minatory sea. It could also have been a maritime version of casting the runes; there is a long tradition of rings thrown into the sea as an act of divination. All these meanings converge in this ancient rite of union with the sea, performed in spring at that place where the "inside" and the "outside" embraced. At a later date one of the punishments for heresy was death by drowning, when the condemned were rowed out to sea and despatched into the waters. These maritime executions might in turn be seen as sacrifices to the sea-gods.

At the close of one of these Ascension ceremonies, in 1622, there was a violent earthquake in Venice. Just as the doge and his courtiers returned from their voyage of celebration, a slow and regular thunder beneath the earth lasted for several seconds. Everything trembled but nothing, apart from a chimney, fell. There have been other quakes in the lagoon. It is an unstable area in every sense. An earthquake is recorded in 1084, when the campanile of S. Angelo was dislodged. Towards the end of the twelfth century there were simultaneous upheavals in Saint Mark's Square and on the island of Torcello, suggesting that there is a "fault" lying between them. There was a great earthquake on Christmas Day 1223, and then again in 1283 when the shock was followed by a great inundation. On 25 January 1384, another earthquake set all the church-bells of Venice pealing at the same time; it was followed by another shock on the following day, and these quakes were repeated at intervals over an entire fortnight. The Grand Canal was empty, but the streets were full of water.

The weather of Venice is sea-weather; the air is damp and salt-laden, conducive to fog and mist. If the climate is equable, that may in part be the position of Venice. Averroes, the twelfth-century philosopher, was the first to calculate that Venice was at a latitude of forty-five degrees, at the middle point between the equinoctial and the northern Pole. It is another example of the extraordinary balance of Venice between the geographical regions of the earth. The climate is mild, compared with much of North Italy, because it is environed by the sea. The spring is delicate and fresh, the energetic wind blowing from the Adriatic. The summer can be sultry and oppressive but, once the sun has gone down behind the Friulian mountains, the air is freshened by the breezes from the sea. The autumn is the true season for Venice. It has an autumnal air, the air of melancholy and departure. The Venetian painters, Carpaccio and Bellini, bathed their canvases in an effulgent autumnal light.

There is, especially in autumn, the possibility of rain. A subdued greyness then haunts the air, and the sky is the colour of pearl. The rain can be persistent and torrential. It soaks through the most protective clothing. It can be blinding. Then the rivers may burst their banks, and the rising waters around Venice turn to a jade green. The best description of the Venetian rain is found in Henry James's *The Wings of the Dove*, where he describes "a Venice of cold lashing rain from a low black sky, of wicked wind raging through narrow passes, of general arrest and interruption, with the people engaged in all the water-life huddled, stranded and wageless. . . ." The city of water is blockaded by water, as if the natural elements were pursuing their vengeance against the most unnatural city.

The "wicked wind" may come from several points. An east wind blows in from the sea, refreshing in the warmer months but crueller in the colder seasons of the year. A wind from the north-east, the *bora*, brings the colder air from the northern region of the Adriatic. A humid wind comes from the lagoon, known as the *salso* because of its salt-laden content. Some people say that it smells of the algae and seaweed of the surrounding waters. The salt and damp penetrate the houses of Venice; the paint flakes, and patches of plaster fall from the walls. The bricks crack and eventually crumble.

There are gusts of wind that pass very quickly, and eddies or squalls of circulating air. Sir Henry Wotton wrote of "flashing winds." All this is of the nature of the sea. There is a south-westerly wind, too, once called *garbin*. It may be of this wind that Saint Bernardino of Siena wrote in 1427. He asked a correspondent, "Were you ever at Venice? Sometimes of an evening, there comes a little wind which goes over the face of the waves and makes a sound upon them, and this is called the voice of the waters. But what it signifies is the grace of God, and the breath breathed forth by Him." Even the weather of Venice was once deemed sacred.

But the most celebrated wind is the *scirocco*, the warm wind that comes from the south-east and can persist for three or four days. There is a *scirocco di levante* and a *scirocco di ponente*, a hot *scirocco* and a cool *scirocco*; there is even an elusive wind called the *scirocchetto*. The *scirocco* itself has been blamed for the Venetian tendency towards sensuality and indolence; it has been accused of instilling passivity and even effeminacy within the citizens. Why should people not be moulded as much by climate as by history and tradition? The outer weather can make or unmake inner weather.

Yet some weeks of the winter can be harsh, a potent reminder of the Alps and the northern snows. The most frequent weather lament concerned the bitter cold. In the winter of 1607–08 those who went fowling in the lagoon were on occasions frozen to death, and there were reports of travellers being surrounded and killed by packs of starving wolves. At the beginning of the eighteenth century came a famous "Year of the Ice" in which provisions were brought to the frozen city by sledge. In other winters the lagoon also froze, and the Venetians could walk over to the mainland. In 1788 great bonfires were lit on the Bacino, the basin of water in front of the piazzetta; stalls and booths were erected on the ice, in the Venetian equivalent of a Frost Fair. In 1863 great sheets of ice went up and down the Grand Canal, flowing with the tide, for a month. Venice was then truly the frozen world, the ice covering the houses and palaces as well as the water. The light was blinding. Venetian houses were not built for the cold; the great windows and the stone floors of the larger dwellings made them almost intolerable during the blizzards of winter. Yet there is still something inexpressibly delightful about Venice in the snow, the whiteness creating an enchanted kingdom where what is fluid has become crystal; the quiet city then becomes wholly silent beneath the panoply of snow.

But there are winter weeks of not quite snow and not quite rain. These may become the weeks or days of fog. The iridescent mist or haze is then enveloped by the myriad fogs that creep in from the sea. The grey Istrian stone becomes an outpost of the fog, a sentinel of consolidated fog looming out of the gloom. As the Esquimaux have

many words for ice, so the Venetians have many names for the fog—
nebbia, nebbietta, foschia, caligo. In the midst of the *nebbia*, it is as if heavy
rain-clouds had come to rest upon the earth and water. Nothing can be
seen or heard. The fog sometimes shrouds the city so that the only
sounds are those of bells and muffled footsteps; if you take the
vaporetto, or water-bus, that goes around the city you disappear within
the white curtain about fifty yards (about 45 m) from the shore; all that
is visible of Venice are the posts carrying lights. The city only rises
before you when you arrive at the next stage.

There are portents for flood. The air becomes heavy and still; the
roar of the sea can be heard breaking against the Lido. The waters in
the canals stir uneasily, and become more green with the influx of the
sea. The tide is driven forward by the wind. The water rises to the edge
of the *fondamenta* but then, more alarmingly, it begins to well up
beneath the city itself. It spouts up through the storm drains and
between the paving stones; it seeps through the foundations, rising
higher and higher; it washes against the marble steps of the churches.
The city is at the mercy of waves that seem to be of its own making.
When the sirens sound, Venice prepares for another *acqua alta*.

This high water, flooding the *fondamenta* and the *campi*, making a
lake of Saint Mark's Square, invading houses and hotels, is not unusual
in the city. One chronicler gave an account of a great flood in 589,
although assuredly there were many before that date. They may have
been so common that they deserved little notice. Other floods are
recorded in 782 and in 885, when water invaded the entire city. They
have been occurring ever since. In 1250 the water rose steadily for four
hours and, in the testimony of a contemporary, "many were drowned
in their houses or died of the cold." It was believed that the floods were
provoked by demons and bad spirits, while the only protection lay in
invocations to the saints who guarded Venice. At a later date there was
less recourse to supernatural help. In 1732 the area of the piazzetta,
facing the lagoon, was raised by one foot (0.3 m) on a calculation that
the sea at Venice rose three inches (76 mm) in every century. This was
an underestimate.

The *acqua alta* is part of a natural cycle, occurring when wind and
tide and current converge in what is for Venice a fatal embrace; the
bora and the *scirocco* can both cause surges of storm in the sea. There is
also the phenomenon of the *seiche*, an oscillation or standing wave in

the relatively shallow waters of the Adriatic. But if Venice is sinking, it is in some measure due to the removal of water by industry from artesian wells. When the water was taken from the silt and the clay, the water table was lowered—and, with it, Venice. The deepening of waterways within the lagoon, and the reclamation of marsh-land, have also increased the danger of flooding.

There are several inundations in every century, therefore, but in recent years they have been increasing in size and frequency. In the 1920s there were 385; in the 1990s there were 2,464. In November 1966, the flood reached a height of six feet four and a half inches (1.94 m). The *scirocco* blew for two days, keeping the murky and polluted water locked within the lagoon. At the time some believed that it would mean the death of Venice.

When the rain came, it was collected within the stone gutters of the churches and houses; it ran through the pipes and then through conduits until it reached the underground cisterns beneath every *campo*. There the water filtered through a body of sand before penetrating the well shaft. It was fresh and pure. The wells, or *pozzi*, were ubiquitous. At the middle of the nineteenth century there were still 6,782 remaining in the city, Byzantine or Gothic in construction. An immense well was sunk in the fifteenth century, in the middle of Saint Mark's Square. Two great public cisterns were built in the court-yard of the ducal palace, from where the water-carriers or *bigolanti* would carry their precious commodity. They were the peasant women of the Friuli, who wore bright skirts, white stockings and hats of straw or felt; they wandered barefoot through Venice, with their copper buckets, calling out *"acqua—acqua fresca."* It was a mournful, as well as a melodious, cry.

For a city built upon water, water itself was sacred. It is what in the gospel of John is called "living water." The well-heads themselves were highly decorated as a symbol of their significant content. They were embellished by fragments of altars, pieces of religious statuary, and the stones of ancient temples, as a token of their spiritual presence. There were accounts of miracles being performed by or beside the wells. In the plague of 1464 a monk was saved from extinction by a cup of water drawn for him by a knight from a local well. The knight was later identified as Saint Sebastian and, from that time forward, the *pozzo* became known as Saint Sebastian's Well. Water is holy. The Byzantine well-heads were sculpted with a range of religious symbols, including the cross and the palm tree; they were cylinders of marble, that might have been glimpsed in any eastern city. The Gothic well-heads, which resembled the capitals of great pillars, displayed figures both naturalistic and grotesque. Yet the wells often ran dry. Venice, on water, was often in need of water. After storms the wells were marred by salt water. It was a general practice for boats to be despatched to the rivers Bottenigo and Brenta in order to pick up fresh supplies. Towards the end of the nineteenth century artesian wells were established on the mainland to guarantee a more bounteous flow.

Water was the staple of life, and so the wells became central to the social routine of each parish. The iron lid that closed the mouth of each well was opened at eight in the morning, so there were always knots of people beside it during the day. It is the most common view in photographs of "old" Venice. The well defined the intimacy and density of the parish. Water has always been the great unifier and leveller, and in many respects Venice was considered to be an egalitarian city. The well was a symbol of public beneficence, a visible token of the wise stewardship of the city.

But of course water is the life and breath of Venice's being in quite another sense. Venice is like a hydropic body filled with water, where each part is penetrated by another. Water is the sole means of public transport. It is a miracle of fluid life. Everything in Venice is to be seen in relation to its watery form. The water enters the life of the people. They are "fluid"; they seem to resist clarity and precision. When the more affluent Venetians built villas on the mainland, they always chose sites as close as possible to the River Brenta. The Venetian painter, Tintoretto, loved to depict flowing and gushing water; it expressed something of his own spirit. In the work of Giorgione, and of his Venetian school, there are constant allusions to fresh and running water, to wells and pools and lakes. In myth and folklore water has always been associated with eyes, and with the healing of eyes. Is it any wonder, then, that Venice is the most visually seductive of all the cities of the world?

The endless presence of water also breeds anxiety. Water is unsettling. You must be more alert and watchful in your perambulations. Everything shifts. There is a sense of otherness. The often black or viscous dark green water looks cold. It cannot be drunk. It is shapeless. It has depth but no mass. As the Venetian proverb states, "water carries no stains." This formless water has therefore been used as a metaphor for the human unconscious. In his essay, "The Visions of Zosimos," Carl Jung relates that the spirit is hidden in water like the fish. Venice has been depicted as a fish. This wondrous water, infused with spirit, represents the cycle of birth and death. But if water is the image of the unconscious life, it thereby harbours strange visions and desires. The close affiliation of Venice and water encourages sexual desire; it has been said to loosen the muscles, by human imitation of its flow, and to enervate the blood.

Yet Venice reflects upon its own reflection in the water. It has been locked in that deep gaze for many centuries. So there has been a continuing association between Venice and the mirror. It was the first city to manufacture mirrors on a commercial scale, and by the seventeenth century was fashioning the largest mirrors in the world. The plate glass for mirrors had been created by the end of the fifteenth century. Two of the greatest of all Venetian artists, Giovanni Bellini and Titian, painted young women in the act of gazing at themselves in a mirror. In both of the paintings there is a mirror poised behind the head, and one raised towards the face. The date of both paintings has been given as 1515, only eight years after the government of Venice licensed the making of mirrors on the island of Murano. The artists were publicising Venetian commodities or, rather, they shared the Venetian preoccupation with luxury goods. Yet at the same time they were contemplating in painterly terms the contrast between the true surface and the glassy surface, a duality of which they were well aware in the world all around them. The young woman might have been Venice herself, sitting and admiring rather pensively her own reflection.

The image in the mirror may in some sense be a guarantee of identity and of wholeness. The root of narcissism lies in anxiety, and the fear of fragmentation, which may be assuaged by the sight of the reflection. The Virgin Mary, in the Book of Wisdom, is lauded as "a spotless mirror of God"; Venice always associated itself with the Virgin. But of course the image in the mirror is a false self; it is hard, abstract and elusive. It has been said that the Venetians are always aware of the image of themselves. They were once masters of the display and the masquerade. They were always acting. One of the favourite pastimes of Venetian audiences in the eighteenth century was the use of opera glasses trained upon each other.

It is a place of doubleness, and perhaps therefore of duplicity and double standards. Travelling on the newly built railway Richard Wagner was intent upon "looking down from the causeway at the image of Venice rising reflected from the waters beneath," when his companion "suddenly lost his hat out of the railway car window when leaning out in delight." The reflection is delightful because it seems to be as substantial and as lively as that which is reflected. When you look down upon the water, Venice seems to have no foundations except for reflections. Only its reflections are visible. Venice and Venice's image are inseparable.

In truth there are two cities, which exist only in the act of being seen.

3

Mirror, Mirror

There is in Venice an abiding attachment to the surface. It has become commonplace that in the city only the fronts of houses were worth embellishment or decoration. Most of the Gothic façades are simply that—screens that bear no relation to the organic structure of the buildings themselves. It is one of the strangest aspects of a city that in certain respects resembles an ornamental shell. The rich plaster and stucco may conceal decaying brickwork, and Ruskin speculated on the "duplicity" of Saint Mark's where internal and external ornamentation were quite distinct. The city was built in brick but disguised by marble.

It seemed to matter not at all that behind the sumptuous façades the grand Venetian houses were often cold, dirty and uncomfortable. In similar fashion, among the owners of these houses, there was an outward show of prodigality combined with avarice and penny-pinching at home. That was the Venetian way. It was not at all usual to invite guests, for example, into the house itself; that inward space was confined to relatives and the most intimate friends. The English poet, Thomas Gray, remarked that in their domestic lives Venetians were "parsimonious to a degree of nastiness."

Honour was important in Venetian society, as in others, but the mark of honour was what was known as *bella figura*; it might be interpreted as the art of keeping up appearances. One of the great engines of Venetian life was, and is still, the fear of criticism. Everything must be done according to form, and for the sake of form. That form may hide malfeasance and corruption, but it is important that it remains in place. It resembles the façade or screen of the Venetian house.

The twin imperatives of show and spectacle, design and ostentation, move through every level and every aspect of Venetian society. A sixteenth-century account of a bankrupt banker of the Rialto explained in passing that "this market and the city of Venice are naturally very inclined to love and trust in appearances." The painters of Venice lingered over the rich surfaces of the world. The architecture of Venice had the artifice and outwardness of the theatre. Venetian music has always been concerned with outward effectiveness rather than internal coherence. The literature of Venice was oratorical in nature, whether in theatre or in popular song. No other city-state in Italy was so concerned with problems of rhetoric and style. Venetian ceilings are characteristically false ceilings, suspended somewhere beneath the beams. In the eighteenth century display and spectacle became a way of masking the decay and failure of public policy. It is a constant note, one that provides a clear insight into the identity of the city and its people.

The contemporary restoration of many buildings in Venice is a case history of seeming rather than being. In their devotion to appearances the restorers have created an unreal city, bearing little relation to its past or to its present. The architects and designers were concerned to reprise the aesthetic contours of the city; but these were imagined rather than real, the fruit of wishful thinking and nostalgia. What happened in practice is that they remodelled or modified the architectural language of the past to make it fit their own preconceptions of how Venice really ought to look. Fluting and veneer were removed; horizontal lines were straightened and strengthened; windows were altered to conform to the structure; balconies were narrowed for the sake of overall harmony; attics were taken out, and baroque fixtures replaced by Gothic. For some reason the stronger shades of red and yellow have spread in a city where they did not exist before. The style was known as *ripristino*. It amounted to the creation of fakes. It is an example of a general malaise of modern Venice, first recognised by the German sociologist Georg Simmel in the early part of the twentieth century. He remarked that the city represented "the tragedy of a surface that has been left by its foundation." That does not render Venice superficial. Quite the contrary. The attention to surface, without depth, provokes a sense of mystery and of unknowability.

For many centuries Venice has been famous for its glass-making, now the preponderant industry on the island of Murano. What is the attraction of glass for the city of the sea? Glass is material sea. It is sea made solid, its translucence captured and held immobile. It is as if you could take up handfuls of the sea and turn it into brocade. Venice is the place for this. The first writer on the making of glass in Venice, Georgius Agricola, wrote in the early sixteenth century that the glass was formed out of "fusible stones" and "solidified juices," an apt translation of Venice's position between water and stone. Sand becomes crystal. It is not Venetian sand, however. It came from Syria and then later from Fontainebleau in France. Yet the Venetian glass-makers were the most ancient, and the most skilled, in the world.

Glass-makers had worked in the lagoon from the time of the Romans. There are finds of glass from the fourth to the seventh centuries, and a seventh- or eighth-century furnace in Torcello shows evidence of Roman manufacturing conditions. Folk tradition always asserted the continuity of glass-making on the islands, and there may indeed have been some legacy of inherited skills. Yet much of the expertise derived from Byzantine and Islamic sources. It is another example of the balance Venice maintained between two worlds.

An individual glass-maker, a certain "Domenico," is first mentioned in a document of 982. A Venetian guild of glass-makers was established in the thirteenth century. In that same century, for fear of fires, the glass-manufacturers were transferred to the island of Murano. There they flourished. But they were in a sense imprisoned by the state. They could not move to any other part of Italy. To reveal any of the secrets of Venetian glass-making was to incur the death penalty. Any workman who escaped to the mainland was hunted down and, where possible, forcibly retrieved. It is, if nothing else, a token of the importance of the trade in the Venetian economy. Glass-making was vital to the city's economic success. It would be absurd to suggest that the Muranese workmen believed themselves to be oppressed, or were forced to labour in any climate of fear, but the threat of state punishment is an apt token of the constant presence of the Venetian state in all aspects of Venetian life. It was by no means a free society. It was an insular, and therefore enclosed, society.

They made goblets and ewers, bottles and flasks, beads and chalices, lamps and windows, pitchers and eye-glasses, as well as a range of ornamental objects created out of *cristallo*, a malleable form with all the translucence and brilliancy of rock crystal. They could render a glass so fine that it was reputed to burst into fragments if it came into contact with poison. The workmen of Murano created glass that had the colour of milk, glass that mimicked the texture of ice, glass threaded with copper crystals. Types of glass resembled marble or metal or porcelain. From the fifteenth century forward, in fact, Venetian glass grew ever more elaborate and ornate. It became a luxury, at a time when Venice had become the provider of luxuries of every description. Objects became ever more useless and ever more expensive. In 1500 one contemporary noted of the Muranese glass industry that "there is no kind of precious stone that cannot be imitated by the industry of the glass-workers, a sweet contest of man and nature."

Venice had already been involved in that contest, sweet or otherwise, for many hundreds of years. It is another reason for its perfect adaptation to the trade. An early seventeenth-century English traveller, James Howell, marvelled how a furnace fire could "convert such a small lump of dark Dust and Sand into such a precious clear Body as Crystal." But had not Venice wrought such a transformation upon itself, from the dark dust and sand of its origins? Out of that dust and sand came a crystal city, its churches and bridges and houses billowing out and growing ever more expansive. When the travellers came to Murano, in order to observe all the arts of glass-blowing with spatula and pincer, they were peering into the nature and growth of the translucent city.

The lagoon was often described as resembling molten glass, and indeed glass became a metaphor for Venice itself. There was a saying that "the first handsome woman that ever was made was made of Venetian glass." Glass is translucent, weightless; it is not a dense material, but is a medium for colour and light. Glass has no content. It is all surface, infolded in crests and waves, where the inner is also outer. Venetian painters learned from their fellow citizens who worked at the furnaces. They learned how to mingle colour, and how to create the impression of flux and molten form. They borrowed material in a literal sense. They mingled tiny pieces of glass with their pigments, to convey the shimmer and transparency they observed all around them. It glimmers; it is flecked by foam; it ripples and undulates; it possesses a giant translucent calm; it has currents of darker colour; it is fluid. So the glass is, like Venice, of the sea.

II

The City of Saint Mark

4

The Saint Comes

There was one great transformation in the early history of Venice. In 828 an object was brought to this place that entirely changed its character and its status. It is supposed to have been the body of the great evangelist, Saint Mark himself. The essential story remained unchanged through the centuries. It concerned some Venetian merchants—a class who, from the beginning, took the lead in all the affairs of the Venetian state. Buono of Malamocco and a companion, Rustico of Torcello, had gone on a trading mission to the port of Alexandria. In that alien land they entered into a discussion with the custodians of the church of Saint Mark, who were responsible for protecting the body of the martyred saint lodged in an ancient sarcophagus. These priests bitterly resented the persecution of the Catholic community by the Saracens, and expressed the fear that their precious church might be pillaged and damaged. The Venetians listened with great sympathy, and then suggested to the priests that they might like to return with them to Venice; they might also care to bring the body of Saint Mark with them. That could be considered the price of their journey. It was a piece of business. Despite certain misgivings, the custodians agreed.

The body of Saint Mark was taken out of the sarcophagus and unwrapped from its silk shroud, the relic being substituted by another and less eminent saint. It was then placed in a chest and taken on board the Venetian ship, the merchants first ensuring that the saint's remains were covered by a layer of pork and cabbage. When the Muslim officials asked to inspect the chest, they cried out *"Kanzir, kanzir"* (Oh horror) at the sight and smell of the pork. The sainted corpse was first concealed in a sail and suspended from the yardarm but, when the holy cargo had reached open sea, the saint's body was placed on the deck surrounded by candles and thuribles. Thus the evangelist was safely conveyed to Venice, but not before a number of miracles eased his passage across the Mediterranean.

His arrival could not have been more propitious. By mysterious means Mark informed his guardians that he wished to be taken to the ducal palace rather than to the cathedral church then rising in Olivolo. He was lodged in the banqueting hall, but a chapel dedicated to his memory was erected in an open area where the basilica of Saint Mark's now stands. It was then a grassy field, planted with trees, as well as a garden and fruit orchard. All this was removed and filled, so that the chapel of Saint Mark might rise.

The devotion to Saint Mark soon outstripped that to the previous saint, Theodore, and the great basilica was eventually raised in his name. The ducal palace needed a shrine to bolster its legitimacy, and it could be suggested that the shrine required a palace; the covenant between them instantly magnified both the status of the doge and the power of the community. If anyone were rash enough to question the account of the divine prize, according to a later Venetian historian, then "let him come to Venice and see the fair church of Monsignor S. Marco, and look in front of this fair church" at the mosaics that faithfully tell the whole story. This may not be evidence that would stand up in a court of law, but it was enough testimony for the pious and the credulous. The mosaics were only the most prominent examples of the cult of Saint Mark. On the great arch, above the right-hand singing-gallery of the basilica, can be found the scene of the embarkation of Mark's body; there is the ship sailing for Venice; there is the reception of the body in the city. These are mosaics from the end of the twelfth century, made luminous by the decorum and formality of the Byzantine tradition. Mosaics are the filigree upon the silver surface of Venice.

From the beginning, the cult of Saint Mark was as much a secular as a sacred affair. He became the icon and emblem of Venice (together with his winged lion), but he was always associated with the doge rather than the bishop. The open theft of the relic was not an issue. There soon grew up a legend that Mark had been bishop of Aquileia, to the north of the lagoon, before ever becoming bishop of Alexandria. And in any case the fact that the transition had been made with the blessing of Mark himself proved its benefaction. God's will had been done. Otherwise the theft would not have succeeded. It is one of those circular arguments that are very difficult to break. In the thirteenth century another layer of the story was added. It was claimed that Saint Mark, on one of his missions, sought refuge from a storm and providentially took shelter on the island of Rialto. Here, in the future Venice, an angel appeared to him and proclaimed *"Pax tibi, Marce. Hic requiescet corpus tuum."* Be at peace, Mark. Your body will one day rest here. There is of course no historical record of the evangelist ever visiting the lagoon.

There are in any case many problems with the original account, not the least serious being the fanciful chain of events that led to the *translatio* of Mark. That there was some kind of theft seems clear. That a sacred relic was lodged in Venice is also clear. It may or may not have been the body of Saint Mark himself. It might have been any ancient body, wrapped in pious fraudulence as heavy as any shroud. It is likely that the merchants had in fact been sent to Alexandria by the doge, precisely in order to purchase the relic. Its removal to Venice would heighten the sacred authority of the doge as well as the importance of Venice itself. Venice and Mark might rival Rome and Peter. It is interesting that Mark had been secretary to Peter, and that Peter had quarrelled with Mark for being insubordinate and insufficiently devout; these were precisely the charges raised against Venice by successive popes. From the time of the *translatio* Venice had a most uneasy relation with Rome, never conceding the primacy of the pontiff in its religious affairs.

Many other consequences flowed from the *translatio*. The presence of the saint was supposed to guarantee Venice from assault or blockade, and thus lend credence to its claim of invulnerability. Venice did survive, unscathed, until the time of Napoleon. The blessing of the saint would also unify the islands of the lagoon under the leadership of Venice, a political and social transition that did indeed take place over the course of two or three centuries. There were rumours that the head of the evangelist had been left behind at Alexandria, but the Venetian accounts insist upon the wholeness of the body. Insecurity in the spirit demands completeness elsewhere. The wholeness of the relic was also an analogy for the organic interdependence of the islands of the lagoon.

It is important, too, that the saint arrived by sea. The sea had become Venice's true element, and there was no better way of sanctifying it than by claiming it as the shining path of divine protection. The mosaics in the basilica emphasise the image of the ship upon the waves. In a later legend a trio of saints—Mark, George and Nicholas—commandeer a fishing vessel and quell a storm in the lagoon that has been brewed by demons. On his disembarkation Mark presents a gold ring to the fisherman, who in turn gives it up to the doge. Power over the sea is transferred from saint to fisherman to leader. It is one of the formative myths of Venice, engaged in its continual fight against the waters.

There is also the question of free trade, upon which Venice depended. At the time of Mark's *translatio*, the Byzantine emperor had imposed a trade embargo between Christians and Saracens. But in defiance of that prohibition the two merchants had transported their holy cargo from Alexandria, perhaps clearing the way for other less precious commodities. It was a hit against the emperor and a good omen for the merchants. If you cannot farm, as the Venetians used to tell the pope, who also complained about their trade with the infidel, you must fish. And that included fishing for saints. It was said that at the time of the opening of the sarcophagus in Alexandria a delicious odour as of "sweet spices," filled the city. Venetian traders were well known for their bartering of spices.

The relic also secured the independence of Venice. The city's previous guardian, Saint Theodore, was of wholly Byzantine provenance. By supplanting Theodore with Mark, Venice was asserting control over its own destiny. So Saint Mark became a synonym for Venice itself. It would seem that half of the Venetian males are still christened Marco. The red flag of Mark became the Venetian standard. The winged lion is everywhere. The essential and eventual autonomy of Venice was assured by the remarkable, if not miraculous, events of 828.

There was a great fire in Venice in 976, in the course of a rebellion against the reigning doge. In that conflagration the church of Saint Mark was utterly destroyed. It would have been supposed, then, that the combustible relic would itself have been consumed in the flames. In fact it was to all appearances "lost" until 1094, when by curious chance a piece of column fell away revealing the last remains of the evangelist. It was certainly a miracle that he had withstood the great fire. And, against all the odds, he is still with us. Until recent years it was reported that his body lay beneath the high altar of Saint Mark. In the summer of 1968 Pope Paul VI handed certain relics of the evangelist to a delegation of Coptic church-leaders, but confirmed that the rest of the body was still in Venice. The thumb of Saint Mark, as well as the famous gold ring given to the fisherman, are still preserved in the treasury of the basilica. The old bones still live in the imagination of the people.

There is a further reminder of the saint throughout the city. The lion of Saint Mark is the emblem of Venice; it can be found in stone and in bronze, carved in relief or in the round. The lions are to be found on the ducal palace and the doge's chapel; they stand in front of the shipyards of Venice; they guard various grand houses and communal spaces. Every public building in Venice once bore an image of the beast. The winged lion stands on a pillar at the harbour. The lion was a symbol of both religious and political intent. The leonine symbol is one of authority and of paternalism. It is also a token of justice. All of these associations come together in the ubiquity of the lion on Venetian stones and walls.

As a companion of the Evangelist, the spiritual connotation of the lion was clear. But the lion could also be ferocious. It could be aggressive. It was a way of symbolising the might of Venice, if it were ever roused. An inscription of the mid-fifteenth century reads: "Behold the winged lion! I pluck down earth, sea and stars." The lion of Saint Mark was often depicted with its hind legs in water, and its front legs upon the land, an apt indication of Venice's pretensions to lordship both of the sea and of the mainland.

5

Refuge

Venice has been construed as a great ship upon the sea. Sometimes, among the restless motion of the waters, there is a sensation that the ground of Venice is also in motion like the deck of a ship. Ralph Waldo Emerson wrote in his *Journal*, of his stay in Venice, that "it is as if you were always at sea."

The image of the ship of state is a familiar one, but it has a particular pertinence in the case of a city that seems almost to float. When a doge of the early fifteenth century, Francesco Foscari, spoke of guiding the republic he reverted instinctively to the language of the sea. He discoursed upon sails and upon cordage, upon the wind and current, with all the experience of a practised sailor. It was a language that the Venetians intimately understood. The analogy was made, for example, between the building of the city and the building of a ship. When a ship was constructed, with keel and ribs of wood, it was not easy to say when the form first emerged; in similar manner, it was not easy to specify the origins of Venice.

The tip of the Dogana, or custom house, sitting on the edge of land that leads to the Grand Canal, has often been compared to the prow of a ship. On the church of S. Maria Salute, immediately behind the Dogana, a statue of the Virgin has been clothed in the uniform of a *capitano da mar* or admiral of the Venetian fleet. Venetian buildings have often been compared with ships, with their cylindrical forms and rectangles, ships turned into stone and permanently moored. The wooden roofs of some Venetian churches have been erected *in forma di galea* or as a "ship bottom roof." The circular apertures, everywhere in Venice, are like portholes.

Yet the most important allusion can be saved to the last. The ship was once, for the early settlers, a place of refuge. The ship of Venice was, from the beginning, a haven for exiles and wanderers. It was an open city, readily assimilating all those who came within its borders.

One fifteenth-century traveller noted of Venice that "most of the people are foreigners," and in the following century a Venetian recorded that apart from the patricians and the citizens "all the rest are foreigners and very few are Venetians." He was referring principally to the shopkeepers and artisans. In 1611 an English diplomat, Sir Dudley Carleton, described Venice as a "microcosmos rather than city." It was created in the fashion of *orbis* rather than of *urbis*. And so it has remained for the rest of its history.

There were French and Slav, Greek and Fleming, Jew and German, Oriental and Spaniard, as well as assorted citizens from the mainland of Italy. Certain streets were named after them. All the countries of Europe and of the Levant were represented. It was something that all travellers noted, as if quite suddenly they had come upon the Tower of Babel in Saint Mark's Square. No other port in the world held so many strange peoples. In many nineteenth-century paintings the gabardine of the Jewish merchants, the scarlet caps of the Greeks, and the turbans and robes of the Turks are seen jostling among the more severe costumes and top-hats of the Venetian gentlemen. It might be said that the Venetians fashioned their own identity in perpetual contrast to those whom they protected.

The Germans were granted their own "miniature Germany" in a complex known as the Fondaco dei Tedeschi at Rialto which contained two halls, for dining, and eighty separate rooms. The merchants were supervised and monitored by the government, but it was said that "they love the city of Venice more than their native land." In the sixteenth century the Flemish settled in large numbers. The Greeks had their own quarter, with their own church dedicated to the Orthodox faith. After the fall of Constantinople in 1204, and the abandonment of that city to the Turks in 1453, there was a further flow of Byzantine Greeks—among them soldiers, mariners, artists and intellectuals looking for patrons. The Armenians and the Albanians had their own districts. Eventually an Armenian monastery was established on the island of S. Lazzaro, where Byron travelled to learn the Armenian language as a way of exercising his mind among the more sensual pleasures of Venice. There was a colony of Turkish merchants, established as the Fondaco dei Turchi, where a school for the teaching of Arabic was maintained. So Venice was the setting for a thriving cosmopolitan life. It was not altruism or generosity that occasioned this inviting embrace. Venice could not have survived without its immigrants. Some of them were raised to the rank of citizens; some of them intermarried with the indigenous people.

They were not all, of course, well protected. Many thousands of poor immigrants were cramped into cheap housing, sharing the corners of rooms with others of the same race or nationality. Many of them came as refugees from Balkan wars, or from impossible poverty; some of them were escaping from plague. They congregated in the poorer parishes and by the sixteenth century, as a result of the influx, Venice had become the most densely populated city in Italy. The immigrants also provided cheap labour for the city, and were even employed in the galleys of the Venetian warships. They did the work that the Venetians themselves preferred to avoid.

In the fourteenth century the Italian poet, Petrarch, celebrated Venice as the "sole shelter in our days of liberty, justice, and peace, the sole refuge of the good." As a port, the city attracted such epithets as "shelter" and "refuge." They were natural images. Pietro Aretino, himself an exile from Rome who had found safe haven in Venice, put it another way. In an address to the doge in 1527 he declared that "Venice embraces those whom all others shun. She raises those whom others lower. She affords a welcome to those who are persecuted elsewhere." There were, after all, refugees who travelled to Venice for reasons other than commercial. There was a toleration in this open city that was unknown in other regions. That is why it became, from the eighteenth century forward, a resting place for what Henry James called "the deposed, the defeated, the disenchanted, the wounded, or even only the bored." The deposed were a particular speciality of Venice. Many of the dethroned princes of Europe made their way here. At one time in 1737 there were five dispossessed monarchs living in the city, one of them being the young Charles Edward Stuart.

It was also a haven for those of broken spirit, for wanderers, and for exiles. Venice became the home of the dispossessed and the deracinated. Its watery and melancholy nature suited those who were acquainted with sorrow. It became a haven for those who were uncertain of their origin or of their true identity and for those, perhaps, who might have wished to escape from them. It was like a mother, endlessly accessible and accommodating. It was a womb of safety. The people were known for their placability and civility. Venice was a city of transit, where you might easily be lost among the press, a city on the frontier between different worlds, where those who did not "fit in" to their native habitat were graciously accepted. In the nineteenth and early twentieth centuries, for example, it became attractive to male homosexuals who were lured by the opportunities for boys and gondoliers. There came here, too, swindlers and fraudsters of every description; there were failed financiers and statesmen, shamed women and soldiers of fortune, alchemists and quacks. The rootless were attracted to the city without roots.

Venice was also a frontier between different faiths, Catholic and Orthodox, Islam and Christianity. So it attracted religious reformers of every description. A secret synod of Anabaptists was established here in the middle of the sixteenth century, and the German community harboured many Lutherans among its number. Venice always kept its distance from Rome, and protected the independence of its Church from the depredations of the pope; so it became, in theory, an arena for religious renovation. There was even a time when the English government believed the republic to be ready to join forces with the Reformation. In that, of course, it proved to be wholly mistaken.

If you had failed, then Venice was a good place to forget your failure. Here you were in a literal sense insulated from the outer world, so that its scorn or simple inattention could no longer wound you. Venice represented an escape from modernity in all of its forms. And, like any port, it offered anonymity. If you were an exile in Venice you could lose your identity; or, rather, you could acquire another identity entirely in relation to the floating city. You, too, could become fluid and elusive. Tell me who I am. But not who I was. That still holds true.

For a place that afforded refuge for the foreign or the dispossessed, it is perhaps ironic that Venice gave the world the name of the ghetto. A ghetto, a small and insular community, seems naturally to arise from Venetian circumstance; indeed the Venetian ghetto became a Venice in miniature, and will thus help us to understand the nature of the city itself.

There had been Jews in the city from the twelfth century, at the very latest, and in 1152 a population of thirteen hundred is recorded. They were not permitted to live in Venice itself, but were settled upon the adjacent island of Spinalunga; its name was changed later to Giudecca. Two centuries later they were given permission to reside in the city. A burial ground was prepared for them in the sand of the Lido, with a palisade to protect the Jewish dead from the "enormities" of the Venetians. But the Jews were always subject to the prejudice and hysteria of the larger population, prompted by superstition or greed to strip them of their wealth. They were forbidden all professions except that of medicine, and were denied all trades except that of money-lending; then they were reviled for the very business they were obliged to take up.

By the early sixteenth century their dwellings were scattered over the city; a series of military defeats in the same period, in battles with some of the Italian cities of the mainland, were believed to spring in part from the Venetian tolerance of the Christ-killers in their midst. God's wrath was directed against His chosen city, exacerbating the anxiety that the Venetians always seemed to feel. So, on 29 March 1516, the Jews were enclosed in the first ghetto. It was located on the edge of the northern district known as Cannaregio, some distance from the sacred places of the city. It seems to have taken its name from the previous use of this remote enclave as a foundry for cannon; the word for the casting of metal was *gettare*. The noun for the cast is *getto*. Two other adjacent neighbourhoods were eventually added to its domain. It was a complex of ghettoes.

It was not an altogether novel development. The German merchants had already been consigned to their own quarters, where they could be supervised and taxed without difficulty. The Turks would soon follow. The policy of separation and enclosure had, in addition, previously been tested in the Venetian colonies of the Mediterranean. The administration of Venice was a pragmatic business. But of course that pragmatism, under other skies and in other cultures, could become brutal and murderous. The Venetians had always been preoccupied by the definition and creation of space. What could be more natural, therefore, than their invention of the ghetto? It was not, however, the most benign concept. The sacred state had, in certain respects, become a rationalised state. The combination elsewhere might prove fatal.

But the Venetian ghetto had certain special and defining features. It was, or it became, poor and overcrowded. It was surrounded by a wall, a small island with one bridge connecting it to the rest of Venice. The inhabitants of the ghetto were allowed to leave when the *marangona* bell in the campanile of Saint Mark's rang at daybreak, but they were obliged to return by sunset. At that time, the drawbridge was raised. The Jews were locked in for the night. Space was so limited, and the influx of residents so large, that buildings grew higher and higher to eight or nine storeys. The buildings were divided into a number of apartments, with four or five families residing in each of them. It is reported that some people had to sleep at separate times of the day or night, since there was too little floor space. Rilke recites a story of one block in the ghetto that rose and rose ever higher until its inhabitants could finally glimpse the sea. That is a significant Venetian fable.

Yet in truth all the windows looked inwards, to the central *campo* or courtyard. There was to be no visual contact between Jews and Christians. It was deemed inadvisable, for example, that the Jews should be allowed to see the sacrament as it was paraded through the adjacent Christian streets. Such was the measure of the latent Venetian anxiety. So, from the outside, the unusually tall edifices were bare cliffs of stone. Guards were posted at the gates of the bridge by night and by day. The adjacent quays were walled in. Two boats were employed to patrol the immediate area. The ghetto resembled a fortress or a prison. The city itself had become a kind of prison for some of its inhabitants. The Jews were obliged to wear a sign of their race. It was at first a circle of yellow cloth, the size of a fourpenny loaf, stitched onto the breast of an outer garment; then it became a yellow hat; then a red one. Sexual congress between the two communities was forbidden. Any Jewish male discovered *in flagrante* with a Christian female was punished with the removal of his testicles.

By the end of the sixteenth century there were complaints that the ghetto had "become by day and night a den of thieves and harlots, troubled by rows, clashes of weapons, and threats." But in the sixteenth century this might have been the definition of any city. Three hundred years later the French writer, Théophile Gautier, condemned it as a "fetid and purulent district." But this was a period when much of Venice might have answered to that description. The ghetto reflected the nature of the larger city but, in this microcosm within a microcosm, it did so in an intense and garish way.

There were gambling dens in the ghetto, as there were in the larger city, where large sums were won or lost. The ghetto harboured a community of as many tongues and accents—Spanish, Portuguese, Greek, Italian, German, Levantine—as the city itself. The ghetto was closely organised and controlled by the Jewish leaders, imitating the example of the Venetian patricians. On the feast of Purim the Jews put on masks and disguises in true Venetian fashion. It became known as the "Jewish Carnival." The inhabitants of the ghetto excelled in music and in singing, as did the Venetians themselves. By the early seventeenth century there was even a musical academy within the walls. The Jews put on elaborate theatrical performances. Many Jewish women dressed themselves in the latest fashion, with velvet and plush, velveteen and lace. They had been thoroughly Venetianised, in other words, to the extent that the stricter rabbis would condemn their general dissipation and sensuality. The ghetto had become another Venice.

This was one of the secrets of the city. It reproduced itself effortlessly in all of its various districts and institutions; its nature and its structure were endlessly imitated in a perhaps unwitting act of homage. Every community within Venice, whether a trade guild or a manufactory, became a miniature republic. The image of the city was so powerful that it became a paradigm, drawing everything towards itself. A thousand cities of Venice comprised the city, just as a thousand flames may make up one fire.

The ghetto was not despised by the Jews themselves. It became a home, a haven, just as Venice itself had once been to the first settlers. It became a resting place. The Jews of Spain and Portugal, for example, were happy to find refuge there. It became a centre of Hebrew studies, and the principal site of Hebrew publishing in Europe. It was a fixed point of rabbinic culture. Despite its somewhat noisome reputation it remained for some Jews a central place of prayer and spirituality, reflecting the sacred destiny of Venice itself. It also offered a welcome defence, on a practical level, against outbreaks of anti-Semitism among the populace.

Jews and Christians would mingle in the ghetto during the day, and in fact the ghetto exercised a peculiar fascination for some members of Venetian society. The government of Venice tried to prevent its citizens from attending the Purim plays, for example, but in the face of mounting protest gave up the attempt. There was simply too much enthusiasm. Certain Venetians would also regularly attend the synagogues, when a renowned or gifted speaker was about to deliver the sermon. In turn rabbis would listen to the sermons in Venetian churches. There may in fact have existed an affinity deeper than either the Jews or Venetians would care to confess. There were many similarities. Both people were intent upon custom and ceremony; the Venetian patricians were often described as "grave" and "dignified," in a fashion similar to Jewish elders. And the mercantile Venetians, like the Jews, were subject to vulgar prejudice. Other countries accused them of "insatiable cupidity" and of "conspiring the ruin of everyone." The rest of the world believed that Venice was extraordinarily wealthy, even though it took great pains to conceal its wealth. Similar charges had been levelled at the Jews in all ages. There was a fellow feeling. They were both hated.

So in Venice the Jews were tolerated in a manner not evident in other European cities. There is no example of popular execration or maltreatment, although it was reported that Venetian drunks or Venetian children would sometimes dance in the Jewish graveyard on the Lido. The Jews were tolerated, perhaps, because they were profitable. You can never ignore the principle of commercial calculation running through all of Venice's affairs. Jews were allowed to open business premises only on the payment of large fees. The trade that Jewish merchants and shopkeepers brought to Venice was of immense service to the Venetians themselves. The relatives of the Venetian Jews often sent their capital to the city. At times of crisis, not infrequent, heavy taxes were levied against the ghetto. In the first decades of the seventeenth century it has been estimated that the net revenue received from the ghetto was approximately 220,000 ducats; the sum was much higher than any collected from Venice's overseas or mainland colonies.

Yet a more exalted association can be placed beside this talk of taxes and ducats. It is significant, for example, that both Venetians and Jews had a solemn sense of law and a sacred belief in nationhood. They both shared a preoccupation with their native territory as a common heritage. They both believed that their constitution was in essence a covenant between deity and people. They both reverenced their forefathers, and had an inordinate respect for custom and tradition. The Jews knew themselves to be mutually interdependent, part of a communal life rendered ever more sacred by a common purpose and the necessity of self-preservation. Does this not remind us of the Venetian state? The two cultures were images one of another.

6

Against Nature

There were once many gardens in Venice. In the sixteenth century there were five hundred of them nestling within the city, spreading their own refreshing and aromatic life. Yet by the eighteenth century Casanova remarked that "a garden is a rarity in Venice." In the middle of the twentieth century it was estimated that there were sixty remaining. That number may have since been revised. Yet there are still gardens, secluded and still, protected by walls and gates, creating little pockets of green in the stony life of the city. In previous centuries the smaller gardens might have shrubberies of larch or cypress or laurel. The larger gardens were planted with flower-beds and avenues of fruit-trees, complete with cages of singing birds to maintain the illusion of nature. There were also, in the largest of them, temples and fountains as well as elaborate loggias. The fugitive scent of fruit and jasmine and banksia roses trailed through the *calli* and the *campi*.

The Venetians evinced a great love for flowers, matched only by their love of buildings. There were itinerant sellers of gladiolas and tuberoses, and other blossoms harvested from the mainland. On describing these merchants in 1623, Sir Henry Wotton coined the English word florist. It entered the vocabulary effortlessly. On Saint Mark's Day it was the custom for each young Venetian man to offer a rosebud to his sweetheart. In painted representations of Venice in the fifteenth century, there are innumerable pots of carnations cluttering the window-sills. But tastes change. In the early decades of the twentieth century, the aspidistra became the flower of Venice. There was, however, one native flower. It was the flower of the lagoon, *fiore di barena*, clothing the level marshes with a purple robe. It is a token of that time when Venice itself was merely a heap of wild and uncultivated nature.

On the lagoon itself there were garden islands. In the fifteenth century there were vineyards and monastery gardens. The island of

Giudecca was until recent years a paradise of gardens. The island of Torcello was the home of the vine and the pomegranate, the oleander and the acacia, the fig and the elder tree; it also provided the rich soil for maize and artichoke. Once there were olive trees all over Venice. The island of Castello, where the cathedral of the city stands, was once known as Olivolo. Olive oil was a profitable commodity.

Yet in the city itself there is no sense of regeneration or rebirth that accompanies the presence of flora and foliage. It has been said that the Venetians prefer marble to vegetation. In Venice architecture must take the place of nature. It must allude to nature in a pious and consolatory manner. It is one of the secrets of Venetian building. The stone of the buildings is sculpted with leaf and branch. The hundred columns of Saint Mark's comprise a solemn forest. The wood becomes stone. The stone becomes wood. The great houses have also been compared to coral reefs.

It needed art to re-create nature. There was a fashion among Venetian painters of the early sixteenth century for pastoral scenes. But the natural world is pictured without life. It is not worked or populated. There are sheep. There are picturesque rustic buildings. There are groves and springs. There are nymphs and shepherds in the foreground. The inner reality of rural life is not understood. The grass is depicted as if it were velvet, for example, just as in Venetian manufactories velvet was created to resemble grass.

The natural life of the city must be imagined rather than seen. It must be intuited beneath the layers of stone. Byron called Venice "the greenest isle of my imagination," a paradox only he could sustain. George Aschenbach, the protagonist of Thomas Mann's *Death in Venice*, sees in vision "a landscape, a tropical marshland . . . a kind of primaeval wilderness-world of islands, morasses and alluvial channels." It is a vision of Venice itself in its original state. But it is a city that no one else will ever see.

And what kind of animals prowl in this city of stone? There were once sheep and oxen. There were foxes, and even wolves. There were horses and mules in the streets of Venice. In 1177 a mule carried Pope Alexander III through the streets of Venice, and in 1361 the doge and eleven patricians entered the city on horseback. The Veneti of early time had been known for their skill on horseback, and the latter-day Venetians continued their practice. Eighty horsemen were deployed in

An early map of Venice,
devised in the late fifteenth
or early sixteenth centuries;
looks small, fragile and
defenceless in its watery world.

A perspective plan of Venice,
painted with oil upon panel,
displays the city at its most
stately and noble.

The interior of the basilica of Saint Mark, glowing with the radiance of gold. The roof is a sea of gold. The mosaic work, covering forty thousand square feet, is a skein of iridescence thrown across the walls and arches.

A mosaic of the Virgin Mary, from the beginning of the thirteenth century, from the basilica of Saint Maria Assunta on the island of Torcello. Mosaic is the true art of Venice.

A mosaic of the Flood in the western portico of the basilica of Saint Mark. The fear of encroaching waters was a Venetian obsession.

The Stealing of the Body of Saint Mark, by Tintoretto. Only in Venice can the artist's fieriness and extravagance be properly realised. His art is Venice in its purest and most spiritual form.

The Lion of Saint Mark, painted on panel in the fifteenth century. It is the image of Venice, seen everywhere in the city. The leonine symbol is one of authority and of paternalism. It is also a token of justice.

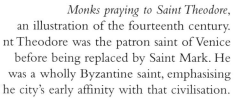

Monks praying to Saint Theodore, an illustration of the fourteenth century. nt Theodore was the patron saint of Venice before being replaced by Saint Mark. He was a wholly Byzantine saint, emphasising he city's early affinity with that civilisation.

A photograph of the piazzetta San Marco, with the pillars of Saint Mark and Saint Theodore guarding the holy space. The piazzetta was redesigned in the sixteenth century as a stage set, with the pillars as the frame.

A religious procession in front of the basilica, completed by Gentile Bellini
in 1496. Such processions had both a civic and spiritual significance. They were
the living embodiment of sacred and secular governance in Venice.

A photograph, taken in the 1880s, of the crowds in Saint Mark's Square.
The Square became known as "the finest drawing room in Europe."

The Miracle of the Cross on San Lorenzo Bridge, painted in 1500 by Gentile Bellini. Venice was itself a city of miracles. No city in Europe, with the possible exception of Rome, has witnessed so many. The survival of Venice itself, on the waters, was deemed to be a miracle.

The departure of the doge's ship, the "Bucintoro," towards the Venice Lido on Ascension Day. This scene, painted by Francesco Guardi in the 1760s, depicts the marriage of the city and the sea. The doge halted at the part of the Lido where the waters of the Adriatic and the lagoon meet. Here a large flask of holy water was emptied into the mingling currents.

The Healing of a Possessed by Vittore Carpaccio, painted in 1494. Here can clearly be seen the Rialto bridge spanning the Grand Canal. The artist faithfully depicts the wooden bridge, the sign of the Sturgeon Inn, the houses and institutions along both banks of the Canal. His is the poetry of urban detail, with its bricks and balconies and chimney-tops.

Saint Mark's Square, in 1310, to maintain public discipline after the discovery of a conspiracy against the state. There were tournaments in the square, and at one such display in 1364 Petrarch was moved to remark that the Venetians demonstrated horsemanship and weapon-handling enough to equal "the fiercest fighters on earth." There were horse-races across the Rialto bridge until they were banned by edict in 1359. It was a city where one of the principal sounds was that of the clangour and neighing of horses. This did not endure, however.

In 1611 the English traveller, Thomas Coryat, reported seeing only one horse in the entire city. Horses were eventually barred from the streets. There was simply not enough room, and the spread of stepped stone bridges was a further impediment. Such was their rarity that, in 1789, Mrs. Thrale noticed a line of Venetians queuing to marvel at a stuffed horse. Indeed by the eighteenth century the patricians of Venice were ridiculed for their inability to ride on anything except gondolas. It shows that a native skill may disappear from sheer lack of practice. The only horses now to be seen in the city are those with the rigid composure of metal. The four bronze chargers panting on the façade of Saint Mark's, the spoils of war looted from Constantinople, are a token of a city where natural life is coming to an end.

Cats and dogs were, and are, popular in Venice. Once the city was filled with watch-dogs and hunting dogs for deployment in the lagoon. But over the centuries they have become more discreet. They are relatively small and domestic. They consort well with the spaces of the city. The dogs in particular enjoy the savour of old stone. They have a distinct sense of territory, as Venetians also do. The Venetian painters loved dogs. Carpaccio enjoyed their company on canvas. In one of his most famous paintings, now to be found in S. Giorgio degli Schiavoni, a small terrier looks up expectantly at Saint Jerome (or perhaps Saint Augustine) lost in divine rapture. Nature looks on, bemused, at the supernatural. But he also paints dogs on guard, dogs asleep, dogs on verandas and dogs on gondolas. They were not reserved for patricians. Almost all of the numbers of the local newspaper in the eighteenth century, the *Gazzetta Veneta*, contain advertisements for lost dogs. The Venetians embraced them because they were one of the tokens of the larger natural world that they had forfeited in their struggle for survival. In the modern *vaporetti*, the dogs are all safely muzzled.

The cats were celebrated as the "little lions" of Venetian life. They are part of the territory. They are naturally lazy. They are naturally observant, and can spend much of their day simply looking on. Yet cats, unlike most breeds of dogs, do not like water. They can still be found in feral groups, scattered across the city. They haunt the fish-market. They can be seen on ledges, on steps, under bridges and in the squares. The square of S. Lorenzo is particularly graced by cats. They are useful, of course, in catching the rats. Rats are one of the curses of Venice, but one surprisingly little mentioned in the literature of the place. There is a saying in Venice that every house has a rat; by which is meant that every family has a renegade member. But it can also be taken literally.

The efficacy of cats against the pests may have prompted the Venetian superstition that he who kills a cat will die within a year, and that he who hurts a cat will suffer an accident. This did not deter the more serious cat-haters. There were once mysterious outbreaks of cat-poisoning in the republic, and a curious ritual in which a cat tethered with a board was killed by systematic head-butting from the Venetian crowd. Yet there has always been a general celebration of animal life in the republic. Late medieval and early Renaissance painting is filled with animal studies; Carpaccio and Crevelli, Tintoretto and Veronese and Bellini, depict cats and dogs and falcons and deer and pheasants. Titian painted white rabbits. In every case there was a desire to embrace a natural world which was in truth out of reach, all the more fervently loved for being elusive.

There were aviaries and cages of singing birds all over Venice, another reminder of a natural life elsewhere. Brightly coloured birds—finches, canaries and parrots—were the favourites. All these birds had, of course, to be imported. In the sixteenth and seventeenth centuries the apothecaries of the principal shopping street, the Merceria, kept cages of nightingales to advertise their trade. John Evelyn reported that "shutting your Eyes, you would imagine your selfe in the Country, when indeede you are in the middle of the Sea." The pursuit of nature was for the Venetians a way of forgetting the unnatural and precarious position in which they lived.

Browning loved the seagulls of Venice, although they are seldom mentioned in the annals of the city. Yet the seagulls should be named with the cranes and the wild ducks as the native birds of the lagoon. They are also part of the myth of the city, like the flight of birds that led the earliest settlers to the islands of the lagoon. There is a legend that the pigeons of Saint Mark's Square are a direct descendant of those flocks that followed the exiles from the town of Oderzo in their flight from the barbarians. The swallows provide another blessing. They come in summer, and swoop down upon the mosquitoes that are the plague of the shallow waters.

No one can visit Venice, however, without being aware of the pigeons. Those in Saint Mark's Square are the most pampered and preserved birds in the world, to the extent that they have acquired an absolute immunity from the passing human population. In times of frost or heavy rain they will literally form a pile, one upon the other, creating and maintaining warmth in their huddled masses. They know that they are not at risk from predators, and that they will not be disturbed. So they have developed a unique form of animal behaviour, like some remote island species on a distant sea.

They are protected by ancient custom. And custom, in Venice, is sacrosanct. It is said that on one Palm Sunday they were released from the basilica of Saint Mark, with small weights tied to their legs. Hampered in this manner, they became easy prey for the dinner-tables of the Venetians. But some of the birds still somehow managed to escape, and found refuge on the various ledges and alcoves of Saint Mark's itself. So they were preserved by the intervention of the saint. After that, they became a cult bird. So the story goes. It is certainly true that a daily supply of grain was provided to them from the public granaries, as was the custom in Persia and in southern Russia, and that it became an offence to injure or molest them in any way.

There are now forty thousand "doves of Saint Mark" in the city. The vendors of corn, in the square, maintain nineteen Venetian families. The birds themselves do seem to enjoy some divine dispensation, and Elizabeth Barrett Browning referred to them as the "holy pigeons." There have over the years been several attempts to curb their numbers, on the grounds that they constitute a menace to public health and that their excrement corrodes the precious stone of the city; there have been attempts at poisoning, at trapping, and even at contraception. All have failed. They have been flying and fluttering in Saint Mark's Square ever since it was fashioned. Why should they depart now? And if they were to be removed, would the square itself be any nobler or safer? The case is arguable. Trafalgar Square, now that its own pigeons have been eliminated, looks like a denuded and almost empty space. The birds are part of the spirit of place. They are the grey stone come alive and rendered soft to the touch.

There were many ways in which Venice fought against nature. Its whole soul and being were devoted to the battle against the sea, and that rivalry by a process of transference affected other areas of Venetian life. It is remarkable, for example, how expert the Venetians became at "forcing" flowers. They were adept at making roses and gilliflowers blow unseasonably; they had sweet-scented roses in January. It was also common, in the first part of the twentieth century, for Venetians to dye their flowers; orange and blue roses were displayed for sale, as well as pink or purple daisies. But these are no doubt examples of a very old practice. The Venetian love of colour is well enough known. Why should it not spread from the canvas to the more transient world?

The Venetians were entranced by artificial gardens, the more complex the better. In their villas on the mainland, by the Brenta, the gardens were formed in symmetrical shapes with every variety of water sculpture in grottoes and caves. The greenhouses were filled with rare plants and with foreign flora, and the hedges were fashioned into the shapes of boats or animals. The marble statues of nymphs and goddesses were the natural or unnatural extension of the pastoral landscapes that were fashionable in the early sixteenth century. In this same period, too, there was a general and genuine interest in the practice of horticulture, in the constant striving to control and to improve the natural world. Everything was of a piece. The Venetian patricians revelled in their triumph over nature—or, rather, their native skill in manipulating it for their own purposes. It was, after all, the principal lesson of the republic's history. The city represents in the most delicate and disquieting way the ambiguous domain between the natural and the artificial, suggesting that there may be some third entity.

7

Stones of Venice

If it is a city of stone rather than earth or leaf, for example, does that make it an unreal city? Oswald Spengler believed that the development of civilisation could be marked by the transition from plant to stone, and in that sense Venice might be considered the most civilised of cities. From the beginning of the fifteenth century, when the wooden city was slowly dismantled, it became a little kingdom of stone. It has all the appearance of solidness and stability, all the stronger because of its constant companionship with water.

There is no natural stone in Venice. So it had to be bought or stolen. It is the old story of the floating city. There was a time, after the capture of Constantinople, when every boat sailing to Venice from that city was obliged to carry a consignment of stone. It was used as ballast. Yet much had to be purchased. The marble of Venice came from Carrara and from the island of Paros. Trachite stone, from the Euganean hills, was used for paving the *calli* and the *campi*. Dark or red stone was imported from Verona; it was mottled with chips or pebbles of harder stone that resembled islands surrounded by channels. The lighter stone of Verona, pink and grey, changes tone according to the seasons and to the light. It is perfectly suited to the city. Pink granite, and porphyry, came from Egypt. And there was abandoned and disused stone, stone from the old churches and houses of the lagoon islands. Stone was so precious that it was used and used again. The spoils of ruins laid the foundation for new buildings in a continual process of regeneration and reinvention. The gravestones of the Roman dead became parts of Christian churches. An altar to the sun god, taken from Aquileia, was re-employed in the baptistery of Saint Mark's. It can truly be said that Venice was built upon antiquity. It harbours past ages.

There are also more exotic stones. The Venetians loved the coloristic effect of agate and malachite, amethyst and cornelian. The ultramarine used on the façade of the great house on the Grand Canal, known as the Ca d'Oro, was made of powdered lapis lazuli from Badakhshan. The Venetians loved coloured and richly veined stone— green porphyry and black granite, stone with red stripes on a white ground, stone with white stripes on an orange ground. In the church of Saint Mark, there are more than fifty different types of stone.

But the principal stone of Venice was quarried in Istria. Istrian stone endures heat and cold; it is easily worked and, most importantly, it resembles its sister stone, marble. Once it has been smoothed and polished, it can scarcely be distinguished from that material. It is an example of Venetian show. It was used as foundation for the great houses and churches. It was used for sculpture, for framing doors and windows, for columns and for keystones, for quays and coats of arms.

There is one important fact about the stone. It is a limestone. It comes from the action of the sea, made up by the unimaginable compound of billions of marine creatures. It represents the compacted time of the sea. It is the essence of sea. When Auden imagined a limestone landscape, he could hear the murmur of underground streams. It is indissolubly connected with the life and history of water. Marble itself is also limestone, hardened and changed so that it is more resistant to the sea air. That is why it was often used upon the façades of the churches and greater houses. So the sea has become, by metamorphosis, the stone of Venice. The stone glows with the inner translucence of the ocean. It glistens. It gleams. It shimmers. It has been described as a forest of marble, springing upward from the petrified trees within its foundations. Ruskin devotes many paragraphs, in the aptly entitled *Stones of Venice*, to the designs of foliage and flowers sculpted in stone; the ornamentation is so careful that the stone leaves of a vine are every one varied in position. There are branches and twisting tendrils, drifting leaves and bunches of grapes; every rib and vein of the foliage may be copied exactly. It is a way of commemorating nature, but it is also a way of mocking it.

The visitors come to Venice precisely because of its stone. For the traveller, it is a city of buildings rather than of people. Stones are the life of the city. There is a tradition of sacred stones. Stones in the form of Byzantine crosses were set into the front of palaces. Arrangements of oval stones and stone crosses are found on many churches and houses. Above the Gothic doorways are generally to be found tympana of stone, carved with angels or with saints. Stone was a way of giving form to spirit. There are stones of faith and there are stones of scripture, with passages from the Bible inscribed upon lintels and gateways; there are stones of the law, on which legal precepts and decrees were carved; there are stones of punishment, the sites of public justice and of execution; there are stones of infamy to mark places of treachery and disgrace, the words on one stone column declaring that it "was erected, in view of the public, to be a terror to others, and a warning for ever to all." These tokens go very far back, to the primitive belief in stone as the image of God found in cultures as diverse as those of India and Celtic Europe, Melanesia and the Americas. It happens that these beliefs were perpetuated by the very special circumstances of the floating city. Precious stones were also magical stones. Rilke once described Venice as a "stone fairy tale."

The Venetian painters lavished their wealth of colour and of invention upon stone. In Carpaccio and Veronese, in Bellini and Tintoretto, there are vistas upon vistas of stone. It is the landscape of their imagination. The public buildings of Venice elicited from them a profound veneration and respect. The staircases and columns, the hallways and turrets, are their real subject. Their sensibility lies behind Canaletto's later meticulous rendering of the city's architecture. Canaletto's painting "The Stonemaker's Yard" is a meditation upon the power and potential of stone. His canvases were generally prepared with a brick-red ground.

But Venice has a secret. It is also accurate and appropriate to describe it as a city of masonry. It is in large part built with brick, artfully faced with marble or with stucco. In the most profound sense, it is deceptive. The great palaces are constructed out of brick. The churches, and the dwellings, are of brick. It is in truth a city of baked clay, taken from the earth of the mainland. Yet it is clothed with marble and limestone in homage to the sea rather than to the earth.

The brick and stone of Venetian buildings have on occasions been compared to the flesh and bone of the human body. The glow of limestone has been likened to the glow of flesh. So the stones may live and move. The stones of Venice seem light. The buildings are aerated, ready to rise from their moorings and soar into the empyrean. When the narrator of Proust's *Time Regained* stumbles in the entrance of the Hôtel des Guermantes in Paris, he is thrown back in time to the moment when he stood upon two uneven paving stones in the baptistery of Saint Mark's; the moment of vision afforded him overwhelming happiness, obliterating time and space in a euphony of sensation between past and present. The stones of Venice brought him joy and indifference to death.

Many legends and superstitions surround the stone of Venice. In some veined marbles strange shapes appear. On a wall of Saint Mark's, for example, two slabs of marble were sawn apart; they revealed the image of a bearded hermit with his hands folded in prayer. There is scarcely a stone in that edifice that has not been sanctified by legend or report. Here is to be found the rock from which Moses drew water. Here are stones upon which Christ walked, or upon which His blood was spilled. On the wall facing the piazzetta, beside the basilica, are two groups of porphyry images. It is believed that they are four Saracens who were turned to stone in the act of robbing the basilica of its sacred treasures.

In another part of Venice, by the Salizzada del Pignater, there is lodged above an arch a heart made of brick; if two lovers touch it, their passion will last for ever. Statues suddenly move or vanish. On the night of Good Friday the statue of Judas, in the Madonna dell'Orto, was said to rise in flight for Jerusalem; he was accompanied by the stone images of Justice and of Faith on the roof of the same church. The statue of a merchant, still to be seen in front of one Venetian house, was supposed to cry in February when the air was colder than any stone. The good and the innocent, if they placed their hands upon the breast of the merchant, would hear his heart beating. Many of the legends of the city are preoccupied with one central fear—that the stone will come alive. There are stories of stone lions bounding into life, of wizards that could turn stone into flesh, of a column by Saint Mark's that on foggy nights secreted blood. If Venice has turned the natural world into stone, its secret longing might be to reverse the miracle and once more to become fresh and yielding. Stone represents the longing to die, a tendency and a yearning to be found in every city. God created the natural world, as the Venetians were taught, but humankind made the city. After his murder of Abel, Cain became the founder of cities. Cities represent the primal curse, and the abandonment of natural ties. Venice is their avatar.

III

Ship of State

8

"Let it be everlasting"

The cry in Saint Mark's Square was always that of "Marco! Marco!" invoking the saint of the city. On his deathbed the greatest theologian of Venice, Paolo Sarpi, breathed the words *"Esto perpetua!"*—let Venice last for ever! Yet by the time he murmured this blessing, in 1623, the city had become a state in more than name. It had become one by deed and example. The abstract concept of the state did not emerge until the first half of the sixteenth century, but the idea of the common good was of course very much older. The common good had created Venice in the first place.

The first mention of the *commune Venetiarum* can be traced to the beginning of the twelfth century, when civic dignitaries wished to supplant the power of doge and people. From this time forward we can chart the growth of a bureaucratic state with its administrators and its diplomats, its governors and its laws. The local ties of parishes and the wards known as *contrade* were weakened, with a decline in the number of religious ceremonies designed to celebrate them; instead there emerged the notion of a unified and united city, expressed in numerous public works and relayed by public decrees. A new form of urban life was being created, at once more efficient and impersonal. Public order was confirmed and controlled by public means. The people had once created the city; the city now created the people. Or, more exactly, the people of Venice now identified themselves in terms of the city. The private had become public. The city had become a totality. Certain criminal acts, for example, were described as being "contrary to the public will" thus conflating the people with the city. By the fifteenth century, at the latest, we may speak of the formation of the Venetian state. It was known as the "Signoria," roughly meaning sovereignty or lordship.

So how did this city become a state and, indeed, a forerunner of the modern state? It is a perplexing question, related to complex rituals of self-awareness and communal self-respect. It emerged together with a well-supervised system of public finance, sustained by such mechanisms as credit and bills of exchange. Some of the first banks in the world were located in Venice. The first public loans were issued in that city in 1167. The Banco del Giro was established in 1619. A state cannot survive without internal stability, governed by law. The Venetians were always proud of the nature of their justice, however flawed its administration might become. Yet the law behind all laws was, in the words of one English ambassador at the beginning of the seventeenth century, "reason of state." The state was eternal. The state was the source of all morality. It had an almost Byzantine rigour and prestige.

But there are more practical matters to consider. A state needs a broadly defined elite that will exercise power in the apparent interest of all. By the end of the thirteenth century the governance of Venice was vested in the hands of a patriciate that was legally defined. And of course the security of the constitution was intrinsically important to the security of trade. Power and commerce were inseparable. Such a general administration needs a bureaucracy, to supervise such matters as public health and public order. The bureaucracy of Venice was one of the wonders of the western world. Everything was committed to writing, as the overflowing archives of modern Venice will testify. At a time when other cities, or other nations, had only the most rudimentary internal organisation Venice was already a model of administrative expertise. The census of population was carried on more frequently, and with more efficiency, in Venice than in any other city. It was said by Jacob Burckhardt, in *The Civilisation of the Renaissance*, that "Venice can fairly make good its claim to be the birthplace of statistical science." Every aspect of social and cultural life was closely ordered. Even the sale of fruits in Saint Mark's Square, and of flowers on the steps of the basilica, was monitored and controlled. The rise of bureaucracy helped to foster accounts and treatises on the arts of government, texts that played a large part in the formation of what has become known as civic humanism. Of course in the actual practice of government and statecraft there were always large doses of opportunism and corruption, of relativism and pragmatism; but they flourished all the more for being easily concealed behind the imposing order of the public administration.

A state needs a measure of conformity among its inhabitants. The city can survive with rowdy or antagonistic citizens—in some ways, it thrives upon them—but the early Venetian state needed a measure of internal control. No city had more success in ordering its people than Venice. The doge and the various councils exercised in a literal sense the art of power. Any words of offence, or what we might now call speech crimes, were prosecuted for being *"contra honorem huius civitatis"*—against the honour of this state—and rewarded with a period of imprisonment. Foreigners who spoke disparagingly of *la Serenissima* were banished. In the secret correspondence of a Venetian diplomat, published by Alfred de Musset, was found the entry to "pay to Signor A, the sum of fifty scudi, for having killed the Signor S, who spake ill of the Republic of Venice."

It was the state that the Venetians were meant to serve. It was continually asserted that it had been bequeathed to them by their diligent forefathers and that they should deem it more precious than their own lives. They were in honour bound to preserve it. The key to Venice was exactly there—preservation. The city itself was from the beginning a miracle of preservation, and it felt the need to invoke that miracle again and again. In its threatened and embattled position, as the public edicts suggested, it needed a coherent and obedient body of citizens to sustain it. This is the reason for the relative tranquillity of Venice over the centuries. It springs from its origin. Power sprang from the place itself, in the constant awareness of collective survival.

But the state emerges from an awareness, and a celebration, of power. Venice became strong because its immediate neighbours were weak; there was no city to challenge its authority over the adjacent mainland. Yet eventually it became a city-state depending on its command over other cities. It was never a question of a natural territory, outlined by rivers and mountains, but a confederation of separate urban entities. It created an empire of cities in northern Italy, now won, now lost, now exchanged.

So we are presented with an image of a highly authoritarian, very well organised, and exceptionally efficient enterprise. This may not consort well with the modern picture of a beautiful and serene if on occasions drowsy city; but it is the necessary pre-condition of its contemporary form. Venice is now, and for ever will be, because of what once it was.

★

The Signoria thereby became the object of a secular religion, honoured and commemorated in literally hundreds of communal rituals spread through the year. A large bureaucracy was created precisely to organise and to administer these festivals. Even at the time of the siege of Venice, surrounded by Austrian troops in 1848, scarcely a month or even a week passed without the celebration of a fête or pageant. It was in the blood.

The Venetian people were temperamentally inclined to spectacle and display. The city itself was designed for elaborate ceremony and in Saint Mark's Square, the theatre of operations, gifts were presented and greetings were exchanged. It is a measure of the order of the state that strict custom and formality guaranteed the order of the rituals. Various groups carried variously coloured candles. The banners flown had their own code; white when Venice was at peace, green when a period of truce had intervened, and red when open warfare had been declared.

The ducal processions, in particular, were viewed as the Venetian constitution in motion. They were the living embodiment of sacred and secular governance. In other cities and in other states, according to a Milanese observer in 1494, "the moment the Prince has passed all go pell-mell and without any order." But in Venice "everyone goes in the best order imaginable." There were engravings and paintings of the entire sequence, with each participant's role clearly defined by attitude or by costume. In the sixteenth century Matteo Pagan executed a remarkable series of eight woodcuts, detailing every participant in the procession.

There were the eight standard bearers, followed by certain judicial officials; there were the six musicians sounding silver trumpets; there were the squires of the foreign ambassadors, followed by the ducal squires. There were more musicians, followed by minor officials such as the clerks and the notaries. And so it goes on, the procession itself fashioned into three large groupings in which religious authority and state power were weighed and balanced. It was not a procession of persons, but a procession of office-holders. In the middle walked the doge; the centre was the heart of power. Radiating out from that centre, rippling through the procession, were the classes and hier-archies in due order. The citizens walked before him, in ascending levels of rank; the nobles walked after him, in descending levels of rank. It was observed by some that the patricians were notably benevolent; they smiled a great deal. There was a general atmosphere of calm and serenity. On certain occasions in Venetian history, that was the greatest act of all.

The celebrations were not necessarily of an uplifting nature. At the festival of the Epifania, on 6 January, certain rowing men were dressed as old women; wearing carrots strapped to their noses, and trailing old stockings, they raced to the Rialto bridge. At the feast of Giovedí Grasso, in February, a bull, and several pigs as well, were ceremonially slaughtered by the guild of locksmiths in Saint Mark's Square. In a later part of the ceremony the doge and certain senators attacked with staves, and then knocked down, some lightly built wooden castles. The ceremony was in effect the reproduction of a Venetian victory over the parent city of Aquileia. Is politics transformed into game, or is the game a form of politics?

There were other festivities when the doge visited various quarters of the city. When he entered the parish of S. Maria Formosa, for example, he was given a hat of gilded straw, a bottle of wine and several loaves of bread. At the close of the proceedings twelve wooden statues of women were taken in procession to the church, whereupon they were pelted with turnips. The ritual was said to derive from an occasion when twelve Venetian maidens were carried off by pirates before being rescued by the young men of the parish. It is all most improbable. It is more likely to represent a primitive phase of Venetian experience, when the young women of wealthy families were all married on the same day as part of a fertility ritual. But thus do folklore and festivity take on strange shapes. It was the custom in the city to call a frigid or disdainful woman "a wooden Mary." The word marionette may spring from the same source.

There were so many Venetian festivals that, in the end, one day was chosen to commemorate several different celebrations. It had become in essence a ritual city. That is why certain pathways were chosen. Churches were sited at focal points, where theatre and piety converged. Public spaces became ceremonial axes, part of the vast geometry of the sacred city. It was a society of the spectacle. Land and water were conjoined in a variety of festivals. Visually and emotionally the various districts or *sestieri* were also woven together in acts of

homage and of celebration; the processions represented the collective
hope of the city, just as they memorialised the collective experience of
the city. Ritual promised continuity and harmony. Ritual also assisted
in the shaping of time within the city. It was seen to obey ceremonial
law rather than the diurnal round of minutes and of hours. Ritual also
helped to codify and identify the past. There were perhaps less elevated
aspects of the show. The pageantry impressed foreigners and ambassadors with the solidarity and wealth of the Venetian people. These
festivals, like those of modern Venice, also helped to lure tourists to the
always alluring market-places of the city. The Venetians never lost a
chance for making money. The same practicality lay behind the
institution of the Carnival, and of course all the art and film "biennales"
of more recent years.

The festivals, therefore, brought much of the city into play. The
paintings of the sixteenth and seventeenth centuries show all the
windows and balconies of the houses draped in ornate carpets.
There were many elaborate "floats" and wheeled chariots displaying
the cardinal virtues or the saints of the city; there were large displays of
decorative architecture; there was music and singing. There were
paintings and sculptures and recitations. There were stages or
"scaffolds" for theatrical performances in which the political events of
the day were reinterpreted in the form of allegory. At the festival of the
"Sempiterni," in 1541, a painted globe of the universe was floated upon
gondolas along the Grand Canal; within the globe, a masked ball was
conducted. The pageant was a method of reinventing life as a form of
art. It represented the very highest form of popular consciousness,
which is why all classes of Venetian society participated in it.

So the population of Venice walked in measure along the sacred
routes, with each person knowing his or her own place in the general
enterprise. It was hoped too that the common people, the *popolani*,
would in the general mood of rejoicing forget that the liberties they
once enjoyed had been lost irrecoverably. Spectacle was of course
another way of procuring social order. The same Milanese observer of
1494 mentioned that "one single person appeared to me to direct
everything, and he was obeyed by everyone without protest." Only the
great hierophantic societies, such as those of Egypt or of ancient
Mexico, have achieved such order. It is one of the singular facts about
Venice that its religion should have such an atavistic hold upon its

people. The reason for it may lie in the peculiar merging of place with piety. The earth of Venice was sacred, miraculously saved from the waters of the world. The people of Venice were part of that earth.

The government of Venice thereby perfected the art of self-presentation. It became an exercise in style. It evolved into a unique form of rhetoric by which all the actions and decisions of the state were hallowed by tradition and sanctioned by divine authority. The especial providence of Venice was invoked, together with the concepts of glory and resolution and independence. The immortality of Venice was also assured. It could most kindly be described as a means of emphasising idealities. But it could also be criticised as a wilful disregard of realities. It might also be seen as a fog of fine sentiment, no less dense than the fog coming in from the sea, veiling the greed and ruthlessness of *la Serenissima* in most of her dealings with the outer world.

No other people placed so much reliance upon the devices of rhetoric. It was a city of performance. Poetry was understood, and considered, as a form of oratory. In an essentially pragmatic culture, such as that of Venice, the whole art of literary education was to inculcate the techniques of rhetoric. The artistic life of the city, in music and in painting, was attuned to expressive performance; it emphasised that which was shown rather than that which is meditated or intuited. Whether we are listening to the music of Vivaldi or gazing at the canvases of Tintoretto we are engaged with an art of "effect," of dazzling virtuoso performance, of bravura exercise. The facility of Tintoretto, and the fluency of Vivaldi, may also be understood in terms of the rhetorical concept of *copia* or plenty. The textbooks of Venetian rhetoric demonstrate a native form of eloquence depending upon "moderation" and "propriety"; in the manner of the state itself *"variazione"* or "variety" must be used to temper extremes and avert the dominance of any one style. It was part of Venetian reserve and discretion.

In an eighteenth-century treatise, *An Account of the Manners and Customs of Italy*, variously attributed to Giuseppe Baretti and Samuel Sharp, it is remarked that "the Venetians value themselves much on their forcible eloquence, and think that their advocates are the only legitimate offspring of the ancient Roman orators." An earlier legal advocate, Leonardo Giustiniani, declared in a letter of 1420 that "there is no kind of case, no type, no topic, finally no precept of the entire art [of rhetoric] in which I must not be proficient." From the earliest times the administration of Venice was steeped in rhetoric.

That is the reason why, of all the Venetian arts of government, the most finely tuned was that of diplomacy. The ambassadors of Venice were unrivalled in the arts of graceful self-presentation, with the attendant emphasis upon appearance and demeanour. These were the elements of *sprezzatura*, which can be defined as the ability to create an effect while concealing the art or skill involved in so doing. Concealment, and double nature, came instinctively to the representatives of Venice.

It was the first city to maintain a continuous diplomatic presence outside the confines of Italy; it had established an embassy to the court of France in 1478. The principle and stated aim of *la Serenissima* was to maintain peace with all parties; only in those circumstances could trade truly flourish. War may have been good for the armament trade, but not for the convoys of spices and other goods that were carried across sea and land. When in 1340 Edward III of England desired that Venice should pledge not to lend assistance to his enemies, the doge replied: "It is not the custom of the Venetians to interfere between disputants or belligerents, except for the sake and purpose of making peace." The Venetians were expert at the polite rebuff. From the sixteenth century their policy was one of strict neutrality, a non-committal approach to all who wished to involve Venice in the affairs of other states or cities. The Venetian system of government was established upon a coherent pattern of equivalence and balance. It seems likely that they applied the same notion to foreign affairs. In the days of political decline, however, this apparent neutrality was condemned as the cover of timidity and irresolution.

Venice's diplomacy was described as *occhiuta* or many-eyed— prudent, discreet, circumlocutory, conciliatory and practical. It was cloaked by *dolce maniera*, a term for mildness or sweetness derived from music. But behind that mask the Venetian ambassadors probed for weakness and prejudice; they were not averse to bribery and other forms of corruption; and they watched everything, looking for grievances they might exploit; they were masters of intrigue. They played state against state, not scrupling to incite one city against another if it suited their purpose. They were dishonourable in their pursuit of Venetian honour.

The most famous diplomatic innovation of the Venetians was in fact the report that all ambassadors were obliged to present to the senate after their tour of duty was complete. These were called *relazioni*, utterly unlike any other ambassadorial documents, in which the diplomat was obliged "to report if he has learned anything of the country from which he comes worthy of being heard and pondered by prudent senators for the benefit of the fatherland." His survey would include such matters as military preparedness, economic conditions, the health and character of the sovereign. No detail was considered too trivial to be overlooked, on the principle that knowledge is power.

Venice was a city of foreign ambassadors, too, who came to the city seeking for information. They were greeted with elaborate ceremony and all the panoply of state. But this was the rhetoric rather than the substance of their welcome. When Sir Henry Wotton, the English ambassador of the early seventeenth century, made a proposal for submission to the doge, he received the most nebulous possible response; the doge was forbidden by law to make any specific reply and, in the words of Wotton, could only "float in generalities." So the ambassadors needed all the guile and patience they could muster. Wotton also noticed that the doge and his advisers favoured delay and stealth in matters of state. Ambivalence and ambiguity were the ground of their considerations. This may have been beneficial in times of peace but, in times of danger, it was a positive disadvantage. It is perhaps instructive that it was Wotton who offered the famous opinion that "an ambassador is a man of virtue sent to lie abroad for his country." Only the atmosphere of Venice could have prompted such a conclusion.

9

The Chosen People

Venice has always been a city of myth. The collective need of the people, for reassurance and identity, has the consequence of creating a fantasy city based upon idealised self-representation. By the thirteenth century it had created a closed political order that allowed it to claim unity and inviolability. By the fourteenth century the Venetians had assumed the mantle of "the chosen people." By the early fifteenth century Venice had fashioned itself as the "new Rome" with its own mainland empire.

But the real "myth of Venice" arose in the early sixteenth century, in the years immediately following the city's struggles against an alliance of its enemies, known as the League of Cambrai, when the European powers were ranged against it. The defeat of Venice, followed later by the restoration of most of its territories, had a double consequence. It was felt that the city was vulnerable but that it was also invincible. From this potent mixture of anxiety and reassurance there emerged a doctrine that expressed the permanence and harmony of *la Serenissima*. The idea of an aggressive and victorious republic was replaced by the myth of an illustrious city of peace. It was in this period that the architecture of the city took its classical shape. The plan of the city became a metaphor for order and grandeur. The city became known primarily for its art and for its music. Ruskin believed that the myth of a nation or tribe is formulated at the time of its utmost power. But that is not necessarily the case. The myth of Venice was prompted by observable weakness that had somehow to be concealed from the outside world. Even after it had effectively forfeited its authority, it still displayed itself as a proud and powerful city.

The ingredients of this myth can be distinguished in a close reading. The Venetian state was founded by miracle and governed by providence. It was immune from external invasion. It was immutable. It had survived for a thousand years, according to a chronicle, "without ever changing." Every other city in the world had lost its liberties, frequently or infrequently, but Venice had never once been oppressed. In 1651 James Howell wrote in *A Survey of the Signorie of Venice*, "Were it within the reach of humane brain to prescribe Rules for fixing a Society and Succession of people under the same Species of Government as long as the World lasts, the Republic of Venice were the fittest pattern on Earth both for direction and imitation." Venice represented an idea that was itself eternal.

It was supposed to embody a harmonious mingling of all forms of government. It was at once democratic, with its great council, aristocratic, with its senate, and monarchical, with its doge. The idea of balance, and of stability, is of course paramount for a city resting upon the sea. Thus James Howell could write that Venice "is as dextrous in ruling men as in rowing of a gallie or gondola." It aspired to be a veritable commonwealth of liberty. It was free from civil unrest and internecine warfare. Its political debates were conducted in an air of refinement and sagacity. It was a city, therefore, devoted to the common good. There was no room for individual ambition or private greed. The princes of other lands were ruled by the passion for self-aggrandisement and by the imperatives of temporary necessity. But, as Pope Alexander VI told the Venetian ambassador in Rome in 1502, "you are immortal insomuch as your Signoria [government] never dies." It was compared with the phoenix, the bird that regularly renews itself. So the city was self-conscious, and confident, enough to turn itself into one continual allegory.

The rulers of Venice were acclaimed as epitomes of wisdom and fraternity. In the ceiling panels of the ducal palace they are shown at the feet of the Saviour or in the light of the Holy Spirit. It was related that there was no discord between them, all united in the cause of the republic. They were devoted and impartial in their dealings, never allowing private interests to affect their judgement. There was no room for corruption or individual ambition. Effectively they were anonymous servants of the divine order of the state. That is why they conventionally dressed in black, and in public were urged to preserve a decorous and dignified appearance. The doge was invariably of great age, confirming the notions of wisdom and experience. It was a great play. But it served its purpose, particularly in fooling foreigners.

And what of the citizens? Philippe de Commynes, an ambassador from fifteenth-century Flanders, was astonished to see the Venetians lining up to pay their taxes, at such a rate that the tax collectors could not keep pace with them. The motive here may have been fear rather than devotion. Yet this much is true: the city did indeed have the capacity to instil fervour in the hearts of its inhabitants. As early as the thirteenth century a Paduan chronicler exclaimed: "Oh happy commune of Venice, that happy city where the citizens, in their every manifestation, have the common interest so much at heart that the name of Venice is held as divine!"

It was the seat of wisdom. The ducal palace was considered to be another palace of Solomon. It was the home of justice. The sculptured image of Venice was based upon the figure of justice with the sword in one hand and the scales in her other. It was the seat of learning. It was the seat of liberty. It had never been the subject of any other power or empire; it had ceded no authority to West or East. Its inhabitants were bound together in a mutual covenant. In the seventeenth and eighteenth centuries that liberty took a different form, in the carnivalesque society of art and theatre and sex that became notorious throughout Europe. But the later liberty was based upon the perhaps more virtuous original.

The city quickly acquired Olympian characteristics. The great staircase in the ducal palace, known as the Scala dei Giganti, was surmounted by the images of Mars and Neptune. Venus was always part of the myth of Venice. The images of Jupiter and Minerva, Mercury and Apollo, are still to be seen in Saint Mark's Square. The great paintings depicting the figures of classical mythology were created in Venice rather than in their more natural home of Rome. Mount Olympus was to be found in the heart of the city.

By the mid-seventeenth century the myth of Venice had become in England a paragon of harmony and continuity, all the more alluring in a country that had witnessed civil war and regicide. It was seen as a model of republican virtue in which patrician and citizen (for which the English read "lords" and "gentlemen") shared authority. It also became a model for the intellectuals of the Enlightenment, who saw in its proceedings a genuine compact between rulers and ruled. It became an inspiration to the makers of the American constitution.

It is the nature of humankind to idealise, to indulge in excessive praise as well as unjust condemnation. The daily texture of life in

Venice was neither harmonious nor free. The government was often corrupt and ineffectual. There were many who disparaged the city all the more fiercely because of its pretensions to grandeur. In the seventeenth century it was depicted as the home of assassins and sodomites. Far from being free, it was an oligarchy. It was a tyranny. Its symbol was the torture chamber of the council of ten. Its true emblem was the dungeon. In the late twentieth century, too, some revisionist historians emphasised the greed and oppression endemic in a ruling class based solely upon birth.

A parade of triumphalism provokes hate and resentment. There were many scholars who considered Venice's version of its history mere trumpery. It was a fake. The Venetians, holding themselves aloof from the rest of Italy, were derided as misers and fishermen. They were as treacherous and unpredictable as the water on which they lived. The city of merchants was denounced for its insatiable cupidity. Cosimo de' Medici described them as unblushing liars. Indeed their rulers and ambassadors were known throughout Europe for their double-dealing; they had so great a reverence for the state that they would stoop to the lowest practices in order to maintain it. There is some truth in all of these allegations. At a later date D.H. Lawrence described it as an "abhorrent, green, slippery city." Many visitors have been unmoved by its charms, professing to find it superficial, tacky and unhealthy.

It is hard to know whether the people themselves, or the rulers, of Venice were ever gullible enough fully to subscribe to the myth of Venice. But that myth has never wholly died. In the early seventeenth century Giovanni Priuli apostrophised Venice as "a terrestrial paradise." Two hundred and fifty years later John Ruskin, one of the many Englishmen who have been entranced by Venice, described it as "the paradise of cities." He was speaking in a time when Venice had lost its authority, its trade and its independence. So the myth goes on. Venice still remains the exemplary city.

It is unique. There is no doubt about that. That is what led to its success. The location of the city is, obviously, singular; and, from this, everything else in its history sprang. You may see in the seed the whole created being. The union of water and earth allowed it to neglect, or to transcend, the ordinary practices of European states. It had to invent a new way of life. Venice belonged to no particular element, just as it belonged to no other authority. Goethe decided that the peculiar circumstances of the city in the lagoon required that "the Venetian is bound to develop into a new kind of being." The Venetian political system, of incredible complexity and subtlety, designed to balance and harmonise the various councils and jurisdictions, was like no other on earth. In the endless letters of travellers the predominant note is one of wonder at its difference. Thus Lady Mary Wortley Montagu wrote, in the middle of the eighteenth century, that it was a "great town, very different from any other you ever saw, and a manner of living that will be quite new to you." In 1838 the American author, James Fenimore Cooper, observed that he was "in the centre of a civilisation entirely novel." The abiding charm of Venice lies in the fact that it is always new and always surprising. It is, somehow, always renewed by the enthusiasm and wonder of its visitors. So it is that the Italian writer of the early twentieth century, Gabriele d'Annunzio, asked "if you know of any other place in the world like Venice, in its ability of stimulating at certain moments all the powers of human life, and of exciting every desire to the point of fever?"

The Venetians were well aware of their uniqueness, too. They had a lively conviction of their own difference. They believed that their city was born as a place of refuge, from the barbarians no less than from the sea, and enjoyed the especial status it conferred upon them. They trusted in their especial, and superior, destiny. If this resulted in a certain arrogance towards other Italian city-states, then so be it. It might also lead to complacency, of course, which had less certain consequences.

So for others it enjoyed a visionary quality. It was the city of earthly beauty. It seemed so fragile, and yet it was in reality very strong. It floated upon the water like an optical illusion. Petrarch described it as representing "another world," by which he might have meant a double image of this world. This was the effect it had upon Rilke, upon Wagner, and upon Proust. In *Invisible Cities* (1972) Italo Calvino describes a visionary city with the steps of marble palaces descending into the water, of bridges and canals without end, of "balconies, plat- forms, domes, campaniles, island gardens glowing green in the lagoon's greyness." Kublai Khan asks the narrator, Marco Polo, whether he has ever seen a city such as this. The Venetian replies that

"I should never have imagined that a city such as this could exist." In this context Calvino himself said, of *Invisible Cities*, that "every time I describe a city I am saying something about Venice." Venice is in that sense the purest city of all.

It is invariably associated with dream. Henry James described his sojourn in Venice as a "beautiful dream." "Venice," he wrote, "is quite the Venice of one's dreams, but it remains strangely the Venice of dreams, more than of any appreciable reality." To those visiting the city for the first time it seems strangely familiar. In this, it resembles the landscape of dreaming. So for Proust the city "was one that I felt I had often dreamed before." The *calli* are so labyrinthine that the passers-by seem suddenly to disappear. It is a common experience for visitors, after a perplexing walk, to find themselves back at the place from which they started. But this may be a dream of oppression, a dream of being beguiled into a maze. This induces fear as well as amazement. Charles Dickens, in *Pictures from Italy*, invoked his whole journey through the city as an oneiric adventure—"I passed into my boat again and went on in my dream"—but it is one that has the qualities of nightmare with intimations of horror and of darkness; beneath the surface of the fantasy or vision lie "dismal, awful, horrible stone cells." It is an unreal city because it seems to have no foundations, like the landscape of a dream.

"Never did a city seem so dream-like and unreal" (William Dean Howells) . . . "her aspect is like a dream" (Byron) . . . "dream-like" (Hugo von Hofmannsthal) . . . "this dream-like town" (Rainer Maria Rilke) . . . "the life of a Venetian is like a dream" (Disraeli) . . . "When you are at Venice it is like being in a dream" (John Addington Symonds) . . . "Dreamlike and dim, but glorious" (John Ruskin) . . . "The city of my dreams" (George Sand) . . . "That waking dream of beauty" (Frances Trollope) . . . "We have been in a sort of half-waking dream all the time" (Mark Twain). It is perhaps significant that these testimonies all date from the nineteenth and early twentieth centuries. They are part of a culture in which the interior life first came to prominence as an object of study. Once more the city, infinitely malleable and fluid, satisfied the cultural expectations of a new period. It breathed the spirit of the age. Sigmund Freud visited Venice on several occasions. He mentions the city in *The Interpretation of Dreams* as the site of one of his own most disturbing dreams. It was of a warship passing over the lagoon.

It can hardly be doubted, then, that Venice still exerts some strange power over the human imagination. To walk around the city is to enter a kind of reverie. Water instils memories of the past, made all the more real by the survival of the ancient brick and stone. The presence of water may also induce the emergence of unconscious desires and fantasies. The uterine embrace of the womb has already been mentioned. It has always been a city of luxuries, and luxuries are dreamed-of things.

The most important Venetian text of the early modern period is entitled *Hypnerotomachia Poliphili* (1499), or the strife of love of Poliphilus, as veiled in a dream. It is a recondite and anonymous work, the meaning of which remains unclear, but it is concerned in large part with the transition between illusion and reality. There are dreams, and dreams within dreams, revealed in a series of architectural conceits. In this respect, it is wholly Venetian in spirit.

IO

The Prison House

When Byron apostrophised Venice in the fourth canto of *Childe Harold's Pilgrimage*, his tone was ambiguous:

> I stood in Venice, on the Bridge of Sighs;
> A palace and a prison on each hand . . .

He did not know, or failed to recollect, that the palace itself also contained a prison. An American visitor in 1760, James Adams, was appalled and discomfited by the atmosphere of the city. "For God's sake let's see to arrange affairs," he wrote, "and get out of this vile prison."

Fynes Morisson, in the early seventeenth century, reported that Venetian women were "locked up at home, as if in prison." Dickens dreams of dungeons when he floats along the canals of Venice, and meditates upon scenes of dreadful night when "the monk came at midnight to confess the political offender; the bench where he was strangled; the deadly little vault in which they tied him in a sack . . ." In the nineteenth century Venice became a true image of horror. The most famous adventure of the city's favourite son, Giacomo Casanova, concerns his escape from the Venetian prison to which he had been consigned. With its slops thrown into the canal, and the scent of bilge water, the city sometimes had the smell of the prison-house.

Some of the most famous prisons in the world are to be found in Venice. The Bridge of Sighs itself, named after the laments of those about to be gaoled, is the most picturesque of all penitential emblems. It was not in fact given that name until the nineteenth century, largely by the happy inspiration of Byron; yet it serves the purpose, and the image, of Venice very well. When William Beckford rode in his gondola beneath the bridge he invoked the memory of Piranesi, the artist born in the Republic of Venice, whose enduring fame lies in his shadowy and vertiginous drawings of imaginary prisons. Despite his great success and renown in Rome, Piranesi liked to sign himself as "*architetto Veneziano.*" From his gondola Beckford looked up at the highest part of the prison and, snatching his pencil, "I drew chasms and subterraneous hollows, the domain of fear and torture, with chains, rocks, wheels and dreadful engines. . . ." These are some of the images summoned up by *la Serenissima.*

The most feared and hated institution of the city was a judicial committee known as the "council of ten." It was created in 1310, as a direct result of a political conspiracy by a group of patricians, and it soon became an indispensable part of the machinery of state. By the fifteenth and sixteenth centuries it had acquired a power equivalent to that of the senate itself. It concerned itself with the threat of lawlessness and unrest within the confines of the republic, and thus its remit stretched very far. It was an internal police force, small and flexible enough. It met in secret, every day of the week. Its members wore black mantles and became known as the "black inquisitors." It employed secret agents in every part of the city, and relied also upon a network of anonymous informants. It never allowed the evidence to be given to the accused, and its witnesses could not be cross-questioned. The examinations of the accused were generally conducted in darkness, and from the room of the three leaders of the council was a staircase leading directly to the dungeons and the chambers of torture. Its verdicts did not permit any appeal. Banishment or death, by strangulation or by drowning, followed very quickly. It was, according to Rousseau, "a tribunal of blood, equally horrible to the patricians and the people." There is no doubt an element of exaggeration in Rousseau's account, and in those of others who liked to foster the myth of Venice as a dark and vicious place, but there can be no doubt that the reputation of the small council was the single most important element in the understanding of the Venetian polity. It symbolised the secret life of the city.

Prisons were in a real sense part of the literal and metaphorical world of the Venetians. A fourteenth-century notebook, kept by a merchant, contains a list of all the gaols of the city. The most notorious prisons in Venice were in fact part of the palace of the doge. It was ordained that the doge himself should hold the keys, with the unspoken suggestion that prisons supported the legitimacy and authority of the state. There were prisons on both sides of the Rio della Paglia that flowed past the palace; those on the ground floor were known as "the wells," for the reason that water often collected in them, while those on the upper storey were called "the leads" after the slabs of lead that covered the roof just above them. Some of the individual dungeons had names, such as "the lion" and "the volcano." The wells in particular had a reputation for noisomeness, with the suggestion that it were better to be entombed alive than to be lowered into these holes. But, as with most aspects of Venetian life, there is more than an element of fantasy and myth-making in these accounts. The supposed horrors of the Venetian gaols may be related to their proximity to water, but they can be construed as part of the shadow world behind the ritual and masquerade that touched every aspect of Venetian life. What depths of torture and depravity might somewhere lie concealed in this fair city? What is being masked? The answer may be—nothing at all. When the French forces invaded and overwhelmed Venice in 1797, only one prisoner was found in the wells. He had been imprisoned for sixteen years and, on re-entering Saint Mark's Square in broad sunlight, he was struck blind and died shortly thereafter.

Casanova was imprisoned in the leads, and from the grating of his cell he saw rats of a "fearful" size wandering unconcernedly in the garret. When he asked his gaoler about the "scoundrels" imprisoned with him he was told that, on the contrary, they were respectable people who for reasons known only to the authorities "have to be sequestered from society." It emphasised to him the "horrible despotism" to which he, too, had become a subject. Yet he escaped; he fashioned an iron bar into a spike, and cut his way out onto the rooftop. His narrative of imprisonment and flight is a central story of Venice itself.

It is generally believed that Casanova died in Bohemia on 4 June 1798, but there is an unofficial story that he secretly returned to Venice after the French Revolution and lived there in anonymity. It is also said that he practised certain necromantic rites that guaranteed him immortality. Some argue that he still lives in his uncorrupted body; others believe that he is reborn in every Venetian infant. He really does represent, therefore, the *genius loci*. He never really escaped, after all.

The image of the prison has often been used to conjure up the mood and setting of the city. Like the Jews in its ghetto its citizens are in a sense incarcerated, surrounded by water as if they were confined in Alcatraz. No citizen was allowed to leave Venice without official permission. That is why there is relatively little crime in the city; in a place where everyone is watching everybody else, there is nowhere to hide. The route to the mainland can easily be sealed off. The Venetian people were, in addition, heavily policed. By the fourteenth century there was one policeman for every two hundred and fifty citizens, with the laws enforced by the council of ten and the *signori di notte* or "lords of the night." There were also the chiefs of the wards, and a secret force known as the *sbirri*. It was reported that the *sbirri* dealt with offenders by throwing their cloaks over them and then, having muffled them, led them directly to the prison. The elements of silence and concealment consort well with the popular image of the city. They are of a piece with coercive legislation and constant observation.

There is, or was, very little privacy in Venice. The people are packed closely together. The small communities of every parish were woven flesh to flesh. The private space is small indeed. Just as private interests were subordinated to public needs, and the individual subsumed within the larger community, so privacy itself was considered to be of little importance. All this may induce acute feelings of claustrophobia. The people cannot escape one another, let alone the clusters of islands on which they are immured.

II

Secrets

The shade of the prison house may also induce secrecy. If privacy is a luxury, then the keeping of secrets may become ever more urgent or obsessive. The city of masks must, in any case, also be the city of secrets. The Venetians, despite their apparent sociability, are notoriously reticent. They do not invite casual visitors into their homes. In the portraits of Venetians there is a general air of inscrutability; they are painted for their office rather than for their person, and their actual temperament or personality is not to be divulged. They are impenetrable. It was said of one doge that "one never knows whether he loves or hates anything." One public lecturer, from another part of Italy, found it impossible to engage his audience of young Venetian nobles in any form of political discussion. "When I ask them," he wrote, "what people think, say, and expect about this or that movement in Italy, they all answer with one voice that they know nothing about the matter." Was this silence the result of fear or of distrust? In a city where you could be banished on the evidence of suspicion alone, who would willingly open their mouths? After Napoleon had conquered Venice in 1797 he instigated a survey of the newly captured people. He asked, in particular, what were Venetian prejudices and opinions. The native writers of the survey could not enlighten him since, they said, such questions admitted no answer. No other city had so effectively silenced its inhabitants. There were times, in fact, when indiscretion exacted a high price. When two glass-blowers escaped to foreign capitals with the secrets of their trade, in 1745, the senate decreed that they should be assassinated by means of poison.

It was observed that, on the Rialto, the bankers and merchants customarily spoke in hushed voices. The government of the city was conducted in secrecy. We might almost describe it as an Oriental secrecy, with secret meetings, secret payments, secret audiences, secret decisions and secret deaths. When new nobles were introduced to the business of government their oath of allegiance included the promise of "faith and silence." It is highly characteristic of Venice. One of the allegorical paintings in the doge's palace is that of taciturnity. There is a strange figure of stone on the edifice of Saint Mark's; it is of an old man, leaning on crutches, who has a finger to his lips. It was said that Venice was a secret oligarchy; it not only kept its secrets, but the nature of its own identity was also a secret.

The oath for the council of ten was *"jura, perjura, secretum prodere noli"*—swear, foreswear and reveal not the secret. There are pages in the annals of government where the words *"non scribatur,"* let it not be written, are to be found. Other chronicles of Venice were burned. The archives of the government were secret; the doge himself could not consult them, unless he were accompanied by an official. The keeper of the archives was a man who could neither read nor write. In an eighteenth-century text, *The Chinese Spy*, it is stated that "silence is the emblem of this government; everything is secret and cloaked in mystery. Political doings are covered by a thick veil of darkness. In Venice those who talk are buried alive in a tomb covered with lead."

Thus it was said by a seventeenth-century historian that "the Venetians are apt to be jealous of all ambassadors, and to interpret all their Actions as Mysteries tending to Conspiracy." They discussed every word and action "from whence they make great conjectures and draw mighty consequences of State." No Venetian official could speak to a foreign diplomat, on pain of death or life imprisonment. The boxes at the opera had little "withdrawing rooms"; diplomats felt obliged to visit one of the several opera houses, if only to discover secrets which would otherwise be hidden from them. Paradoxically the mute stealth of these proceedings encouraged suspicion and conspiracy. Venice was known as the city of conspiracies.

There was a violent altercation at a meeting of the senate in 1511, which the council of ten deemed to be so shameful that it was never to be mentioned; oaths of secrecy were demanded from the members of that body. Many proposals and discussions, put before the senate, were also considered under strict vows of silence. Some dignitaries were imprisoned or sent into exile so that they could not speak out. Secrecy was for the public good. When the senate deliberated for a month over the imprisonment of a Venetian admiral, for incompetence or mal-feasance, not one word reached the admiral himself until the moment he was seized and bound; his friends, who had argued passionately in his defence, had not warned him. When rumours of a great military defeat began to filter through Venice, in the early part of the sixteenth century, the council of ten refused to discuss the issue and imprisoned anyone suspected of a loose tongue.

And there was, at the end of the eighteenth century, the case of "the Venetian secret." It was a secret that Sir Joshua Reynolds, for example, pursued to his death. It concerned the warm texture of Venetian painting. How did the artists fabricate that golden and glowing tone? Reynolds even scraped down one of Titian's canvases in search of the secret. One woman, Ann Provis, declared that she possessed it. She said that it was contained in a copy of a lost text concerning the method and practice of the great Venetian painters. Miss Provis promised to reveal it, but only in exchange for ready cash. Of course it was a confidence trick. James Gillray caricatured the whole affair in a print entitled "Titianus Redivivus; – or – the seven-wise-men consulting the new Venetian oracle."

So Venice was well known as a city of secrecy, of mystery, and of silence. Henry James described it as a place of "endless strange secrets" and in *The Portrait of a Lady*, partly set in Venice, there is the almost unbearable tension of what has been left unsaid. Such an atmosphere perfectly suits the Venetian genius for intrigue. Casanova said of his Venetian contemporaries that their "most prominent characteristic is to make a mystery of nothing." In the past the Venetians made a mystery of government, or a mystery of love; now they were happy to create mystery for the sake of mystery. The gondolas were designed for secrecy, with little cabins draped by blinds or by black cloth. A Venetian writer, Giovanni Maria Memmo, wrote in 1563 that the houses of Venice "should have some secret doors where one can enter and exit without being seen by anyone." Venice is still in part a secret city. It is a secret city of the living, unseen by the many thousands of tourists who take up the public spaces. That is why good restaurants are hard to find; the Venetians reserve them for themselves. There are still streets that seem in retreat, silent and secluded. The watery element deepens that sense of seclusion and secrecy. The canals render the streets remote and unfamiliar.

But secrecy is also the companion of anxiety and of shame. Those who preserve secrets may wish to conceal their real nature. Secrecy leads to dissimulation and play-acting. It was said that Venetians never discussed their true motives in the affairs of the world. Yet secrecy is also an aspect of power. That which is spoken can be denied or repudiated. It can be tested and contradicted. That which is unspoken remains most powerful.

The secret city takes the shape of a labyrinth. It is a maze that can elicit anxiety and even fear from the unwary traveller. It lends an element of intrigue to the simplest journey. It is a city of dead-ends, and of circuitous alleys; there are twisting *calli*, and hidden turnings; there are low archways and blank courtyards, where the silence is suspended like a mist. There are narrow courts that terminate in water. The natives do not lose their way, but the traveller always gets lost. It is impossible not to get lost. But then suddenly, as if by some miracle of revelation, you find that for which you have been searching—a small church, a house, a restaurant will suddenly present itself to you. The city gives you a present. But, then, it is unlikely that you will ever find that place again. Kafka would have understood Venice.

The concept of the maze or labyrinth is an ancient one. It is a component of earth magic that, according to some authorities, is designed to baffle evil spirits. The Chinese believed that demons could only ever travel in straight lines. It has also been said that the dead were deposited at the centre of the mazes. That is why they retain their power over the human imagination. The labyrinth of classical myth is that place where the young and the innocent may be trapped and killed. But the true secret of the Venetian maze is that you can never observe or understand it in its totality. You have to be within its borders to realise its power. You cannot see it properly from the outside. You have to be closed within its alleyways and canals to recognise its identity.

The scheme of house numbers is difficult to understand; in each *sestiere*, they begin at number one and then snake through every street until they finish. They reach into their thousands without the benefit of any reference to street or square. The names affixed to the streets seem in any case to be different to the names printed in the maps of the city. In fact the reality of Venice bears no relation to any of the published guides and maps. The shortest distance between two points is never a straight line. So the network of Venice induces mystery. It can arouse infantile feelings of play and game, wonder and terror. It is easy to believe that you are being followed. Your footsteps echo down the stone labyrinth. The sudden vista of an alley or a courtyard takes you by surprise; you may glimpse a shadow or a silhouette, or see someone standing in a doorway. Walking in Venice often seems as unreal as a dream or, rather, the reality is of a different order. There are times when the life of the past seems very close—almost as if it might be around the next corner. The closeness of the past is embodied in the closeness of the walls and ways all around you. Here you can sense the organic growth of the city, stone by stone. You can sense the historical process of the city unfolding before you. There is a phrase, in T.S. Eliot's "Gerontion," to the effect that history has many cunning passage-ways. These are the passages of Venice.

News travelled fast through the echoing *calli*. Venice was at the centre of news, from East to West and from West to East. In the early modern era it was the primary conduit of news in the world. The correspondence of merchants, from the thirteenth century, was a significant source of information. He who heard the news first—of an important transaction, or the scarcity of a certain commodity—would profit most. Speed was of the essence. The roads must be in good repair, if possible, and the ships swift. Venice was one of the first cities to organise a postal system, the *compagnia dei corrieri*, in the fourteenth century. Nevertheless it took four days for the mail to travel from Nuremberg to Venice.

It was the news and speculations that generated half the business of the Rialto. In fact Venice would not have been the centre of commerce if it had not been the centre of news. It came from all sides—from couriers on horseback, from the reports of diplomats, and from the letters of administrators. Information descended in torrents upon the market-place. Once the news was known, it was discussed. There was an inn, the Golden Ship, where Venetians would meet "to recount their Intelligences, one with another . . . thither also came Merchants that were strangers." Some of the earliest coffee houses were established in Venice, for the particular reason of conveying information. The human city could itself be described as a medium for the reception and exploitation of information. Venice, the pre-eminent city, was also surely pre-eminent here.

So the Venetians ran after the latest news and the latest sensation. Yesterday's news was of no account. The entries in the diaries of Marino Sanudo, in the early sixteenth century, were often prefaced with the phrase that "news came that. . . ." The Venetians listened with "elevated ears" for the latest word or information. There were reports known as *notizie* or *avvisi* read aloud to the populace, who paid a small coin known as a *gazzetta* for the chance of hearing the latest rumours. It is perhaps not surprising that this appetite for news was considered by some to be a contagion or a distemper. Sir Henry Wotton described "news" as "the very disease of this city." Yet some news was more important than most. In a letter of 31 March 1610 Wotton wrote from Venice to his employer, Robert Cecil, of "the strangest piece of news . . . whereof here all corners are full." It was the news of the new universe penetrated by Galileo.

One resident of Venice has been celebrated, if that is the right word, as the first of all journalists. Pietro Aretino came to Venice in 1527, in exile from the papal court at Rome, and for the next twenty-nine years threw himself into the public discourse of the city. He wrote comic plays, pornographic dialogues and religious works; but he also thrived in the world of the weekly newspapers then circulating through Venice. An early biographer described him as the "first great Adventurer of the Press." He thrived upon the art of public self-imaging and described the affairs of the day in the language of the street. He wrote pasquinades or flysheets that were distributed everywhere in the city, and he refurbished the form of the *giudizio* or almanac. Local and immediate news was now the staple of the public prints. He wrote on demand. Aretino turned "news" into a commodity, in the style of any merchant of Venice. His writing smells of the turbulent city. He thrived in the city, and repaid the compliment by extravagantly praising his hosts in plays and letters. So he was tolerated. In truth he could have existed nowhere else.

It is not perhaps surprising that the first newspaper in the world, the *Gazzetta*, emerged in Venice at the beginning of the seventeenth century. At various times in the following century one of the first modern journalists, Gasparo Gozzi, published *L'Osservatore Veneto* and *La Gazzetta Veneta*. The latter, established in 1760, was published twice a week; its editor received news, and subscriptions, at four bureaux in the city. There were news items, advertisements, conversations overheard in Saint Mark's Square, menus, questions and pleas by "lonely hearts." All Venetian life is there, from the story of the drunken porter who fell to his death from an open window to a list of the rates on the exchange. It was one of a number of news-sheets and newspapers and newsletters. Many of them simply publicised private scandals and quarrels; they indulged in rumour and innuendo; they reprinted personal letters, and created a climate of acute social embarrassment for certain prominent Venetians concerned about their good name or *buona fama*. They were of a piece with the topical satires that were circulated through the streets, the token of a city that was obsessed with its own communal life. Yet there is one thing missing. The political debate of the city goes unnoticed and unremarked. The government of Venice was masked.

Nevertheless Venice was filled with rumour and intrigue. There were spies everywhere. The courtesans were spies. The gondoliers were spies. The state inquisitors had spies. The council of ten had spies. There were spies for the trade guilds, who informed on any craftsmen or workers infringing the rules of business. There were political spies, employed to denounce any corruption in the processes of election or of government. The spies spied on other spies, and were in turn followed and watched. There was heavy surveillance at the docks, the point of entry for people as well as goods. The abiding rule, for foreigners and other interested parties, was to stay silent. As long as you did not talk, you remained at liberty.

There is the story of Vivaldi walking in Saint Mark's Square with a violinist from Dresden, Johann Pisendel. He suddenly broke off the conversation, and asked his friend to go home with him at once. Behind closed doors Vivaldi then told Pisendel that he had been observed by four officials. Vivaldi told his friend to remain within the house until he had discovered what offence, if any, Pisendel had committed against the majesty of Venice. It turned out to be a case of mistaken identity. But the fear had been there. The mere experience of being observed had induced it.

One of the secretaries to the council of ten was an expert in the breaking of codes and secret ciphers. Every foreign embassy or foreign household in the city had one or more resident spies. The foundations for foreign merchants, like the Fondaco dei Tedeschi for the merchants of Germany, were packed to bursting with spies; the Venetian weighers and brokers on those premises were known to work for the government in a semi-official capacity. One great lady of Venice, Elisabetta Zeno, held a salon for certain important senators; behind a screen were hidden two clerks, who for her later benefit noted down everything that was said. When the Venetians became informed of the conspiracy, they suspended the senators from any public office. Elisabetta Zeno herself was exiled for life to Capodistria. Every Venetian on foreign soil was expected to take on the role of spy as part of his or her civic duty. The prelates of Venice, when in Rome, were expected to spy upon secret papal enclaves. The Venetian merchants who travelled to other lands or other cities were especially useful; it is apposite, too, that in a mercantile state, the language of merchants was used as a code. The Turks, for example, might be described as "drugs" and the artillery as "mirrors" in a fictionalised commodity market.

Spying was a Venetian employment and pastime. People were always, and still are, watching other people in the city. The state of the houses was such that surveillance could take place through cracks in the walls or floors. The houses of the powerful were not exempt. Three youths were found to have broken through a section of the senate ceiling, so that they could listen to an address by an ambassador recently returned from the Ottoman court. There were examples of professional, and amateur, informants throughout the city. There was incentive, too; the accusers were rewarded if their information proved to be correct, and their names kept secret in the honoured Venetian fashion. The Venetians invented this particular form of harassment, known as *denuncia* or *denontia segreta*. It is still true that Venetians, if they find it necessary, will inform on one another. In a small place, humiliation is the greatest punishment of all. It was sometimes only necessary for the government to "name and shame" a culprit for the necessary sentence to have been executed.

Of course the administration of the city thrived on the undermining of personal loyalties. It was a measure of the success of the state that its people should conform to the greater good. Indeed the habit of denunciation might be seen as a thwarted or twisted expression of civic pride and civic belonging. It is embodied in the *bocca di leone*, the lion's mouth, to be found in various parts of the city. The mouth, generally carved on a grotesque and offensive head, was a postbox for accusations against any Venetian. The accuser was obliged to sign the paper and include the signatures of two witnesses to his or her good name; but the information could include anything, from financial extravagance to licentiousness. Anonymous accusations were meant to be burned, but in fact could be entertained if they involved matters concerning the security of the state. This lion's mouth was of course another Venetian invention. It was the mouth of the city, a capacious orifice of whispers and rumours. It meant that there was a general atmosphere of surveillance, even in the most private quarters of the city. There were even specific mouths, designed to implicate those who cheated on their taxes or who adulterated oil. A wife could inform upon a husband, a son upon a father. The practice was continued in Venetian dominions. In some Venetian country houses, on the mainland, there was a *bocca delle denoncie segrete* where informants could accuse individuals working on the estate.

Gossip and scandal were thereby the fuel of Venice. It was a network of small neighbourhoods; each one resembled any country village, in itself, but packed together on an island the atmosphere of rumour became ever more intense. "All Venice will know" became a common-place sentiment. Casanova complained that he was "the talk of the city." Rumour spread very rapidly, so that the street urchins knew the name of the next doge before it had been officially announced. There was a general awareness of "murmuring in the city." The sister-in-law of one of Byron's Venetian amoratas, according to the poet, "told the affair to half Venice and the servants . . . to the other half." Rumour had a thousand tongues and, as one Venetian patrician put it, "everyone says what he pleases, dreaming up something at night and spreading it in the morning." Rumour was the excrement of Venice. If you spread it thickly enough, anything might grow. W.D. Howells, in his *Venetian Life* (1866), commented that you must "figure the meanness of a chimney corner gossip added to the bitter shrewdness and witty penetration of a gifted *roué*, and you have some idea of Venetian scandal." The Venetian gossips knew every trifle. The talk was some-times known as *ciaccole* or chit-chat, and the word itself expresses the littleness of the discourse. The victims, of course, were excessively humiliated. Many of the popular songs of Venice were concerned with the harm wreaked by mischievous gossip and by "perjured tongues."

Some victims were inclined to call upon divine protection; a picture of a "swooning Madonna" was to be donated by one Venetian if his wife gave birth in time to avoid "malicious gossip." When a secretary of state in Venice, Pietro Antonio Gratarol, believed that he was being ridiculed in a play by Carlo Gozzi, and had tried unsuccessfully to have it banned or censored, he fled to Padua, without the permission of the Venetian authorities, and was eventually condemned to death in his absence. But the ultimate penalty did not balance the fear of rumour and mockery. He could not bear the malicious gossip.

Nevertheless gossip was accepted as evidence in the courtroom. It had a privileged status, and was generally considered to be the prerogative of women and of servants. But fruit-vendors, street-sellers and gondoliers were also called to give witness to what they had seen or heard. There were "murmurs" about this or that. The witnesses testified that "the whole courtyard was there" or that "if one person says it, everyone says it." The most intimate secrets of a marriage were known to the community, which was generally not averse to taking sides in any marital dispute. It was quite common, too, for neighbours in such circumstances to enter the house or crowd the doorway. The Venetian idea of the "common good" was here lent a visible identity. The comedies of Goldoni are a perfect image of this unusual social life. People come and go from one house to another. Doors and windows are perpetually open. Taverns and shops are close by, so the conversation can be continued from living room to inn without any disturbance. The *campo* or *campiello* is one large domestic space. It is a curious fact that in Venice public matters were held in inviolable secrecy, while private affairs became public knowledge almost at once. Gossip may then have been a form of compensation.

Neighbours and domestics would come into court in order to testify on oath. They considered their evidence to be "public knowledge." So the people watched one another, morning and night. They studied one another. It helped that they already knew each other by sight. At the opera, the opera glasses were characteristically trained upon the audience rather than the performance. From a certain perspective, however, the members of the audience were the performance. The Venetians are still marked by their propensity for gossip. Strangers in a familiar setting are noted and, if necessary, reported to the police. The telephone lines are always busy.

12

Chronicles

Venice was the most conservative of societies. It revered tradition. It reverenced authority. The city was always searching for an historical origin, so it worshipped origins. It venerated the past. The respect for custom permeated every level and every aspect of Venetian culture. Custom represented the inherited will and instinct of the people. Custom was the embodiment of the community. There was a formulaic phrase used in public pronouncements, to the effect that new legislation was simply following "the most ancient customs" of the city. It was a form of reassurance. Custom was also considered to transcend positive or systematic law. Experience was always more important in Venice than theory. There would never be a revolution in the city.

The social life of the people was dominated by customs. To disregard costume, in matters such as church-going or hospitality, was to invite criticism. Of all the things the Venetians most dreaded, the worst was public obloquy. That is why they were often so lavish in public acts of generosity, but frugal to the point of miserliness at home.

The artists of Venice used a common and narrow range of iconography. The architecture of the city is of course known for its traditionalism. The form of the houses, large and small, remained unaltered for many centuries. There was no change in structure or decoration. If they fell down, they were rebuilt on the same spot with the same principles and even with the same materials; the remains of the previous building were used in the construction of the new one. The foundations could always be re-employed; petrified wood did not decay or burn.

In building instructions there is a consistent theme—rebuild this room according to its original dimensions, do not let this wall be any higher than its predecessor, reconstruct this house where it was previously. Perhaps it was the fear of fluidity, of mobility—the fear of water—that instigated this stasis. Casanova said that the patricians of Venice trembled at the mere idea of novelty. Power is itself a conservative force. A Venetian historian from the early seventeenth century, Paolo Paruta, noted that states are preserved by continuing the same traditions with which they were founded. Change encourages corruption.

Even in the sphere of mercantile activity, where the city was most expert, there was a pronounced aversion to change. It is often said that the Venetians invented the art of double-entry book-keeping; in fact the technique was invented in Genoa. The Genoese minted the first gold coins, drew up the first insurance contracts, and made the first marine charts; Venice characteristically lagged fifty or more years behind. It borrowed from others. It did not create *ab novo*. It feared and distrusted innovation. Only the forceful intervention of Napoleon brought an end to a system that had endured for five hundred years without noticeable change. It was until 1797 the sole example of a medieval city-state. It was, after all, an island.

The Venetians were obsessed with their history. They produced the largest body of chronicles in the Italian world. Extant from the fourteenth century are more than a thousand such texts. The diaries of Marino Sanudo, detailing the most inconsequential or tedious events of the late fifteenth and early sixteenth centuries, filled fifty-eight volumes in folio. It is reported that, at the age of eight, he was making an inventory of the pictures in the ducal palace. He, like the other chroniclers, was fascinated by the life of his city—its laws, ceremonies, trades, customs, treaties, were considered to be of fundamental importance and interest. It was a parochial vision, perhaps, but an understandable one. The spirit of place spoke through him. He could only truly be himself by acting as a medium for Venice.

After the chronicles came the histories. By the middle of the fifteenth century there were volumes with titles such as *De origine et gestis Venetorum*. The "origin" was just as important as the "deeds." The origin explained the deeds. In 1515 Andrea Navagero was appointed to be the first official historian of Venice, a post in which he was expected to celebrate the "constancy and invincible virtue" of the city. This was precisely the moment when the "myth of Venice" was being formulated. The concept of a state historiographer is itself an interesting one, suggesting that the task cannot be left to free enquiry.

As with "official" biographers, the art lies in concealment as much as revelation.

Unfortunately Navagero did not entirely succeed in his purpose, and in his will he ordered that his notes and papers be burned. He had, perhaps, revealed too much. There then followed a succession of state historians who, like the narrative painters of the sixteenth century, united minute detail with a general celebration of Venice's sacred history. They were always reshaping the myth to accommodate present circumstances. They were descriptive and prescriptive, with the sure belief that they were offering a practical guide of governance to those who came after them. Everything was to be explained, and understood, in terms of the historical ideal. The historiographers were convinced that to chart the history would also be to reveal its manifest destiny. Tradition is the key. In a city constantly nervous of its own survival in the sea, duration itself was considered to be worthy of honour. If it has endured, it must be laudable.

The reverence for custom and tradition was not necessarily benign. The political and economic decline of the city was not wholly of its own making, but the inherent conservatism and traditionalism of the authorities impaired the possibilities of improvement and renewal. The patricians, reassured by their own claims to superiority, often made signally disastrous decisions. Their exploitation and sack of Constantinople, in the company of allies, led directly to the Turkish conquest of the city on 29 May 1453. Venetian industry was injured by the restrictive practices imposed by the government. As Joseph Addison put it, the Venetians were "tenacious of old Laws and Customs to their great Prejudice, whereas a Trading Nation must be still for new Changes and Expedients, as different Junctures and Emergencies arise." They wished to guarantee, for example, their reputation for manufacturing luxuries. So they emphasised quality at the expense of cost and quantity. In an enlarging world economy, this was a mistake.

There was a deep reluctance among the rulers of Venice to confront a world of change. That is why the Arsenal, the shipbuilding enterprise that had for a long period been the home of technological efficiency, had become by the seventeenth century hopelessly out of date. There was no renewal, and no true renovation. It may be that Venice distrusted itself too much to be capable of change, and made a strength instead out of sheer survival. That is still its most enduring attraction.

So the city took on various historical guises to suit the imperatives of the period. It reinvented itself as Roman. In the second quarter of the sixteenth century buildings were raised in the Roman manner of public architecture. These were heralded by the triumphal gateway to the Arsenal itself; it was the first exercise in Venetian monumentality. In the 1480s shields and helmets of stone were attached to the bas-reliefs of the ducal palace. In the face of threats from two empires, of the Hapsburg Charles V and of Suleiman the Magnificent, Venice laid claim to the inheritance of the greatest of them all. Rome was the context for her particular historical mission. Even the constitution was said to be derived from Roman originals.

The patrician families of the city began to find Roman ancestors, through whom they could plausibly hope to inherit ancient *virtus*. The Cornaro family traced their clan to the Cornelii, and the Barbaro to Ahenobarbus. The dark gown of the governing class was known as a toga, as if the senators of Venice would be as much at home in the Forum as in Saint Mark's Square. The historians of the city identified their founding fathers with the refugees from Troy, who were supposed to have established Rome itself. It was all a great charade, but there comes a time when a nation or nation-state will embrace the most absurd or extravagant claims in order to bolster its sense of identity. So by the sixteenth century the Venetians were calling themselves "the new Romans."

There was in any case a fascination for antiquity. There were antiquities, begged or borrowed or stolen, everywhere in Venice. Classical sculptures and trophies were set up in public places. There were many famous antiquarians. There were also notorious forgers who could knock up a piece of Roman statuary or a classical bronze without any difficulty. In a similar spirit the governors of Venice would sometimes proclaim that a certain activity—let us say education—had been preserved "from the foundation of the city." This was normally quite untrue, but the fraudulence betrayed the reverence for antiquity in itself.

The Venetians were primarily interested in the material remnants of the ancient cultures of Greece and of Rome; they were not interested in their intellectual prowess. Greek for the Venetians was the language of business, rather than the language of Plato. Latin was a necessary *lingua franca*, not an agent of revelation. In Burckhardt's *The Civilisation of the Renaissance in Italy* there is a long section on "The Revival of Antiquity" as an agent of moral and spiritual awareness. Venice is not mentioned in this context. Burckhardt simply praises it as the home of a flourishing publishing trade and the centre of "affectation and bombast" in funerary inscriptions.

The Venetians were understandably proud of their history. "I observe," Lady Blessington wrote in the 1820s, "that the Venetian cicerone [guide] and gondoliers often refer to the past prosperity of Venice, and always in a tone that shows a knowledge of its history, and a pride of its ancient splendour not to be expected from persons of that class." It was, and is, a city based upon memory. It is a city of nostalgia. It lives by remembering, and representing, its past. In the same way visitors are invited to admire buildings and scenes that are so familiar that it is as if they somehow "remember" them.

It is wholly to be expected, therefore, that the Venetian archives are the second largest in the world. Only the archives of the Vatican are more extensive. Yet none are more rich or more detailed than the Venetian papers. Some date from the ninth century. Everything was written down, in the hope that older decisions and provisions might still be useful. It is the measure of the efficiency of a state that it preserves its official documentation. In that sense, Venice was very efficient. The Archivio di Stato, just one of the many official archives, contain 160 km (one hundred miles) of files and documents. When the German historian Leopold von Ranke first came upon them in the 1820s he was, like Cortez on a peak in Darien, staring at an ocean; from his encounter with the papers sprang the first exercise in what was known as "scientific history." They are still an infinite resource for contemporary historians and sociologists, who find there stories and dramas of Venetian life in more profusion than in the scenes of the *commedia dell'arte*.

IV

Republic of Commerce

Area delle Fabbriche Vecchie

13

The Merchants of Venice

The genius of the Venetian state lay in commerce and in industry. Trade was in its blood. The city was sustained by what has been described as the first capitalist economy, but the phrase needs refining. It represented the first great triumph of mercantilist capitalism in Europe, the commercial paradigm for seventeenth-century Amsterdam and for eighteenth-century London. In this market-place everyone came to buy or to sell; the artist and the priest, as well as the merchant, sought for profit. The system of trade defined the social and cultural systems of the city; it subsumed them. Fashion and innovation became the key concepts. Rational calculation, and the abstract relations of credit and exchange, fashioned a wholly new kind of society—a society of commodities and a society of consumers. It has been said that the modern economic spirit sprang from the experience of the city. Paris only took on an urban form, for example, when *mercatores* or merchants settled beside the existing schools and monasteries.

All the actions of Venice, in war and in peace, were determined by the interests of commerce. It conquered only for profit, not for glory, and calculated with cold eye the financial gain to be acquired from the pious aspirations of the Crusades or the brutal sack of Constantinople. Its diplomatic treaties are wrapped in the language of "recompense" and "reparation." In a private document of the fifteenth century, known as the *Morosini Codex*, there is a formulaic sentence for disaster—"many people died and much merchandise was ruined." The essence of trade lies in further and further expansion, but Venice itself could not grow. So it exploited territories overseas from mainland Italy to the island of Cyprus. At the height of its power, it was the third largest state in Europe. It was also the richest. That is why commercial self-interest became a foundation of national ideology.

The earliest example is that of salt. The dwellers of the lagoon, long before the immigrants from the Veneto ever arrived, had traded in that substance; the lagoon was a perfect place for salt pans, with the brine of the low-lying sea all around. But the Venetians pursued that business with a vengeance. They decided to create a monopoly in the supply of salt to the mainland. By force and by conquest Venice appropriated the other centres of salt production in the territories closest to it. Then it applied itself to the salt producers of the entire Adriatic, compelling or bribing them to close their manufactories; if any salt was produced in overseas territories (as it was in the Venetian colony of Cyprus) it was taken to Venice and stored in great warehouses from where it was despatched to consumers at monopoly prices. Effectively the city put down any hint of competition. This was the Venetian way of doing business. In similar fashion it exploited the appetite for spices that re-emerged in the twelfth century, when the Mediterranean became once more open to traffic. Within a short time it dominated the trade. In the sixteenth century, for example, it imported almost six hundred tons of pepper annually from Alexandria. It even had its own pepper officers.

The greatest source of profit lay in trade over long distances; the more the possible risk, the more the possible benefit. It has been calculated that, in the early fifteenth century, there were some 3,300 vessels within the city's mercantile marine. The ships of the Venetians left in convoys; each year there were seven trading expeditions sailing for different destinations. One fleet travelled to the Crimea, for example, and another to Cyprus and Egypt. Venice itself owned the galleys, and rented them out to the highest bidders. It is a perfect example of the city's commercial instinct. The freight, and the dates of travel, were arranged well in advance. Merchants at home would then invest in the journey of the travelling merchant, in return for a large proportion of any subsequent profit. There was much profit to be obtained. On the return of these argosies the quays of Venice were piled high with carpets and silks and perfumes, sacks of cloves and bags of cinnamon. Argosy is indeed the most appropriate word. It derives from the port of Ragusa (Dubrovnik in what is now Croatia), a Venetian colony in the sixteenth century.

In the fourteenth century wax and pepper, sandalwood and ginger, were despatched to Europe by Venetian merchants from the Indies and Syria, Timor and Malabar. The East did not know the market prices of the West, nor did the West know the prices of the East. But the Venetian merchant understood, and calculated, both. Metals and manufactures were despatched to the East, while cotton and spices travelled in the opposite direction. The Venetians exploited opportunities that other cities and other states did not see or to which they were indifferent. Venice is the fulcrum between what we call the medieval, and the early modern, ages.

Some of the earliest banks in the world were established in Venice. There are private banks mentioned in official records from 1270. In the thirteenth century, too, Venice created the first publicly funded national debt, known as the *Monte*. The *Monte* meant literally a "pile" of coins. Until the fourteenth century moneylenders were free to practise in the city, although they were forbidden in most other cities. In the twelfth century charging large interest was said to be "an old Venetian custom." The counters for the money-changers, covered in cloth or carpet, were set up at the base of the campanile in Saint Mark's Square. Truly the Venetians made a religion out of money. On the bills of exchange was often inserted the phrase, "And may Christ watch over you." There was a public bank in the city by 1625, 107 years before the foundation of the Bank of England. Venice became the largest bullion market in the world.

The merchant of Venice was the master of Venice. The founders of Venice were merchants or, rather, they were forced to trade in order to survive. The doges themselves engaged in trade. So there is the curious anomaly that the earliest nobility of the city were wholly involved with commerce; there was no hierarchy of birth, dependent upon a feudal system of honour, but a social framework entirely fashioned out of commercial speculation. As an English ambassador wrote in 1612, *"Omnes vias pecuniae norunt."* They know all the paths of money. Fortunes were not made out of landed property but out of skill in business. This accounts in part for the evident sense of equality that the Venetians experienced, one with another; in the realm of King Money, all subjects are intrinsically equal. Money knows no duty or honour.

Yet in practice it was government of the rich, by the rich, and for the rich. There was no merchants' guild in Venice, for the simple reason that the city itself was one grand guild. It was a government of merchants. Much of its commerce was in fact controlled by a relatively small number of families who had always been in business. They were characterised by their acumen as a family unit so that, for example, the Dandolos were known to be audacious and the Giustinianis were benevolent. The domestic partnership whereby brothers, or fathers and sons, traded together was known as *fraterna*; its account books could pass through many generations, like a piece of family furniture. Household accounts were not separated from business accounts. They amounted to the same thing. The senate was essentially a board of directors, with the doge as the chief executive officer.

The government of the city was practical and efficient; it was moderate in its spending, and vigilant over its auditing of costs. The resources of the city were managed with extreme caution. The Venetians, for example, had great skill in the drawing-up of contracts, which became almost an art form. There was not the expense of a standing army; soldiers were purchased when necessary. The council of ten were charged with the administration of the Mint. The bankers kept their coins in the offices of the state treasury.

The government could only safeguard trade by maintaining liberty and security; liberty in the removal of restrictions, and security in the domination of the sea. The originality of Venetian governance lay in its unique ability to fuse politics and economics into a new form of power. It can be called state capitalism, or communal capitalism, or corporate government. The point is that it worked. In administrative terms, it was the equivalent of the philosopher's stone. The Venetian merchants could also take comfort from Isaiah's disquisition on Tyre that it was "the crowning city, whose merchants are princes, whose traffickers are the honourable of the earth . . . and her merchandise and her hire shall be holiness to the Lord."

The image of the merchant is central to any understanding of Venice. It was even said that all Venetians were merchants. Why should that be so? The merchant is in part a speculator, ready to take acceptable risks for the sake of future profit. He rises to a challenge, but will decline a mere escapade. He is ambitious for supremacy, and competitive if not coercive towards his rivals. But he is also thrifty, and cautious. If these are paradoxical qualities, they are part of the paradox of Venice. The love of commerce, and the desire for gain, are essential to its nature. There were many Venetian proverbs on the subject of money—money is our second blood, money makes money and lice make lice, a man without money is a corpse that walks.

Merchants calculate. They are economical with their time, as well as with their words. Within them are wells of secrecy and duplicity. They have little use for culture unless, that is, a profit can be made out of it. They are interested in peace; but they are, in essence, dispassionate observers of the affairs of the world. An opportunity, after all, can arise out of any situation. War itself can be a source of immense profits, if it is handled in the correct manner. New markets can be opened, and new resources exploited. But the Venetian merchants were more interested in the short, rather than the long, term. They shifted with the ever-shifting scene. That is why they were described as foxes in a world of lions. There is another Venetian proverb: With truth and lies you sell the merchandise.

From the fourteenth to the eighteenth centuries Venice became the city of luxury goods. Luxury may be defined as a form of erotic display, a deep response to the refinements of sensation. It suggests delicacy and rarefied pleasure. One need hardly add that it encourages further and further consumption. We need many things as the staples of life, but we desire even more. Desire lies in the open mouth of the consumer. Venice has always been known as a sensual city, whether in the ubiquity of its courtesans or in the lush canvases of its painters. Both artist and prostitute reflect the underlying reality of the city in which colourful display and material value are sacrosanct. The popular festivities of Venice might also be considered to be an expression of luxury.

Venice possessed no natural resources, and so it relied upon manufacture; the only way of maintaining its supremacy was in the creation of more various and more rarefied items. Luxury was prodigality, whether in spices or perfumes or dye-stuffs or ornaments of gold and rock crystal. Venice traded in them all. It made the glass and the silk and the soap. It manufactured the marzipan as well as the wax. Venice was a centre of silk manufacture, while the neighbouring island of Burano was the home of lace-making and Murano of mirrors and glass. The manufactories of Venice created the first glass window pane, which was undoubtedly a luxury on its arrival. In 1615 it became the first western city to market coffee. The fork was also a Venetian invention, one of the panoply of luxuries that emerged upon the dining table. Venetian households, in general, were known for their ornamentation and luxurious furnishing. The whole city was a hive ever active, relying to a large extent upon rapid and small transactions. You may see the merchants in the paintings, many of them young and eager, surrounded by pens and papers and balances. Each one is in a little world of striving and risk. Lorenzo Lotto finished "Portrait of a Young Man with Account Book" by the early 1530s; from various signs and tokens it is clear that the young man, after an unhappy romance, is seeking for consolation in the perusal of household accounts. He turns the pages of a double-entry register. Never have the blessings of business been more poignantly stated.

But we can move closer to the merchant. We can glimpse more of his life. A manuscript notebook of the early fourteenth century, known as the *Zibaldone da Canal*, has survived. It was compiled by a merchant, of unknown name, and is filled with arithmetical and geometrical notations together with what the merchant calls "many beautiful and subtle calculations." There are medical remedies of an eminently practical nature, together with the most egregious superstitions. He notes that cheese becomes lighter as it dries out, so that it must be weighed carefully at the end of a voyage. He estimates the profit to be earned from gold smuggled into Tunis. He calculates the length of voyages. He recommends that a traveller, on first boarding his ship, should invoke saints Oriele and Tobias. He remarks, also, that there is "a time to threaten and not to fear." The heart of the merchant is thereby laid bare.

In Venice according to one senator, "everything is up for sale." He was referring in particular to political office, when the state itself became the object of commercial speculation, but he was entirely correct in a wider sense. Venice became the market of the world. "Indeed it seems," one visitor wrote in 1494, "as if the whole world flocks there, and that human beings have concentrated all their force for trading." This notion of "force," the energy and power released by commerce, is the perfect word for the tempest of Venetian business. To Venice came the wines of Crete and the cinnamon of the Indies, the carpets of Alexandria and the caviar of Caffa, the sugar of Cyprus and the dates of Palestine. Cloves and nutmegs arrived from the Moluccas by way of Alexandria; the camphor of Borneo was brought to the lagoon together with the pearls and sapphires of Ceylon; the shawls of Kashmir lay beside the musk of Tibet, while the ivory of Zanzibar was unloaded with the rich cloths of Bengal. The Venetian ambassadors signed commercial treaties with the soldan of Egypt and the khan of Tartary, the sultan of Aleppo and the count of Biblos. The sons of nobles became apprentices at sea. Marco Polo was a merchant.

Fernand Braudel, in *Le Temps du Monde* (1979), characterises Venice in 1500 as the centre of the world economy. In 1599 it was described by Lewes Lewkenor as "a common and general market to the whole world." In Coryat's *Crudities* (1611) Saint Mark's Square itself is called the "market-place of the world." The city dominated the Adriatic, and insisted that all of its trade passed through its own ports. Venice fought off all other claimants. It was the quintessential merchant city, the ultimate bazaar.

The early trade fairs of Europe were conducted in Venice, perhaps from the examples of Egypt and Syria. The annual fair of the *Sensa*, with its origins in the twelfth century, was devoted to luxury goods; there were no less than twenty-four shops, for example, reserved for the goldsmiths and the silversmiths. It took place in Saint Mark's Square, lasted for fifteen days, and welcomed some hundred thousand visitors. There were glass-blowers and painters and armourers; in fact, craftsmen of every kind. Trade then became a carnival and an entertainment. It became the object of festive ritual, just as the harvest rites of the countryside had a spiritual as well as a secular importance.

Yet there is a sentence from Voltaire that underlines the economic significance of this trade in luxuries—"*Le superflu, chose très nécessaire*"; luxury was necessary because it stimulated trade. The possession of luxuries, for example, was a vital element in the attainment of status. It has been argued that the growth of luxury is largely responsible for the rise of modern capitalism, in which case Venice was a pioneer capitalist in more than one sense. In its exploitation of raw materials, in its obsession with profit, in its rational organisation of trade and manufacture, and in the size of its operations across the known world, it was the very model of capitalistic enterprise. These urban merchants and shopkeepers learned how to diversify, to create new occupations and products, to seek for simplicity in all forms of exchange.

Luxury is the stepmother of fashion. There were sudden "crazes" in the city and the great chronicler of Venice, Pompeo Molmenti, noted that "no nation ever showed itself so insatiable in the matter of fashions." In his *Treatise of Commerce* (1601) John Wheeler remarked that "all the world choppeth and changeth, runneth & raveth after Marts,

Markets and Merchandising, so that all thinges come into Commerce."
This was the situation of Venice. So here we may see the beginnings of
what has become known as consumer demand. The consumer
emerges in Venice. Fashion was the goddess of this turning world.
Vivaldi was disparaged as yesterday's composer, according to an
eighteenth-century observer, "for fashion is everything in Venice,
where his works have been heard for too long and where last year's
music makes no money." At a later date Margaret Oliphant, the
Scottish novelist, described it as "the sensation-loving city." The ladies
of Venice always wore the latest style, and in the street of merchants
known as the Merceria there was a doll dressed in the latest Parisian
mode. The shop itself became known as "The Doll of France." Fashions
created luxuries; luxuries encouraged trade; trade prompted industry.

Venice was built from gold. It was the golden city. The desire to grow
rich led to an obsession with gold. It was both a solace and a treasure.
It was an investment and a defence. It was glorious. It was pleasing to
the eye. The Venetian protagonist of Ben Jonson's *Volpone* rises with
appropriate words upon his lips, "Good morning to the Day; and, next,
my Gold." In the Mint of Venice there once stood a statue of Apollo
holding gold ingots. Petrarch, in an encomium upon Venice,
enumerated all the wild and distant places to which its merchants
travelled. "Behold," he wrote, "what men will do for the thirst of gold!"
One early fifteenth-century doge spoke of Venice as holding the
"*signoria dell'oro*" or lordship of gold. Venice was golden in the manner
of Jerusalem or of the celestial city.

   Gold was one of the principal glories of Venetian painting. The
artists worked with gold thread and gold dust and flakes of gold. The
Virgin, in Bellini's "Frari Triptych," is enthroned beneath a gold mosaic;
she is suffused by a golden light that seems to contain the sweet breath
of eternity. This is the light that can be experienced in Venice itself.
The same painter, in his "Agony in the Garden," bathed Christ's back
with powdered gold. In his "Resurrection," at the Scuola di S. Rocco,
Tintoretto has gilded the branches of the fig tree so that the light of the
miracle may be seen to touch and transfigure the natural world. Gold,
believed to be engendered by the sun in the bowels of the earth, is a
sacred commodity.

   The most celebrated *casa*, or house, in Venice is surely the Ca d'Oro.

Its façade, constructed between 1421 and 1437, was so embossed and gilded that it became a glittering wall of light. There were 22,075 sheets of gold leaf fixed upon its surface. It was matched in the city only by the "golden coffer" of the Fondaco dei Tedeschi and the "golden basilica" of Saint Mark's. In the basilica itself is displayed the *Pala d'Oro*, the gilded altar screen encrusted with precious jewels. The fame of Venetian goldsmiths was such that their work became known as *opus Veneticum*. Gold was used in the decoration of Venetian glass, and was of course part of the texture of the cloth of gold worn by the doge. When dressed in gold the doge became an emblem of the city and a token of its wealth. The precious material represented dignity and moral power. Even the performers in Venetian operas were dressed in gold.

There is the less lovely topic of land, to which the Venetians applied a form of agricultural capitalism. In the fifteenth century Venice acquired much territory on the mainland. A century later, the landscape had been transformed. The patricians had in part eschewed maritime trade, and concentrated instead upon their investments on *terra firma*. The labourers in the fields worked under the eyes of supervisors. The barns and the wine-presses were organised for the maximum efficiency. Land was reclaimed, systems of irrigation were introduced. The Venetians applied the techniques used for the creation of the city itself. It marked the end of feudalism, and the new exploiters of the land eventually became known as the *capitalisti*. At the same time the appetite for bucolic poetry, and the affection for pastoral landscapes, became more pronounced. Culture followed economics.

In the seventeenth century, as trade became ever more difficult and uncertain in a world of change, the patricians of Venice saw land itself as the major source of income. Rice and maize were exported; mulberry trees were cultivated. By the eighteenth century agriculture had become the single most profitable enterprise in Venice. There were those at the time who lamented this flight from mercantile trade to farming. It was wrong to abandon the sea, the mirror of Venice, in order to harvest the land. Or so it seemed. But the Venetians had always sought profit rather than honour. By exploiting the *terra firma*, they remained true to their first principle. Yet of course there were consequences. The partial withdrawal of Venice from the international world of trade inevitably led to a decline in influence and in status. The Venetians became more provincial.

The principal market of the city, however, remained that of the Rialto. It was the power station of Venice. It was the seed, the origin. It resembled the City of London, the centre of London's energy, but on a more local and much more intense scale. Here the first settlers were supposed to have come ashore and, by the strange alchemy of the city, here the first negotiators or merchants began their trade. Commerce seems to have sprung up, fully armed, from the ground itself. It enters the public records of the city at the end of the eleventh century, when the patrician families of Gradenigo and Orio gave up their properties in the neighbourhood of the Rialto for use as a public market; the area had been a commercial centre for some time, primarily used by butchers, and the gift to the Venetian commune was a recognition of that fact. In the twelfth century the private houses in the neighbourhood were converted into shops and warehouses. It became truly a bazaar. Such was the importance of its commerce that, in 1497, the council of ten decreed it to be a *sacrario* or sacred precinct. On Ash Wednesday and Good Friday there were ducal processions to the two principal churches of the Rialto. Trade could have no finer commendation. It had been enshrined.

The Rialto grew and grew. Outlying streets were cleared and widened; the canals were improved, and docks constructed. In the 1280s the Rialto Nuovo was erected to the west of the original market and, thirty years later, the Campo di Rialto was enlarged. There was a general desire to bring harmony and even dignity to this commercial scene; a great map of the world was placed on the wall of its principal colonnade. There was a prison, and a pillar for public proclamations. There were warehouses, too, and government offices for the administration of trade. The patricians met and mingled within a loggia or open-sided gallery at the base of the Rialto bridge. When much of the neighbourhood was destroyed by fire in 1514, it was rebuilt on the same pattern with the streets or "blocks" running parallel to each other. The essential conservatism of the Venetians required that they should preserve the old forms. The passageways of the Rialto, like a *souk* out of the East, had become the natural expression of trade.

The main street was lined with shops selling luxury goods, but there were areas for banking and for shipping insurance. There were separate markets for diverse commodities, and "specialist" stalls such as those for leather goods. The more expensive the items, the closer they were to the heart of the Rialto; this central spot was marked by the little church of S. Giacomo di Rialto. Taverns and brothels were on the periphery, where they were joined by rag-sellers and dealers in second-hand goods. It was an island of money-making, from the highest to the lowest. It was a little Venice within the larger Venice, a vivid instance of the commercial life.

There was already a wooden bridge linking both sides of the Grand Canal in the vicinity; it was rebuilt on two separate occasions but it could hold out no longer against the tide of improvement. The first stone of the existing bridge was laid in 1588, and the work was completed within three years. Two rows of shops and stalls lined its span of eighty-nine feet (27 m), but the higher significance of commerce was not neglected. On its side were sculpted the figures of the Archangel Gabriel and the Virgin Mary. Hail, money, full of grace.

The city's topography, therefore, was defined by its centres of trade. The larger *campi* became open-air markets. The Merceria, the route linking Saint Mark's Square and the Rialto, was lined with 276 shops of every kind. It was, according to John Evelyn, "one of the most delicious streetes in the world." There were also pedlars and street-sellers, hucksters and itinerant craftsmen; sales and auctions were held in the streets, beneath porticoes or in the shade of the churches. Shops themselves became places of assembly. It was a great carnival of commerce.

There were traders of every description. There were no less than forty trading guilds, ranging from apothecaries to weavers, from victuallers to barber surgeons. There were also hundreds of different occupations without a guild, from wet-nurses to porters and latrine-cleaners. It has been surmised that virtually the whole population of Venice worked. It was a desperate obligation for those below the level of the patrician. The existing street names of the city bear witness to the forgotten world of work and trade—a street of the sheet-metal workers, a street of soap-makers, a street of wax factories, a street of dyers. The street of the goldsmiths became, at the end of the nineteenth century, the street of the greengrocers. The tailors and the jewellers worked together in the same quarter. Jacopo Bellini, the progenitor of the great Bellini family, executed many drawings and studies of the itinerant labour of his city. He knew that these tradesmen and hucksters were the essence of Venice itself.

A large proportion of Venetians worked in the textile industry. There were the lace-makers, their eyesight ruined by their labour. Children, from the age of five, were enrolled in the trade. The exquisite refinement of the art, prized by the rich matrons of Europe, can be measured in human suffering. Other workers turned raw English wool into finished articles. The looms of the city produced damask and cloth of gold. There were weavers of tapestry and spinners of cotton. Of course women and children were part of this enormous trade. The workshop knows no gender. Despite the severe restrictions placed upon the movement and freedom of patrician women, the females of the lower orders were treated as fuel for the fire of the Venetian economy. Women were employed as printers and sail-makers, iron-mongers and chimney-sweeps.

There were also female hawkers. Gaetano Zompino published *Cries of Venice* (1785) in which he listed sixty different varieties of hawker. Similar books were written in London and Paris, but in Venice the endless sound of human voices would have a distinct and different quality. There was no other background noise, apart from the hurrying feet of the passers-by and the calls of the gondoliers. The cries of the wood-dealer and the chair-mender and the man with the performing monkey would have echoed through the streets of stone, joyful and mournful, intense and intimate. Tomatoes a little sour, perfect for the salad! Women, you must make water with lemons! The pears that wet the beard!

In this climate everything could be raised, or lowered, to the status of a commodity. As Venice grew richer the churches became ever more ornate, as ornamented and encrusted as the jewel boxes of the great Venetian ladies; it was reported that, at the time of the creation of Venice, the Almighty had been promised "a hundred temples of gold and marble." The reverence for show and splendour began early. That is why Venice was the showcase of the world. Information became a commodity, as Venice became the centre for the trade in printed books. Knowledge could indeed be packaged like a consignment of pepper. Albrecht Dürer, a resident of Venice for a time, executed a sketch in which books are being produced en masse as if they were loaves of bread. As a result there were more literate people in Venice than in any other part of Italy. Incipient capitalism had its uses. It is appropriate that the manufacture of spectacles, for the purpose of reading, was begun in Venice.

There was a thriving trade in human flesh. By the twelfth century the slave trade in Venice far surpassed that of other cities and other countries. The Venetians were incorrigible slave traders, and the markets of the Rialto and S. Giorgio were centres of slavery. They were eager for this particular source of income, since the profit on each item was said to be 1,000 per cent. They sold Russians and even Greek Christians to the Saracens. Men and women and children were bought or captured in the region of the Black Sea—Armenians and Georgians among them—before being despatched to Venice where they were in turn sold on to Egypt and Morocco and Crete and Cyprus. They sold boys and young women as concubines. One doge, Pietro Mocenigo, had in his seventies two young Turkish men in his entourage.

Many of them were consigned to Venetian households. No patrician family was complete without a retinue of three or four slaves; even Venetian artisans owned slaves, and used them in their shops or workshops. Venetian convents possessed slaves for domestic service. The galleys were stocked with slaves. But the city always needed a fresh supply; servile status was not inheritable. Many slaves were freed in the wills of their masters or mistresses. Marco Polo manumitted one of his slaves, Peter the Tartar, before his own death in 1324. In 1580 there were three thousand slaves in the capital. The black gondoliers in Carpaccio's paintings of Venice are all slaves.

The solemn benefits of the Church could also be bought and sold, with the purchase of altars and windows and commemorative masses. In 1180 a stall was set up in Saint Mark's Square for the sale of indulgences from time spent in Purgatory. Relics could be purchased. The seamless robe of the Saviour was valued at 10,000 ducats. The island of Crete was slightly cheaper. It was sold to Venice for a thousand silver marks.

Music and art, sculpture and opera, were all appraised by the criteria of profit and loss. The point was put plainly enough by the quintessentially Venetian artist of the eighteenth century, Giambattista Tiepolo, who suggested that painters should "please noble, rich people . . . and not other people who cannot buy paintings of great value." Yet this could be construed as a moral, as well as an economic, imperative. Artists might, in the process of appealing to the wealthy, "be directed towards the sublime, heroic, towards perfection." In Venice there was every reason to believe that the possession of money was compatible with the pursuit of glory. It might even be argued that the Renaissance itself, springing from the social and cultural life of the Italian cities, was the first movement towards the commodification of the western world; it was composed in part of art objects that could be ordered and purchased, that could be transferred from place to place, that were not unique to one city or one society. In Venice we can witness the rise of cultural materialism, which in turn created the first cosmopolitan culture. Music was part of the market, too, in which Vivaldi and Galuppi drove hard bargains. Opera was notably successful in Venice because, from the beginning, it was highly profitable. Speculators even made money from the leasing of boxes. It is hard to name one activity in the city that was not commercial in origin or in nature.

The painters of Venice, in their portraits and in their more expansive urban scenes, provided an inventory of costly material goods. The sitter is seen with his or her possessions, and the city is decked in ornate splendour. Bellini's paintings depict the fine porcelain, and the sumptuous carpets, currently available in Venetian shops. These canvases were in turn placed within gilded and elaborate frames. It is not accidental that Venetian houses were known for their plenitude of pictures. Everything promised richness.

Artists came to the lagoon in order to learn the techniques of powdered gold, used in painting and in manuscript illumination. In Venice they would also find the finest pigments, brought from the East. Venetian painters, too, were well known for their skill in depicting the texture and appearance of the velvets and satins that were sold in the city itself. In a portrait of one doge, Bellini clothes him with the costly damask that had only recently been imported from the Levant. The sign of art as a commodity is the surface. In many cases the surface is without content or, more precisely, the nature of the subject is subordinated to the imperatives of surface decoration or ostentatious costliness. It is one of the attributes of capitalist enterprise that an object is no longer significant for its essence but for its exchange value. Here we may see one of the abiding characteristics of Venetian painting.

The notion of art as trade is of intrinsic importance to the cultural history of Venice. Most works were commissioned directly from the patron or patrons, and so the artists responded directly to what we might call consumer demand. There was an association, in the fifteenth century, between artistic theory and trading practice. There were manuals instructing the merchant on the right shades of dyes and spices, couched in precisely the terms that the artist would understand. In the activities of trade and art, objects become separated from the world; they are more intensely seen and judged. The consumer, too, judges by the senses.

There was also a connection between mercantile calculation and pictorial geometry; Piero della Francesca, after all, wrote *A Treatise on the Abacus* as well as one entitled *On Perspective in Painting*. When a Venetian merchant calculated the volume and appearance of his goods he was engaged in the same process as the Venetian artist. Sebastiano Serlio and Andreas Vesalius both lived in Venice, or in the Veneto, in the 1530s. One wrote a treatise on human architecture, and the other completed a treatise on the human body; the finely shaded illustrations in both books bear a striking resemblance.

A steady supply of paintings was despatched along the trade routes of the city, on both sides of the Adriatic; in a literal sense art followed commerce. The establishment of trade between Venice and the Netherlands, for example, heralded the profitable interchange between two schools of painting. When Venice and Germany joined in commerce, they also joined in art. The good citizens of Augsburg and Salzburg had many paintings of the Venetian school; the collectors of Venice possessed many works from German and Netherlandish painters.

There was also a market for "utility art," with panel paintings used as devotional props and easel paintings as interior decoration. The material, rather than aesthetic, quality of the work was the important consideration. By the sixteenth century there were already "dealers" operating in Venice, mediating between artist and client, or between seller and purchaser. The contracts drawn up between consumer and supplier often specified the amount of gold, or expensive pigment, to be employed in any one painting. They ordained the nature, as well as the dimensions, of the work. They included a "deadline" for completion as well as penalty clauses for late delivery. Some contracts even included a clause in which the artist agreed to surpass the work of another named artist. Tintoretto, from a family of dyers, had all the skills of the merchant. He habitually undercut the prices of his rivals, thus assuring a steady supply of commissions. He worked quickly as well as cheaply. The letters of Titian are filled with money matters, with haggling and demanding and complaining. Canaletto, two centuries later, was a master of the export trade. Tiepolo concentrated upon the production of historical and allegorical painting on the very good grounds that only they provided him with a reasonable profit margin.

There was a passion for collecting in Venice; anything, from Roman coins to freaks of nature, could be taken up and placed in cabinets or cupboards. So the city could become a market in another sense. Private collecting was a Venetian phenomenon of the sixteenth and seventeenth centuries. It created new forms of demand, and new methods of accumulation; it made the act of possession intrinsically worthwhile. The consumer could pose as the connoisseur. The sybarite could become a humanist saint. He was called a virtuoso. The first known collections were Venetian, dating from the fourteenth century. But the obsession with *studioli* or curiosity shops just grew and grew. The collection of the Venetian patrician Andrea Vendramin included sculptures and medals, urns and gems, lamps and shells, plants and manuscripts, costumes and mummified animals. The whole world could be purchased and displayed. Another Venetian patrician, Federigo Contarini, aspired to possess a specimen of every thing or being ever created; in this, of course, he could not be assured of success. During the course of the seventeenth century possession became more specific and specialised. There was a market for antiquities and a market for landscape paintings; there was a market in natural marvels, such as the many-headed hydra valued at six thousand ducats, and a market in ancient musical instruments. Coins and medals were also popular. The collection of Apostolo Zeno, for example, contained 5,900 medals. We must never forget, however, the commercial instinct of the Venetians. Zeno's medals were a financial investment as well as a scholarly marvel. A collection could also be a portfolio. That is perhaps why it was an enduring, as well as a widespread, passion in the city. The last great Venetian collector, Conte Vittorio Cini, died in 1977.

Niccolò Serpetro's *Marketplace of Natural Marvels* was published in

The Battle of Lepanto, painted by Paolo Veronese in 1571. This work was completed just a few months after a famous victory of the Venetian forces (among others) over the Turks. Two hundred and thirty Turkish vessels were sunk or captured, with only thirteen losses for the Europeans. Lepanto was the last battle in which the use of the oar held the key. In later engagements the sails were raised.

Plan of the Arsenal in the seventeenth century. The Arsenal of Venice was the largest shipbuilding enterprise in the world, with its own network of docks and system of production lines. Ships were turned out from the shipbuilding yards of the Arsenal fully rigged and fitted, in the first version of the capitalist factory.

Detail of a Venetian warship, taken from the mausoleum of Girolamo Michiel completed in 1559. The image of the ship, and the circumambient sea, can be glimpsed everywhere in Venice. The city itself can be seen as a ship upon the waves.

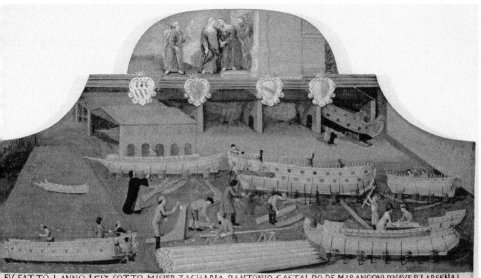

FV FATTO LANNO 1517 SOTTO MISIER ZACHARIA DANTONIO GASTALDO DE MARANGONI DNAVE D'LARSENAL
FV RINOVATO D'LANNO 1753 SOTTO LA GASTALDIA DI FRANCESCO ZANOTTO GASTALDOE COMPAGNI

he sign for the Marangoni family of shipbuilders, painted on panel in 1517. Shipbuilding s of course one of the principal crafts of a city surrounded by water. Ship–builders offered defence, and protection, against the watery element.

1 van Grevenbroeck's painting of a workman dredging a canal, an image of the eighteenth century. In all periods of Venetian history the government was involved in major efforts concerning health care and sanitation.

Jan van Grevenbroeck's painting of an oar-maker at work in Arsenal. Oar-making wa one of the many Venetian trades springing from the sea. The oar was used in the perp ual battle against the natural world and in warfare against the city's competitors.

A painting of a Venetian doctor during time of plague, by Jan van Grevenbroeck. the time of pestilence the doctors clothed th selves in black robes, coated with wax and matic oils; they wore a hood and cowl their heads, large glasses to protect their and a long beak-like nose with a filter a end. They looked themselves like ghou

The shop of a Venetian bell-maker, at the end of the eighteenth century, painted by van Grevenbroeck. Venice was a city of be all of them pealing together at the time of processions. They also had a more practica use. The bells rang out at precise times of to coordinate the activities of the populac

owroom with lamps and vases. For many centuries Venice has been famous for its glass-
king, now the preponderant industry on the island of Murano. What is the attraction of
glass for the city of the sea? Glass is material sea. It is sea made solid, its translucence
captured and held immobile.

Lace workers on the island of Burano, photographed at the end of the nineteenth
century. Burano has been for many centuries the home of lace-making in Venice.
Lace is a Venetian specialty; like the mosaic it is an art of elaboration and intricacy.

A Venetian courtyard at the
end of the nineteenth centu
Venice is a city of dead-end
and of circuitous alleys; ther
are twisting *calli*, and hidden
turnings; there are low arch
and blank courtyards, where
silence is suspended like a n

A photograph of a fu
gondola, taken at the begi
of the twentieth ce
Venice has always
associated with death, ar
gondola itself has often
viewed as a floating h

...ew railway bridge ...he lagoon, depicted in ...ddle of the nineteenth ...y. The bridge ...ented perhaps the ...adical change in the ...y of Venice. It became ...cted to the mainland. ...ity was no longer ...nd, and had lost its ...ved status as a refuge ...he world. It meant, ...at the prime signifi- ...of the water had gone ...r. It became a city ...chanical, rather than ...ural, time.

The remains of the ...panile, which collapsed ...7 July 1902. It buckled ...lded upon itself, neatly ...loding into a large pile ...of rubble. It fell, as the ...netians said at the time, ...ke a gentleman." There ...ere no fatalities, except ...at of the caretaker's cat.

LA DOMENICA DEL CORRIERE

| ABBO. . . . . L. 5 — | L. 8 — | SI PUBBLICA A MILANO OGNI DOMENICA | Uffici del giornale: |
| Semestre . . . . » 2.50 | » 4 — | Dono agli Abbonati del " Corriere della Sera " | Via Pietro Verri, 14 MILANO |

Anno IV. — N. 30.   27 Luglio 1902   Centesimi 10 il Numero.

CIÒ CHE È RIMASTO DEL CAMPANILE DI SAN MARCO, A VENEZIA, DOPO IL CROLLO AVVENUTO IL 14 CORRENTE.
(Disegno di A. Beltrame, dal vero).

An illustration taken from *The Stones of Venice* by John Ruskin, displaying types of the wind
from the early Gothic palaces. The style was dominant in the fourteenth and fifteenth centur
surviving even into the sixteenth century and giving an unmistakeable aspect to the city th
still survives. Most of the well-known palaces or great houses are created in the Gothic mc

Venice in 1653 with the entirely appropriate notion of placing the curiosities of nature in an imaginary piazza not unlike Saint Mark's Square; here, amid the porticos and shops and stalls, the wonders of the world could be purchased. The market is the metaphor, and the reality. Everything is on display. The display, rather than any intrinsic worth, is the point. Serpetro's imagined world was re-created in the late eighteenth century, when a great wooden oval was constructed in Saint Mark's Square entirely for the display of goods. The Venetians were celebrated for their skill at window-dressing, and created the first glass shopfronts in the world. So their markets were great exhibitions. From the fairs of the twelfth century onwards, the goods of the city were paraded. At a later date works of art were put up for sale in the square, classical and contemporary works hanging side by side in the open air. It is entirely appropriate that the Venice Biennales—of art, of film and of architecture—are still flourishing at the beginning of the twenty-first century. They are continuing a great tradition of showmanship.

The first factories of capitalism were the silk manufactories of Venice. Ships were turned out from the shipbuilding yards of the Arsenal fully rigged and fitted, in the same fashion as the automobiles of a later date. Glass-making and mirror-making were full-blown industrial enterprises, in which the division of labour was matched by the economies of scale. These were family trades, too, with the son taking over from the father.

The authorities of the city also invented the concept of "zoning," whereby industries were despatched to separate locations. It would be possible to construct a map of Venice in which every trade and industry is given a separate territory, cloth-stretchers to the west and tin-smiths to the north-east. The area of Dorsoduro was taken up by fishermen and silk-workers, while that of Castello was inhabited by sailors and by shipbuilders. This rationalisation of urban space continued well into the nineteenth century, when it was decreed that the Lido should be devoted to recreation and become a seaside resort.

The industrial power of Venice, pre-eminent in the sixteenth century, is attested by the fact that its technical innovations soon reached other parts of Europe. The manufacture of gold cloth in France was introduced by the weavers of the city. Luxury soap-making came out of Venice. The type fonts of the Venetian presses were copied in other cities. Venetian workers revolutionised the production of fine woollen cloth. The city became the unlikely setting for technological change and innovation. For more than a century it was the first industrial city in Italy and, indeed, the centre of European industry. At the peak of its development, in the third quarter of the sixteenth century, its population reached 180,000.

In the end that industry declined. The nature of any decline in the human world is interesting. As a spectacle, it is arresting; as a lesson, it is invaluable. A nation in decline is always more intriguing than a nation at the summit of its power. Sorrow and humility are always more attractive than triumph. But was this the case with Venice? There seems to have been very little sorrow, and no humility at all.

The reasons for the industrial decline of the city are many and various; they may be said to be part of changes in the human world as a whole. The discovery of new trade routes, and the emerging supremacy of Amsterdam and London in the late seventeenth century, have been cited as explanations. The merchants of England, Holland and France were able to undercut the prices of Venetian suppliers. The Venetian government refused to compromise on the quality of its luxury goods; its competitors had no such scruples. The cloths and metals of the north were cheaper. It was, in essence, the global transition from the Mediterranean to the North Atlantic. The compass of the world had changed. That is why in the seventeenth century the wool market, the staple of Venetian trade, was perilously close to collapse. The Venetians, too, were temperamentally averse to innovation; as we have already noticed, the patricians and merchants were traditionalists. The habits of control and regulation, born from the earliest communal fight of Venice to survive, could not be changed in a generation. Other economies were more open, and more flexible. By the beginning of the eighteenth century, therefore, Venetian industry had been curtailed.

Yet it cannot be said that the standards of living, among the various sections of the Venetian populace, were notably affected. Certainly it would be wrong to talk in anthropomorphic terms of "weakness" or "decay." Perhaps, after all, talk of decline is unwarranted. There may simply be transition. Venice merely changed its nature, to deal with changing circumstances, and attained commercial success in a different guise. It is still a rich, and richly endowed, city. It is the home of biennales and of tourists. It has in effect marketed and sold its ultimate commodity—itself. Its history and memory have been transformed into luxury goods for the delectation of travellers and visitors. It traded in goods and in people; now, finally, it trades upon itself.

14

The Endless Drama

Venice might be described as a series of box-like stages, opening out one into another. It is the merest cliché that it resembles a vast stage set, against which the citizens engaged in carnival and parade. The paintings of Carpaccio and of Longhi, the drawings of Jacopo Bellini, depict it as a form of sacred theatre; in the work of these Venetian artists the city is a *tableau vivant*, suffused with what W.D. Howells in *Venetian Life* described as "the pleasant improbability of the theatre." The citizens are displayed in groups, with actions and attitudes taken from the stage or from the pageant. It has always been a place of artifice, where even the natural has a sprinkling of stage dust. It glitters. The houses and churches have the air of stage properties, sited for the convenience of the eye. The arches and the stairs are mere effects. The palace of the doge, and the basilica of Saint Mark, take their place before the proscenium of Saint Mark's Square.

The pageant masters made full use of the square for floats and parades, mummeries and processions; on great state occasions, the theatrical possibilities of the city were exploited to the full. The square was also the stage on which acrobats and magicians performed. Puppet theatres were especially popular, in a city that was itself often described as a puppet show. Venice welcomed actors dressed in motley. There were even stages on the water, during the pageants and festivities. Stages were erected on the Grand Canal for the performance of serenatas. There were ornamental barges, too, for singers and musicians. The water was a perfect auditorium as well as a stage.

The façades of the Venetian churches were often eminently theatrical, with fantastic ornaments of stone loaded upon them; the curved mouldings vie with the contorted columns; volutes and pinnacles, capitals and cornices, are piled high in wedding-cake fashion. The church of S. Moise, built by Alessandro Tremignon in 1688, is a riot of whimsical excess. The more famous Salute invites awe rather than admiration. The religious services of Venice were theatrical in conception and execution, with music more suitable for an opera than for a sacred occasion; the congregation was an audience, chattering and gossiping through the proceedings, and the ritual was a performance. The recesses of the churches create an authentic air of mystery; the confused light and darkness, the brilliance of marble and precious stone, the air steeped in the perfume of incense, are all what Ruskin termed the "stage properties of superstition" in Venice. They are to be found in the basilica of Saint Mark, for example, which Ruskin considered to be of a theatrical nature "unexampled in any other European church."

Yet the theatricality of Venice was sometimes a cause of complaint among Venetians themselves. When at the end of the sixteenth century new pillars were added to the square one senator, Federigo Contarini, compared them to theatre props. In the twenty-first century the newly rebuilt theatre, La Fenice, has been criticised by some Venetians as a contrived pastiche of the previous building destroyed by fire. Theatricality is everywhere.

The convents of Venice became a form of theatre, with the nuns sitting behind gratings watching the rest of Venice cavort before them; masked balls, with the characters of Pierrot and Harlequin, were performed for their delectation. The private trials of Venice were conceived in theatrical terms. During one hearing of the Inquisition the walls of the chamber were draped in black; the curtains were suddenly thrown back to reveal a strangled corpse. The deliberations of the council of ten depended upon surprise and suddenness. The head of the police in the late eighteenth century, Missier Grando, always dressed in black. The various receptions and meetings, conducted within the ducal palace, were occasions of intense theatricality. At an ambassador's reception the doge sat wrapped in a golden cloak, with the various councillors ranged about him. Upon the death of a doge a great procession circled Saint Mark's Square, each member carrying a large candle or torch; in front of the basilica the coffin was raised and lowered nine times while the bells of the city tolled. On Good Friday torches were lit beside the houses and palaces that lined the canals, so that all the waterways of Venice were illuminated by fiery reflections. The power of visual spectacle was more important to Venice than to any other European city.

There was a long history in Venice of collaboration between art and theatre. Jacopo Bellini was a pageant master and stage designer as well as an artist; at the time there would have been no need to distinguish his different roles. He was simply *festaiuolo* or organiser of festive play. The art of Veronese and of Tintoretto is in part the art of staging; theirs was an intensely theatrical vision. The work of Veronese was known as *"maestoso teatro"* or majestic theatre. He in turn has been associated with the great architects of Venice, Sansovino and Palladio, who share with the artist a sense of space and structure. When Sansovino redesigned the piazzetta in the sixteenth century he intuitively defined it as a stage set with a one-point perspective; from the *bacino*, the basin of water before it, the buildings on both sides diminish towards the "vanishing point" of the ornate clock tower. From the other direction, looking from the piazzetta towards the *bacino*, the two great pillars frame the watery landscape. Here some of the great set scenes of Venetian life were conducted. This was the site, for example, of the public executions. The rituals of Venice were surrounded by stage fire.

Tintoretto acquired the habit of placing small figurines, of wax or clay, in illuminated boxes. This was the brilliantly lit arena of his imagination, prior to his work on canvas. But the light is that of the stage spotlight. Tintoretto and Veronese also designed, and sketched, costumes for the stage. They needed to look no further than their canvases for inspiration. Tiepolo, too, revealed an interest in decorative costume; he also favoured exaggerated theatrical gesture and facial expression. The characters depicted in his paintings are often grouped together in the fashion of a dramatic chorus; they are earnest, purposeful and emotional. They have the bearing of actors, figures of *commedia dell'arte* under the impress of strong feeling.

This can only happen in a culture where no distinction is made between nature and art, between what is real and what is artificial. Or, rather, the distinction does not matter. The importance of anything lies in the gaiety and brilliance of its surface. Expression and activity are of more consequence than essence or being. That is perhaps an inevitable consequence of urban life, where everyone must signal his or her role. But it also seems peculiarly appropriate to Venice. Wagner, an adept at scenic mysteries, recognised the truth of the city at once. He remarked that "everything strikes one as a marvellous piece of stage-scenery," and that this unreality created a "peculiar gaiety" that could not help but affect any visitor. The "chief charm," he added, "consists in its all remaining as detached from me as if I were in the actual theatre."

Detachment is the key. It is actually the reverse of what Coleridge once called "the willing suspension of disbelief." We know that it is a real city, with real people, but we will proceed as if it were unreal. It was often noticed that the people of Venice were themselves detached from the world beyond their city. The government of Venice, by the eighteenth century, was considered too remote from the ordinary dealings of the world to be of any consequence. It was, you might say, trapped in its theatre. As the power of Venice declined in absolute terms, in that century, its capacity for life and display was never more exalted. The glorious past and the uncertain future were obscured by carnival and festival. This was not an isolated phase in the city's history. During the Austrian siege of Venice in the early nineteenth century, when suffering and hardship and famine became the lot of all citizens, the people crowded on balconies and rooftops to watch the bombardment. The summits of the campanili and the towers of the churches were filled with Venetians bearing spy-glasses and telescopes so that they might more clearly see the destruction being inflicted upon their own city.

In foreign productions, as, for example, in the theatres of London, Venice was often viewed as a stage set. The Christmas pantomime at Drury Lane, in 1831, included a diorama entitled "Venice and its Adjacent Islands." When Byron's plays, *Marino Faliero* and *The Two Foscari*, were produced the stage sets were considered to be the most considerable element of the entertainment. When Charles Kean played Shylock in *The Merchant of Venice*, in 1858, the sets were praised for their realism. But what reality were they reflecting other than the theatrical image already in the public mind? This is the context for Edward Lear's disappointment with the buildings of Venice, from which he derived "not one whit more of pleasure from seeing them there than in any of the many theatre scenes, dioramas, panoramas, and all other ramas whatever." He knew them all already.

There is no scene in Venice that has not already been painted. There is no church, or house, or canal, that has not become the subject of an artist's brush or pencil. Even the fruit in the market looks as if it has been stolen from a still-life. Everything has been "seen" before. The traveller seems to be walking through oils and water-colours, wandering across paper and canvas. It is no accident that Venice has also become a traditional setting for twentieth-century, and twenty-first-century, fiction or film. It is the natural home for the sensational and the melodramatic. Narratives of intrigue and mystery are commonly set in the *calli* and *campi* of the city, and Venice is the obvious setting for an international film festival. Venice is not so much a city as the representation of a city.

So what were the Venetians themselves but actors, characters against a celebrated backdrop? Henry James, in *The Aspern Papers*, described them as "members of an endless dramatic troupe." There is the gondolier and the lawyer, in their characteristic costumes; there is the housewife and the beggar. All of these people live in public. They delight in self-expression. They share the same language of gesture and attitude. They talk continually. They describe and imitate one another. They watch one another against the background of little shops and houses. They live in an intense and circumscribed space. It is another example of the Venetian life of the surface, where the primacy lies with what is seen. Hence, in the last century of the republic, the sublime importance of the mask or *bauta*.

The transcripts of trials, now held in the abundant archives of Venice, demonstrate the extent to which instinctive and unforced drama entered social and domestic life. The demeanour, as well as the evidence, of the witnesses was recorded. One book-keeper was described as wiping his face with his handkerchief, and twisting himself about, under the strain of testimony. There were dramatic phrases in the courts. "I never wanted him. I said yes with my voice but not with my heart." "I do not even talk with her or her friends, because they are not meat for my teeth." It is reported that the actors who performed in the various *campi* were employed to coach witnesses in the arts of speech and gesture.

It is always possible to see urban life as a form of theatre. When Wordsworth described London, in the *Prelude*, he reached for theatrical metaphors; he wrote of "shifting pantomimic scenes" and "dramas of living Men." London was for a him a "great Stage." But Venice possessed these qualities *in excelsis*. The masquerades of the Carnival were participating in one giant dramatic performance of which the city was the centre. The spectators become part of the play, and the crowd swirls in and around this living theatre. The memoirs of that quintessential Venetian, Giacomo Casanova, demonstrate the facility with which life in the city can be turned into self-conscious and self-serving drama. The individual Venetian, without mask or cloak, can become a lithe performer. Goethe noticed a man by a quayside, telling stories in Venetian dialect to a small group of bystanders. "There was nothing obtrusive or ridiculous about his manner," he wrote, "which was even rather sober; at the same time both the variety and precision of his gestures showed art and intelligence."

Venetians delighted in costume. They sometimes seemed to be dressed up as actors playing in a particularly sophisticated city comedy, and in 1610 a volume of illustrations was published with the title *Outfits of Venetian Men and Women*. They had a keen eye for fashion and for striking colour. They manifested an almost child-like delight in dressing-up. The patrician women of Venice in particular loved sumptuous attire. Indeed they seem to have been almost obliged to do so by the state. For one feast in honour of the French ambassadors, in 1459, the senate ordered all female guests to arrive in bright clothing and to wear as many jewels as possible. The appearance of wealth, and luxury, was all that mattered.

Evelyn described the garb of Venetian women as "very odd, as seeming allwayes in Masquerade." Fynes Morisson gave a more graphic description, noting that they "shew their naked necks and breasts, and likewise their dugges, bound up and swelling with linen." Their hats boasted many accessories, including butterflies and flowers and stuffed birds. But this was the Venetian talent for outward show. It seems, from certain allusions, that it was not customary to change under-garments very frequently. They were scrupulous in one respect, however. They wore veils, white for the young and black for the middle-aged or the old. But the Venetian women were most notorious, and conspicuous, for their shoes or *zoccoli*. These were effectively stilts, as much as eighteen inches (457 mm) in height, upon which they were balanced by attendants. They looked like giants in a pantomime. Venetian women were said to be half of flesh and half of wood. The preposterous footwear has been explained by the muddiness of the streets, or by the Venetian male restriction on female roaming. It also allowed the presence of gaudy or decorative trains. It is more likely, however, to have been a fashion that got out of control.

It might be mentioned, in passing, that Venetian women had the general practice of dyeing their hair yellow. One of the ingredients in the process was human urine.

But the quest for *la bella figura* ran among both genders and among all classes. The women of the poorer sort wore simple gowns and shawls, but they had a liking for small rings of chain which they wore around their wrists and necks. The fishermen wore large brown hooded cloaks complete with scarlet lining. The gondoliers wore white shoes and red sashes. Female servants wore frocks of dark brown or peacock blue. The beggars were self-consciously picturesque, and would often wear a cloak in imitation of the richer citizens. The working men dressed in blue tunics, with wide sleeves narrowed at the wrists, and the trousers that were first worn in Venice became known as "Venetians" or "pantaloons." The favourite colour of the people was azure blue, translated as *turchino*, and known to Cassiodorus in the sixth century as the "Venetian colour." It was possible, from the dress of each Venetian, to know his exact position in the political hierarchy.

The patricians obeyed strict rules in all matters of dress. Only the doge was permitted to wear gold. He also had the widest sleeves, since the width of the sleeve was a mark of status. The Venetian patricians wore sober black gowns as an image of their presence as perpetual guardians of the state. They were the priests of the polity. Those of higher rank dressed in scarlet or violet or purple; the members of the senate, for example, wore purple. But these, too, are grave and official colours. Over their gowns they wore hooded cloaks. They also wore black caps or *bereti*. Since the priests, the more important citizens, the doctors and the lawyers of Venice also wore black it is not difficult to see a city dressed in mourning. Many of the women, poor and patrician, also wore black. It was essentially a uniform or, in other words, a costume with which to express uniformity.

The long robe also impeded quick movement, so that the walk of the patrician was generally slow and deliberate. In 1611 Thomas Coryat, the English traveller, recorded how "they give a low congie to each other by very civil and courteous gestures, as by bending of their bodies and clapping their right hand upon their breasts." So black was the colour of gravity. Black was the colour of anonymity. Black also held elements of intimidation. It represented death and justice. The predilection for black lasted a thousand years, its endurance a measure of the intense conservatism in all matters of Venetian social custom. Indeed the taste has lingered. It is not wonderful to see, in the streets of twenty-first-century Venice, young men wearing large black capes. There is still something odd, something theatrical, about the dress of contemporary Venetians.

There was one group of Venetians who showed off tremendously. The young patricians of the Renaissance city belonged to one of the numerous city clubs or *calza* guilds, from the Triumphanti to the Valorosi, the Immortali to the Principali. The hose or *calza* on the right leg was sewn with gold and silver, and besparkled with pearls and jewels; it was drawn over tightly fitting breeches and reached the hip. It was set off by a doublet of velvet worn over a flowing shirt of silk. Their long golden hair was, as often as not, dyed. And then there was the perfume. It might be expected, in a most unnatural city, that everything was scented—hats, shirts, socks, handkerchiefs. Even the money was scented.

The *calza* guilds were best known for their presentation of theatrical performances, for fêtes or wedding celebrations, at which the young men and young women (known as *compagne*) excelled. "We wore the stocking of the club," one of them, Giacomo Contarini, wrote to his brother in January 1441, "as well as mantles of Alexandrian velvet brocaded with silver, doublets of crimson velvet with open sleeves, zones of the same colour, and squirrel fur linings, on our heads caps *alla Sforzesca*." *Sforzesca* can be interpreted as in the style of Francesco Sforza, a celebrated *condottiero* or leader of mercenaries; before his success it had been the fashion in Venice to wear hats *à la Carmagnola*, after the name of a renowned general. It is an indication of the Venetian love of the trivial and the triumphant, all expressed in the most theatrical possible manner.

The Venetian patrician, at his noblest, had a long aquiline nose and high cheek-bones; he was the statesman as ascetic. His skin was the palest white. But a singular change can be dated precisely to 1529. In that year Venetian men began to cut their hair short, and to wear beards. Before that time they had worn their hair long, and beards were only allowed as a sign of mourning. Once one or two tentatively made the change, all the others duly followed. There were other and more general changes. By the late sixteenth century, for example, costumes became looser and fuller where once they had been stylised and close-fitting. The reasons are obscure, buried somewhere in the human appetite for novelty and transformation. It is no part of our purpose to write a history of fashion. It is important only to recognise that, for Venetian men and women, clothing was essentially dramatic costume.

In the eighteenth century criers walked through the streets of Venice, calling out the casts and performance times of the latest plays. Venetians were known throughout Europe for their love of theatre. It was a passion that touched all classes, from the gondolier to the patrician, and is nowhere more evident than in the extraordinary success of *commedia dell'arte*. This form of improvised comedy first emerged in the Veneto of the sixteenth century although its ancient origins, whether in classical drama or festive ritual, seem undeniable. One of its principal figures was Pantaleone or Pantalone, a Venetian name attached to the recognisably Venetian figure of a sprightly if sometimes foolish old merchant. (Venice was effectively ruled by old men.) He was dressed in a red costume and black cape with red Turkish slippers, as token of the fact that he traded with the East. Thus the sixth age of man, according to Jaques in *As You Like It*, is represented by "the lean and slipper'd pantaloon." He always spoke in Venetian dialect. It has been surmised that his name comes from a corruption of *pianta leone*, to plant the lion, in reference to the lion of Saint Mark on the flag of Venetian merchants. His besetting vice is that of avarice, the avarice of the wealthy man who fears to lose what he has rather than that of the poor man who wishes for more. He is fearful, a pacifist who nonetheless wishes to conquer the world by trade, jealous of everything, a fanatical patriot, desperate wooer and miser, high-principled but subtle, so fearful of being gulled that he runs headlong into situations that will guarantee his gulling. He represents Venice's uneasy conscience.

From Pantaloon, too, springs the name of pantomime; we have Venice to thank for a still popular English art. The characters of the *commedia* were indeed pantomimic figures, with Arlecchino in his chequerboard costume and Doctor Graziano in his black robe. The female parts were played by young men. They wore masks, and spoke in Venetian dialect mixed with Greek and Slavonic words. Arlecchino spoke in the dialect of Bergamo, the town in Lombardy from which many of the porters and labourers of Venice came. The actors were shown the scenario of the play but, as soon as they stepped onto the temporary stage, they invented the dialogue with a wit and vitality that were wholly native. They were often obscene, and always playful. They engaged in fevered and acrobatic dances to the accompaniment of the lute and guitar.

The performers of the *commedia* were not averse to mocking contemporaries and contemporary types. The audiences for these comedies could recognise themselves. They screamed with laughter, and applauded, and cheered, whenever a familiar allusion was made. There were courtesans among the characters of the *commedia*, and many courtesans among the audiences. The themes of these improvised plays—unhappy children, miserly fathers, disloyal servants— were the stuff of Venetian social life. It was a curious mixture of magniloquence and parody, loud lamentation and broad farce. These were plays about play-acting. It can be called the comedy of mercantile capitalism, similar in spirit to the "city comedies" of early seventeenth-century London. Comedy thus became the mirror of the world.

And then of course it spilled over into the perception of real people and real events. Some of the cases conducted before the courts of Venice have the ingredients of a farcical sketch. A French diplomat of the early seventeenth century mocked the grave Venetian statesmen of the period as "these pantaloons." So there may have perhaps been something risible about the spectacle of these solemn figures all secretly pursuing profit for themselves.

The Venetian people were themselves often derided as *pantaloni*. Byron noticed, too, the "naivete and Pantaloon humour" of the Venetians. There is still a phrase in Venice, *paga pantalon*; Pantalon pays, meaning the state or the taxpayer pays. Casanova records how he donned the costume of Pierrot, "assuming the gait of a booby." In the masquerades of the Carnival, you had to maintain the character of the person whose costume you had donned. The early visitors to the Carnival noted that the local citizens liked to dress up as the natives of other countries. A Venetian could become an actor without a moment's hesitation.

It has sometimes been suggested that out of the songs and scenes of the *commedia* emerged the opera itself. It is perhaps not surprising, then, that Venice became the first centre of opera in Europe. The opera and the *commedia* embody the spirit and attitudes of the people. They come out of the same circumstances, and fulfil the same desires. Both arts spring from the spectacle inherent in the religious and civic rituals of the people. The popularity of opera in Venice is of course well documented. Never has an art so suited the temperament of the people. The first public opera house in the world was created in Venice; in 1637 the patrician Tron family opened one within the premises of its grand house, and began to charge entrance fees for all who flocked there. A second opera house opened two years later and, within fifty years, there were seven of them. For librettists and composers there was now a flourishing trade. The post of the impresario was born. Dancers and singers were hired under contract. The structure of the opera itself became standardised, with each of the principal singers awarded five arias, and it was manufactured as quickly and as proficiently as a glass vase on Murano or a ship in the Arsenal. Between 1680 and 1743, 582 separate operas were produced and staged.

Opera flourished in Venice because, in many respects, it was an urban art. It was an art of contrast and heterogeneity in a city filled with contrasts between rich and poor, squalor and splendour; it was an art of the scenic and spectacular, in a city filled with the energetic display of festival and carnival. Opera is concerned with external life, life on display, with the great general drama of the human spirit taken up in music and in song. Opera has to do with energy and splendour, with ritual and melodrama. It was thoroughly Venetian. It also sustained the myth of Venice. There were operas in which Venice was hailed as a new Troy or a new Rome; there were operas that dramatised the origins of Venice among the exiles; many of the stage sets were of Venice itself. The audiences clapped, and whistled, and yelled. The gondoliers obtained free entrance; they applauded by stamping their feet and uttering loud cries of "Bravo!" Once they had heard a favourite aria, they would stamp their feet so loudly that the singer would be obliged to return to the stage with a reprise. After the aria was over, flowers would rain down from the boxes, together with scraps of paper on which laudatory poems had been written. There were even occasions when doves, with bells around their necks, were released within the opera house. One traveller noted the reaction of a Venetian patrician in his box. *"Ah! Cara! Mi butto, mi butto!"* Oh my darling, I'll jump, I'll jump!

Venetian stagecraft was renowned throughout Europe for its subtlety and elaboration. John Evelyn noted with approval "a variety of scenes painted and contrived with no less art of perspective, and machines for flying in the aire, and other wonderful notions; taken together, it is one of the most magnificent and expensive diversions the wit of man can invent." This fascination with the marvels of stagecraft was of a piece with the Venetian predilection for fairy-tale plots and Oriental settings. There were shipwrecks and sea-monsters, fire-breathing dragons emerging from the depths and classical deities gently lowered from the sky. The "cloud machines" of Venice were especially praised. It was art as play.

Burckhardt, in *The Civilisation of the Renaissance in Italy*, quotes one Venetian to the effect that "the fame of the scenic arrangements (*apparati*) brought spectators from far and near." But he went on to note that the skill and effectiveness of these engines of display were used only for "comedies and other cheerful entertainments." Scenic display had helped to kill tragedy. There never has been room for tragedy in Venice.

The first European theatre, specifically built for the production of plays, was erected in Venice in 1565. By the end of the seventeenth century there were eighteen public theatres, a large number catering for a population that was never more than 150,000. In the same period London possessed only six, and Paris only ten, theatres. In the sixteenth century, according to the Italian composer Girolamo Parabosco, the citizens "would climb walls, break open doors, or swim the canals to force their way into the place where some famous comedian was acting."

The members of the audience were as much part of the play as the players. They gossiped, and laughed, and even gambled, through the course of the drama. People moved from box to box in search of conversation and entertainment. The noise of their chatter was compared to that of a bush filled with birds. The lighting was always dim, and the boxes were almost wholly dark; the desks of the musicians were illuminated by candles of Spanish wax, and the stage was lighted by lamps fed with olive oil. The spectators in the boxes spat upon the spectators in the pit. This was a custom endured with good spirit. Those in the pit were allowed to wear hats; those in the boxes were not given that privilege. The gondoliers, the favourite sons of

Venice, entered free of charge, as in the opera houses. They in turn set up claques for particular actors or particular playwrights. They were often bribed to clap, or to jeer, on cue. Others merely waited at the back, with lanterns, for their masters. Between the acts vendors would pass among the people, selling oranges and biscuits, aniseed water and chestnuts, coffee and ices.

The curtain would rise upon a classical temple, a forest, or a royal palace. There would be processions and parades, banquets and battles. But there was one favourite subject. It was the city itself. The whole audience cheered any and every allusion to Venice, and they were delighted by amorous or mercenary dramas set in the streets and houses of the city. It was an intensely local drama. The spectators loved, in particular, the more reassuring emotions of family life. If a character or scene violated the decorum of real life, the audience would object in the most strenuous manner. Goethe witnessed a production which was stopped by the spectators when a young man was supposed to kill his wife with a sword; the actor then stepped forward, apologised, and confirmed that the scene would after all end happily. Were they not, after all, part of one big if not entirely happy family?

This is nowhere more evident than in the work of the most famous of all Venetian playwrights, Carlo Goldoni. His was the comedy of Venetian social life. He held a mirror up to Venetian nature. It was so congenial to him that, in one year, he completed sixteen three-act comedies; in the course of his theatrical career from 1734 to 1776, he wrote 250 plays. Like his compatriots Tintoretto and Titian and Vivaldi, he worked at high speed. He was filled with verve and energy. In the language of business, he managed a quick turnover. He began by writing formulaic dramas established upon the pattern of the *commedia*, and then by happy instinct migrated to the mild comedy of Venetian life. He captivated his public with portraits of gondoliers and of servants, of shopkeepers and housewives. Everything was staged on an intimate scale, with that compactness and neatness intrinsic to the Venetian character. The typical setting is the *campiello* or little square; the background is of familiar shops and houses. He reproduced the language and the manners of the people with the utmost fidelity. The larger world is of no consequence to his characters. In one of his comedies a Londoner talks of the canals of his city, with the suggestion that Goldoni believed London to resemble Venice. His characters do not concern themselves, either, with the politics of their city. That was a task left to others. They comprise a small group of people who steer their way through quarrels, misunderstandings, and awkward domestic moments. Households and families become unstable for a moment; then they steady themselves and sail on.

The first stage directions of *The Fan*, one of his most famous comedies, reveal a wholly Venetian scene.

> Evarist and the Baron sit towards the front at a little table drinking coffee, Limonato serves them, Crispino is cobbling in his booth, near to him Coronato sitting beside his door, writing in a notebook. The Boots cleans the restaurant windows. Geltrude and Candida on the terrace, knitting. To the right Tognino is sweeping the square. Nina is spinning before her house door, beside her stands Moracchio holding two hunting dogs by a cord. Every now and again Timoteo puts his head out of the pharmacy; in the background Susanna, sewing before her shop.

It is a perfect miniature.

Goldoni was true to the spirit of the people, too, in his ability to see the absurd aspect of serious things. There was much mockery, and some impertinence, but no malice, in his humour. There is no violence upon his stage. Goldoni carefully refrained from the frank obscenity of the earlier *commedia*. His characters idle and gossip; they are lively, and witty; they talk about the latest play and the most recent scandal. They are very interested in money. But they are generally amiable and convivial. All of these qualities may be said to be characteristic of the Venetian temperament in the first half of the eighteenth century.

There is no inwardness. There are no meditations or monologues. We may call Goldoni's drama superficial, therefore, but it is not meant to be anything else. It is a drama of surfaces. The Venetians on the stage are not properly individualised; they think, and act, like a community. They are not known for their eccentricities. They express no great passions. Everyone is affected by the same sentiments, and has much the same identity. That is why Goldoni's comedies are couched in the genial poetry of domesticity. They do not record the exploits and sensibilities of outstanding individuals or aberrant types. All is light and graceful. Goldoni celebrated the inherent dignity of ordinary human nature.

And what, then, were the characteristics of the Venetians themselves? They were universally reported to be cheerful, with an innate gaiety and spontaneity of address. Henry James believed that they "have at once the good fortune to be conscious of few wants" and thus allowed their lives to be measured by "sunshine and leisure and conversation." They had a freedom of manner, although it is something of a paradox that they were governed by one of the most severe systems of government in Europe. There may be some connection between public discipline and private liberty. George Sand described them as a "gay, unthinking people, so witty and so full of song."

They were also described as frivolous, mercurial and naive. That may be the darker aspect of gaiety. They were considered, by other Italian city-states, as inept and unreliable. They were deemed to be fickle and unjust. They had a propensity to forget even the most recent and the most grave misfortunes. It may be the forgetfulness of excessive vivacity. The naivety, however, may have been characteristic of the people rather than of the patricians. By the government they were treated almost as children. Hence their trust of the state, and the climate of submissiveness in which they seemed to flourish. Addison believed that the senate of Venice encouraged sports and factions among the "common people" in order to preserve the safety of the republic.

They were, then, ambiguous. They were difficult to "read." Ambiguity, reflecting the ambiguous status of a city on the water, may be the key. In the eighteenth century a nun could also be a prostitute. A gondolier might be a very wealthy man. A richly clad patrician might have no money. Albrecht Dürer reported that among them were "the most faithless, lying thievish rascals, such as I could scarcely believed could exist on earth; and yet if one did not know them, one would think that they were the nicest men on earth." It could be argued that this is true of humankind in general, under whatever sky, but in a city of masks and secrets this ambiguity becomes manifold and pervasive. It becomes more intense.

It is certainly the source of the charge of duplicity that was always being levelled against them. They possessed a talent for dissimulation in their dealings with other states, and indeed with each other in the business of law and government. They disguised their greed with the semblance of honesty and piety; they hid their guile under the mask of polity. It became their nature, in the phrase of one English observer, "to sew a piece of Fox tayle to the skinne of S.Mark's Lyon." There were many stories of their duplicity. When the king of Hungary came to Venice, in the fifteenth century, he begged the body of Saint Paul the Hermit from the canons of the church of S. Zulian. They did not wish to offend the sovereign, and so they gave him the body of one of the Grimani family. The Hungarians then worshipped this worthless body as a holy relic.

The city of masks was adept at the art of concealment. That is why the Venetians were always polite, evincing what was known as their characteristic *dolce maniera*; they were celebrated for their good manners. They were formal and reserved in their public demeanour, perhaps recalling the Venetian proverb that "he who loves foreigners loves the wind." There was a certain courtliness, from which the Venetian patrician could keep his distance. The memoirs and records suggest that they were courteous, and composed, even in their private dealings. They loved form, and surface, above everything. In company Venetians were observed to be "stiff," relying entirely upon propriety and correctness of behaviour. Unlike other Italians, for example, they were not known for extravagance of gesture or language. There were certain significant catch-phrases adoped in the official texts of the city. Councillors were called *"prudentes et cauti,"* prudent and cautious; an officer of state was *"sapiens et circumspectus vir,"* wise and circumspect. They were pious, for example, but they were not zealots. Savonarola would not have been welcomed in Venice.

Their humour, however, was unambiguously coarse. There is a Venetian saying to the effect that, if you want to laugh, talk about shit. The statue of one famous and over-productive author, Niccolò Tommaseo, is known as *el cacalibri* or book-shitter. The vulgarity, as in England, has much to do with a culture of practicality and common sense. There was, for example, a certain harsh realism in their state-craft. In this "romantic" city there were few romantics. The humour is often at the expense of hypocrisy and pretence; it was often dark and, on occasions, bitter or savage. The Venetians were great deflaters of the pompous or the preening. This may have been the instinctive reaction of a population inured to the hypocrisies or pious pretences of public life. It was a way of striking back, of showing that they were not really fooled.

15

Wheels within Wheels

In 1605 Venice was described as "the summary of the universe," because all that the world contained could be found somewhere within it; if the world were a ring, then Venice was its jewel. It is in some respects the model city, the ultimate city defying nature and the natural world. It is the most urban of cities, occupying a realm of meaning very different from those communities rooted on earth and soil. As such it offers lessons to other cities. Lewis Mumford, in *The City in History* (1961), notes that "if the civic virtues of Venice had been understood and imitated, later cities would have been better planned." The system of transport, for example, with the fast Grand Canal cutting across the slower-moving smaller canals, was a model of its kind. The waters of the lagoon have also ensured that the city remained of a manageable size; it did not sprawl, and its only suburbs were the other islands that had an intrinsic life of their own.

It has also become a paradigm of European culture. One may claim plausibly that the first industrial revolution occurred in Venice rather than in England, with the management of shipbuilding, glass-making and mirror-making. It was the first centre of commodity capitalism, the focal point of a vast urban network that spread across Europe and the Near East; it was a city dependent upon, and also sustaining, other cities. It represented a new form of civilisation that had moved from agrarian to mercantile life. It has always been an emblematic place. In the late sixteenth and early seventeenth centuries, for example, it was interpreted as the ultimate city—perverse, unnatural, reducing its population to servile status. In our own century it may also be classified as the first post-modern city, the city as game. In that sense Venice may be the harbinger of a common human destiny.

Its polity itself became a model for others. Hobbes wrote his *Leviathan* after an extended residence in Venice; that book has in turn been seen as an apologia for the burgeoning market economy. The political reformers of the puritan Commonwealth, in the seventeenth century, looked towards Venice as a viable model of a modern republic. So did the founding fathers of the United States.

The administration of the state was paradigmatic in another sense. It became the model for all other forms of rule and order in the city. The election procedures of the guilds were established upon the elaborate rules for the election of a doge. The meeting halls of the fraternities were based upon the halls of the ducal palace, and were similarly decorated with historical and mythical painting. The diamond lozenges on the façade of the ducal palace are locked into a mesh. Venetian madrigals of the sixteenth century are known for their complex of overlapping voices, each singer distinctly heard in a dense and undulating body of sound.

The topography of the city itself—with its small bridges, canals and narrow *calli*—reflects the intricacy and interlinked dependency of republican institutions. The multiplication of magistracies and agencies, in the supervision of Venice, was often described as "labyrinthine" as the streets and alleys themselves. The members of the various committees were replaced every six months or every twelve months, giving a shifting pattern to the polity much like that of the movement of the sea. Did the territory determine the polity, or did the polity form the territory? It is an unanswerable question, so deeply implicated in the origins of human behaviour that it must for ever remain unresolved.

So what was the secret of this polity that crept into every feature of Venetian social life? Dudley Carleton, the English ambassador in Venice in the early seventeenth century, had an analogy with one of the commodities the city traded. The republic "is a clock going with many wheels, and making small motions, sometimes out of order, but soon mended, and all without change or variety." These wheels, and wheels within wheels, were the various organs of the state.

The earliest guardians of Venice, from the first settlement of the lagoon, were the tribunes of the various islands; they were elected annually. Yet this loose structure proved unworkable, and in 697 the first doge was elected; Paoluccio Anafesto was chosen and acclaimed by all the people in a general assembly on the island of Heraclea. It was believed that the spirit of republican Rome had been reborn. Yet, as in Rome, the power of certain leading families was used to destroy any incipient democratic spirit. Only the rich and powerful merited the awards of office. In the tenth and eleventh centuries there were many feuds between the aristocratic families; doges were assassinated or expelled from office. In the middle of the twelfth century a group of officials was formed to help and advise the doge. It was known as the "commune," although it had none of the revolutionary implications of the later use of that word.

It was not enough. At the end of the twelfth century a council of the aristocratic families was formally instituted to check the activities of the doge. It was they who now elected the leader, and the doge was merely presented to the people for their "approval." He came upon the balcony to the words "This is your doge, if so it please you." At a later time even this acknowledgement of the power of the people was removed. There were further restrictions placed upon the nature of government. In 1297 a law was passed that allowed access to the great council only to those patrician gentlemen whose fathers or paternal grandfathers had already sat in the body. It was to be an exclusive club, and Venice became an hereditary aristocracy. By 1423 the nomen-clature of the commune had been dropped, and the state was for ever after known as *dominio o signoria* signifying power or lordship.

So by the beginning of the fifteenth century the essential structure of Venetian government was shaped and determined. There were some constitutional changes in the sixteenth century, but the principles remained the same until the end of the republic in 1797. It was as if eighteenth-century England were still governed by the polity of Richard II and Henry IV.

This structure had evolved over many centuries and, like the mammalian life of Australia, it was a unique phenomenon born out of relative isolation. It was made up of a series of councils and official bodies, each of which participated in some kind of mystical unity like the threefold divinity of the Trinity. At the base of a complex and striated pyramid was the general assembly, which met only to ratify essential legislation. Above them lay the great council, which in theory elected the various magistracies, the members of the lesser councils, and the doge himself. The councils included "the forty," a specialised body of patricians, and the ducal councillors. The members of these councils comprised the senate. At the top of the pile stood the doge. It would tax the reader too far to elaborate further upon the wearisome and complex organisation of the various councils and assemblies and magistracies. It was scarcely understood by the Venetians themselves.

But an insight can be gained into the labyrinthine Venetian mind by describing the process by which a doge was elected. On the morning of the election the youngest member of the Signoria, one branch of the administration, fell on his knees to pray in the basilica; then he went out into Saint Mark's Square, and stopped the first boy whom he met. This child then became the *ballotino*, who drew the nomination slips from the urn in the ducal palace. In the first ballot the great council chose thirty of its members. In a second vote nine were chosen out of this original thirty. In turn the nine chose forty, each of whom had to receive seven nominations. A new ballot would then reduce this forty to twelve, who voted for twenty, who voted for nine, who voted for forty-five, who voted for eleven. These eleven then voted for forty-one. The final forty-one voters would then elect the doge. No more cumbersome and intricate procedure could have been devised. Its only purpose was to eliminate individual chicanery and special interests, but it suggests an almost obsessive preoccupation with communal solidarity.

The cohesiveness was maintained by a myriad of overlapping powers and offices; this fostered a sense of equilibrium, so important in the floating city, and of adaptability. It also afforded a measure of judicial oversight. It was government by debate and by committee. What it lacked in novelty and excitement, it made up for in prudence and continuity. It was patient, and it was thorough. That was why it endured. The rapid turnover of magistracies, most of them lasting for only six months, meant that the patricians were trained very quickly in various fields of administration. There was inevitably inefficiency and confusion, together with a bewildering number of bureaucratic procedures, but they were considered to be a price worth paying for good order. The secret of success, perhaps, lay in the curious fact that no one could really know where true power resided. There was no single authority.

Venice was in name a republic, but in practice it is best described as a plutocracy. Only one hundred families were allowed to participate in the government; the citizens and the *popolani*, or lower class, were excluded. The polity also had all the features of a gerontocracy.

Patricians under the age of forty were excluded from the senate; in the fifteenth and sixteenth centuries, the average age of a doge on the day of his election was seventy-two. The doges were always older than the popes, the only other office in Italy where the leader was elected for life. This might be an advertisement for the healthy air of the republic, but it is also a reflection of the emphasis that the Venetians placed on tradition and experience. The road to leadership, being a long one, required patience and obedience; the length of service to the republic fostered conformity and compromise. It was also a precautionary measure. No doge would rule for a very long time, or acquire too much power. The military commanders, and the principal members of the government, were old. Domenico Contarini, for example, was seventy-five when he was elected general of the Venetian forces in 1526. He was not exceptional. A government of young men—we may take as an example the medieval English monarchy—creates a culture of impassioned fervour, of sudden violence and intense rivalry. None of these occurred in Venice.

There were rivalries, of course. In the last decades of the sixteenth century there were tensions between the representatives of the "old" families, dating from the first years of the republic, and of the "new" families who had arrived at a somewhat later date. The "new" families were opposed to the encroaching power of the council of ten and wished to refurbish the trade of Venice by finding new markets. There was in fact a gradual change of emphasis, in the administration of the city, but it was a slow and cumulative process. There was no descent into party or faction. Everyone depended on everyone else to maintain the smooth working of the governmental machine. No individual ambition, or familial rivalry, was allowed to undermine the safety of the state.

Corruption was general and widespread. "Every office," Marino Sanudo wrote in October 1530, "is filled for money." It was common for rivals vying for a particular post to come into the great council carrying bags of gold. "Loans" were offered to individual electors. There was an old Venetian saying that to give a favour is to receive a favour. There were over eight hundred offices to be filled in the city, and a major preoccupation of the patrician class lay in lobbying for position; this was especially true of the poorer members of the governing class, known as the *svizzeri* after the Swiss mercenaries, who had no other source of income or status. Legislation was continually passed against electoral corruption, and the intricate procedures for the choice of even the most minor official were designed to circumvent the more obvious forms of bribery. But the elaborate precautions are themselves significant. They suggest a deep awareness of the possibility of corruption. A city that is deeply corrupted will go to extraordinary lengths to seem incorruptible.

The word for plot and chicanery, imbroglio, derives from the very topography of Venice. The *brolo* or *broglio* was the garden laid out before the ducal palace. Here the patricians would walk, and plot their latest moves. It was the place for lobbying and for intrigue, where a smile or the tug of a sleeve was the only necessary sign.

The doge, therefore, was the most senior member of the government. In the earliest times he wore a biretta or bonnet, like the ancient kings of Phrygia. He was dressed in a mantle of silk fringed with gold, and secured by golden buttons. His shoes and stockings were red. He was elected for life, but he was surrounded by restrictions and regulations. There would be no Caesar in Venice. The doge could not open his own mail. He could not receive foreign visitors in private. He could not discuss matters of policy without consulting his councillors. He could not leave the city without permission. He could not even travel in the city without gaining approval. He could not buy expensive jewellery, or own property outside Venetian territory. He could not display the ducal arms beyond the confines of the ducal palace. He was never to be called "my lord" but only "messer doge" or "sir lord." No one was to kneel before him, or to kiss his hand. It was said that he was essentially a "tavern sign" swinging in the wind. The more true power he forfeited, the more he was loaded with pomp and ceremony.

Yet he possessed power of a kind. He was after all the figurehead of the state. Sir Henry Wotton declared that "like the sun he doth effect all his purposes *in radio obliquo*, not by direct authority." He presided over all the elective councils, including those of the senate, the great council and the council of ten; he was the general supervisor of all the organs of government. He had to preside twice a week at public audiences, and his ceremonial duties were onerous. He was the symbolic representative of the Venetian state. In a literal sense he embodied the health of the nation. His dress, and demeanour, were scrutinised for any change of emphasis. When during a debate on the conduct of a difficult war the doge left his seat in order to urinate, his action caused a sensation. But part of his power lay elsewhere. He knew all the secrets of the city.

On his death the same formulaic words were pronounced. "With much displeasure we have heard of the death of the most serene prince, a man of such goodness and piety; however, we shall make another." The signet ring was removed from his finger and broken in half. The dead doge's family had to leave the palace within three days, and their furniture was removed. Three inquisitors were appointed to scrutinise all the actions of the doge and, if necessary, to punish his heirs for any fraudulence or wrongdoing. Only in that way could the state resist the rise of powerful families.

The doge was the patrician among the patricians. The social structure of Venice was in essence very simple. The patricians comprised 4 per cent of the population; the citizens represented a further 6 per cent; the rest, approximately nine tenths of the population, were simply the people or *popolani*. Each group had its own functions, and its own privileges. It was a highly structured and deeply hierarchical society— a society of legally defined estates and orders—made up of a number of interlocking networks and affinities bound together for the greater glory of God and the city.

Yet how was it possible that 10 per cent could effectively master and control 90 per cent of the population? They bribed them; they deceived them; they created internal rivalries; they consoled them for their lack of power by weaving myths of origin and identity. It is the story of human history itself.

We may begin with the largest number of the Venetians. The *popolani* were made up of tradesmen, artisans and labourers, and the poor. They formed a social, rather than an economic, category; so there were differences in wealth between the *popolo grande*, the richer landowners and merchants, and the shopkeepers or artisans of the *popolo minuto*. There were so many local variations, in fact, that we cannot entertain a description of "the people" in any political sense. There was no feeling of "solidarity." As the Spanish ambassador put it in 1618, the *popolani* "is made up of so many elements that I do not think it can ever start a riot, even though it is large enough to occupy and fill the whole of Venice." The people were generally believed to be loyal and tractable, with an affection for their native city that far outweighed any tendency to protest or rebel.

There were other good reasons for the maintenance of social order and stability among the people. There was always enough cheap food, except on unusual occasions of emergency and famine, and through the centuries the wages of the workers maintained a relatively high level. There was none of the endemic distress, for example, that characterised the lower class of Paris or London. It would have been impossible to write *Les Misérables* in Venice.

The people could be fierce, however, but only with one another. The poorer people, the fishermen and the gondoliers and the servants and the labourers, formed two great factions across the city known as "the Castellani" (also named the "Arsenalotti") and "the Nicolotti." It was an ancient division, born from the enmity between the fede-rated townships of the Veneto, Jesolo and Heraclea, from which the Venetian settlers first came. Well into the twentieth century the Nicolotti wore a black cap and a black sash around the waist, while the Castellani wore red. The Nicolotti also had their own version of political power, since from the fourteenth century they had acquired the custom of electing their own leader known as the *gastaldo grande* who was solemnly taken in procession to greet the doge in the ducal palace. The Arsenalotti had their own privileges. The workers of the Arsenal were deputed to stand guard when the general council was in session, and they acted as a bodyguard for the doge. By these means the *popolani* were drawn into the life of the state. So the Venetian people were not accustomed to, and indeed had a hatred for, political sedition.

Their territories were clearly divided, with the Castellani to the east and the Nicolotti to the west, centred around the parishes of S. Pietro di Castello and S. Nicolò dei Mendicoli. The boundaries were a clear indication of the fact that in the earliest days the city itself was a collection of independent communities. One church straddled the common frontier, S. Trovaso, but the Castellani entered by the south door and the Nicolotti by the west door. There were often street fights between the two factions, tolerated by the government on the assumption of "divide and rule"; by fighting among themselves, they minimised the chances of general urban riot against the authorities. In a series of battles, in 1639, over forty combatants were killed. But in succeeding years these encounters were gradually turned into staged games and contests such as the regattas. In true Venetian fashion aggression was softened into ritual.

The *popolani* had no political power, but they enjoyed a different version of hierarchy and degree in the membership of guilds or confraternities. All of the ordinary occupations of trading life had their representative organisation. There were over a hundred of them, registered in the thirteenth century, and they offered exclusive rights for dyers and coopers, masons and carpenters, rope-makers and fruiterers. There were guilds of hemp-spinners and fustian-weavers, two hundred altogether throughout the city maintaining an intricate occupational web that kept every worker in his or her place. So it was a covert way of maintaining control of the working population.

Like other medieval guilds throughout Europe, they were exclusive and hierarchical. They moved against strangers or foreigners working in the city; they laid down standards of good practice, and punished those who ignored them. They had their own officers, and their own courts; they organised the markets and, perhaps most importantly, they provided financial support for any member who was out of work for reasons of accident and illness. No male Venetian could practise his craft without joining the appropriate guild. No man could join his guild without first swearing an oath of allegiance to the city, but of course no member of the guild had any status in the political life of the republic. It is pertinent and significant that none of the most important professions, such as lawyers and merchants, had or needed to have guilds in order to protect their interests. The state performed that role for them.

The guilds maintained the "rights" of the workers, but they were also insistent upon the duties involved. They had, for example, to furnish conscripts for service in the galleys. Through the agency of the guilds, too, the state could enforce discipline within the various trades. The guilds were also brought into the devotional life of the state by becoming involved in specific religious rituals and processions. They adopted certain saints as their patrons or patronesses, before whose shrines they would light candles on days of festival. By these means the morality of state power was enshrined in popular consciousness. So were the independence and the status of the workers, as maintained by the guilds, part of some grand illusion? It all depends on the observer.

The trades of the *popolani* were, in a literal sense, one of the pillars of Venetian life. The two pillars of the piazzetta, holding up Saint Mark's lion and Saint Theodore, had on their granite bases carved images of the workers of the city—the wine-sellers, the cattle-dealers, the smiths, the fishermen, the basket-makers, the butchers, the fruiterers, all had their place. These images have now been effaced by time and weather. Like their counterparts on the Venetian streets, they have disappeared. The craftsmen of Venice have now become so many tourist shows.

When the trades marched in procession to greet a new doge, they arranged themselves in predetermined order; the glass-blowers led the way, followed in turn by the smiths, the furriers, the weavers, the tailors, the wool-carders and others. In the rearguard came the fishmongers, the barbers, the goldsmiths, the comb-makers and the lantern-makers. Each trade had its own liveries, its own symbols, and its own band of musicians. It has been estimated that in the late sixteenth century the unskilled labourers and artisans of the city, below the level of guild membership, comprised some ten thousand men and women; if the members of their immediate families are taken into account, they comprised a quarter of the entire population. They were essentially the proletariat feeding Venice's mercantile capitalism.

The class above the *popolani* was known as the *cittadini*. It was a distinction afforded by birth and by residence, and by the duty of paying certain taxes; it was not an economic group in any meaningful sense of the word. An aspirant had to prove that both his grandfather and his father had been born in Venice, and that the family had for three generations been untainted by any form of manual labour. At a later date it was sufficient for a man to have lived in the city for fifteen years and to have paid all the requisite taxes. Once this was determined the citizen was free to enter the ranks of the bureaucracy, for example, that lay behind the Venetian state machine. The *cittadini* were in large part the civil servants of the city, with all the virtues and vices of that group; but they provided the continuity and efficiency necessary for the business of government. Little or nothing is known of them as individuals. Throughout the history of Venice they were the anonymous and uncelebrated servants of the state. They dressed like, and copied the solemn manners of, the patricians.

At the top of this unified society stood the patricians themselves, the exclusive class or caste that governed the republic throughout its history. Never have so few ruled so peacefully over so many. They have already been described, with their black gowns and stately manner, in previous pages of this book. In the extant portraits they resemble one another in gesture and expression—or, perhaps, in the lack of those elements. Since they are depicted as possessing no interior life to speak of, they are inscrutable. It was said of one doge that no one knew whether he loved or hated anything. Yet their gravity and self-control afforded a sense of continuity and firmness in a floating world. In a world of shifting appearances, they were changeless.

There were poor as well as rich nobles, but the largest number of patricians always wished to retain the exclusivity of their rank. In the late thirteenth, and early fourteenth, centuries the great council was closed to all those outside the charmed circle; it was a form of government by virtue of inheritance. A list of the chosen families was then inscribed in a register that became known as "the golden book." There were twenty-four of them, recorded in 1486, who had been part of Venetian life from at least the seventh century; they included the Bragadin, the Polani, the Querini and the Zorzi. By the seventeenth century there were approximately 150 families, or clans, coming together in various informal associations of interest. This multiplicity of factions ensured the stability of the state, since no one family or interest could achieve supremacy. Yet they were so relatively few in number that they knew each other very well. They knew the virtues, and the weaknesses, of all those aspiring to high office.

The last surviving relics of the patrician class are still standing. They are the great houses of Venice. Until the sixteenth century even the grandest houses of the patricians were simply known as dwellings, *casa* or *ca'*; after that date they were often given the more distinguished appellation of *palazzo*. Some of them indeed were palaces, of noble rooms and rich furniture. "I never saw palaces," William Hazlitt wrote in 1824, "anywhere but at Venice." Their façades can be seen beside both banks of the Grand Canal, while others are lost in the tapestry of alleys and smaller canals that comprise the rest of the city.

In the fourteenth and fifteenth centuries these mansions had a utilitarian function. They were trading post as well as domicile. They represented the collective identity of the family. They represented the honour of the succeeding (male) generations. There were rules encouraging the members of the same family to retain possession of the house, a fixed point in a floating world. Some of the houses looked away from the water, and were assembled around an inner courtyard. The ground floor or central *portego* was used as a storeroom and as business quarters, opening onto the canals for the easy traffic in goods; there was a water-entrance, and a land-entrance. On the upper floors were the living quarters. The central hall on the first floor, the *sala*, opened onto suites of rooms on either side. There were also a myriad of small rooms, for the various members of the extended family, as well as "private" staircases. In the fifteenth and sixteenth centuries the hall was made grander, its furnishings more ornate, and its interior decoration more sumptuous. This was the period when the patricians were moving from involvement in merchandise to investment in estates on the mainland.

It was in fact only in the late fifteenth and early sixteenth centuries, when Venice deemed itself to be the new imperial city, that the great houses with grand incrusted façades were built for display. The mouldings, and capitals, and filigree, were part of a public attempt to emphasise the grandeur of the city. Many were decorated with frescoes devised by artists such as Titian and Giorgione. Others, like the Ca' d'Oro, were encrusted with precious metals. Venice looked like a city of marble and gold. It should be recalled that these were palaces rather than castles; unlike the houses of the nobility in the rest of Italy, they were not fortified or defended in any way. There was no need.

V

Empire of Trade

16

The Lion City

As Venice grew richer, it became more powerful. A city needs a ruling authority, and the acquisition of authority invites arrogance and belligerence. It encourages the will for further power. Venice, surrounded by the sea, could not grow out of its own frontier. But it could be enlarged and enriched by its extension in other lands and in other cities. It could become an empire.

In earliest times *la Serenissima*, the city of the Virgin, had been given a masculine identity by its citizens. It was the Lion City. The very conditions of its existence made warfare an inevitable part of its history. There was warfare against the natural world and then warfare against its competitors. It was obliged to fight for its survival. Venice had archers and oarsmen and maritime warriors. Sea powers are natural competitors. While land powers may agree to the division of land into frontiers, the ocean has no frontier. Wherever there is sea, there are hostile ships. Throughout its long history, Venice could never rest.

The drawing books of Jacopo Bellini, composed in the mid-fifteenth century, contain many studies of cavaliers and crossbowmen preparing themselves for combat. Half of Bellini's lifetime was spent in the battles of Venice against other powers. "This nation of sailors," Petrarch wrote, "was so skilful in the handling of horses and weapons, so spirited and so hardy, that it surpassed all other warlike nations whether by sea or by land." So it can indeed be construed as a masculine city. The history of Venice was conceived, and composed, as the history of patriarchal families. The government of Venice was patriarchal in all of its elements. The society of Venice was considered to be patrilinear in nature. The image of the city was wholly dependent upon the exercise of paternal authority.

The patrician youth were trained to use the bow, and to command galleys at sea. They were educated in all the knightly virtues, in a period when the chivalric code of warfare was honoured throughout Europe. The first jousts, in Saint Mark's Square, are recorded as early as 1242. From that time forward they were staged at regular intervals. In Bellini's drawing books, chivalric opponents dash upon each other in spectacular tournaments. On these occasions the city was given up to the celebration of militarism and the military virtues. It provided the theatre of war. Painters were employed to embellish shields and armour as well as icons and portraits. Artists, among them Bellini himself, were used to design fortifications and draw military maps. In the sacred paintings of Venice the saints are often seen wielding swords. Saint George, one of the patrons of the city, was the archetypal military saint. This is very different from the picture of Venetians as quick-witted traders or as earnest statesmen. But knightly valour was once an aspect of their culture. How else could the Venetians have created an empire?

So they knew how to use force when it was required. They were quick to strike, when the opportunity presented itself. One conquest led to another conquest. In fact, one conquest demanded another conquest. In a state that never felt itself secure, the condition of the world was always perilous. Unsuccessful generals and admirals were imprisoned, exiled, or killed. When they employed the newly invented cannon against a recalcitrant Italian town, an old chronicle reported that "one would think that God were thundering." One cannon was named "the Venetian Woman who Casts down Every Wall and Spike."

The first colonies of Venice were in the lagoon itself; originally the smaller islands had self-ruling or self-sustaining communities. Once each island had its monastery, and its church. But, soon enough, they all became part of Venice itself. The leaders of the city might then take comfort from the opening words of the ninety-seventh psalm: "The LORD reigneth; let the earth rejoice; let the multitude of isles be glad thereof." The multitude of islands were swallowed up by the great city growing in their midst. Or their communities simply withered away.

Torcello, seven miles (11 km) to the north of the most serene city, was once a thriving place. Before the city of Venice ever rose from the waters, it was a great civic centre for the exiles from Venetia. They had first come in the middle of the fifth century. A cathedral of Byzantine form was raised here in the seventh century. It was built as a refuge and a strength by exiles fleeing from the mainland; the windows of the church have shutters of stone. Wealthy monasteries were founded on its fertile soil. In the tenth century it was described by the Emperor Constantine VII Porphyrogenitus as *"magnum emporium Torcellanorum."* Yet the success of Venice led ineluctably to the decay of Torcello. There was no room for two thriving centres of trade in the lagoon. There are some, however, who say that it was poisoned by the malarial waters of the lagoon. The sea was silted up, and the island was surrounded by stagnant ponds. There may be truth to this, but the visitation of disease added only the final blow to a long process of disintegration. Ineluctably Torcello sank in the significance of the world. In the nineteenth century a nobleman of spurious or dubious origin was dubbed as "a count of Torcello." Now the once thriving island supports a handful of people; all around are wastes of mud-filled creeks and rivulets and what Ruskin described as "salt morass." The brick campanile, and the mosaics within the cathedral itself, are the only remnants of its faded splendour. The civic square is covered by wild grass. Yet the silence of this island, interrupted sometimes by the soughing of the wind through the reeds or the rustle of rippling waters, is a vivid token of the primeval lagoon to which the first Veneti came. Another symbol can be found here of the Venetian world. There is a restaurant on the island, frequented by the tourists who journey to Torcello as an outdoor museum. It is really no more than that. And might it then somehow anticipate the fate of Venice itself?

On the majority of the islands could once be found a tall campanile and brick-built church; there was a small piazza, with the image of the lion on wall or pillar; there were little clusters of whitewashed houses, their gardens protected from the depredations of the salt wind by neat red fences. Then they were touched by decay more insidious than the wind. The island of Ammiana once boasted eight churches; then it was depopulated and turned into a salt farm. And where did the inhabitants go? They migrated to Venice. All of these dead towns and cities and settlements could once have been proposed as alternatives to Venice; they might have flourished and grown strong, as Venice did. If we were to follow the precepts of Italo Calvino's *Invisible Cities*, we might create the possible cities of the lagoon; the distinct customs and dialects of each island might then have created several different cities, resembling and yet not resembling Venice itself. But, then, this would be a fantasy.

Other islands, once under Venetian control, have disappeared. The island of Constanziaca was engulfed by the waters. It had once contained monasteries and churches. It became so woeful, however, that it was turned into a burial site where the bones of the dead were left to bleach in the sun. Then with all its churches and bones it simply subsided into the sea. No one knows its precise position. Other islands suffered a similar fate, among them Terra dei Mani and Terra dei Soleri. Five little islands encircling Murano have been washed away by tides and currents. There is seaweed now where once tall cypresses grew. Some islands were overcome by earthquakes or tidal waves; others were claimed by a slow and general desuetude. They could not compete against the most serene city.

The Venetian authorities turned some of these once flourishing islands into prisons or hospitals. It was one way of pushing the undesirable elements of the population to the margins. It was also an exercise in total power. The island of S. Servolo was turned into a lunatic hospital for men, while the island of S. Clemente was a mental asylum for Venetian women. Sacca Sessola was a place of exile for those suffering from consumption, while the Isola della Grazia held those who burned with fever. On the island of Poveglia were laid out huts for the lepers banished from the city. All these islands were known to the Venetians as *"isole del dolore"* or the islands of sorrow.

The island of S. Biagio, now called Giudecca, was once a green haven of orchards and gardens; here were a convent, a home for penitent prostitutes and a pilgrims' hostel. But the secular world of Venice intervened. It became essentially a suburb of the city. Other islands were used as agricultural factories for the markets of the Rialto. In the second half of the fifteenth century the island now known as the Lido became an extension of Venice's port. It became part of the economic zone that now encircled and sustained the city.

The beginning of the Venetian empire beyond the lagoon can be found in the ninth century. Venice was not as yet a leading sea-power. That position was reserved for the Spanish and for the North Africans. But it needed to control its immediate environment. It had to find, and maintain, a reliable food supply for an increasing population. It needed to secure access to water and to agricultural land. It needed to control the lifelines of its trade. So Venice turned to the mainland. The people of the sea were obliged to conquer *terra firma*.

Towards the close of the ninth century Venice sacked the rival cities on the Italian coast and took control of the mouths of the Adige and Po rivers. The rivers gave them access to the markets of northern Italy; within a short time the bargemen of the city were offering their wares in Pavia, the capital of Lombardy. The merchants of Venice were prominent, too, in the markets of Verona and Cremona. In the tenth century Venetian markets and warehouses were built on the banks of the rivers Sile and Piave. The Venetians occupied a castle beside the Livenza river, so that their goods could reach the German traders coming down into Italy. By 977 the Venetian traders had a colony in Limoges, and by the next century they had diffused themselves into Marseilles and Toulouse. The corn-growing areas of Treviso and Bassano were acquired. In this period, too, the Venetians began the slow process of purchasing mainland property and territory. Some of the great families of Venice, like the Badoer and Tiepolo, acquired land around Treviso. The larger monasteries purchased estates along the coastal plain. This gradual enlargement of Venetian property continued for seven centuries. The key issue, as always, was that of commerce and in particular of the supply of grain.

Once the trade with northern Italy and much of Europe was considered secure, the governors of Venice turned their attention towards the sea. The merchants already effectively controlled the trade in eastern goods, but the success of that trade demanded that the routes to the East should be strengthened and defended. The sea was to be made safe for the mass transport of goods. The principal cities of Istria, immediately across the sea from Venice, submitted. The northern part of the Adriatic became known as the Gulf of Venice. Then the Venetian navy worked downwards. By the end of the tenth century it effectively controlled the Middle Adriatic, and set about the conquest of Dalmatia (now part of modern Croatia). The islands and cities of the region surrendered to the superior force and numbers of the Venetians. Some cities, more alarmed by the depredations of the pirates who found safe haven in the small islands and inlets along the Dalmatian coast, invited the doge and his troops to enter their gates. Other cities were tormented by the demands of the petty despots, characteristically living in fortress outposts, and preferred the more benign sovereignty of Venice. Other places were simply happy to enter stable trading relations with the great sea-city. All of them were treated as allies, rather than as subjects, of Venice. Yet in truth the empire was being born. The pirates were defeated. The marauding Slavs were pushed back from the coast. In 998, the doge added the honorific of "dux of Dalmatia" to his title.

The seaway was open for increased traffic with Egypt and, more particularly, with Byzantium. Venice had already become that ancient city's single most important trading partner, sending slaves and timber in exchange for wine, oil and wheat. In 991 Greek and Arab envoys travelled from the East to pay respect to the new doge, and a year later a treaty confirmed that Venice had been granted "most favoured" status by the Byzantine emperor. It confirmed what was already known. Venice had become the dominant trader of Europe, its commercial supremacy sustained by a vigorous and expanding navy. In return Venice offered its ships as transport for Byzantine soldiers crossing the Adriatic. The city was also, for all practical purposes, inviolable. At the time of the Magyar invasions of Lombardy, at the end of the ninth century, a stone wall was built to defend the islands of the Rialto. A great chain was placed across the water to prevent enemy ships from entering the Grand Canal. But the precautions were unnecessary. The Magyars could not reach the sea-girt city. They were beaten off in the shallow waters of the lagoon, where their ships foundered and sank. The great wall itself was demolished in the fourteenth century. It was not required.

By the eleventh century, therefore, Venice had become an autonomous and influential state. In the latter part of that century it fought with the troops of Byzantium against the Norman invaders of Sicily. The reason for the Norman adventure, as well as all the other policies and actions of Venice in this period, was very simple. No other state or city could be allowed to block the mouth of the Adriatic, thus imprisoning Venice within its own waters. This was the great fear and the abiding preoccupation.

It has become customary to describe the eleventh century as the period in which Latin Christendom emerged triumphant. This is nowhere more powerfully evinced than in the history of the Crusades. They have been construed as a direct attack upon the Muslim world, or as a form of spiritual imperialism, but the participation of Venice in the First Crusade had no such motives. The Venetians were waging economic warfare by other means. They were not concerned with the cross, or with the sword, but with the purse. The point was that rival trading cities, Genoa and Pisa in particular, were already taking part. Venice could not permit its competitors to gain an advantage in the lucrative markets of Syria and Egypt. To have a permanent presence in Antioch, or in Jerusalem, would be a source of innumerable commercial benefits. So, in the summer of 1100, a fleet of two hundred Venetian ships arrived at Joppa (Jaffa); the Venetian commanders agreed to help the crusaders on condition that the merchants of their city were given the rights of free trade in all dominions recovered from the Saracens. The terms of this practical bargain were accepted. The Venetians were then despatched to besiege the town of Caifa (Haifa) and, having achieved the surrender of that place, they returned to the lagoon before the end of the year. They were not content, however, with this single and relatively simple victory. They wished to acquire more profit from their participation in the holy cause. They established trading stations within the Syrian ports, and began a lucrative business in transporting pilgrims to the newly captured Jerusalem.

On their way to Joppa, too, they had engaged in a peculiarly Venetian piece of business. The fleet had cast anchor at the ancient Lycian town of Myra (Bari), in search of the bones of Saint Nicholas who had been bishop of that place; the saint is now better known as the progenitor of Santa Claus but, in the eleventh century, he was revered as the patron saint of sailors. The Venetians, naturally enough, wanted him. It is alleged that they arrived in the town and put to the torture four Christians, the keepers of the shrine. They learned nothing of any consequence from these unholy proceedings, however, and made do with the theft of the bones of Saint Theodore. Theodore had been the patron saint of Venice before the arrival of Mark; he was a good second-best. Yet before their departure, according to the Venetian chronicles of Andrea Morosini, a wonderful fragrance issued from a recess beneath an altar in the church itself. The scent was that of Saint Nicholas. So he was removed, too, and brought back in triumph to Venice where his bones were lodged in the monastery of Saint Nicholas on the Lido. That is the story, at least. In fact the remains of Saint Nicholas, if such they are, have remained in Bari to this day.

Whether the tale reveals more of Venetian mendacity, or of Venetian greed, is an open question.

The crusading venture had been a success for Venice, and in 1108 the Venetian fleet once more sailed under the flag of the cross. It may be noted that the governors of the city were particularly interested in the seaports of the Mediterranean, and that Venetian merchants were established in Acre, Jerusalem and elsewhere. Yet the attentions of the doge and senate were not confined to the principalities and powers of the Middle East. They thought it prudent to maintain and consolidate their presence on the mainland. They took Ferrara and Fano under their control, and moved against Padua. In the process they reasserted their rights over the principal rivers of the territory. On the other side of the Adriatic, they struggled with the Hungarians over the coastal regions of Dalmatia. They now had many enemies. The cities of the mainland were jealous of Venetian wealth, and fearful of Venetian power. The Norman kingdom of Sicily had long regarded Venice as a foe. The German empire of Hohenstaufen still laid claim to northern Italy.

There emerged one other formidable enemy. In 1119 the new emperor of Constantinople decreed that the trading privileges of Venice were at an end. He ordered all Venetian residents within the boundary of his empire to remove themselves and their business. He also proposed a treaty with the king of Hungary, thereby recognising Hungarian claims to the Venetian settlements in Dalmatia. The reaction of Venice was slow but assured. The Venetian fleet raided and sacked a number of Byzantine territories; Rhodes, Chios, Samos, Lesbos and Modon were some of the objects of their vengeance. They had set out to prove that they were now the single most important sea power in an area previously deemed to be the preserve of Constantinople. The emperor signed a new trade agreement with Venice in 1126.

The Venetian empire could justify its existence with the claim that trade, and not conquest, was its purpose. It naturalised its subjects with a spirit of enlightened commercialism. The motive was one of constructive self-aggrandisement. There was no true cult of empire, as there was in nineteenth-century London or in third-century Rome. There was no interest in massiveness or monumentality for their own sake. The only concession to the appetite for glory lay in the construction of gateways at key points in the city—the Torre dell'Orologio, the Porta della Carta, and the Arco Foscari among them. The gateway to the Arsenal is in every guide to the city. These were the Venetian equivalent of the triumphal arch, all the more striking in a city without a defensive wall.

Yet the Venetians who lived and traded in Constantinople, and in the other markets of the kingdom, became increasingly unpopular. They were judged to be arrogant and greedy. Away from Venice, the Venetians became insecure and fractious. They attacked their Genoese and Pisan rivals in trade, and refused to obey Byzantine edicts. They even stole the relics of saints from the churches of Constantinople. They were generally considered by their hosts to be vulgar, mere merchants looking for bargains. In turn the Venetians despised the Greeks, as effete and indolent. Then in 1171, on the command of the emperor, all the Venetians in Constantinople and elsewhere were arrested and imprisoned. A Venetian fleet, despatched to threaten the lands of the emperor, was reduced to impotence by the onset of plague. The commander of the unsuccessful expedition, on his return to Venice, was assassinated in the streets. It was the condign justice meted out to all perceived failures. The Byzantine emperor then sent a message to the doge in which he asserted that the Venetian nation had acted with great foolishness. He noted that they were "once vagabonds sunk in the utmost poverty" who had somehow claimed the right to imperial ambitions. But their abject failure and "insolence" had rendered them "a laughing stock."

The leaders of Venice reacted cautiously. They formed alliances with some of the emperor's enemies, and began an insidious campaign against Byzantine territories. There were secret talks and clandestine meetings. An accord was eventually reached and in 1183, twelve years after their arrest, the Venetian merchants were finally permitted to leave the prisons; a formal peace treaty between Venice and Byzantium was signed. It had represented a great crisis, and a vivid token of the real enmity between Constantinople and Venice; one city was dying, and the other was impatiently waiting to emerge supreme. Over the next few years there were pacts and agreements and messages of mutual confidence between the two cities. But in truth there could be no end to the struggle other than a fatal one.

The new eminence of Venice was exemplified by one of those

scenes of living theatre at which Venice excelled. The characters in this lavish spectacle were the leaders of Latin Christendom. One was the emperor of Germany, Frederick Barbarossa, and the other was Pope Alexander III. Barbarossa laid claim to the Lombard states, and in particular to Milan; Pope Alexander strenuously resisted the claim, and allied himself with the Italian cities. The emperor was excommunicated. Nevertheless Barbarossa, spurned by the Church, had success with the sword. The Lombard cities were taken. Milan fell, and was largely destroyed. Yet the dominion of Germany over this part of Italy was constantly being threatened by internal rebellion and by the open hostility of other Italian cities that looked to the pope for leadership. The weariness of continual warfare, and the inevitable cycle of victories and defeats, eventually disheartened both sides. The pope and the emperor contemplated the principles of an agreement. But where should they meet formally to ratify their pact?

Venice had largely kept itself aloof from the hostilities, on the very good ground that it is better to remain neutral in any battle between such powerful enemies. Venice did not in any case concern itself with the affairs of Italy if its own interests were not directly touched. So the most serene city became the most appropriate setting for the reconciliation of Barbarossa and Alexander. On 23 March 1177, the pontiff landed at the Lido and was received at the monastery of Saint Nicholas; he was no doubt shown the so-called "relics" of the saint himself. On the following day he sailed into Venice, where he was received by the doge. There were now long and difficult negotiations over the terms of the peace, with the emissaries of both sides raising objections and proposing alterations. Yet the pact was finally sealed. On 23 July the emperor was welcomed to the monastery of Saint Nicholas. On the following day he sailed to Venice, where Alexander awaited him. The pope sat in state upon the papal throne, which had been placed before the central gates of the basilica; he was surrounded by his cardinals, like some crowd scene from the sacred plays of the period. The emperor, disembarking from the glittering barge of the doge, walked in stately procession towards the pontiff. Before him walked the doge himself. Saint Mark's Square was filled with spectators, eager to see the play unfold. When the emperor reached the papal throne he took off his scarlet cloak and, bowing to the ground, kissed the feet of the pope. Alexander, now weeping, raised up the emperor and gave him the kiss of peace. The audience now began to sing the *Te Deum*, and all the bells of the city rang out. It had been a great performance.

This dramatic scene was also used by Venice as an advertisement for the city's strength and sense of justice. It was the seat of a general reconciliation. The city was the place of impartial judgement and of equity because it was subject to God alone. It played no part in the power politics of popes or emperors, except to heal the wounds caused by them. That, at least, was the message of the Venetian chroniclers in reporting these events from the summer of 1177. For that moment, when the bells pealed, Venice was the centre of the world. There were more immediate benefits also. The emperor granted trade privileges to Venice throughout his empire, and the pope gave Venice ecclesiastical dominion over Dalmatia.

The spectacle itself might have acted as an overture for the grander opera that was about to be performed. In the years that followed, Venice entered another, and greater, phase of its imperial power. It conquered and stripped Constantinople. A new scenario began with another holy war. The pope had declared a fourth crusade against the infidels and, in the early months of 1201, the French princes who had taken the cross came to Venice to plead for the ships that would transport them to the Holy Land. They were received in great state by the doge, and were asked to plead their case before the people of Venice in the basilica. So, after mass had been heard, one of their number stepped forward and declared that "no nation is so powerful on the seas as you"; after that piece of flattery, he implored the aid of the Venetian people. The princes then knelt down and wept. Immediately there were cries all around the basilica. "We grant it! We grant it!" It was a fine piece of stage management, in the best traditions of the city.

The doge, Enrico Dandolo, was already old and nearly blind. He was elected at the age of eighty-four, but he was one of those Venetian patriarchs whose tenacity and singleness of purpose were the visible proof of the city's own ruthlessness. It was said that he had nourished a grievance against Constantinople ever since the mass imprisonment of 1171. According to one Byzantine Greek chronicler, "he boasted that so long as he failed to take revenge on them for what they had done to his people he was living under sentence of death." It was even reported, in later chronicles, that he had been blinded by the

Byzantines themselves when he had once travelled to the city as an ambassador; this is the stuff of legend only.

The carpenters of the Arsenal were set to work, engaged to build and equip enough ships to carry 4,500 horsemen and 30,000 soldiers. In return Venice demanded 84,000 silver marks. The efficiency of the shipbuilding yards was by now well known throughout Europe, and all of the ships were delivered on time. But there was one problem. The crusaders had been unable to find the money to pay for them. So a new arrangement was concluded. The Venetians would waive full payment, on condition that the crusaders would assist them in subduing the rebellious city of Zara on the Dalmatian coast. It was a diversion from the Holy Land, but the leaders of the forces of the cross considered it to be a necessary one. Three hundred ships left the lagoon in October 1202, to the chant of the *Veni Creator*, and sailed down the Adriatic. Zara, after a siege of five days, surrendered. Christian had turned against Christian rather than the common enemy of the Saracen. The pope, incensed by this unwelcome development, excommunicated the forces of the expedition. It is not reported that the Venetians, in particular, were in any way cowed or humbled by the papal wrath.

Once the Venetians were fully in possession of the town, they were surprised by the arrival of an unexpected guest. The son of the deposed emperor of Constantinople, Alexius Angelus, came to Dandolo in search of justice. He wished the crusaders to overthrow the usurper, on the throne of the empire, and reinstall his father. For his part he pledged to finance and otherwise assist the armies in their high purpose. It was an offer that could not be refused. It has often been surmised that Dandolo had held this aim in mind throughout all the preparations for the crusade, and that he had already determined that Constantinople rather than Syria was to be the destination of the Venetian fleet. There can be no doubt that Dandolo saw a great opportunity for advancement and enrichment in this war at the expense of Constantinople. But there are elements of adventitious chance in all the affairs of men. Dandolo could not have known that the French crusaders would be unable to honour their obligation, although it is likely that he knew in advance of the arrival of Alexius in Zara. The Venetians were always adept at taking advantage of chance and circumstance. Yet in another perspective the great events of the world seem, on close scrutiny, to be made up of a thousand singular elements and accidents and coincidences. In the midst of this swirling world it would be hard to detect a pattern. So we may say that *it just happened*. As a consequence of these events the power of Byzantium was extinguished, its city and empire weakened beyond repair.

The Venetian fleet, in aid of Alexius, moved against the city. On 24 June 1203, it sailed beside the walls. A French attack by land seemed to have failed and so, under the command of Dandolo, the Venetians tied their galleys together to form a united front; from the decks and turrets of the vessels, military engines discharged their fire into the city. Constantinople was in flames. Dandolo himself stood at the prow of the first ship that struck land. He was dressed in full armour, and the standard of Saint Mark flew at his side. At his urging the Venetian soldiers leapt from their vessels and scaled the ladders swung against the walls. There was some combat, but the forces of the Byzantines were overwhelmed by this swift attack from the sea. The banner of the republic was fixed on the rampart. The city was taken. The deposed emperor, on whose behalf Alexius had pleaded, was rescued from his dungeon and placed upon the throne. Alexius himself was crowned in the basilica of Saint Sophia, and took his place as co-ruler of the empire.

Yet the fatal decline of Constantinople was about to resume its inevitable course. Alexius had promised the crusaders more than he could achieve. He lacked finance and, more importantly, he had forfeited his authority among his countrymen by relying upon the forces of the crusaders to obtain the imperial crown. The citizens of Constantinople, instigated by fear and rumour, rebelled against the new emperor. Alexius was cut down, his father abandoned to his grief.

The Venetians and their allies now had to extinguish this rebellion, and bring the city under their rule. They had not come so far to be simply asked to leave. So once more, in March 1204, they laid siege to the city. On the eve of the assault Dandolo declared to his men that they must "be valiant. And with the help of Jesus Christ, milord Saint Mark, and the prowess of your bodies, you shall be tomorrow in possession of the city, and you shall all be rich."

Once their victory was assured, the Christian armies, inflamed by greed and anger, began a general sack of the city. Constantinople was pillaged and burned. The wealthiest city of the world, filled with art and sculpture, was laid bare. Its citizens were slaughtered, the frenzy of blood-lust such that it seemed that the gates of hell had been opened. The palaces and houses of the city were ransacked. The churches were despoiled. The statues were melted down, and the pictures ripped apart. The tombs were opened, and the sacred vessels removed. It is reported that a prostitute was enthroned in the chair of the patriarch, in the basilica of Saint Sophia, from where she "hurled insults at Jesus Christ, and she sang bawdy songs, and danced immodestly in the holy place." One chronicler claimed that the rapine exceeded any other since the creation of the world. And the Venetians were the principal agents of this despoliation. Much of the plunder found its way to Venice. The four great horses that surmount the basilica of Saint Mark's are part of the fruit of that brutal victory.

There were other spoils. The crusaders claimed the dominions of Constantinople, and carved up its empire among the victors. Venice negotiated its portion with its customary merchant zeal, and was rewarded "the fourth part and the half of the Roman empire"; that is, it commanded three-eighths of the old empire. It already claimed Dalmatia and Croatia, and now it took possession of the Aegean coasts and islands as well as parts of the Mediterranean. It controlled Crete and Corfu as well as the islands of Modon and Coron. It took the western part of Greece and the islands of the Ionian Sea. It demanded the coast of Thrace, as well as the ports on the Hellespont. It seized Negroponte in the Aegean. While the other crusaders were unsure of their geography, the leaders of Venice knew exactly what they wanted. Many of the islands were then granted to various patrician families of Venice, who held them as fiefdoms of the republic. There was now also a large Venetian colony within Constantinople itself, which acquired a large measure of independence from the home city. There were even reports that the capital of the new empire was about to remove from Venice to Constantinople, but these were discounted. Yet one central fact was clear. The markets of the east were beckoning. All thought of the war against the infidel was forgotten and, indeed, the crusaders never did reach the Holy Land. It was the last of the crusades.

The strategy of Venice was that of a sea power intent upon strengthening its command of the sea. That is why the first great conquests were in the Levant, or eastern Mediterranean, where Venice might pose as the begetter of "an apostolic empire of the East" as a fitting successor to the Christian empire established in the East by

Justinian and Constantine. It is a typical example of Venetian rhetoric masking policy. To the victors, the spoils. So the imperium of Venice was largely confined to the islands and to the coastal regions. The Venetians wanted no part of the inland empire of Byzantium, whether in Asia or in Europe. The city could never have become another Rome. Instead it settled for secure trading routes across the seas, with a series of ports under Venetian control linking the market of the lagoon to the markets of the Levant. These were not so much colonies as trading posts, stretching from Venice to the Black Sea. The nature of Venetian dominion was now clear for all to observe. The power of Constantinople was effectively gone for ever. The consequences of the Venetian adventure, however, were by no means beneficent. That which is born in fire may die in fire. A weakened Constantinople became the prey of the Turks; the newly established Latin empire endured for only sixty years; the colonial possessions of Venice also left it exposed to attack in a long sequence of wars that tested its strength. For the next seventy years the serene city would be engaged in almost constant warfare with its rebellious subjects and with its rivals, with the Saracens and with the pirates of the Mediterranean.

17

Cities in Collision

There was one other significant competitor with which Venice had to deal. Genoa was known to the world as *"la Superba,"* Genoa the proud. Petrarch had described Venice and Genoa as "the two torches of Italy"; but fire can drive out fire. Both cities were known throughout Europe for their rapacity and acquisitiveness. The Genoese were more individualistic and inventive; the Venetians were more communal and conservative. The Genoese had a history of internecine warfare and rebellion; the Venetians were quiescent. Could they ever have lived at peace with one another?

For many centuries the merchants of Genoa competed with those of Venice in the eastern markets. But the success of the Venetians materially hindered the commerce of the rival city. It had been decreed, after the fall of Constantinople, that the Genoese were to be excluded from trade throughout the empire. But the Genoese fought back. They, too, were a seafaring people who had built up a great fleet that could challenge Venice on the seas of the known world. There were open clashes between the rival cities on the coasts of Crete and in Corfu, where the native inhabitants welcomed the arrival of the Genoese. A truce was agreed in 1218, but this was merely a prelude to further and more fatal struggles.

The tension between the two cities remained constant throughout the century, with skirmishing and assaults in all the markets where they competed; in 1258, after some particularly bloody fighting in Syria, the Venetians expelled the Genoese merchants from their quarter in Acre. There was then, for the Venetians, an unfortunate and unexpected development. In 1261 the Greeks, under the leadership of Michael Palaeologus, regained control of Constantinople. The Venetian fleet was at sea and the city was relatively unprotected. Under these auspicious circumstances the emperor's forces mounted a rapid attack on the Latin contingent, and gained the defensive walls.

Three weeks later Michael walked in glory to the basilica of Saint Sophia. He owed much of his success, however, to the Genoese who had supplied him with fifty ships; in return for their support they wished for unrestricted trade access in the markets of the city. They wanted revenge upon the Venetians for their forced departure from Acre. When the Venetians returned, they could do nothing except rescue their compatriots whose shops and dwellings had been destroyed by fire.

The Genoese were not faithful allies. Their merchants were, according to report, arrogant and avaricious. Their fleet proved unequal to a naval challenge from Venice. More importantly their representatives in Constantinople were accused of mounting a conspiracy against Paleologus himself. Ever ready to supplant a rival, Venetian envoys were sent in secret to the court of the emperor. A new trade pact was concluded. The Genoese were to be expelled from the empire, whereas Venice would be granted free privileges. In addition the Venetians were allowed to retain the former Byzantine possessions of Crete, of Negroponte, of Modon and Coron. These were sufficiently generous terms, and the emperor now understood that Venice itself was the greater power.

The Venetians were becoming accustomed to empire. At the beginning of the fourteenth century the doge, Pietro Gradenigo, made a speech to the great council of patricians in which he declared that "it is the duty of every good prince, and of every worthy citizen, to enlarge the State, to increase the Republic, and to seek its welfare by every means in his power." It was the responsibility of the state, too, to seize every favourable opportunity for aggrandisement. Gradenigo had the mainland of Italy particularly in mind, where now the Venetians were actively promoting a policy of aggressive warfare. They had once sought neutrality in the battles between pope and holy Roman emperor over the cities of Italy. They had once wanted simply to preserve their trade routes. But now the experience of imperial expansion had hardened their sinews. They had become more belligerent. The mainland of Italy was in any case changing its nature. The principal cities no longer saw themselves as vassals of superior powers, such as the papacy, but as sovereign regions or city-states. There were some eighty of them throughout the land of Italy. Some were under the control of individual families, such as the Este of

Ferrara, and others were in theory republican communities. Yet the central point was their independence. Independent cities want power and territory. They compete with each other for trade and influence. They even fight each other.

In 1308 Venice fought on the mainland in order to maintain its commercial rights within Ferrara and gain control over the Po. It allied itself with Florence and Bologna in order to fight back the expansive policies of Verona, and in the process captured much mainland territory. It fought against Padua and by its victory gained the provinces of Treviso and Bassano as well as the city of Padua itself. It won Verona and Vicenza. The Italian cities that came under Venetian domination were not subjugated. Venetian civil and military commanders were dispatched to the cities, but municipal government continued in the familiar fashion. The Venetian ruling class had a genius for administration and government. Its power was neither too lax nor too onerous. There are some indications of an imperial style but in the colonies overseas the rulers were blended within the native landscape. There was no ruling ideology of conquest. There was no attempt to impose new standards of value or new principles of belief. They came not as conquerors or as missionaries but, essentially, as traders. Their true belief was in the efficacy of commerce. They were a very practical people. They were unpopular enough, but they were resented rather than hated.

It would be wrong to assume, however, that there was no internal discontent. The immediate fact of conquest was, for the conquered, hard to bear. The example of Crete is representative. The lands of the local Byzantine magnates were expropriated, and given to Venetians. There were neither finances nor resources to maintain a standing army on the island, so a number of Venetian patricians were sent out as colonisers who retained their lands as fiefdoms on condition that they defended them. These Venetians tended to inhabit the towns and cities of the island. They were accustomed to cities. Cities were their natural habitat. In due course a predominantly agricultural economy was in part turned towards urban trade, trade directed almost exclusively to the mother-city. And of course the Venetian authorities imposed heavy taxation upon every transaction. They encouraged trade for the purpose of exploiting it. Yet merchants began to flourish on the island. There was also a growing market for the wares of Cretan icon-painters.

It has been estimated that 95 per cent of the icon-painters, throughout the Venetian empire, originally came from the island.

The Venetian strategy was to remodel the governance of the island on the example of Venice herself. Crete was divided into *sestieri*. There was a *duca* in the principal role, modelled on the doge. The major decisions of security and trade, however, were still the prerogative of the Venetian senate. There were more visible changes. The principal square of Candia, the capital of Crete, was renamed Piazza S. Marco. It became the meeting place and market of the island, with its own basilica and ducal palace. It was remodelled and restored to lend dignity and seriousness to the new administration. It became the stage for festivals and public celebrations. A processional way was constructed between the entrance gate of the port and the basilica. Venice was re-creating its theatre of trade and of politics in a new environment. The Byzantine palaces and monuments were reused, their symbolic meaning subtly altered to reflect Venetian hegemony. Some of them were given new, "Venetian," façades.

Venice saw itself as the natural heir to Byzantium. There was no sudden disruption but, instead, an orderly transition. The religious traditions and the public ceremonies of the old empire were appropriated and adapted. As always Venice lived by assimilation. The example of Crete is again instructive. The ecclesiastical rites of the Latin Church, in ceremonies and processions, were moulded with the rites of the Greek Church. The Venetians adopted the cult of the local saint of the island, Titus. So there were no religious wars. The Venetians were not like the Spanish. There were endless reconciliations and compromises, simply in order to maintain the momentum of what was essentially a vast trading regime. Cretans married Venetians. Venetian merchants migrated to Crete. Cretan scholars and painters migrated to Venice. A new culture emerged, of the West and of the East. After the fall of Byzantium Crete became the centre of Hellenism in the West. There were, naturally enough, influences of opposite tendency. There are still Venetian dialect words embedded in modern Greek, among them the words for steel, armada, velvet, the acacia tree and the wedding ring. Indeed there was a revival of Greek letters under Venetian rule. It was Venice, rather than Byzantium, that preserved native Greek culture in the early modern period. Its poetry was composed by men whose political, racial, spiritual and cultural allegiances were to Venice.

There were revolts and rebellions, as a result of local grievances and factions, but the island remained in Venetian hands for more than four centuries. It can be concluded, therefore, that the Venetians were effectively the first modern colonial power.

Yet in a world dominated by war and empire, there could be no end to rivalry and struggle. In the letters and chronicles of the late fourteenth century the optimism of the Venetians is in some part replaced by intimations of gloom and melancholy; the world seems more uncertain, and the role of providence ill-defined. The loss of confidence is accompanied by the search for greater security in the world. The acquisition of empire, then, brought its own burdens. In 1364 the native inhabitants of Candia rebelled against their Venetian overseers; several Venetian patricians also joined in the revolt. The insurrection was put down, its leaders executed, but it had been a troubling moment for Venice. Petrarch was in the city when the victorious force returned to the lagoon. "We augured good news," he wrote, "for the masts were garlanded with flowers, and on the deck were lads, crowned with green wreaths and waving flags over their heads . . ." Relief, as well as triumph, was the emotion of the day. A high mass was celebrated in the basilica, and a great festival was organised in the square itself. Petrarch was present on this occasion, too, and remarked upon the magnificence of the ceremonies. As the empire of Venice became more assured, so the taste for spectacle and ceremonial grew more intense.

Genoa was not quelled by its expulsion from Constantinople. Its traders were dominant in the Black Sea. It held the pre-eminent position in Syria and Palestine. There was never any chance of an enduring peace. In 1350 a Venetian admiral surprised a fleet of fourteen Genoese vessels at the port of Negroponte, and captured ten of them. The other four were allowed to flee simply because the Venetians were too occupied in plundering the cargo of the others. The Venetians and their Greek allies then confronted the Genoese fleet in the Bosphorus, but the battle proved inconclusive. In 1353 the Venetians defeated the Genoese off Sardinia, but a second Genoese fleet began a journey of destruction through the Adriatic and the Aegean. A year later a Venetian fleet was sabotaged and sunk by the Genoese in the port of Modon; the Venetian commanders and their men were taken into custody. It was a signal victory for the Genoese but, even in defeat, the Venetians proved to be expert negotiators. A truce was agreed by means of which each side promised not to attack the other.

The subsequent peace was not, for Venice, a peace at all. It was obliged to cede Dalmatia to the king of Hungary, because of that sovereign's superior force of arms; it was impelled to withdraw its merchants from Famagusta in Cyprus when the Genoese took over that town. The Venetian fleet kept the Adriatic as its territory, but it was engaged in constant confrontation with the Genoese in the Black Sea. When Venice seized the vital island of Tenedos, controlling access to that sea, the Genoese once again declared war. The Fourth Genoese War was to prove the most terrible, and the most fatal, of all.

The hostilities began in 1378 when a Venetian admiral, Vettor Pisani, sailed west and won a great victory over the Genoese in Genoa's own waters. But there were complications closer to home. The king of Hungary invited the Genoese to use the Dalmatian coast, opposite Venice, as their centre of operations. It was an opportunity not to be missed. Pisani was obliged to return to the Adriatic, in order to protect Venetian convoys in a gulf that the Venetians had always claimed as their own. His base was at Pola, in Istria, and at the turn of the year the vessels of the fleet were being fitted up and cleaned for future hostilities. But a battle was forced upon them before they could muster all of their ships. The Venetians first had the advantage, when the Genoese admiral was killed, but a reserve force of Genoese ships came forward unexpectedly and overwhelmed the Venetians. Hundreds were killed or captured.

With their fleet effectively out of action, it was the moment that the Venetians most feared. Their enemies closed in upon them from every side. The king of Hungary closed the routes of the northern Adriatic; the lord of Padua blocked the western trade routes on the mainland. The fleets of the Genoese were protected, and were being augmented all the time. They were even able to enter the lagoon, and burn towns along the Lido. This had never before happened in the history of the serene republic. When the Paduans and Genoese joined forces, and took the extensive port of Chioggia to the south of Venice, the armed circle around the city was complete. The Venetians were now effectively under siege. They might even be invaded. Business on the Rialto came to a halt. The salaries of public officials were suspended. The poor were told by the doge that they would find food in the homes of the rich. When threatened, the Venetians came together as a coherent body. The Venetians proposed negotiations but the Genoese replied that they would not talk to their enemies until the horses of Saint Mark's had been bridled; by this time the bronze horses, taken from the spoliation of Constantinople, had become a symbol of Venetian pride and greed.

It was a moment of the utmost peril for the Venetian authorities, who knew that they would need the support and co-operation of all the people to avert a fatal outcome. At the insistence of the crowds they released from prison Vettor Pisani, who had been incarcerated for his defeat at Pola. He now became the popular champion and the principal defender of the city. The doge himself, Andrea Contarini, helped to train crews for the new galleys that were being built.

The plan, outlined by Pisani, was to sink barges and boats laden with stone in the deep channels around Chioggia; this was a way of cutting off the port, and its Genoese invaders, from the mainland and from the Genoese fleet still at sea. The scheme was a success. The Genoese found themselves blockaded, with dwindling supplies of food, water and gunpowder. The Venetians were also suffering from privation, but they had one advantage. They possessed hope. Even as Pisani harried and outmanoeuvred the Genoese, trying desperately to leave Chioggia, another Venetian admiral returned to port. Carlo Zeno had completed a military expedition that had captured the cargos and booty of many Genoese ships in the Mediterranean. Then he received instructions to return to the lagoon and assist his city in its trial of strength with Genoa.

It was he who helped to prevent the increasingly desperate attempts of the Genoese to fight their way out of Chioggia. There were great battles on the sands and the Genoese commander, Pietro Doria, was killed when a cannon ball struck the tower from which he was observing the proceedings. Then, in June 1380, the Genoese surrendered. There was still work to be done in the Adriatic and in the Mediterranean. But Genoa never challenged Venice again. Genoese vessels never returned to the Adriatic. In this year of defeat a Genoese friar delivered a homily to his congregation. The Genoese, he said, were like donkeys. "When many are together, and one of them is thrashed with a stick, all scatter, fleeing hither and thither." The

Venetians, on the other hand, resembled pigs. "When a multitude of pigs is confined together, and one of them is hit or beaten with a stick, all draw close and run unto him who hits it."

The victory had enormous consequences for Venice. In the fourteenth century it became one of the principal cities of the known world. Where in previous centuries it had been aligned with the East, in cultural and mercantile terms, by the end of the fourteenth century it had emerged as a properly European power. After the war was over it went on to claim by right of conquest or dominion Durazzo and Scutari, Lepanto and Patras, Argos and Athens. These were the homes of wine and wheat. The Venetian empire of Italy also grew, or rather was accumulated, step by step. In the early years of the fifteenth century Verona and Padua despatched ambassadors to Venice to make the formal act of submission. They were followed by Ravenna and Friuli and a host of other towns and cities. From the Alps in the north to the Po in the south, from Bergamo and Crema in the west to the sea itself, Venice claimed dominion. It might even be claimed that the city had refashioned the ancient province of Venetia, from which its ancestors had come.

Governors were sent to the towns and cities under its control, and a "captain" was appointed to administer military affairs. High service on the mainland became a prelude to political authority at home. But each city was able to preserve its local privileges, as well as its customary assemblies and magistrates. Only gradually was there a movement towards more professional and bureaucratic structures, with the increasing significance of a small number of aristocratic families. The pattern of Venice was, ineluctably, beginning to repeat itself. The greater bears down upon the lesser. But the dominant city—the *inclita dominante*, or illustrious mistress, as it was known—did not seek to impose union on these territories. The Milanese and Florentines were far more ready to assert their authority over their subject cities. The Venetians were more cautious or, perhaps, more conservative. There was some confusion over the status of local law, as it related to Venetian law, but that was perhaps inevitable. The empire of the mainland was driven by pragmatism and expediency. There was no Venetian state. There was only a trade confederation, relying heavily upon the revenue accruing to Venice through the proceeds of indirect taxation.

The Venetians also discouraged any enterprise that might challenge the commercial supremacy of their own city, as, for example, the weaving of luxury textiles, so that according to an English observer in the 1760s "every other town in the territory of the Republick appears poor in the comparison of the mother-city." The innate conservatism of the Venetian state, too, actively discouraged the modernisation of the general economy of the mainland territories. This led directly to Venice's eventual financial decline. The Italians were not able to compete with the resurgent English and Dutch. The inability or unwillingness to create a state, and a modern state at that, may also have encouraged the fissiparous qualities of the Italian peninsula. In one sense the opportunity for unification and centralisation had been squandered. So Italy remained a prey to foreign powers.

Yet Venice was still secure. It was protected by the lagoon while the plains and hills of northern Italy gave it space against the rival city of Milan; the deep valleys and mountains of the Alpine region afforded it protection against northern rivals. The further the dominion spread, the more jealously it was protected. Issues of self-defence as well as commercial gain were used to justify the absorption of towns and regions. Inaction was no longer possible.

In the first quarter of the fifteenth century, therefore, Venice aligned itself with Florence in order to fight the Visconti family of Milan; this was its first departure from its policy of splendid isolation. There was much opposition to this alliance in Venice itself. Venetian merchants traded very successfully with the Milanese territories and any overreaching by Venice would require the presence of a standing army. Yet the leaders of Venice determined to form an alliance with the free republic of Florence against the tyrants of Milan. The strategy was successful and, with the removal of the Visconti family, Italy reached a state of broad equilibrium amenable to Venetian pressure. There were now no more than five territorial states with their claims and resources finely balanced—Venice, Naples, Florence, Milan and the papal state. Each ruling city and its dependent territories was given the name of *lo stato* or the estate. In time the word developed to mean the collective existence of a nation or people. In the beginning these *stati* depended upon the personality of the ruler or ruling family; eventually, of course, they would be politically and scientifically organised to merit the description of a "state." The interests of the state then became paramount. Of these new Italian powers von Ranke, the German historian, wrote that "they were neither nations nor races; neither cities nor kingdoms; they were the first States in world." And Venice was one of them, opening the way for the development of the modern world order.

Milan was still the dominant city of Lombardy, and Florence of Tuscany, but in the phrase of William Wordsworth only Venice did also "hold the gorgeous East in fee." The eastern association was evident in the streets and houses of the city; even its national basilica was Oriental in inspiration. By the fifteenth century it was the richest city in Italy, with an annual budget equal to that of Spain or of England. There were many more palaces in Venice than in any other city. Its navy was arguably the finest in the world. It was also a much more stable city than any of its rivals on the mainland, with a strength and persistence that derived from its earliest instincts for survival in the battle against the sea. While the Genoese in particular were plagued by civil war and internecine rivalries, Venice remained a model of constancy despite periods of plague and of economic depression. The strength and security of its constitution rendered it powerful. The trade of the city revived, particularly in its intercourse with India and with China, and the revenues of the Rialto were never more strong. It was triumphant.

18

A Call to Arms

At the height of its intervention on the mainland, Venice could maintain a force of forty thousand troops. It was estimated by the reigning doge, in 1423, that the city possessed thirty-five galleys, three hundred round ships and three thousand other vessels; they required a complement of thirty-six thousand sailors, almost a quarter of the entire population of 150,000 people. There were ships christened *La Forza*, *La Fama* and *La Salute*. They were used to protect the armed galleys of the trade convoys that left Venice on prearranged dates; they were used to combat pirates and to harass enemy traders. No foreign ship was safe in the waters Venice considered its own. The officers were elected from the patrician class of the city. Service at sea was an indispensable part of the education of the young patrician.

The crews were at first all free men, volunteers found in Venice or in Venetian possessions. By the beginning of the sixteenth century conscription had been introduced. This of course so lowered the status of galley labour that it became a burden to be avoided. To be an oarsman, a *galeotto*, was considered to be part of a "low" profession. So by the middle of the sixteenth century there was a change in the nature of these crews. It was said that they comprised drunks and debtors, criminals and other outcasts. The courts of Venice sometimes consigned the guilty to the galleys rather than the cells. By 1600 prisoners made up the principal part of the crew. The measure of their servitude can be computed by the records of the Venetian courts—eighteen months of galley service was considered equivalent to three years of close imprisonment and a period in the pillory, while seven years in the galleys was considered to be equal to twelve years of confinement. Their rations were made up of biscuit, wine, cheese, salt pork and beans. The diet was designed to feed the sanguinary humour. A Franciscan friar was always on board to rouse them. Yet there are reports of disease and of early death, of exhaustion and despair. Carlo

Gozzi, in the eighteenth century, saw "some three hundred scoundrels, loaded with chains, condemned to drag their life out in a sea of miseries and torments, each of which was sufficient by itself to kill a man." He noticed that, at the time, "an epidemic of malignant fever raged among these men." It is not clear, however, that the changed personnel were in general any less proficient as oarsmen. They helped to win a famous victory against the Turks at Lepanto.

The maritime marvel of Venice was the Arsenal, the greatest ship-building concern in the world. The word itself derives from the Arabic *dar sina'a*, or place of construction, thus affirming the strong con-nection of Venice with the East. It was built at the beginning of the twelfth century, and was continually being extended and expanded until it became a wonder of technology. It was variously described as "the factory of marvels," "the greatest piece of oeconomy in Europe" and "the eighth miracle of the world." The epithets are a measure of the respect in which new technologies were then held. Its famous gate, made up of Roman and of Byzantine elements, was raised there in 1460. The Arsenal had become the centre of another empire. It was the engine of trade. It was the foundation of naval might. It was a token of the supremacy of industrial enterprise in the most serene city.

Eventually two and half miles (4 km) of walls, and fourteen defensive towers, surrounded sixty acres (24 ha) of working space. It was the largest industrial enterprise in the world. A population of skilled workers and labourers grew up around the site. The number of workmen has been estimated at anything between six thousand and sixteen thousand; in any event they worked in large numbers. This shipbuilding neighbourhood in the eastern part of Venice became a recognisable part of the city, with its own prejudices and customs. People lived and died, were baptised and married, within the three parishes of S. Martino, S. Ternita and S. Pietro. It is still an area of tiny houses, crowded tenements, small squares, dead-ends and narrow alleys.

The inhabitants became known as *arsenalotti*, and such was their importance to the state that the male population of ship-makers was also used as a bodyguard for the doge. They were also employed as fire-fighters. Only the *arsenalotti* were allowed to be labourers in the Mint. They alone rowed the ceremonial barge of the doge. Proud of their status, they never united with the other artisans of Venice. It is a case of divide and rule. It is also a signal example of the subtle way in which the leaders of Venice co-opted what might have been an unruly group of people within the very fabric of the city. The loyalty of the *arsenalotti* materially helped to secure the cohesion and the very survival of Venice.

The Arsenal was the first factory established upon the assembly line of modern industry, and thus the harbinger of the factory system of later centuries. One traveller, in 1436, described it thus:

> as one enters the gate there is a great street on either side with the sea in the middle, and on one side are windows opening out of the houses of the arsenal, and the same on the other side. On this narrow strip of water floated a galley towed by a boat, and from the windows of the various houses they handed out to the workers, from one the cordage, from another the arms . . .

It was known as "the machine." The armed galleys were constructed here. The relatively unarmed "round" ships, with sails instead of oars, were also made here. The key to its efficiency lay in the division, and specialisation, of labour; there were shipwrights and caulkers, rope-makers and blacksmiths, sawyers and oar-makers. Thirty galleys could be built and fitted within ten days. When the French king visited the place in 1574, a galley was built and launched in the two hours it took him to eat his dinner. The whole process of industrial collaboration, however, might be seen as an image of the Venetian polity itself. Everything is of a piece.

Dante visited the Arsenal in the early fourteenth century, and left a description of it in the twenty-first canto of the *Inferno*:

> As in the Arsenal of the Venetians
> Boils in the winter the tenacious pitch . . .
> One hammers at the prow, one at the stern,
> This one makes oars and that one cordage twists
> Another mends the mainsail and the mizzen.

It may not be coincidence that Dante places this vision in the eighth circle of hell, where corrupt public officials are punished eternally. The blatant sale of public offices became a problem in Venetian governance.

Eventually the Arsenal was outmoded. The development of craft technology in the seventeenth century rendered it obsolete. It continued producing galleys when no galleys were needed. It became inefficient, its labourers underpaid and underworked. Yet it did not finally close until 1960, when eleven thousand families were removed from their ancient neighbourhood. Now the factories and production lines are used to house exhibitions for the various festivals that visit Venice. It is an apt token of the nature of the city.

The Venetian army was as effective by land as the Venetian navy on the oceans. By the middle of the fifteenth century it could afford to maintain a standing force of twenty thousand troops, with extra militia ready to be called up in an emergency. By the beginning of the following century, that number had doubled. It was of mixed identity. Venetian engineers were well known for their skills in siege weaponry, but it was said that the Venetians themselves did not make good soldiers. To a large extent, therefore, the city relied upon mercenaries for its defence. Its soldiers came from Dalmatia, Croatia and Greece as well as from Germany and Gascony; there were light horse from Albania and cuirassiers from other parts of Italy. When some Venetian gunmen were captured at Buti in 1498, and their hands cut off, some of the unfortunate troops were from England and Holland.

The acquisition of a land empire, at the beginning of the fifteenth century, was the direct motive for the creation of a standing army. Yet such an army posed problems for the leaders of the city. An army could move through its streets. An army could threaten its mainland possessions. That is why no Venetian was ever made general or commander. The danger of a military coup was always present to the administration. Venetian patricians were not allowed to command, at any one time, more than twenty-five men. It was a safeguard against faction. Instead a foreign commander was always chosen, although he held his office under the watchful care of two senior patricians in the field with him. It was not an ideal arrangement, especially in the very heat of battle, but it served Venetian interests well.

The foreign generals were known as *condottieri*, from the Italian word for contract. They were contracted men. But they were also adventurers, and sometimes brigands, who were suited to the theatre of Venice. They aspired to the type of the classical Roman general, ferocious in war and gracious in peace; they were deemed to be no less wise than courageous, no less virtuous than judicious. And they were paid well. Venice was known as a generous, and prompt, employer. The *condottieri* were given ornate houses along the Grand Canal, and were granted large estates on the mainland. They seemed to be indispensable to the state, but there were some who questioned the wisdom of employing them. They could be persuaded to change sides, if large enough bribes were offered, and they could sometimes be feckless and excessively independent. Machiavelli blamed the collapse of Venice, in his lifetime, on the use of mercenaries and mercenary commanders. If the Venetians did not excel at warfare, they would soon become deficient in the arts of peace. Sir Henry Wotton, at the beginning of the seventeenth century, commented that "by the lasciviousness of their youth, by the wariness of their aged men, by their long custom of ease, and distaste of arms, and consequently by their ignorance in the management thereof" the Venetian state was in sad decline. Yet decline was always being predicted for Venice, even at the acme of its power.

VI

Timeless City

19

Bells and Gondolas

The Venetians needed to control time, just as they controlled every other aspect of their insular world. The bells rang out at precise times of day, to co-ordinate the activities of the populace. Within the campanile itself, in Saint Mark's Square, there was a system of five bells—the *marangona* that announced the beginning and end of the working day, the *nona* and the *mezza terza* that rang the hours, the *trottiera* that invited the patricians to vote in their various assemblies, and the *maleficio* that called the spectators to the latest public execution. The bells were a form of social control, creating areas of forbidden time. An edict was announced in 1310 that "no person whatsoever shall be suffered, without special licence, to walk abroad after the third bell of the night."

In the private and public institutions of the city every phase of activity was signalled by the ringing of bells; the people were summoned for waking, for washing, for praying, for eating and for sleeping. It is another indication of the paternalism, or authoritarianism, of Venetian society. Yet since bells were intimately associated with religious devotion, it was a way of making life itself a sacred activity. It was a qualitative, as well as a quantitative, token.

Yet time seems to shift in the city. The tokens of various periods appear together, and various times modify one another. In Venice there is no true chronological time; it has been overtaken by other forces. There are occasions, indeed, when time seems to be suspended; if you enter a certain courtyard, in a shaft of sunlight, the past rises all around you. This is not necessarily a private or individual sensation. The organisations of the city were believed by the people to be "perpetual." In their work on the public monuments of the city the Venetians were concerned to accrue various layers or levels of time, with borrowings and adaptations from earlier cultures. Theirs was never meant to be an architecture of the present, but rather of the past and present conflated. The city affords visitors a glimpse of the porousness of history.

There is indeed a different sense of time in the city, as any visitor will testify. No one can hurry in Venice; no one can "make up" time. There is no transport except by water, and there are many hindrances to a pedestrian's rapid journey. It is a city that slows down the human world. That is another reason for the sense of enchantment or dream that it induces. There is a great will to wander and be lost. The official institution of time was also different. The beginning of the next day was dated from the hour of the evening Angelus, or six o'clock. Thus 6:30 p.m. on Christmas Eve was, for the Venetians, already Christmas Day. This system continued until the Napoleonic conquest.

The continuity of the city and of its administration impressed upon the inhabitants a different sense of time, also, calculated in centuries rather than in decades. Venice measured itself in historical rather than chronological time. The centuries are, as it were, enclosed on the island; they are imprisoned in the labyrinth of the *calli*. Time on the mainland has the room to spread outward, so that it becomes flatter and thinner. In Venice it echoes and re-echoes. The Irish writer Seán O'Faoláin described it as "a projection of the Schopenhauerian will, a timeless essence."

It might be truer to say that there are continuities through time. A Venetian of the sixteenth century, if not earlier, would have no trouble in finding his or her way through the streets of the modern city. That is true of few other cities on earth. The churches, and markets, are still in the same place. The ferries still cross the Grand Canal from the same stations that they used five hundred years ago. The same religious festivals are celebrated. Of all cities, Venice is the one that most fully manifests continuity. It has become its reason for being. It is reassuring because it represents permanence and stability in a world of change; that is why its survival has become so important to variously concerned groups in England and America. Some of the cityscapes of the sixteenth century, by Carpaccio and others, can still be identified in the contemporary city. There is a famous view by Canaletto of a stone-mason's yard, by the bank of the Grand Canal where now the Accademia bridge has been erected. From the painting itself, approximately of the Campo S. Vidal and the church of S. Maria della Carità, it is possible to identify still existing houses, a small bridge and a little canal. The painting is dated to 1727, so the territory has remained stable for almost three hundred years.

The most obvious sign of continuity is also the most familiar. The gondolas have been plying the waterways of the city for a thousand years, with only the smallest modifications in shape and appearance. John Evelyn described them in the seventeenth century as "very long and narrow, having necks and tails of steel . . . some are adorned with carving, others lined with velvet, commonly black . . . while he who rowes, stands upright on the very edge of the boate, and with one oare (bending forward as if he would precipitate into the sea) rowes & turnes with incredible dexterity."

The gondolas are first mentioned in a document at the end of the eleventh century, although they must have been in existence for many decades before that date. The word itself has been granted many derivations, from the Latin *cymbula* or Greek *kuntelas* (both meaning small boat). But the actual origins of the boat have been variously found in Malta, Turkey, and, improbably, Avignon. It found its definite, and still modern, shape by degrees. Originally it was shorter and squatter than the modern version, with a cabin placed in the middle of the boat often protected by blinds or curtains. This was the mode of transport used by the patricians of the city, who might have many gondoliers in the pay of the household. By the seventeenth century these cabins or *felzi* became places of assignation and intrigue, adding to the legend of Venice as a city of hidden pleasures. They were removed in the 1930s. There was one other modification in the middle of the eighteenth century, when the right side was made nine inches (225 mm) longer than the left; this adjustment increased the little boat's speed and manoeuvrability. Then the gondola sailed on through the centuries, growing slightly longer and slimmer so that it might accommodate the growing number of tourists. It was still a boat of pleasure, but no longer reserved for the few.

There were ten thousand gondolas in the sixteenth century, many of them festooned with ornaments and carvings. This encouraged displays of showmanship and rivalry among the wealthier Venetians, who were allowed few opportunities of conspicuous consumption in public. Such a spirit was of course to be resisted by a Venetian state that curbed individualism of any sort in the name of collective brotherhood. So the ornamentation was, in a decree of 1562, forbidden. That is why the gondolas became black. Even though black was not considered by the Venetians to be an unfavourable colour, the gondolas ever since have regularly been seen as floating coffins. Shelley compared them to moths that have struggled out of the chrysalis of a coffin. James Fenimore Cooper felt that he was riding in a hearse. Wagner, fearful in a time of cholera, had to force himself to board one. Goethe called it a capacious bier. And Byron saw it:

> Just like a coffin clapt in a canoe,
> Where none can make out what you say or do.

Byron is here describing the amours that might or might not take place in the private space of the cabin. The gondolier penetrating the interior canals of the city has also been given a phallic importance, so that in Venice sex and death are once more conflated. Henry James wrote of the experience that "each dim recognition and obscure arrest is a possible throb of your sense of being floated to your doom. . . ." A ride on a gondola can prompt some very powerful instincts.

The metal beak at the prow, the *ferro*, has a complicated history. Some believe that its six teeth represent the six *sestieri* of the city. It has also been considered to be a replica of the beak of a Roman galley; given the Venetian fondness for antique copy, that has the ring of truth.

The gondoliers are the most famous of the city's native sons. Their characteristic uniform of straw hat and black-and-white striped top, together with the red or blue scarf, was really only formalised in the 1920s. But their *braggadocio* is very old. They seem to enjoy the sound of their own voices, on land as well as on water. They bawl; they bellow; they sing. But when they are hushed, and the only sound is that of the gondola gliding through the water, then the deep peace of Venice begins to reign.

The gondoliers have been celebrated in song and ballad from the sixteenth century. They were praised for their discretion. When the gondola was used as a place of assignation, the gondoliers were silent about their customers; if a gondolier had denounced a lady to her husband, he would have been drowned by his colleagues. They were employed to deliver sensitive letters. Foreign visitors often denounced them as foul-mouthed cheats or pimps, but they received more praise from their compatriots. They appear as good-hearted heroes, for example, in the comedies of Goldoni. Here is part of a typical setting from his play, *The Good Girl*: "two gondoliers arrive at the same moment from opposite directions . . . Each insists that the other shall give way by dropping back." There then follows a dialogue of threat and insult known to all earlier travellers to Venice. Yet their high spirits were part of the air of the city. They were incarnate of the will to live, and to survive, upon the water.

The cries and songs of the gondoliers have been endlessly recorded. In *Stones of Venice* Ruskin himself devotes his first appendix to "The Gondolier's Cry." It might be the title to an opera. *"Premi!"* to pass on the left, *"Stali!"* to pass on the right, and *"Sciar!,"* to come to a halt. The gondoliers love to call to one another across the water, although such marine repartee is now as much of a theatrical act as the singing of "O solo mio" or "Torno a Sorrento." Although in the city itself they are still a powerful and sometimes disruptive force, they are now principally the delight of tourists. They have in a larger sense become part of the self-conscious mannerism of contemporary Venetian life, their costume little more than fancy dress. It has been said that no Venetian would be seen dead in a gondola, except perhaps in those that are used as ferries from one bank to another.

There are now only four hundred gondolas at work in the city. Only four are made each year. The boat cannot last for ever. After twenty or so years of service, its woodwork will warp and weaken. It is then taken to the island of Murano, where its wood is used to kindle the flames of the glass-works. It becomes part of another city industry, its energy transformed into Venetian glass.

20

Iustitia

On one of the three exposed corners of the ducal palace, there is a sculpture concerning the judgement of Solomon. On the west façade of the palace is the figure of Iustitia, with the sword of justice upright in her hand; here also is the word "Venecia." Venice and Justice have been combined in one eternal image, with the inscription "Strong and just, enthroned I put the furies of the sea beneath my feet." Above the Porta della Carta, in the same complex of public buildings, is enthroned the virgin image of Venetia and Iustitia with sword and scales. The crowning figures of the palace are also those of Iustitia. The justice of Venice is one of the myths of Venice. It is deemed to be ancient. It is deemed to be divinely inspired. It is related, in ultimate form, to the judicial salvation of humankind.

The actual nature of Venetian law is less glorious, but perhaps more interesting. As in all aspects of the Venetian polity, it was of mixed inheritance. Elements of it came from Roman jurisprudence, and from Byzantine legislation. Other elements were taken from the Lombard and Frankish codes. Having no firm territorial foundation, Venice was forced to adapt or borrow the traditions of other peoples. It could be said that the Venetians created a patchwork coalition of various legal principles, flexible and accommodating for any circumstances. Venetian law was, above all else, efficient. A nation all at sea must first save itself.

The first code of jurisprudence was promulgated at the close of the twelfth century, and the laws were collected in the following century within the pages of five great books. The majority of statutes, as might be expected in a city of merchants, dealt with matters of wealth and property. Commercial law was the most voluminous. The five books might be said, in fact, to embody a mercantile attitude towards law. Despite the reverence for the customary image of Justice, the practice of the Venetians seems to have been largely empirical and pragmatic.

The laws were often acknowledgements of what already existed in practice. Customary law, unwritten and on occasions anecdotal, seems to have been pre-eminent. It was even declared that custom might override the written law. This is in part evidence of the merchant spirit, distrusting legal niceties and quibbles. The offender must pay for dishonour done to God, and disrespect shown to the city. These were the important matters.

It was often said that Venetians were more fond of talking than of doing. Certainly it is true that no other city-state produced so much legislation. The contents of these laws are sometimes confusing, inconsistent and contradictory. They were passed and then not enacted. They were issued, or reissued, when the very same laws were already on the statute books. The leaders of Venice legislated too much. There is an air of fantasy, or of unreality, about their search for legal formulae. Some of the great council believed or thought that they remembered a certain law. When it could not actually be found, it was drawn up and entered anyway. There was a saying that "seven days suffice before time obscures a Venetian law":

> Una leze veneziana
> Dura una settimana.

The sumptuary laws, in particular, entered the minutiae of social life where no practical supervision was possible. So they were largely ignored. They remain, however, the most bizarre example of the lengths to which the Venetian state would go to influence social conduct. If the city were a large family, as was often claimed, then it was of a harshly paternalistic kind. Thus, in 1562, it was decreed that "at any meal of meat not more than one course of roast and one kind of boiled meat may be provided. This may not include more than three kinds of meat or poultry . . ." The legislation was designed in part to curb the enthusiasm for large family parties, for gatherings of kin, which could be considered as a threat to the state. That is why the particular focus of legislation was directed at feasts and banquets where great numbers of people might gather. Oysters were not permitted at dinners where there were more than twenty guests. There were rules on the number of pastries and fruits that could be served; peacocks and pheasant were forbidden. The slaves who served at such banquets were invited to spy on their masters. The cooks were obliged to report in advance to the authorities what food they had been asked to prepare.

The legislation was also designed to arrest the tendency towards excessive flamboyance; the common people, faced with the extravagance of the rich, might become restless. In Venice, internal dissension had to be avoided at all costs. That is perhaps the reason for the general disregard of sumptuary legislation; it was seen only as a gesture to mollify the populace, not as a serious attempt at enforcing law.

There was also the spiritual argument. The example of vanity and greed would invoke the anger of the Almighty. At times of defeat, on sea or land, the Venetians often blamed the debased morals of certain of the citizens. This was of course a common trope in the medieval and early modern periods, but it applied all the more aptly and sharply to a city that believed itself to be chosen by God. The rules applied to the strictest regulations of dress. No man or woman could possess more than two fur cloaks. In 1696 it was forbidden for anyone to wear lace ruffles on the neck or wrists; brocade and silk clothes were forbidden, and no more than two rings could be worn upon the fingers. Three patricians were chosen as magistrates or sumptuary police, to enforce these regulations. It is not known whether they were successful in their attempts to curb extravagance and excess.

The practice of Venetian law was in theory equitable. Anyone who owned property, whether patrician or citizen or artisan, was treated in the same manner. Patricians could not plead, or expect, any especial favours. There was also a system of appeal established upon principles of fairness. Solicitations could be made to the doge himself. There was a Venetian saying, *"pane in piazza e giustizia in Palazzo"*; bread in the piazza and justice in the palace. Venetian justice had a reputation for strictness, on occasions to the point of barbarity, but also for impartiality. The state provided counsel for those who were poor. Even the slaves of Venice could approach the legal tribunals, and obtain redress from any grievances. In May 1372 a Venetian artisan, Antonio Avonal, and Giacobello, a tanner, whiled away the time by pricking with a long pin the slaves who passed them on their way to vespers at Saint Mark's; they were taken before the authorities. Avonal was sentenced to three, and Giacobello to two, months in prison.

Almost uniquely in Italy, too, the lawcourts conducted their business in the vernacular. The court records are filled with the voices of ordinary Venetians, arguing, pleading, complaining about neighbours and employers and servants. The tribunals were like family courts. Venetian life was one of almost continuous litigation. In fact the sturdy tradition of the vociferous courts helped to stabilise Venice throughout its history. That is why the people of Venice were known to be "law-abiding." Rulers and ruled knew the common ground on which they stood. Saint Bernard of Clairvaux is supposed to have told the doge, Cristoforo Moro, that "the republic would last as long as the custom continued of doing justice."

We have the intriguing spectacle of practical success and ad hoc or muddled legal theorising. Laws were made or unmade, or ignored, or thwarted, or disobeyed. There were so many laws that no one could remember them all. The patrician judges had not received a legal education, except that which they had picked up by observation. They were politicians employed for a relatively short term. So they relied upon the promptings of conscience, conjecture, and common sense. They were, in one sense, amateurs. There must of course have been abuses of power and of principle; there must have been bribes and blackmail. That is the nature of life. Yet the pragmatic workings of the legal system, established upon custom, prevailed. The bond of equality before the law kept the city together. It is a measure of the Venetian temperament.

21

Against the Turks

Even as the sun of Genoa set, in the summer of 1380, a new enemy rose over the eastern horizon in the shape of the Ottoman Turks. The Venetians had been accustomed to underestimate the challenge of the empire of the Osmanlis; they considered it to be locked up by land, and unable to threaten by sea. But then the waters of the Levant became the prey of Turkish pirates who could never be successfully put down; the gradual encroachment of the Ottoman Empire meant that Venetian trade routes were also being encircled. The Ottoman advance threatened the Venetian merchant colonies in Cyprus, Crete and Corfu; the islands had constantly to be defended with fortresses and with fleets. The two empires had their first confrontation in the waters of Gallipoli where, in 1416, the Venetian fleet routed the Turks after a long fight. The Venetian admiral later reported that the enemy had fought "like dragons"; their sea skills, then, were not to be underestimated. The proof came in 1453, when the Turkish forces overwhelmed Constantinople itself. It had been an ailing city, ever since the Venetian sack in 1204, and its defenders could not match the overwhelming forces of the Turks. The Osmanli dynasty was now knocking on the door of Europe. Constantinople, now for ever to be known as Istanbul, became the true power of the region.

There was, for the Venetians, business to be done. It would be better for them to turn putative enemies into customers. The pope might fulminate against the infidel, but the Venetians saw them as clients. A year after the fall of Constantinople a Venetian ambassador was despatched to the court of the sultan, Mehmed II, "the Conqueror," declaring that it was the wish of the Venetian people to live in peace and amity with the emperor of the Turks. They wished, in other words, to make money out of him. The Venetians were duly given freedom of trade in all parts of the Ottoman Empire, and a new Venetian colony of merchants was established in Istanbul.

But the relationship could not endure. Mehmed increased the tariffs to be paid by Venetian ships, and entered into negotiations with the merchants of Florence. Then in 1462 the Turks seized the Venetian colony of Argos. War was declared between the empires. It was considered that by strength of numbers the Turks would succeed on land, while the Venetians would maintain their old supremacy at sea. The Venetians may have been hoping for an eventual truce, from which they could secure concessions. But Mehmed had a more formidable navy than the Venetians had expected. After much fighting, the Venetian fleet was expelled from the central Aegean. It was no longer a Latin sea. The island of Negroponte, in the possession of Venice for 250 years, was occupied by the Turks. The Turks conquered the region of the Black Sea, also, and turned that sea into the pond of Istanbul. The Venetians were forced on the defensive, fighting rearguard actions much closer to home in Albania and Dalmatia.

The Florentines told the pope that it would be for the good of all if the Turks and Venetians fought each other to a state of exhaustion. Yet Venice was exhausted first. It was finally obliged to sue for peace in 1479, seventeen years after the hostilities had begun. Venice kept Crete and Corfu. The Corfiote capital was described by Sir Charles Napier in the early nineteenth century as "a town fraught with all the vice and abominations of Venice"; but the real power of Venice in the Levant was gone for ever. The Turks now held the Aegean and the Mediterranean. The grand vizier of the Turkish court told the representatives of Venice suing for peace, "You can tell your doge that he has finished wedding the sea. It is our turn now." A contemporary diarist, Girolamo Priuli, wrote of his countrymen that "faced with the Turkish threat, they are in a worse condition than slaves." This was hyperbole, but it reflected the disconsolate mood of the people. This was the moment when Venetian ambitions in the east effectively came to an end. The eyes of the city were now turned towards the mainland of Italy.

The equilibrium in northern Italy could not endure. There were leagues and counter-leagues drawn up between the territorial powers, too weak to strike alone against their neighbours. The peace to which Venice aspired could be upheld only by the sword. While there was still empire, there would never be any rest. There were fears among other cities that the appetite of Venice had no limit, and that the city was intent upon the conquest of all Italy north of the Apennines. The republican alliance between Venice and Florence broke apart. There were endless tirades against the city's cupidity and duplicity. The duke of Milan, Galeazzo Sforza, declared to the Venetian delegate at a congress in 1466, "You disturb the peace and covet the states of others. If you knew the ill-will universally felt towards you, the very hair of your head would stand on end." Niccolò Machiavelli was moved to comment that the leaders of Venice "had no respect for the Church; Italy was not large enough for them, either, and they believed that they could form a monarchical state like that of Rome."

The world around Venice was changing. The rise of the great nation-states—of Spain, of France and of Portugal in particular—altered the terms of world trade. The strength of the Turkish Empire, and the intervention of France and Spain on the mainland of Italy, created further burdens for the most serene city. When the French king, Charles VIII, invaded Italy in 1494 he inaugurated a century of national unrest. His failure to take over the kingdom of Naples did not deter the other great states of the European world. Maximilian of the Hapsburgs, and Ferdinand of Spain, were both eager to exploit the rich cities of northern Italy. These states had large armies, fully exploiting the new technology of siege guns and gunpowder. The city-states of Italy were not prepared for the novel conditions of warfare. Milan and Naples came under foreign control. Then at the end of 1508 the great leaders of the world turned their gaze upon Venice. The French, the Hapsburgs and the Spanish joined forces with the pope in the League of Cambrai with the sole purpose of seizing the mainland dominions of the city. The French delegate condemned the Venetians as "merchants of human blood" and "traitors to the Christian faith." The German emperor promised to quench for ever the Venetian "thirst for dominion."

The allies met with extraordinary success. The mercenary forces of the Venetians were comprehensively beaten by the French army in a battle by the village of Agnadello, near the Po, and retired in disarray to the lagoon. The cities under erstwhile Venetian occupation surrendered to the new conquerors without a fight. Within the space of fifteen days, in the spring of 1509, Venice lost all of her mainland possessions. The response of the Venetians was, by all accounts, one of panic. Citizens wandered the streets, weeping and lamenting. The cry went up that all was lost. There were reports that the enemy would banish the people of Venice from their city, and send them wandering like the Jews over the earth. "If their city had not been surrounded by the waters," Machiavelli wrote, "we should have beheld her end." The doge, according to one contemporary, never spoke but "looked like a dead man." The doge in question, Leonardo Loredan, was painted by Bellini and can now be seen in the National Gallery; he looks glorious and serene.

At the time it was widely believed that God was punishing Venice for her multiple iniquities, amongst them sodomy and elaborate dress. The nunneries had become whore-houses. The rich lived in pride and luxury. None of this was pleasing to heaven. So, as a direct result of the war, the doge and senate introduced sumptuary legislation, to curb the excesses of the rich, in the hope of reconciling their city to God. Men were forbidden to make themselves physically attractive. The nunneries were locked up. The wearing of jewellery was strictly curtailed. It was necessary, according to one diarist of the time, "to imitate our ancestors with all possible zeal and care." This ancestor worship had one particular dimension. There were some in the city who believed that the Venetians should have remained a seafaring people, as they were in the beginning, and that the ventures onto mainland territory had constituted a singular and perhaps fatal error.

There was the threat, after the battle of Agnadello, of an imminent siege by the imperial forces; food and grain were stored in makeshift warehouses. The doge sent envoys to the court of Maximilian, offering to place all the mainland dominions of the city under imperial control. He even despatched ambassadors to the Turks, requesting aid against the imperial forces. It is a measure of the desperation of the Venetian leaders that they invoked the aid of the infidels against their co-religionists—unless, of course, the true religion of the Venetians consisted in the worship of Venice herself.

Once the initial terror had subsided, however, the city once more came together. Its tribal instinct revived. It manifested the unity for which it would become famous in the sixteenth century. The ruling class drew together in a coherent body. The richer citizens pledged their fortunes to the defence of the city. The poorer sort remained loyal. The state reasserted itself. It was able to sow discord amongst the ranks of its enemies. Some of the mainland cities, which had come under French or imperial control, discovered that they preferred the more benign Venetian rule. Venice in fact recovered Padua with the active assistance of that city's inhabitants. There were Venetian victories on the battlefield, too, and by the beginning of 1517 it had recovered almost all of its territories. It would not forfeit them until the time of Napoleon. It had also reached an agreement with the pope, on matters of ecclesiastical power, following the precept of a Venetian cardinal to "do what he wishes and later, with time, do what you will." In what seems a typically ambiguous and duplicitous way, the council of ten had already secretly declared the conditions of the agreement void on the grounds that they had been extracted by force. Venice once more made its way in the world.

It had forfeited much valuable territory, in the Levant and elsewhere, but not all was lost. It acquired Cyprus, which it systematically stripped of its agricultural wealth, and it maintained its control of the cities around the Po. The grain of Rimini and Ravenna, also, was indispensable to its survival. And survival was now the key. After the League of Cambrai Venice could no longer extend any further its dominant position in the peninsula. It was surrounded by too many and too formidable foes. There would be no more aggressive expansion. Instead the patricians of Venice continued their policy of buying up parcels of territory as opportunity presented itself. There was soon a definite tendency to exchange the perils of trade for the security of land. Land was a good investment, in a world of ever-increasing population and rising food prices, and concerted efforts were made to make it more and more productive. Nevertheless it represented another form of withdrawal from the world. In the process the Venetians created a new race of landed gentry. The best chance for the state itself lay in watchful neutrality, playing one combatant against another while alienating neither. The only option was that of peace. All the notorious guile and rhetoric of the Venetians were now devoted to that purpose of balancing the Turkish, French and Hapsburg empires. And the strategy was successful until the arrival of Napoleon Bonaparte almost three hundred years later. The remains of the Venetian empire—in Crete, in southern Greece, and on the mainland of Italy—were preserved.

The reassertion of Venice was aided in 1527, by the brutal sack of Rome by unpaid imperialist troops. They raped, and killed, the citizens of the imperial city; they stole its treasures, and burned what they could not steal. Throughout the region waves of plague and syphilis compounded the despair; the ravaged fields could produce no wheat. Once more Venice seized the advantage. Rome had been one of the oldest, and most formidable, adversaries of Venice. The pope who reigned there had put the city under sentence of excommunication on more than one occasion. The papal states were challenged by Venetian power. So the sacking of Rome was welcome news to the administrators of Venice. Many of the artists and architects of the papal court left Rome and migrated to the most serene city where such riot was considered impossible. The reigning doge, Andrea Gritti, had determined that Venice would rise as the new Rome. He flattered and invited composers and writers and architects. One of the refugees from Rome, Jacopo Sansovino, was hired by Gritti to remodel Saint Mark's Square as the centre of an imperial city. Another refugee, Pietro Aretino, apostrophised Venice as the "universal fatherland."

Sansovino restored the public areas of Venice in Roman fashion. He built a new Mint with rusticated arches and Doric columns. He built the great library, opposite the palace of the doge in the piazzetta, in the form of a classical basilica. In the same spirit he built the loggetta, at the base of the campanile, in traditionally classical form. The shacks and stalls of the traders were removed from the square, and in their place was constructed a sacred ceremonial space. Magistrates were appointed to supervise the renovation of other areas as well as the cleansing of the waters around Venice. There was new building everywhere. The quays were refashioned. The symbolism was not difficult to read. Venice proclaimed herself to be the new Rome, the true heir of the Roman republic and the Roman empire. She saw no reason to prostrate herself before the German emperor, Charles V, or the emperor of the Turks, Suleiman the Magnificent. The city itself was conceived as a monument to this new status. According to a declaration of the senate in 1535, "from a wild and uncultivated refuge it has grown, been ornamented and constructed so as to become the most beautiful and illustrious city which at present exists in the world." It was the city of carnival and celebration. There sprang up more parades and ceremonials, more tournaments and festivals.

There were, and are, historians who assert that in this transition the Venetians themselves lost their energy and their tenacity. They became "softer." They were "weakened." They lost their fighting spirit when they embraced the principles of neutrality. They became addicted to the pleasures of comfortable living. It is perhaps unwise to adopt the language of human psychology in such matters. The life of generations is more robust and more impersonal than that of any individual. It is accountable to different laws. All we can say, with any approach to certainty, is that Venice was revived in the sixteenth century. And it was a truly astonishing renewal, first born out of defeat and humiliation. It says much about the ingenuity, as well as the pragmatism, of the Venetian temperament.

There was one more great test. In the first months of 1570 the Turkish forces of Suleiman the Magnificent seized the Venetian colony of Cyprus. Venice unsuccessfully appealed for assistance to the leaders of Europe. Philip II of Spain, fearing a Turkish advance in northern Africa, despatched a fleet; but it arrived too late and proved curiously unwilling to follow Venetian strategy. The demoralised Venetian fleet, under Girolamo Zane, sailed back before ever sighting Cyprus. The island was lost. One of the Venetian dignitaries was beheaded by the Turks, and another was flayed alive. His skin is still preserved in an urn in the church of SS. Giovanni e Paolo. Meanwhile Zane had been ordered to return to Venice, where he was consigned to the doge's dungeons; he died there two years later.

A year after the capture of Cyprus, Pope Pius V devised a confederation of three European powers to contain and to confront the Turks. Venice, Spain and the papacy itself formed a new Christian League or Holy League with the avowed aim of regaining control of the Mediterranean and of banishing the Turkish fleet from the Adriatic. It was a crusade under another name. A naval battle was staged at the entrance to the Gulf of Patras. The battle of Lepanto, as it became known, resulted in a great victory for the Christian forces. There were 230 Turkish vessels that were sunk or captured, with only thirteen losses for the Europeans. Fifteen thousand Christian galley slaves, obliged to work under Turkish masters, were given their liberty. There was another singular outcome. Lepanto was the last battle in which the use of the oar held the key. In later engagements the sails were raised. It was the last battle, too, in which hand-to-hand combat was the chosen method of assault; artillery and, in particular, cannon took over.

After Lepanto, when a Venetian galley returned to its home port trailing the Turkish standard, the city gave itself up to rejoicing. At a funeral oration in Saint Mark's, honouring the dead, it was declared that "they have taught us by their example that the Turks are not insuperable, as we had previously believed them to be." The predominant feeling was one of relief. The Venetians thought it prudent to follow the victory with further assaults on Turkish power, but the pope and the Spanish monarch disagreed. There was an inconclusive campaign in the spring of the following year, but the spirit had gone out of the Christian League. Venice returned to diplomacy, and signed a treaty with Suleiman. Cyprus was lost for ever. Of all the Greek islands colonised by Venice, only Corfu remained free of the Turkish embrace. Yet the victory at Lepanto had emboldened the leaders of Venice. There was some talk of regaining commercial supremacy in the Mediterranean. A new generation of younger patricians came to dominate public affairs.

So by the end of the sixteenth century Venice could pride itself on having survived the encroachments of the Europeans as well as the belligerence of the Turks. It had proved to be a formidable opponent in peace as well as in war. The stability of its government, and the loyalty of its people, had remained steadfast. It was the only city in northern Italy that had not endured rebellion or suffered invasion. The pope compared it to "a great ship that fears neither fortune nor commotion of winds." There emerged now what came to be known as "the myth of Venice." Its antiquity and its ancient liberty were celebrated by Venetian historiographers; it clothed itself in the glory of new public buildings. The republic of Venice, free from faction and guided by sage counsellors, was deemed to be immortal. It refashioned itself as the city of peace and the city of art. Even as its overseas power entered a slow decline, so the spirit of the city manifested itself in another fashion. It is evident in the work of Bellini, of Titian, and of Tintoretto who emerged as the influence of Venice began to wane. But who can speak of decline or decay when the city produced such riches? Venice had merely changed the nature of its power. It now claimed the power to impress—to dazzle. As its imperial power declined, so its image in the world became of vital importance.

VII

The Living City

22

The Body and the Building

The Austrian writer Hugo von Hofmannsthal once described the archetypal city as "a landscape built of pure life." Can this pure life therefore be seen as a living force? Can Venice be shaped and governed by an instinctive existence, which is greater than the sum of its people? Is it more than just a collective?

By the sixteenth century it was already being described as a human body where "the head is the place where the shores are situated; and that part towards the sea are the arms." The canals were the veins of this body. The heart lay in the city itself. So wrote Cristoforo Sabbadino in 1549. Venice was supposed to gaze out at the sea. The English traveller, James Howell, said that no foreign prince had ever "come nere her privy parts." Where were these privy parts? They were presumably the ducal palace and the basilica.

Yet all these references affirm a belief, or instinct, that Venice itself is a living organism with its own laws of growth and change. Does it exist, and survive, by the agency of some inner or intrinsic force that cannot as yet be explained or described? It absorbed the islands that constituted its existence; it had an alimentary system laid out among its canals and waterways. Everything wishes to give form and expression to its own nature; the leaves of the tree aspire to their own shape. So by obscure presentiment, and by the steady aggregate of communal wishes, Venice grew. That is why every part of Venice—its topography, its constitution, its domestic institutions—reflects the whole. Its nervous functions are interdependent. Those who travel to the city for the first time seem to be made aware of a definite personality. Henry James, always susceptible to the subtleties and obliquities of personal sensibility, said that Venice "seems to personify itself, to become human and sentient and conscious of your affection." It was for him mild and interesting and sad.

Does it subdue the lives and affections of the people who inhabit it?

The city is so old, and so encrusted with habit and tradition, that the people can be said to fit within its existing rhythms. The Venetians were often described as actors playing out their various roles. In paintings of Venetian life, the city dwarfs its inhabitants so that it becomes the pre-eminent subject. It has often been said that Venice cannot be modernised. More pertinently, it will not be modernised. It resists any such attempt with every fibre of its being.

On the lower façade of the Palazzo Dario, along the Grand Canal, the owner placed an inscription in Latin announcing "Giovanni Dario to the spirit of the city." So of what, if anything, does the *genius loci* consist? Is there a city god in residence? In other cities the worship of communal values was associated with the worship of place and with the worship of the dead. In the early centuries the Venetian dead were buried in the *campo* of the parish. Thus the passing generations trod upon the remains of their ancestors. Nothing could instil more awe in a Venetian than to stand on the spot where the parish was created. In addition the presence of the ancestors gave a true title to territorial ownership of the land. No stranger could claim the ground where the bones were buried. This may be the clue to the origin of all cities. They began as cemeteries.

It was originally a city of wood. There were so many carpenters, *marangoni*, that the great bell of the campanile in Saint Mark's Square was named after them as the *marangona*. It was a city of wooden tenements, occasional squares, wooden churches, water-lanes, landing stairs and pontoons between islands. Yet the process that formed the modern city was already in evidence; a network of parishes, each with its own church, was slowly forming with their centres accruing together. Wooden bridges were built to connect contiguous islands, and footways were laid over marshy areas.

In the eleventh century this process was intensified; under private rather than public initiative the ponds and marshes were filled or covered, reclaiming all the available land. The burgeoning government systematised the various parishes, creating a core of population from which the city was gradually extended. In the early years of the twelfth century there were proposals for a large market in the Rialto, a great civic square beside the ducal palace, and an arsenal for the maintenance of the Venetian fleet. These public works changed the face of the city, and determined the shape that it would eventually assume. Flood, fire and earthquake shook it from time to time; in 1106 a great fire destroyed almost the whole of wooden Venice. But the process was now too powerful to be reversed. There were many other fires, but the city always rose from them renewed. The great urban project had begun, and it could not be diverted. Venice grew and grew as if it were indeed some natural force.

By the thirteenth century the Venetian state had taken charge of land reclamation. The city was defined as a public space rather than an aggregation of individual communities. The state became the master of the land and of the water. Overseers of embankments, streets and canals were appointed. They were eventually formed into a commission with officers in every parish. Only certain canals were to be used for the transport of wood. Dyers were only allowed to use the water of the lagoon, not of the canals. Thus begins the flood of Venetian urban legislation, dealing with every aspect of life in the city. A system for the management of waste was created. The streets of the city were paved for the first time with flagstones or cobbles. The first permanent bridge over the Grand Canal, at the Rialto, was erected in 1264.

This continual enlargement of the urban fabric continued well into the fourteenth century, at a time when the population had reached one hundred thousand. It was already one of the most inhabited cities of Europe. The major streets of the city were laid out; new quays and bridges were built. Work on a new hall for the great council was approved in 1340; by that date several great churches were beginning to rise, among them S. Maria dei Frari, the basilica of SS. Giovanni e Paolo, S. Maria della Carità, S. Alvise and Madonna dell'Orto. New streets were built. A public granary was instituted.

There was a diminution of activity in the middle years of that century, under the weight of fatalities caused by the Black Death, but the beginning of the fifteenth century saw a wave of new works, private and public. That is how Venice developed—in waves of activity, sudden increases in the temperature of the city, an access of fresh vitality. The temptation to speak in organic terms is strong. Some two hundred palaces, many of them still standing along the Grand Canal, were built in this period. The medieval town of wood had finally given way to a Renaissance city.

The process was finalised, was set in stone, in the sixteenth century. The appointment of Jacopo Sansovino as public architect, in 1527, was the first stage of a deliberate programme of public works to create a second Rome both magisterial and gorgeous. The first general planning act is dated from 1557; it envisaged, among other things, an embankment of Istrian stone encircling the city. Venice became what Lewis Mumford called, in *The City in History*, an "absolute city." It had become the setting for the sedulous dissemination of "the myth of Venice" as an enduring and impregnable polity. The work of Palladio, in the middle of the sixteenth century, added further adornment to a city that would never willingly change again. He reinvented the shape of its sacred architecture with the conception of the churches of S. Giorgio Maggiore and Il Redentore. The city needed only one more thing—the first stone of the great bridge across the Grand Canal at the Rialto was laid on 31 May 1585. The creation of Venice was complete.

Yet despite its manifest grandeur Venice was still an intensely local city. There were divisions, and divisions within divisions. The largest was that which separated "the Saint Mark's side" and "the Rialto side" of the Grand Canal. Then there were the six *sestieri* or divisions of the city that were established in twelfth century; in the late nineteenth century they were still described in popular speech as nations; there was the nation of Castello, for example, and the nation of Cannaregio. Horatio Brown, in *Life on the Lagoons* (1909), noted that the people of the various quarters "are different in build and type of features" one from another; their speech was different. Even the dialects might vary.

Within each district the parishes were congregated. The parish, the *contrada* or *contrata*, was the essential and fundamental unit of Venetian society; in official documents the members of the *popolani* identified themselves in terms of their parish. The parish had its own festivals and rituals, and the parish priest was elected by the freeholders of the neighbourhood. There were small parish markets, and the church was a refuge in times of trouble; many parishes had their own specialised trade. It was an administrative, as well as a sacred, entity. Neighbourhood rivalries between the parishes on either side were common. The identity of each separate parish was also fully formed. So in spirit, if not in structure, the city still reflected its origins in one hundred or so islands.

The square or *campo* was at the heart of the neighbourhood. It spread before the church and was once its burial ground. In each square—or in the *calle* just around the corner—was a fruiterer, a green-grocer, a general goods store, a retailer of pasta, a café, a barber's shop, and various other tradesmen from the mercer to the carpenter. It was a self-contained entity, marked out by its well and its carved well-head where the women of the parish came to gossip. It was a Venice in miniature. If there is indeed a spirit of place within the city, it is still to be found here.

The houses were tightly packed together. The parishioners knew each other's business. Strangers were quickly noted. The city, in other words, was criss-crossed by individual boundaries. Going from one district, or from one parish, to another was like walking into a different town. The people of one district might not know the topography of another. There were parts of the city to which many, if not most, Venetians had never been. It was not unknown for a Venetian to live his or her own life without venturing beyond the bounds of the *sestiere*. There were Venetians who had never entered Saint Mark's Square. The author was told of an old lady of Cannaregio, recently deceased at the age of one hundred, who had only been to the square twice in her life.

The canals are the signs and tokens of division. They are essentially the old streams and rivers that once crossed the territory; the stretch of water dividing the island of Giudecca from the rest of the city was once the mouth of the River Brenta. There are 170 canals threading through the city, ebbing and flowing with the tide for more than sixty-two miles (99.7 km). The Grand Canal itself has a length of two miles (3.2 km). Some allow only one-way traffic, and others accommodate two-way movement; some are dead-ends or blind canals. They have influenced the nature of the people as strongly as the nature of the city. It has been said that the presence of flowing water induces tranquillity. These boundaries of water also inhibited the rapid assembly of people in riot or rebellion. The peace of Venice may derive from its canals.

If the canals are the sign of division, then the bridges are the token of unity. There are more than 450 of them in the city, linking parish with parish. Many of them have honorifics or nicknames, such as the Bridge of Fists or the Bridge of Assassins or the Bridge of the Honest Woman. They were used as battlefields and as places of assignation.

The earliest bridges were simply wooden planks laid across pilings or the hulls of boats, and the first one built of stone was not constructed until the latter half of the twelfth century. In that period, too, the first great wooden bridge or pontoon was erected across the Grand Canal at the Rialto. The sixteenth century was the great age of the stone bridge, when the wooden structures were replaced by their more durable substitutes. They rose on either side to a hump in the middle, and there were no parapets or balustrades. The pedestrian, or horseman, had to be nimble and fearless. The bridge-building has not finished yet. A new bridge has just been put into place across the Grand Canal, linking the two transport centres of Piazzale Roma and Ferrovia in the west of the city.

So out of this medley of disparate parishes and districts emerges the miracle of a sovereign and recognisable city. Out of difference springs identity; out of the parts, related or unrelated, emerges the whole. It is the secret of the city's entire life. One of the first sights that greets the traveller arriving at the *bacino* or pool of Venice are the two columns of Oriental granite standing guard over the piazzetta. On the column closest to the ducal palace stands the lion of Saint Mark. From a distance it looks like a splendid composition. In fact it is made up of separate parts, created in different periods and held together by iron cramps. The age of some of the pieces is not known, but the majority of them can be dated to the late twelfth century. The wings of the lion are the work of restorers, and were originally divided into feathers. So by some instinct or by some compulsion the builders of the column, joining the separate parts of the lion together, represented the creation of the city.

On the other column is poised the statue of Saint Theodore, the original patron saint of Venice. If you were to come closer to this image, you would notice that it is not in any sense the work of one hand. The head is of Parian marble, and is believed to represent Mithridates, king of Pontus; the torso is a Roman piece from the time of Hadrian the Great; the dragon, or crocodile, is in the Lombardic style from the first half of the fifteenth century. It is a glorious, and apparently haphazard, exercise in historical assembly. It deserves to be on its column. Once again it is an image of Venice itself.

The architecture of the city is heterogeneous and apparently random, combining Gothic, Greek, Tuscan, Roman and Renaissance elements; the sum of their combination can be defined as Venetian architecture. Various styles, and stylistic modes, exist simultaneously; the art of Venice lay in amalgamation. It is a reminder of how oddly sorted the appearance of Venice has always been; it is based upon random accumulation of objects and materials. It reflects thoroughly eclectic tastes. There is no consistency, and no uniformity. That is why, for the traveller, Venice can be so fatiguing. It resists interpretation. It denies the single vision. Minarets can become crosses. Byzantine columns can rise towards Corinthian capitals. Parts of one statue can be attached to another. Théophile Gautier, writing of the basilica of Saint Mark, observed that "the singular thing, which upsets any idea of proportion, is that this jumble of columns, of capitals, of bas reliefs, of enamels, of mosaics—this mingling of Greek, Roman, Byzantine, Arab and Gothic styles—produces the most harmonious possible whole." There are endless fragments that, paradoxically, only make sense as part of a perceived unity.

"In this most noble city of Venice," the architect Sebastiano Serlio wrote in 1537, "it is the custom to build in a way which is very different from all the other cities of Italy." It is an insular architecture. It is architecture built on water. Of course it will be different. The buildings of Venice reflect the spirit and the nature of the city. They are the emanations or exhalations of the territory. Ruskin entitled his magnificent appraisal the *Stones of Venice*. The stones are its soul.

So the architecture of Venice is noticeable for its lightness, for its balance, and for its harmony. It represents all the aspirations of its citizens. That is why the architecture is unique and identifiable—the deep central windows, the pattern of recess and shadow, the surface ornamentation, the intricate variety of styles, the preference for curved shapes, the screens of arcades, the general emphasis upon light and space. The thrust is towards the horizontal rather than the vertical, hugging the surface of the lagoon. The façades of Venetian buildings are not load-bearing. The effect is one of magnificence without monumentality. Volume is denied, being always broken up by the effects of glittering light. The façades seem to float freely, as if the architecture itself were a magnificent illusion.

The buildings often seem to be the sum of small parts rather than being dominated by one central conception. It is in that sense a very practical architecture. Venetian builders did not seem to mind asymmetry; they placed together styles that were a century or more apart; they shortened and lengthened buildings according to the exigencies of the site. The emphasis is upon contrast, and variety, rather than uniformity. Different systems of decoration could be employed in the same space; the proportions of the various architectural "orders" were breached. This architecture is one of natural exuberance. There is nothing solemn, nothing portentous, nothing menacing.

One of the essential forms is that of the three-storeyed front decorated with pilasters; it is the basic shape of the houses along the Grand Canal. The focus of the house is towards the exterior rather than the interior. And no one seems to care about the back of the building as long as the front is sumptuous. This is the city of masks. Hence the reliance upon external pattern. It is an ornamental and pictorial architecture. It has elements of the picturesque. The surfaces were encrusted with carvings and coloured marbles, with decorative patterns spreading in all directions. It is as if lace embroidery had been turned to stone.

The first architectural style in the city can be loosely called Byzantine. It is a style of arcades and of domes, of round or inflected arches upon pillars, and of mosaics clothing the walls with beauty. The domed basilicas of Venice were based on an eastern pattern, with the dome hovering over a cube of space in perfect alignment. It was an image of infinity. The Byzantine style in Venice can be dated from the seventh to the twelfth centuries; for five hundred years the city took Constantinople as its inspiration. Then the style renewed itself in the late fifteenth and early sixteenth centuries.

In the thirteen and fourteenth centuries the eyes of Venice turned towards the West rather than the East, and that attention led in turn to the rise of Venetian Gothic. It is significant that at the close of this period Venice was poised to gain a land empire on the mainland of Italy. The churches were now given vaulted naves, although they could not be built very high; the watery foundations of Venice could not sustain any great weight. There was a new interest in interplay of shapes and of materials, in the exfoliation of pillars and pilasters, in great portals, in trefoil arches, in quatrefoil tracery, and in double lancet windows. It was a style of pattern and ornamentation, again deeply congenial to the Venetian genius. Yet it was also a question of self-image, by co-opting a western imperial style, and of a new form of magnificence.

The style was dominant in the fourteenth and fifteenth centuries, surviving even into the sixteenth century and giving a Gothic aspect to the city that still survives. Many Gothic churches replaced their Byzantine predecessors on the same site. They were built in homage to a different God, or to a different conception of God. But it was a secular, as well as a sacred, architecture. Most of the well-known palaces or great houses are created in the Gothic mode. The basilica of Saint Mark is an example of Byzantine; the ducal palace is the embodiment of Gothic.

Ruskin despised the Renaissance architecture of Venice that followed Gothic. He considered it to be a symptom of the city's decline and fall. The classical columns and pediments, the sheer symmetries, were alien to the life and spirit of the place. What had Venice to do with classical antiquity? What had Venice to do with the purity, the austerity, and massive uniformity, that are at the heart of the Renaissance style? The great exponents of the Renaissance style— Codussi, Sansovino and Palladio—were not themselves Venetian. They cast a foreign eye over the city. Palladio did not even like traditional Venetian architecture, believing it to lack *grazia* and *bellezza*. It has been said that the edifices of Palladio do not suit Venice. They do not fit Venice. Yet in Venice everything "fits."

Certain features of Venetian architecture have had a continuous history. The domestic dwellings of the people, for example, have always conformed to a simple pattern. They are not the most inviting aspects of Venetian life. The ordinary Venetian house is a mysterious place. It is the very opposite of the public spaces that seem to be at the heart of the city's life. The house is generally small, narrow and dark. It does not willingly receive guests or welcome strangers. The original timber houses of the city were of one storey, built around a central courtyard, and that sense of inwardness never left the Venetian domain. The innate conservatism of the city was such that by the thirteenth century the essential structure of all subsequent houses had been laid out.

They were simple affairs, of two or three storeys, with one or two rooms on each floor. A wooden balcony ran around the front, and on the roof was the flat enclosed space known as the *altana*. From here the Venetians could take the air, or observe their fellows in the streets below. There were few windows, heavily shuttered or protected by iron bars; the larger windows faced inward, towards the central courtyard. There was very little furniture, but the pieces were richly decorated and ornamented. Flat roofs were preferred. Chimneys were popular. The shutters were painted dark green. There were no Venetian blinds in Venice. And of course there were no cellars.

There were small houses with shops opening onto the street. There were rows of small terraced houses, each room or floor accommodating a family. In parts of the city two identical rows face each other across a narrow street; the effect, surprisingly, is rather like that of industrial housing in the north-east of England—except for the well in the middle of the street. In areas of working-class housing there were also often tunnel-like passage-ways, with arches, known as *sottoportici*.

If the various styles of architecture represented the spirit of the place, as a distinctive and recognisable *genius loci*, that may be because all of them rose directly from the same foundations. The building of Venice was an act of communal perseverance against nature. Beneath the waters of the city lie strata of mud and clay and sand. The foundations of the buildings, piles of tough oak, were driven into that ground with heavy drop-hammers. They reached a depth of between ten and sixteen feet (3 to 5 m) below water. Cross-beams were then laid down, and the interstices between the wooden piles were loaded with cement and broken stone. Then a thick surface decking of wooden planks, bedded in cement, was placed on top of the wooden structure. It became the true ground of the city. A second foundation was erected on top of what was essentially a great wooden raft, two to four feet (0.6 to 1.2 m) below the level of the tide.

From these foundations Venice rose, resting upon a petrified forest. Somehow it manages both to defy, and to make use of, nature. These great trunks of oak and larch and elm had always to be submerged; if they were exposed to the air, they would begin to rot. In their water-logged condition they were sturdy, however, and almost imperishable. The weight they bore was immense. The campanile in Saint Mark's Square, for example, weighs 14,400 tonnes (14,170 tons); yet the piles of wood carry it. The Rialto bridge is supported by twelve thousand piles of elm. The church of the Salute is borne up by 1,156,657 piles of oak and larch. The weight of the building itself helps to stabilise them. There is no complete rigidity. That is impossible in the lagunar waters. Yet even though the piles may shift a little, they do not collapse. Many of them have lasted for a thousand years.

There is a chant sung by the pile-drivers dating from 1069, the latest variant of which was transcribed by an Englishman in the nineteenth century:

> Up with it well,
> Up to the top,
> Up with it well,
> Up to the summit.

The primary materials of construction are brick and timber, with stone used as a decorative rather than a structural necessity. At the waterline is placed a foundation of Istrian stone that is impermeable to water. Ruskin described that stone, quarried on the mainland (there is of course no natural stone in Venice itself), as "smooth sheets of rock, glistering like sea waves, that ring under the hammer like a brazen bell." Above the stone is brick faced with stucco so that the church, or dwelling, also glisters. The absence of stone walls also gives an incomparable feeling of lightness to the material fabric. Venice is a floating world.

In the Galleria dell'Accademia hangs Titian's "Presentation of the Virgin"; it is placed on a wall that was once part of the *albergo* or hall of a notable confraternity; in the foreground of the painting is a great staircase, which the young virgin is ascending. In fact the staircase itself leaves the picture and enters the Venetian world; just to the left of the canvas is the tower staircase of the *albergo* itself, which seems to obtrude into the painting. Among the crowd of people accompanying the Virgin are pictures of recognisable individuals; these are the members of the confraternity. It is typical of Venetian painting to incorporate local detail as part of the overall design. The background wall of the "Presentation" is constructed out of pink and white bricks, set in diamond pattern, as an unmistakable reference to the façade of the ducal palace.

When Carpaccio needed to depict Cologne, in his cycle of paintings concerning Saint Ursula, he simply used the image of the Arsenal in the district of Castello. Tintoretto uses Saint Mark's Square as a setting for biblical miracles. The humble houses and shops of his paintings are directly modelled on Venetian interiors. He placed the image of his contemporary, Aretino, in the company witnessing the Crucifixion. In Veronese's "Conversion of Saint Pantalon" the elderly man cradling the miraculously healed child is the parish priest of the church of S. Pantalon who in fact commissioned the work. There is no attempt here to honour the "individuality" of the priest; rather he becomes part of the company of the blessed, and in so doing reflects beatitude upon the city itself.

When Titian depicted the miraculous draught of fishes, from the narrative of Luke, he ensured that the boatmen took up the character-istic stance of Venetian gondoliers. It is said that in his paintings from the New Testament, Tintoretto always made the Apostles gesture like gondoliers. In his "Miracle of the Relic of the True Cross on the Rialto Bridge" Carpaccio faithfully depicted the wooden bridge, the sign of the Sturgeon Inn, the houses and institutions along both banks of the Grand Canal, and the members of the confraternity of which he was the official painter; it represents the poetry of urban detail, with its bricks and balconies and chimney-tops. More than any other painters in the world, the Venetians readily depicted the environment of their home city. Never has a city and its people obtruded so much on artistic traditions.

23

Learning and Language

The Renaissance came late to Venice. That European revival in humane letters, and in classical scholarship, made a slow and fitful entry into the city. It was not necessarily on congenial soil. The Venetians have never been known for their commitment to scholarship, or to learning for its own sake; they are not inclined to abstract inquiry, or to the adumbration of theory. A humanist on the mainland, Giovanni Conversino, reported to the Venetians in 1404 that "even if you desired to be learned you would not be able to do so; everything you have you possess through drudgery, talent and danger." The sheer necessity of survival transcended questions of abstract principle. It may be true, too, that Venice did not share in the Italian Renaissance because it had never been part of the mainland where classical art and literature once flourished. Literature was not, in a literal sense, part of its territory.

The young patricians were characteristically trained in the arts of practical statesmanship. If they learned Greek, the essential language of the new humanism, it was primarily so that they might administer the Greek colonies of Venice. What did the enlightened leaders of Venice do? They codified the state laws and compiled state papers. Humanism in general was put at the service of the administration; the leaders of "learning" were also the leaders of the senate and of the great council; their concern was to engender political values that maintained and preserved the social system of the city. They were characteristically magistrates, ambassadors, and even doges. There was a great debate in the late fifteenth and early sixteenth centuries upon the rival claims of the active life and the contemplative life in Christian history. The Venetians always espoused the active life. God's providence was a political matter.

If they wrote texts at all, these were concerned with specific problems and circumstances; their theoretical context, if it can be called such, was one of pride in the Venetian state. The only history with which they were concerned was their own history. There were no works that challenged political or economic orthodoxy; there were no volumes extolling the progress of the individual soul in search of beatitude; there were no testaments burning with the chaste flame of aesthetic philosophy. All was rigorous, and severe, and restrained. In Florence the movement of neo-Platonism had its fervent and almost mystical adherents. In Venice, the only interest in Plato sprang from a general respect for authority. There were of course Venetian collectors of coins, of manuscripts, and of antiquities; but they were animated by an acquisitive rather than an intellectual spirit. They were merchants rather than scholars.

When one famous scholar, Cardinal Bessarion, came to the city he was so impressed by its magnificence that he left his collection of rare books and manuscripts to the Venetian state. They were stored in crates in the ducal palace, from which some of them were stolen or sold. The rest were allowed to gather dust for eighty years. Bessarion had bequeathed his collection four years before his death in 1472, but the library for them was not erected until the 1550s. Petrarch, known as the "father of humanism," bequeathed a selection of his library to the state in 1374. In 1635 his manuscripts were found heaped in a small room above the great door of the basilica of Saint Mark's. Damp and decay had got to them.

There was no university in the city itself. The absence might seem a singular omission for any city-state; but there of course was no university in London, either, that other centre of trade and business. In any case it would be wrong to report an utter dearth of learning. There were schools and academies for those of an enquiring mind. The principal disciplines were those of mathematics, geography, physics, astronomy, trigonometry and astrology. Botany was an important discipline, too, with the emphasis on horticulture. There were public lecturers, freelance schoolmasters and private tutors. A school of rhetoric was established in 1460, with the aim of improving the level of public speaking in the city. There were masters of grammar in each of the six *sestieri*, and small schools were also established in the houses of certain patricians; it is not clear, however, how high they aspired. Certainly a large proportion of the population was literate and numerate (perhaps a quarter of the citizenry by the end of the sixteenth century) but it would be hard to claim much refinement or subtlety in a Venetian education. It was designed, really, to increase the efficiency of the state. Cultivate learning, one fifteenth-century patrician told his son, "both for the honour of your country and for the glory and amplification of our family."

Venice was always a city of clubs and fraternities, each one of them a state in miniature with its officers and festivals. So there were in the city thirty or more "academies" where the more educated Venetians might meet and converse. There was an "Academia dei Filosofi" and an "Academia dei Nobili," for example, both situated on the adjacent island of Giudecca; the situation was pertinent, implying that the patricians could escape from the centre of politics and commerce in order to discourse of higher matters. The geography of the lagoon was always important in the Venetian imagination. And there were "salons," formal or informal, where scholars and intellectuals mingled with the leading patrician families. Yet the salon was the home of patronage and, in a city devoted to fashion of every kind, a market-place for the dissemination of novel ideas or fancies. There was singing, reading of poetry, playing of musical instruments, and sometimes even dancing. It is hard to estimate, however, whether the discourse of the salon ever reached higher than the level of informed gossip.

Galileo was one of the learned Italians attracted to Venice. At the age of twenty-eight he was appointed by the Venetian authorities as principal lecturer in mathematics at the University of Padua, a Venetian colony, and he stayed in that institution for the next eighteen years. He devoted himself to the pure and applied sciences, inventing the thermometer and the telescope during his residence there, and his appeals to the Venetian administration for patronage were based upon a very practical determination. He understood the true nature of the city very well. When in 1609 he devised the first telescope, he wrote to the reigning doge that the invention "may be of inestimable service for every business by land and sea; for it is thus possible, at sea, to discover the enemy's vessels and sail at a far greater distance than is customary." He displayed the powers of the telescope from the top of the campanile in Saint Mark's Square, and the Venetian officials were duly impressed. A few weeks later he was appointed professor of astronomy for life, with three times the highest pay ever granted to any lecturer in Padua.

So we may celebrate the practical genius of Venice. There were no visionaries in Venice. They produced no Machiavelli and no Plato. There was no speculation on utopias. There was no concern for dogma or theory. There was no real interest in pure or systematic knowledge as such; empirical knowledge was for the Venetians the key to truth. Experience, rather than reason, was the furnace in which solutions were to be forged. In this they were also very close to the English genius. The Venetians were well known for their adaptability and their common sense; in diplomatic negotiations they were inclined to compromise and to accommodate varying points of view. In the affairs of the world they tended to be efficient and unsentimental.

There may have been no great poetry in the city, but there were important texts on hydrostatics and geography, on hydraulics and astronomy. The Venetians also possessed a practical inventiveness, in pursuits as different as glass- and instrument-making. They invented easel-painting as well as the science of statistics. The real intellectual success of Venice, however, came in the practical manufacture of books. The first licence to print was issued in 1469. Just eighteen or nineteen years after the invention of movable-type printing by Johannes Gutenberg, the Venetian senate announced that "this peculiar invention of our time, altogether unknown to former ages, is in every way to be fostered and advanced." In this, the senators were five years ahead of William Caxton.

The Venetian authorities had sensed a commercial opportunity, and the city soon became the centre of European printing. They created the privilege of copyright for certain printed works in 1486, so the investment of the printers was guaranteed; it was the first legislation for copyright in the world. Venetian bankers underwrote the costs of the new ventures. The paper came from Venetian territory near Lake Garda. All the conditions, for what would now be called mass production and mass marketing, were in place; indeed printing was the first form of mass production technology, creating identical objects at identical cost. It was only right, and natural, that Venice should be the pioneer of that trade. Venice, in 1474, was said to be "stuffed with books." At the time of the Counter-Reformation, too, the authorities maintained a more liberal attitude towards censorship than the other city-states of Italy. At the beginning of the sixteenth century there were almost two hundred print shops, producing a sixth of all the books published in Europe.

Venice excelled in printing, rather than creating, literature. Its most famous printer, Aldus Manutius, was a wandering scholar from Bassanio near Rome. He came to Venice as a lecturer, and despite his great learning he was soon imbued with the commercial spirit of the city. He became aware that knowledge of the classics could be wrapped up in packages like bales of raisins; he could turn learning into a commodity. So in 1492 he formed a workshop for the production of Greek texts. In this pursuit he was aided by the Greek scholars who had fled from ruined Byzantium with the words of the past in their heads. They brought with them, too, manuscripts and commentaries. Almost by accident Venice found itself at the forefront of the revival of learning. Its commercial spirit had consequences in the sphere of the intellect.

In the summer of 1502 an edition of the plays of Sophocles was published with the colophon "Venetiis in Aldi Romani Academia," thus inaugurating a remarkable sequence of all the important Greek authors in meticulously edited versions. The fonts—of Latin, Greek, and Hebrew—were beautiful, and are in fact still in use. The manuscripts were scrupulously copied, in type that seemed aesthetically to rival the original handwriting of the compilers. The printing shop had become an "academy" where visiting scholars were employed to edit the texts and to proof-read the sheets coming off the press. Greek scholars were also hired as compositors.

So by degrees there grew up an "Aldine circle" devoted to the dissemination of learning, in which the spoken language was largely Greek, prompting Aldus to describe Venice as another Athens. Erasmus became a part of that circle, as well as other itinerant scholars and humanists, and at a later date he recalled that some thirty-three employees slept and worked on the premises; he also found the food frugal, and the wine vinegary. Aldus mixed with the Venetian patricians who considered themselves to be patrons of learning; they believed that he added to the glory of Venice. The press of visitors became so great, however, that Aldus put up a notice before his door, at the corner of the Campo di S. Agostino: "Whoever you are, Aldus earnestly begs you to state your business in the fewest possible words and begone, unless, like Hercules to weary Atlas, you would lend a helping hand. There will always be enough work for you and all who come this way."

Yet the turning of knowledge, and learning, into commodities had other consequences. It was said at the time that the abundance of books made men less studious. There were complaints about the "vulgarisation" attendant upon the new technology. In an age of cultural transition, there are always anxieties expressed by those who are still reliant upon the old order. The Aldine press helped to bring the classical authors within the view of a wider audience; the editions were smaller, and cheaper, than any others. For some scholars, this represented a threat to their cultural supremacy.

The printers of Venice also became masters of musical printing, map printing and medical printing, spreading information around Europe. Books on the human anatomy, and on military fortifications, were published. Works of popular piety, light literature in the vernacular, chapbooks, all issued from the city of the lagoon. Printing linked the various strata of the literate classes of Europe together; otherwise there would have been no such general response to the teachings of Luther. The publication of maps helped to create a new international trading economy. The commercialisation of knowledge, as a consequence of Renaissance humanism, indirectly led to religious reformation and the industrial revolution.

The Venetians did have a university but it was located twenty miles (32 km) away in Padua, the city having been taken in 1404. Venice itself would not have welcomed a large body of free-thinking students within its domain. It was also concerned with the loyalty of its own young men, and forbade Venetians to study anywhere other than Padua. So the patrician youth migrated to the mainland city in search of enlightenment, together with students from England, Germany, Poland and Hungary. Sir Francis Walsingham, the famous Elizabethan "spymaster," and Sir Philip Sidney studied in Padua. Many of these foreigners were, by the sixteenth century, followers of the "reformed" religion of Luther and Zwingli; but their apostasy did not bother the Venetian authorities, who were in any case accustomed to the various faiths of the world.

Padua itself was most celebrated for its schools of law and of medicine, and became in the words of Thomas Coryat a "sweet emporium and mart town of learning." There was a chair of agriculture, and a veterinary school. There was a famous department of anatomy, to which the Venetian authorities guaranteed a plentiful supply of corpses. By the middle of the sixteenth century Padua had become the most significant centre for scientific learning in Europe. In a world of institutional faith and individual piety, it offered a secular education. That was the reason for its success. "We despise," one Venetian of the sixteenth century wrote, "knowledge of things of which we have no need."

That is one of the reasons why the arts of literature, as opposed to those of painting and music, were not cultivated. There was a social and political, as well as a practical, reason for this neglect. Literature asks questions and poses problems, whereas art and music celebrate and affirm; writing may encourage disruption and even revolution, whereas art and music aspire towards harmony and balance. Francesco Sagredo was a Venetian patrician and humanist who, in the early part of the seventeenth century, became a companion and associate of Galileo. Sagredo himself had a reputation as a wit and scholar. His own testimony, therefore, may hold the clue to Venetian humanism in general:

> I am a Venetian gentleman, and I have never wished to be known as a literary man. I have good relations with literary men and have always tried to protect them. But I do not expect to grow wealthy or to acquire praise and reputation from my understanding of philosophy or mathematics but rather from my integrity and my good practice in the administration of the Republic . . .

Distinguished writers have been drawn to Venice over the centuries, but the city has not nourished many writers of its own. The two most famous of its native sons are Marco Polo and Casanova, both of whom wrote what were essentially memoirs. Casanova offers an interesting case history of the Venetian genius. "The chief business of my life has always been to indulge my senses," he wrote. "I never knew anything of greater importance." This might be justifiably described as a main article of the Venetian creed. His knowledge did not lead him to any measure of self-awareness, except in the endless duplicity and theatricality of his nature. Despite his many seductions and attempts at rape, he shows no sign of conscience or manifestation of guilt;

Casanova does not indulge in interior reflections of any kind. It is as if he were a character out of *commedia dell'arte*, doomed to continue with the same impersonation in every scene and in every play. It is perhaps no wonder that his story of his imprisonment in the dungeons of the ducal palace, and of his subsequent escape, is a central text in Venetian social history; he was in the prison of his unreflecting self. It is in any case rare to find, in Venetian literature, any attempt at analysis or self-criticism. There is just no interest in the subject, the fruit of a culture in which individualism of any kind was discouraged.

The true literature of Venice was neither tragic nor confessional. There was some epic poetry, but it is wearisome. There was in reality very little poetry of any kind, once more emphasising the low value placed upon self-expression. The real literature was popular and demotic or it was historical and journalistic. The historical tradition was grave, detailed and prosaic. The popular tradition was in love with fantasy and superstition, with wonders and apparitions, with elements of the exotic and the fanciful.

How else to explain the huge popularity of the plays of Carlo Gozzi, the most famous of which is *The Love for Three Oranges* in which three beautiful princesses are born out of three enchanted oranges? It was taken from an old woman's tale to quieten children, and Gozzi said that he wrote it simply to "please so thoughtless a nation as the Venetians." The Venetian audience applauded the first performance "frantically," according to an Italian critic, Giuseppe Baretti, leading him to declare in *The Manners and Customs of Italy* that "The Venetians . . . do not greatly care for the labour of searching after truth, and their imagination runs too often away with them, while their judgment lies dormant." Gozzi's dramas were fantasias of the eighteenth century, with magicians and monsters, knights on horseback and devils in red costume. They were a curious mixture of magniloquence and parody, lamentation and farce, thus continuing the Venetian tradition of *commedia dell'arte* in a more sensational setting. That form is the distilled essence of literary culture in the city.

There was much interest in letters and diaries, too, as if the quotidian life of the city was of paramount importance. To keep a record—this was the Venetian style. Many Venetian patricians maintained diaries of daily events, covering many years and encompassing many volumes. They were not concerned with their individual reflections, in the manner of other diarists, but only in recording the tidings of their city. Nothing was too trivial to be beneath notice.

One of them, Marino Sanudo, wrote some forty thousand pages in minute handwriting. It was a way of celebrating, and commemorating, the city. Some of the more bizarre passages of Venetian history can also make their way into these narratives. On 31 August 1505, Sanudo wrote that

> today the execution took place of the Albanian who foully murdered Zuan Marco. First, his hand was cut off at the Ponte della Late. And note that this resulted in a curious incident: while his wife was saying farewell to him, he moved forward as if he wanted to kiss her. Then he bit off her nose. It seems that she was responsible for revealing his crime to the authorities.

If there is not much poetry in Venice, there is a great deal of song. The folk songs of the city, however, bear no resemblance to the expression of high deathless passion in other folk traditions; there is no pity, and no tragedy. There is pathos and sentimentality. "Would you weep if I were dead?" a mother asks her infant child. "How could I help weeping for my own mamma, who loves me so much in her heart?" Sentimentality is the enemy of true feeling, and suits a city where the mask is pre-eminent. But the folk songs are also filled with gaiety and optimism, a joyful seizing of the day that might be related to the mercantile tradition of the city. There is also an element of shrewdness allied with the fantastical. It was once believed that cities could not create or nourish folk songs—that such songs flourished only in rural areas—but Venice disproved that pastoral myth. In these songs there is much local patriotism, but no politics; there is also satire, and obscenity. Like the Venetian liking for "sweet and sour" in food, the songs are a mixture of acid and honey.

No city in the world has produced so many proverbs as Venice. They go with the capacity of the citizens for sharp retort and instant wisdom. There were many singular expressions reflecting the life and spirit of a mercantile culture. One of them notices with pride that, "Money is our second blood." The conservatism of the people emerges in such phrases as "Novelty pleases those who have nothing to lose," "The first sin is to be born desperate," and "He who loves foreigners loves the wind." Many of them refer to the unique situation and quality of the city and its inhabitants. "Venetians first, then Christians," "The lord of the sea is also the lord of the land," "As soon as a law is made an evasion is found," "Venetians are born tired and live to sleep," "Venice is a paradise for priests and prostitutes." To make an impression—to make a splash—is "to drown yourself in a big sea." "He who looks for help at a gaming table will grow long hair like a bear." "God wants us injured but not dead." "Wine is the milk of the old." This litany could go on for ever, but it is wise to recall another proverb, "The first sign of madness is to remember proverbs."

It is a curiosity of Venetian culture, too, that it is the home of the "rise" tale, a version of folk literature in which a young man or woman battles against poverty and by an advantageous marriage (usually to royalty) becomes rich beyond measure. It is the fairy story of a mercantile society, dreaming of the impossible. One of these stories, the tale of Costantino and his cat, travelled through the English-speaking world as Puss in Boots.

There was always a problem with the Venetian dialect in which these folk tales were generally written. It was not considered to be a serious, or proper, language for literary art. By the end of the thirteenth century the major works of Venetians were being written in the then fashionable language of Provençal. It is a reflection of the fashion for Gothic architecture in Venice during the same period. This literary French then developed into a form of Franco-Italian, the language in which Marco Polo dictated from a Genoese prison in 1298 the memoirs of his exotic journey. It may seem strange that Venetians would write in French rather than a version of Italian, but there is a more recent example to throw light upon this curious cultural phenomenon. In the nineteenth century the upper classes of Russia conversed and wrote in French, considering their native language to be too "low" for refined speech.

In the sixteenth century, too, the Venetian language was demoted in favour of the more literary Tuscan language that had been fashioned three centuries earlier. The language of Dante, and of Florence, became the language of polite literature. The Venetian dialect was reserved for populist drama and popular song. Epics, and histories, were composed in Tuscan. The models of polite discourse were Petrarch and Boccaccio, asserting the dominance of a foreign and archaic tongue over the living vitality of the native dialect. This is perhaps not entirely unexpected. In other cultures, too, a highly stylised or liturgical language has the mastery over the demotic; written Anglo-Saxon was a very different thing from native English. The Venetian dialect was still used for public purposes, however. It was the official language of public administration and of the courts of law. The laws themselves were composed and published in Venetian.

And of course it was—and is still—in use among the people of the city. It varies between districts but, like every other European language, it is becoming standardised and flattened all the time. Is it indeed a language, or is it a dialect? This is a question about which experts differ, but spoken Venetian has very ancient roots indeed. It is a native development out of the low Latin in use in the early centuries of Roman dominion. Each region of the lagoon had an indigenous population that used the common language differently. So the sound of Venetian must surely derive from the speech of the early Veneti. Certainly it is a language older than Italian.

The sound is distinctive. It has been said that the sea-mists and northern winds have changed the timbre of Venetian voices, so that they are harsher than the liquid and sonorous accents of the rest of Italy. The sound of sixteenth-century Tuscan, for example, was described even by one Venetian as "sweeter and more pleasing, lively and fluent." Yet Venetian, the expression of a predominantly mercantile society, is also more powerful and energetic. It can be loud, and it has been said that the Venetians have the loudest voices in all of Italy. It can be raucous, and in the fourteenth century Dante reported that a Venetian woman sounded very much like a man. It has a chant-like or sing-song quality, known as *cantilena*.

So its phonetics differ from those of "standard" Italian. *Madre* becomes *mare*, *signore* becomes *sior*, *figlio* becomes *fio*. Words and phrases are run together, so that the name of the church of S. Giovanni Grisostomo became Zangrisostomo. There was a habit of eliding the last syllable of proper nouns. So the patrician name of Faliero became Falier, having previously metamorphosed from Faletrus and Faledro. *Santo* becomes *San*. *Bello* becomes *beo*, and *casa* becomes *ca'*. It increases the melodic disposition of the words. In that manner *sotto il portico* becomes *sottoportego*. It is more rapid, and perhaps more alive, than other Italian dialects; it is, for example, rich in colloquialisms.

The economy of utterance has another effect. It creates what observers have called the infantine or "babyish" quality of Venetian speech. Byron described it as the language of naivety—he also compared it to the Somersetshire version of English—while the French writer George Sand said that it was destined for the mouths of infants. Two adjectives will be used instead of a superlative to express magnitude, like a child calling out *"bella bella."* Plural subjects have singular verbs, so that in English it might be translated as "the boys does this" and "the girls weeps a lot." Grammar is not the strong point of Venetian speech. Harsh consonants are elided, so that *fagioli* becomes *fasioi.* The "g" ordinarily becomes "z" as in *doze* rather than *doge* and *zorno* for *giorno.* It is in some ways a simple language, lacking sophistication. But that does not make it any the less charming.

24

Colour and Light

It was known as *Venezia la bella*, an incomparable union of art and life.
A Byzantine historian of the fifteenth century compared it to an
exquisitely proportioned sculpture. In its setting upon the waters, it
was born to be painted and engraved. Some have even suggested that
it looked better on paper and on canvas than it ever did in the light
of day. In the drawings and paintings of Venetian life, from those of
Jacopo Bellini in the middle of the fifteenth century to those of
Francesco Guardi in the latter part of the eighteenth century, the
setting and architecture of the city take precedence over the activities
of its inhabitants. The physical space, and the stone face, are pre-
eminent. Who can remember any of the human figures in Canaletto?
In the many images of the public processions of Venice, the spectators
and the participants become part of the architecture; the buildings
themselves seem to embody the harmony and joy of the people. The
stone is a monument to human will but, in the process, the stone itself
becomes revered. The presence of stone—walls, stairways, balustrades
and alcoves—is very noticeable in Venetian painting.

The city might have been composed by a painter seeking symmetry
and contrast, weighing the vertical against the horizontal, combining
shapes and colours in the most harmonious whole. Latin elements are
balanced against Greek elements, Gothic against Byzantine, in order to
symbolise the sway of different empires. The sight lines are perfect, as
in the stage scenery for a play or for an opera, and the perspective
subtly diminished. The details and motifs are carefully mingled. The
co-ordinates of the public buildings were appraised in the light of
Renaissance theories of numbers, so that the vistas have a mystical or
magical enchantment. It was another form of power.

Guardi's paintings of the city are called *vedute* or views, emphasising
the primacy of the eye in the city. Everything is for display. The first
album of Venetian "views," a series of relatively inexpensive

engravings, was published in 1703. Generations of travellers noted that the absence of dust in Venice guaranteed that the great houses and churches would remain relatively bright and clean. One of the reasons why there were, and are, so many balconies and terraces in the city was to provide vantage points from which the beautiful scenario could be observed. It is sometimes hard to know whether the art imitated the reality, or whether the architecture was inspired by the paintings. In Tintoretto's "Paradiso," placed in splendour within the ducal palace, the figures of saints Theodore and Mark, of Moses and of Christ, are arranged one to another in the same positions as their respective principal churches in Venice. So a civic aesthetic is immortalised in paint. Public space becomes artistic space.

Venice was pictorial in another sense, with the frescoes of Tintoretto and Giorgione and others adorning the outward walls of the principal houses. There was a unique appetite in the earliest cities for wall painting, as in the frescoes of Bronze Age Knossos or in the wall paintings uncovered in the ruins of the world's first city, Catal Huyuk in Mesopotamia. It is as if the conditions of urban living prompted the desire for colour and display. In Venice, the essential city, that desire was given full expression. A traveller from the court of Burgundy in 1495, Philippe de Commynes, noted that most of the great houses along the Grand Canal had painted façades; so he dubbed Venice *urbs picta*, or painted city.

In the early part of the sixteenth century Pietro Aretino described Venice as if it flowed from the brush of Titian. "Ever since it was created by God," he wrote in 1537, "never has the city been so embellished by such a lovely picture of lights and shades . . . Oh how beautiful were the strokes with which the brushes of nature pushed back the air, separating it from the palaces in the same way as Titian does in painting his landscapes." The lights and darks "created the effects of distance and relief." The city then becomes a living painting, a work of art in its own right. Yet if a city is a work of art, does it in some sense cease to be a living city? Whistler commented that the people and buildings of Venice "seem to exist especially for one's pictures—and to have no other reason for being!" This of course has been the fate of Venice in more recent years, and it raises questions about its ultimate authenticity.

If we conceive of the city as artefact, something made and not found, then we will understand something else about the nature of Venice. We might say that the cities of the mainland, like London or Rome, were indeed "found." They were part of the natural world before they boasted walls and gates; they were part of the lie of the land, and their growth into cities was a product of many hundreds of generations of settlement and toil. Venice is not that kind of city. It was created. It is a magnificent invention. It is an inspired improvisation at the hands of man. It was from its beginning artificial, a product of a battle against nature itself. The houses did not grow out of the ground. They were built up, piece by piece. The cities of the mainland were always in part defensive structures. Because of the sheltered position of the city of the lagoon, the instinct for defence was displaced by the appetite for display. There was no natural evolution, therefore, but an artificial construct that can only be preserved by further intervention.

The modern restoration of the city offers an instructive lesson in the nature of the artefact. In the latter half of the nineteenth century Giambattista Meduna and his successor, Pietro Saccardo, "restored" large portions of the basilica of Saint Mark's, including the south and west façades; curved lines were straightened, and old marble was replaced with new; the pavement of the left aisle was remade rather than renovated; columns and capitals were scraped clean. It became essentially an imitation or simulacrum of the medieval structure, so that we can say part of the great church was constructed in the 1870s and 1880s rather than the eleventh century. The architects wished to revert to some original state of the basilica; but, in a building created by accretion and assimilation, there never was any original state. The church represents a process rather than an event.

Its new campanile was constructed in the early years of the twentieth century, after the collapse of the original early-sixteenth-century tower. The new campanile may look genuine, to the casual observer, but it is in essence a fake; it is a facsimile designed to maintain the illusion of the tourist that he or she is walking through an ancient city. This architectural quietism never in practice works. Nothing can be rebuilt "as it was"; the very fact of rebuilding precludes that possibility. The larger houses of the city have been restored to look more authentically "Venetian," as already noted, with brighter colours and more regular ornamentation. Such restoration is connected with a loss of nerve, and a loss of identity. After the fall of the republic at the hands of Napoleon, in 1797, the city lost its authority in the world. Its economy was eclipsed with its power. Over the past two centuries it has attempted to create a phantom of its glorious past. It has become in part a fantasy city.

The process has been called, in somewhat ugly terms, the "aesthetification" or "commodification" of Venice. The nineteenth-century French architect, Eugène Viollet-le-duc, suggested that to restore a building is "to reconstitute it in a more complete state than it could have been at any given moment." Thus we have the fullness of the public (rather than the local and private) Venice, more complete than it was in any one period, inviolate, idealised, conceptual, transcending the general inflictions of time. It has never looked more medieval than it does now. Yet in another sense it resembles a visage swollen and unreal after too many face-lifts.

The light of Venice is as important as its space and form. The light on the water casts illumination upwards and outwards. The sunlight plays upon the walls and ceilings, with an incessant rippling effect; it stirs the air and makes everything dance. What is solid is diffused. Buildings shimmer against the surface of the water. Stone becomes colour on the water. It can make the battered marble and the weather-stained brick, the slime on the surface of the canal, seem marvellous. There is a sparkling light, on winter days. But the characteristic of Venice is a pale soft light, like a drifting haze, powdered, part wave and part cloud. It is a pearly iridescent light wreathed in mist. It is drawn from the horizon and the sea as much as from the sun. It lends everything unity.

That is why Venetian painters have always been drawn to the gleam of light upon water, of the reflection of figures and of objects. There are many mirrors, of local manufacture, in Venetian painting. The art of Bellini has always been celebrated for its luminosity, for its ability to charge the air with light. The diffuse sky and the bright horizon contain a glowing world. The surfaces of his canvases emit and receive light. As in the streets of the city itself, even the shadows become sources of light. It is a truism that in Venetian painting colour, rather than contour, is the key. Surely this is related to the vision of reflections in the water?

Light was, in every context, a token of splendour and of nobility. In the twelfth-century chronicles, the basilica of Maria Assunta was celebrated for *pellucida claritas* or admirable lightness. The range of associations is intrinsic to the power of the word. The polished flooring of Venetian houses known as *terrazzo*, compounded of lime and well-powdered stone, was prized for its ability to reflect light; it was buffed and polished with linseed oil until it shone, as everyone testified, "like a mirror." Venetian houses were always designed to catch the light. In the sixteenth century it was noted that the windows were made of glass rather than paper or waxed cloth; according to Francesco Sansovino they "were bright, and full of the sun." There were of course gloomy recesses, dark courtyards, and hidden passages; the Venetians were affected by the chiaroscuro of brightness and shadow. It was part of their nature. It is part of their painting.

There was a passion for artificial light. The chandeliers or *lampadari* of Venice, seeming to float in the great upper spaces of Venetian apartments, were renowned for the myriad and innumerable crystals that seemed to vie with the sparkle of the water outside the windows. Venice was the first city in Europe to have, in 1732, its streets lit by lamps. London followed in 1736. In this period an English traveller, Edward Wright, noted that "the Venetians are excessively lavish of their white wax tapers, in their processions, at their night-litanies." When these lights were seen mingling with the jewels, the gold, the crystal and the silver there was "such a glittering, there was scarce any looking upon them." This is a quintessential Venetian effect, this glittering. It is related to the glittering of the sea all around. Light is the life-giving force. It quickens life. It is an emblem of vivacity and vitality, both associated with the Venetian temperament.

The numinous is luminous. Light is the first created thing. If light is seen as a spiritual substance, then it changes the way we look at the world; the streets and buildings are illuminated by the divine, and are thus themselves sacred. Light has always been depicted as a sign of heavenly grace. There is a light of holiness, and a light of vision. The Renaissance churches of Venice, designed by Codussi and Palladio, exclude any frescoes or mosaics from their interiors; the walls are purely white. In this way the quality of the light was preserved. The Istrian stone of Venice is, in the sunlight, dazzling.

The passion for colour existed, like the veneration of light, as a token of energy and bravura. It was a symbol of being. The harmony of colours was akin to the warmth of the sun. In Venice the term was *colorito* rather than *colore*, intimating the active and expressive possibilities of colour. The nineteenth-century English artist William Etty described Venice as "the birthplace and cradle of colour." In the same century John Ruskin noted that the Venetians resembled the Arabs in "their intense love of colour which led them to lavish the most expensive decorations on ordinary dwelling houses"; in addition they possessed "that perfection of the colour-instinct in them which enabled them to render whatever they did, in this kind, as just in principle as it was gorgeous in appliance." So they coated their palaces in porphyry and gold, where the northern architects employed oak and sandstone. The inner walls of the houses were hung with painted leather or with green and crimson damask. There is expansive colour in the brilliant polychromaticism of their architectural detail, in marble and in mosaic. The basilica of Saint Mark's is a hymn to colour. We may also surmise that this was a culture in which sensory experience was deeper and more intense than our own; in which beautiful colour, and beautiful sound, had a more direct impact upon the human consciousness. Taste, and smell, and sight, and hearing were stripped bare. Life itself was altogether more vivid. The world had not lost its aura.

It was not coincidental, perhaps, that the city itself was the centre of the pigment trade in Europe. The painters of the Netherlands and the rest of Italy would purchase their colours from Venice, where there were merchants who specialised in that trade. Here were the finest orpiment and realgar, used for yellow and for orange, as well as vermilion and lead white. There is the famous "Venetian red," a red earth extracted from the Veneto and characteristically to be seen in fifteenth-century Venetian painting. It was said to be as red as the blood of Christ. The dyeing industries of the city, indispensable in the production of luxury textiles, guaranteed the supply of the pigment known as red lake. The history of fashions in colour—as red lead, for example, gave way to orange at the end of the fifteenth century—would also be a history of human sensibility.

The Venetian painters often pursued the most expensive colours for the sake of their price and rarity. Thus, for example, the profound violet blue of Bellini or Titian was taken from the ground semi-precious lapis lazuli of what is now Afghanistan; red pigments from silver or sulphur were valued very highly. The Venetian republic was the home of saffron imported from the East. In his *Grande Dictionnaire de la Cuisine*, Alexander Dumas *père* remarked that it was "to spices that we owe Titian's masterpieces."

What are the colours of the most serene city? There are of course the sacred colours, Bellini's colours, blue and gold. Many of the public buildings of Venice were decorated with a blue sky of night irradiated by stars of gold. Upon the *Pala d'Oro*, the richly metalled altar screen in Saint Mark's, panels of translucent blue enamel were set within golden borders. It was heaven's colour. Blue is the colour of calm and serenity, adopted in the most serene city. In the paintings of the fourteenth and fifteenth centuries the most favoured colour was a deep blue. There was the violet blue of the sky, and the greenish blue of the soft distance. The colours of salmon, magenta, orange and white are reflected upon the blue and green waters. The sails of the fishing boats, upon the lagoon through the centuries, were orange or crimson.

There is also green, so much wished for in a city of stone. Bellini luxuriated in deep green. The Venetian builders loved green marble. It was an intimation of the natural world, so that we can speak of forests of marble springing up in the city. It was a reminder of the sap and the leaf, of the miracle of rebirth. Ruskin noted that one of the favourite chords of Venetian colour "was the sweet and solemn harmony of purple with various greens." There is the pink of dawn, too, and the pink of evening. Henry James described it as "a faint, shimmering, airy, watery pink; the bright sea-light seems to flush with it and the pale whiteish-green of lagoon and canal to drink it in."

Is this a just description of the water, pale whiteish-green? What is in any case the colour of water? The colours of the sea approaching Venice were once distinguished by the *porti* into which they issued. Thus the waters from the Lido were red, those from Malamocco were green, and those from Chioggia were purple. What is the colour of the waters in the canals and in the lagoon? They have variously been described as jade green, lilac, pale blue, brown, smoky pink, lavender, violet, heliotrope, dove grey. After a storm the colour changes as the water becomes aerated. On a hot afternoon the waters may seem orange. The colours of the sky, and the colours of the city, are refracted in little ovals of ochre and blue. It is all colours and no colour. It reflects, and does not own, colour. It becomes what it beholds.

25

Pilgrims and Tourists

The city needs people. It demands to be seen. The pilgrims of the Middle Ages were the first tourists. They were given guided tours, and certain state officials had the task of inspecting taverns and checking merchandise sold to tourists. These inspectors were also supposed to lead the strangers to the most expensive shops, where they could buy glass beads or silver crosses. There were other guides and agents known as *tolomazi* who offered a range of services from interpreting to money changing. The owners of the various galleys set up booths in Saint Mark's Square, each with the flag of their ship prominently displayed; the masters of these galleys offered snacks of food and glasses of wine to the passing custom while "each abused the other and defamed him to the pilgrims." The pilgrims themselves were lodged in especial taverns and hostelries such as the Little Horse and the Lobster. It was said of some crusaders, on their way to the Holy Land, that they never got further than the Luna Hotel. The Luna was on the quay down from the piazzetta. It was full of guests by 1319. The White Lion opened its doors five years later.

Venice has been the cynosure of all eyes for almost a thousand years; some figures suggest that at the beginning of the twenty-first century it attracts three million residential tourists and seven million "day trippers" each year. Other estimates vary from fourteen to sixteen million annual visitors. It is safe to conclude, therefore, that millions upon millions of people enter a city that has no more than sixty thousand inhabitants. At any one time there are more strangers than citizens. This is not an unusual situation, however, since by the 1840s tourists began to outnumber residents. Yet the imbalance has never been so large. It has been claimed that in twenty-five years, at the current rate of dispersal, there will be no native Venetians left in the city. It will be a city of tourists and of those who serve them. It is no wonder that Venetians feel themselves to be under threat.

Yet through the centuries Venice has passively colluded in its own fate.

At the free fair held on the feast of the Ascension, in the fourteenth century, it was claimed that two hundred thousand strangers came to the city. The authorities invented a season of festivals and fairs, from the end of April to the beginning of June, which could be used to inveigle more visitors. By the fifteenth century there were more than twenty hostelries, most of them situated near Saint Mark's Square and the Rialto. They offered good food, clean linen and a plentiful supply of prostitutes. Engravings, of festivals and of processions, were sold as tourist souvenirs. A city where everything is for sale will naturally wish to sell itself. So the eventual fate of Venice was being decided at a relatively early date. By the end of the fifteenth century a Milanese priest, Pietro Casola, complained that it was a city "about which so much has been said and written . . . that it seems to me there is nothing left to say."

A sixteenth-century tourist, Fynes Morisson, said that Venice was another word for *veni etiam* or come again. The natives were always friendly, and in the early sixteenth century Sir Richard Torkinton said of his hotel in Venice that "the good man of the howse seyd he knew me by my face that I was an englysshman. And he spake to me good englyssh." In a similar spirit the Venetian authorities encouraged any form of entertainment that would entice visitors to the city, including plays and operas and festivals. They also countenanced, even if they did not actively encourage, the belief that the city was the centre of illicit sex. The Venetian courtesan became famous throughout Europe. But anyone, from boys to transvestites, could be purchased in Venice. And of course Venetian hospitality came at a price. A Huguenot tourist of the eighteenth century, François Misson, commenting upon the large number of foreigners in the city, wondered "how much Money all this Multitude must bring to *Venice?*" It was said that every fifth house had a bed to let, and such was the press of boats that "you need but cry out *Gondola* and you have them launch out presently to you." The first guidebook, *Venetia, città nobilissima*, was published in 1581. In the seventeenth century Venice became the centre of the Grand Tour meant to form an essential element in the progress of an English gentleman.

At the beginning of the eighteenth century the English ambassador,

Lord Manchester, reported of the Venetians that "the chief part they intend to act here is to amuse the rest of Europe and do nothing." This was the century in which Venetian artists began to create images of their city expressly designed to appeal to tourists. Francesco Guardi, for example, saw his city as a tourist might see it as a place of romance and of quasi-theatrical scenery. Canaletto specialised in idealised topographical views that were then exported to the rest of Europe in general and to England in particular. In that period there were more than thirty thousand visitors at the time of the Carnival, but the true acme of Venetian tourism was reached in the nineteenth century. The Grand Tour had given way to upper-middle-class travel with Venice as the most desirable destination of all. By the 1840s tourist guides to the city were being written; the first "Cook's tour" of Venice was arranged in 1864. "The Venice of today," Henry James wrote, "is a vast museum where the little wicket that admits you is perpetually turning and creaking . . ."

The city became for the Victorians an acceptable relic of the past, a place of cultural respectability; it offered a refuge from the horrors of industrialism that were even then afflicting England, and a cosy metaphor for an admired and much-lamented past. The "Gothic" architecture of nineteenth-century England found some of its meaning and context in the churches and grand houses of the city. It was already a place of historical nostalgia. The Victorians were in a sense the new pilgrims, the ancestors of those who had gone on a spiritual journey to Jerusalem; yet the pilgrimage now ended at Venice, and its religion was that of art and history. It was in this century, too, that the conventional image of Venice was fixed for ever in the public imagination—the gondolas, the pigeons, the open-air cafés of Saint Mark's Square. It had become a peep-show, a diorama, a bazaar. But there were some who anticipated that the city itself would be altered in the process. In 1887 the English periodical, *The Builder*, warned its readers that the tourists of Venice "had no right to require the inhabitants of any old city that they should be content to reduce themselves to the condition of the custodians of a museum."

In the twentieth and twenty-first centuries the project of Venice may be said to be complete. It has been called the "Disneyfication" of Venice. Venice has been true to its destiny. That is all. It is still a working city but it has acquired a new character. There are those who speak of "decline" or "decay" but there is no real evidence for this. In some respects Venice is the most successful city in the world. Cities are of their nature artificial. Venice will simply take the urban concept to a new height. The nineteenth-century American writer, Francis Marion Crawford, put it best when he declared that "it would not surprise those who know her, to come suddenly upon her and find that all human life was extinct within her, while her own went on, as strong as ever." It is no good pretending that the tourists do not see the "real" Venice in the way that tourists do not see the "real" London or the "real" Paris; the tourist Venice is the essential, quintessential, Venice.

Some tourists are more famous than others. Everyone who is anyone has now been replaced by anyone who is everyone, but in the past the famous and the notorious have been drawn to the city as a stage on which they could perform. Shelley came to lament, and Byron came to ejaculate. Aretino came to celebrate, and Ruskin to denounce. Nietzsche, Proust and Dante all visited the city. Petrarch came here on many occasions, and declared it to be "the most marvellous city that I have ever seen." Turner and Whistler painted Venice, as have hundreds of other foreign artists. In his "Ten O'Clock Lecture," in describing London, Whistler conjured up the image of another city:

> And when the evening mist clothes the riverside with poetry, as with a veil, and the poor buildings lose themselves in the dim sky, and the tall chimneys become campanili, and the warehouses become palaces in the night, and the whole city hangs in the heavens, and fairy land lies before us . . .

By the late nineteenth century there was not an inch of Venice that had not been painted.

It has also been a city of literature, if not exactly a literary city. There are forty references by Shakespeare to Venice and its dominions, not all of them complimentary. Two of his plays, *The Merchant of Venice* (1598) and *Othello* (1602), are set wholly or partly in that city. The first act of *Othello*, with its dark street and its shuttered house, well captures the imaginative ambience of the place. It has been proposed by some scholars that Shakespeare actually visited the city, but that is most unlikely. He did not need to do so. Venice is pre-eminently an imagined city. Sir Politique, in Ben Jonson's *Volpone* (1606), boasts that after the first week of arrival:

> All tooke me for a citizen of Venice:
> I knew the formes, so well.

He is also well aware of the predatory habits of the Venetians:

> For your Venetian, if he sees a man
> Preposterous, in the least, he has him straight;
> He has: he strippes him.

The early nineteenth-century English poets were instrumental in creating what might be called the mythography of Venice. Byron composed two historical dramas set in the city, but his enduring contribution to Venetian sentiment is to be found in poems such as *Beppo*, *Don Juan* and the fourth canto of *Childe Harold's Pilgrimage* where he associates the city with the melancholy outcast who is also the quintessential romantic hero:

> In Venice Tasso's echoes are no more,
> And silent rows the songless gondolier;
> Her palaces are crumbling to the shore,
> And music meets not always now the ear:
> Those days are gone . . .

Yet romance can turn to romanticisation. In the nineteenth and twentieth centuries there appeared a number of somewhat whimsical and self-indulgent travelogues or diaries devoted to the picturesque possibilities of the city. Many writers have composed the same sentence under a Venetian sky—the solemn movements of the gondolier, the market boats at dawn laden with fruits and vegetables, the beautiful children, the marble tables of Florian's, the honeysuckle against a crumbling wall, the solemn mellow tone of the great clock in the piazza, the clangour of the bells of the campanile . . .

In the more serious works of literature, however, Venice appears in quite another guise. It becomes a setting for the secret life. It becomes a place of self-discovery, too, when the usual boundaries between outward and inward, private and public, become blurred. It is a setting where unconscious or repressed desires come forward. It is a place of strange meetings and unexpected encounters. One of the first English novels to be set in Venice, Thomas Nashe's *The Unfortunate Traveller* (1594), has as its plot an adventure in disguise and masquerade when the earl of Surrey exchanges identities with his servant in order to sample the delights of the city unobserved. Venice was already supposed to be the city of lechery and of doubleness or ambiguity. The central part of Ann Radcliffe's *The Mysteries of Udolpho* (1794) takes place in Venice. Although the author herself never visited the city, she imagined it so intently that her descriptions have the utmost verisimilitude. It is a place of intrigue and of danger, of horror and of extravagance.

VIII

The Art of Life

26

Hurrah for Carnival

Byron enters what he considered to be the true and enduring life of Venice, despite his self-dramatising laments at its degradation, by means of the Carnival. "I have hardly had a wink of sleep this week past," he wrote to Tom Moore in 1818.

> We are in the agonies of the Carnival's last days, and I must be up all night, as well as tomorrow. I have had some curious masking adventures this Carnival; but as they are not yet over, I shall not say on. I will work the mine of my youth to the last veins of the ore, and then— good night. I have lived, and am content.

The Carnival was instituted at the end of the eleventh century, and has continued without interruption for almost seven hundred years. After a period of desuetude it was resurrected in the 1970s. "All the world repairs to Venice," John Evelyn wrote in the seventeenth century, "to see the folly and madness of the Carnevall." It was originally supposed to last for forty days, but in the eighteenth century it was sometimes conducted over six months. It began on the first Sunday of October and continued until the end of March or the beginning of Lent. This was also the theatre season. In a city that prided itself on transcending nature, it was one way of defying winter. Yet if the festivities last for half a year, does "real" life then become carnival life? It was said in fact that Venice was animated by a carnivalesque spirit for the entire year. It was no longer a serious city such as London, or a wise city such as Prague.

There were bands and orchestras in Saint Mark's Square; there were puppet shows and masked balls and street performers. There were costume parties in the opera houses, where prizes were awarded for the best dress. There were elaborate fêtes with gilded barges, liveries of gold and crimson, gondolas heaped with flowers. The Venetians, according to William Beckford in the 1780s, were "so eager in the pursuit of amusement as hardly to allow themselves any sleep." In this season, everyone was at liberty.

Evelyn described the Carnival as the resort of "universal madnesse" with "the Women, Men & persons of all Conditions disguising themselves in antique dresses with extravagant Musique & a thousand gambols." But Sir Henry Wotton believed that there was method in the madness; the Carnival was used for "diverting men from talking of greater matters." Another English observer believed that the promotion of pleasure and even of vice, was one of the "main hinges" of the Venetian government. It is, perhaps, the old truism of bread and circuses. But the festivity was directed at strangers as well as natives. It encouraged trade, of course, and the Carnival supported seven theatres, two hundred restaurants and innumerable gaming houses. But the show of joy was also a show of strength, an illusion designed to emphasise the wealth, the independence and the impregnability of the city.

There were bull-fights and bull-runs through the streets. There were firework displays; the Venetians were well known for their skill at pyrotechnics, with the reflection of the coloured sparks and flames glittering upon the water. There were rope-walkers and fortune-tellers and *improvisatori* singing to the guitar or mandolin. There were quacks and acrobats. There were wild beast shows; in 1751 the rhinoceros was first brought to Venice. There were the elements of the macabre; there were mock funeral processions and, on the last day of the Carnival, a figure disfigured by syphilitic sores was pushed around in a barrow. Here once more is the old association between festivity and the awareness of death.

Venetians dressed up as their favourite characters from the *commedia dell'arte*. There was Mattacino, dressed all in white except for red shoes and red laces; he wore a feathered hat, and threw eggs of scented water into the crowd. There was Pantalone, the emblem of Venice, dressed in red waistcoat and black cloak. And there was Arlecchino in his multi-coloured costume. There were masked parties and masked balls. There were masked processions through the streets of the city. The Carnival in fact became intimately associated with the wearing of the mask or *volto*.

It is first mentioned in public documents of 1268, when masked persons were forbidden to gamble. It came out of the East. The most popular form of the Carnival costume was the *bauta*, a mantle of silk or velvet that covered the head and shoulders; a three-cornered hat was worn on top of the hood of this garment. The face itself was covered by a half-mask, of silk or velvet, black or white, or by a white beak-like object known as *larva*. There were some masks that had to be held by the teeth, thus prohibiting speech. Secrecy and silence consorted. The masker, male or female, also wore a black cloak known as a *domino*. The women tended to wear black masks, and the men white. Even if the disguise of the mask was less than perfect the identity of the masker was never to be revealed; he was always addressed as "Signor Maschera." It was all highly ritualised, as befits a ceremony that has its roots in ancient worship.

By the eighteenth century, at the very latest, the masks had become indispensable. During the six months of the Carnival everyone in the city wore them—the rich and the poor, the shopkeepers and the priests, the magistrates and the prostitutes. The priest was in fact denounced by his parish if he did not wear a mask in public. The dignitaries of the city wore them in public ceremonies and processions. Only the money changers were not permitted to wear them. It was reported that a masked mother was seen suckling a masked infant. Even the beggars wore masks.

Altogether it was a curious spectacle. There were assignations. There were betrayals. There was spontaneous sex behind doors and in the corners of alleys. Pleasure is addictive. It can have all the elements and attributes of a fever. Pleasure is a dream. One Venetian described how "women of every condition, married, maid or widow, mingle freely with professional harlots, for the mask levels all distinctions; and there is no filth they do not practise, publicly, with their paramours, young and old." There were also less salacious diversions. Three or four women in masks might go up to various acquaintances and in squeaky, assumed voices tease them for their well-known weaknesses. It was a case of dressing-up and pretending, a game beloved by children of all kinds. The word *bauta* itself is supposed to derive from the childish lisping of "bau . . . bau." And it was often said, of course, that the Venetians were essentially children. Addison believed that the intrigue and "secret history" of the Carnival "would make a Collection of very diverting Novels." Venice always seems to prompt the telling of stories. The Carnival offered the possibility of another world, and of another reality. It represented a second life for those who had been, or who had felt themselves to be, cheated in the first one.

The masked balls were known as *i festini*, and were open to anyone wearing a mask; their location was marked by a lantern garlanded with flowers. Within could be heard the music of the cello and the spinet, and the guests danced the minuet and the gavotte. The kind owners of the house would then go among their guests and demand their fees. Nothing was free in Venice. There were various rules concerning the use of the mask, promulgated through the centuries, but they were generally disregarded. In the nineteenth century, for example, it was decreed that no reveller might touch or walk with a masked person without being given express permission. How was that to be policed?

It is appropriate to speculate about the nature of the mask, so associated with Venice that it has become its unofficial emblem. There are masks, carved out of stone, still to be seen on the bridges and arches of the city. The making of masks, even in the twenty-first century, is one of the most profitable of all Venetian trades. Goethe wrote from Venice that "masks which in our country have as little life and meaning for us as mummies, here seem sympathetic and characteristic expressions." Somehow the mask fitted the Venetian countenance. It became expressive. The mask is an emblem of secrecy in the city of secrets. It suggests that the city itself might, like the maskers, lead a double life. Venice was known for the greed and duplicity that existed beneath the festive or aesthetically appealing surface. It is a city of doubleness, of reflections within reflections, in every sense. The mask is a sign of ambiguity. It has been said that nothing in Venice has a single meaning; everything, from art to government, is open to endless interpretation. The derivation of "carnival" is itself ambiguous. Does *carne vale* mean "farewell to flesh" or "flesh mattered"? *Vale* may have either signification. Some derive it from *carnem levare*, or the giving up of meat. It is also perhaps significant that the mask was known as *larva*; it suggests the secret hatching of life, and the birth of a butterfly from a grub. So the Carnival also celebrates the city as a place of protean identity and delight. Ruskin glimpsed "Proteus himself latent in the salt-smelling skin of her."

The mask itself has perverse connotations. With the black *bauta*, and the black tricorner hat, it has associations with death. It might conceal a grinning death's head. It might conceal nothing at all. Contemporary Venice has been described as "an empty mask." So Sartre wrote that "when I look at the Palazzo Dario . . . I always have the feeling that, yes, it is certainly there, but that at the same time there is nothing there." There is nothing left to find. There is nothing left to describe.

The Carnival also served a social purpose. In a city where the roles of patricians and citizens were well defined, the loss of identity was often very welcome. In the course of their duties the patricians adopted the appearance of severity and gravity as the mark of their public status. The Carnival allowed the release of the social and personal tensions that must inevitably have spread. The Carnival thereby stabilised the people and the institutions of Venice. It encouraged the feeling of community among all the people. It afforded a glimpse of the eternal principles of brotherhood and equality. It was a reminder of the presumed original equality of the Venetian people when they first sought refuge in the lagoons. So the Carnival became a form of public renewal. In other cities, and other states, the celebration of the freedom of carnival life became the occasion for riot or even rebellion. This never happened in Venice.

In the late 1970s, after a period of decline, the Carnival was revived for the islanders of Burano. It then migrated to Venice itself, where the officials quickly realised its value as an enticement to visitors. In this endeavour they have been wholly successful. It is now a Carnival of, and for, tourists. It is of course heavily commercialised, with corporate organisations sponsoring different events. In 2008 it was in fact entirely given over to private hands, and was organised by a company provisionally known as Venice Events Limited. The head of the casino in Venice announced that "sponsors will have at their disposal rooms at the best hotels for their guests, tickets, exclusive tables and deals with the casino." But the Carnival was always a commercial operation, aimed in part at strangers. It has simply fulfilled its essential nature, while in the process becoming unreal and empty.

There were other fairs and holidays. There were trade fairs, such as that of the Festa della Sensa in the middle of May, which were essentially celebrations of trade and of commerce. The mercers of Venice put on display their finest silks, and the goldsmiths put out their finest plate. There were elaborate processions staged by various guilds, where the distinction between commerce and religious ceremony was hard to find. The children blew trumpets of glass. The shops were ablaze with lights and mirrors. The brethren of the guild of S. Rocco held up a banner on which was inscribed "Copious riches, cheerful labour, public joy." A painting by Gabriele Bella shows the fair of the late 1770s, with Saint Mark's Square covered with innumerable shops, tents, booths, stalls and awnings, so that it resembles an Arabian souk.

It is not surprising, therefore, that Venice became known as the city of performance with the multifarious mountebanks and jugglers and acrobats. Saint Mark's Square was famous for hustlers and buskers of every kind. They were freed from oppressive legislation in Venice, and so they flocked there. They were dressed in outlandish gear, singing and dancing on the especially prepared stages. The quacks among them would make elaborate and splendid speeches on the benefits of their elixirs and "soverayne waters." There were illusionists who would pretend to cut open their arms, with much blood, only to reveal that their flesh was untouched. There were snake-charmers and tooth-pullers and magicians who according to Coryat performed "strange juggling tricks as would be almost incredible to be reported." Othello is suspected of drugging Desdemona with "medicines bought of mountebanks." The Venetian kind was notorious throughout Europe.

The Carnival was also the home of voracious and incessant gambling. At the end of the twelfth century the first public gaming tables in Europe were erected by Niccolò Barattieri; they were his reward for raising the two columns of the piazzetta, and his tables were placed between them. It soon became the place of judicial execution, and is still known as a conventionally unlucky spot. But the fever spread. In the thirteenth and fourteenth centuries there were various attempts to organise, and to supervise, the games of chance. It was found necessary, for example, to pass statutes forbidding gambling in the courtyards of the ducal palace and in the basilica of Saint Mark's itself. Yet nothing could stop the obsession with gaming. Playing cards were not invented in Venice, as is sometimes claimed, but the Venetians soon enjoyed something like a monopoly on their manufacture.

There were private *ridotti* or gaming places in many grand houses, and in the houses of courtesans. An edict of 1598 referred to places "with gaming, drunkenness and other dishonesties" to the manifest shame of the state. Servants were asked to denounce masters who set up gambling tables. The patricians were not alone in their predilection for gambling. The people of Venice were also addicted, with dice and cards played in taverns and squares, in wine-shops and barbers' shops, upon bridges, and even in gondolas. They were ready to bet on anything, from chess and chequers to skittles and rackets. One of the most popular forms of gambling involved the results of public elections; money would be placed on one candidate rather than another, and bookmakers set up stalls in the Rialto. Crowds would gather to see who had been elected to the senate, or to the council of ten, but they were not being public-spirited. They were interested only in the outcome of the race. So the authorities of the city decided to control, and to profit from, that which they could not prevent. By the sixteenth century the *ridotti* or public gaming houses were already being licensed for various games of hazard and what was called "honest conversation." Then in 1638 the Venetian state financed a public gambling house, the Ridotto, which became the paradigm or prototype for all the *casinos* of Europe.

In the early eighteenth century gambling was seen as an essential element of the Carnival. It also became the sport of the patricians, run in expensive clubs and under strictly commercial auspices. It was said that "to risk nothing is a thing for a man worth nothing." So gambling was transformed into a sign of magnanimity and nobility. One English visitor to a gaming house noticed that "the crowd is so great that very often one can hardly pass from out of one Room into another; nevertheless the Silence here observ'd is much greater than that in the Churches . . . to see in how much Tranquillity and Gravity very considerable Summs are lost is really so very Extraordinary. . . ." The Venetian gentleman was supposed to suffer loss or gain with the utmost indifference.

There were other public games of chance. At the very beginning of the sixteenth century a city lottery was established. It was a way of turning the attention of the populace from the private diversions of the gaming table into the safer realm of state enterprise. It was of course also a means of raising money. A lottery was conducted at the Rialto, in which the prizes included clothes and furniture, paintings and jewels. In 1590 a lottery was instituted to meet the costs of the newly rising Rialto bridge; tickets went on sale for two crowns, and the prize was one hundred thousand crowns.

When the winners of the public lotteries were announced,

everything else came to a halt. Priests, prostitutes and poltroons were all at the mercy of lottery fever. Pietro Aretino noticed that those under its sway employed the filthiest and most blasphemous language to express their feelings. The losers believed themselves to have been "disembowelled" and "crucified." Yet still they came back for more.

Gambling is a necessary occupation in a city of merchants dependent upon the sea. For the merchant there was always the prospect of enormous future wealth. Yet it depended on the shifting sea. A man might be wealthy beyond measure on one day, poor and ruined on the next. The rise of gaming in the city was often noted as a sign of increasing Venetian decadence, but of course it is the necessary consequence of the atmosphere and ethos of the city. It has been claimed in this book that Venice was the first home of capitalism in Europe; the essence of capitalism lies in risk-taking, otherwise known as financial speculation. Gambling reproduces the essential mysteries of economic fluctuation in a smaller and more intense space.

And then there is the importance of the concept of fortune in Venetian public affairs. The Venetian state was always being urged to avoid *fortuna belli,* the fortune of war, in conflicts where there could be no certain victor. There is some evidence to suggest that, in the course of the fourteenth century, a less sanguine attitude towards fortune and to risk-taking spread among the people. Fortune, too, is the goddess of the Venetian gaming table. "Now all things are subject to fortune," the Venetian historian Bernardo Giustiniani wrote in the late fifteenth century, "and empires are daily changed and transferred. It is fortune which plays this game, fortune which must be obeyed."

When the greatest of all public gaming houses was closed in 1774 by the order of the government, a contemporary reported that "the whole population grows melancholy . . . the merchants drive no trade; the mask-makers perish of hunger; and the hands of certain impoverished nobles, accustomed to shuffle the cards for ten hours a day, have now grown shrivelled and shrunk; in truth vices are absolutely necessary to the life of a State." Gaming was the lifeblood of Venice, just as trading had once been. When all the risk of empire had gone, when all the risk of a great commercial life had disappeared for ever, what was there left to hazard but cards and dice?

The sports and games of Venice have an especial meaning for the students of state power. One famous Venetian pastime, for example, was the "human pyramid." It was known to the Venetians as *forze d'Ercole*, the labours of Hercules, and consisted of men climbing on each other's shoulders, with the number at the base slowly tapering to one man on the summit. It was usually performed upon a raft of boats, thus emphasising an uncanny resemblance to the structure of the state itself where through a complex machinery of association the doge surmounts the people. The human pyramid was also the human image of Venice. It was a feat of equilibrium.

The concepts of lightness and balance are of immense consequence in Venice. So it is perhaps significant that one of the most famous amusements of the Carnival was known as *volo della colombina* or "the flight of the dove." A rope was tied from a moored boat to the top of the campanile in Saint Mark's Square, from which another rope was secured to the ducal palace. An acrobat, dressed as an angel, then climbed to the top of the campanile before sailing down towards the palace and scattering flowers as he descended. In 1680 there was a more daring feat. A boatman, known as Scartenador, ascended by rope to the campanile on horseback.

There were many games and sports, including rackets and fencing; there were wheelbarrow races and horse races and gondola races. In the sixteenth century there was a game known as "Balloon," a kind of aerial football; these games, and others like them, had a reputation for violence. The young Venetian patricians enjoyed shooting matches. All of these amusements were forms of competition, at the end of which a prize was awarded. The Venetians were a highly gregarious, and therefore highly competitive, people. This was not true of Londoners in the same period, for example, who preferred to attend bull-baitings and bear-baitings where there were no true winners and no awards.

There was one game, however, that more than any other symbolised the stability and strength of the Venetian state. It was known as *la guerra dei pugni* or the war of the fists, fought between the inhabitants of the various territories and neighbourhoods. There were the Rialtini and the Cannaruoli, the Bariotti and the Gnatti. But the largest division of all lay between the Castellani—in the western parishes of Cannaregio, Castello, S. Marco and Dorsoduro—and the Nicolotti in the eastern parishes of S. Croce and S. Polo. The dominant factions were the fishermen of the Nicolotti and the shipbuilders of the

Castellani. Their internecine rivalries have already been described. A team from each of these territories met for battle on a chosen bridge, while thousands of spectators lined the streets and houses beside the canal. Dumplings and chestnuts were served to the crowds by street vendors. It was a glorified fist-fight in which the object was to hurl opponents into the water and to gain possession of the bridge.

This became the sport of Venice, according to one sixteenth-century chronicler, "so beloved and esteemed by all the Venetian people, as well as by foreigners." Visiting monarchs were invited to witness the proceedings, as the Castellani and the Nicolotti vied for mastery. When Henry of Valois visited Venice in the summer of 1574 two armies of three hundred men did battle for his amusement; it was said at the time that it was a way of displaying to the Frenchman that the people of Venice were "very fierce, indomitable, headlong and uncontrolled." They wore helmets and carried shields. Many of them came armed with sticks of tough rattan. The fighting could last for several hours. Such violent delights often had violent ends. Many competitors were maimed or injured; they were sometimes even killed.

It was of course an occasion of ritualised violence, in which all the brute force of the populace could be expended; popular energy was being exploited for the purposes of spectacle so that it might not be harnessed for any more dangerous cause. At times of holiday, when the fights took place, there was no other subject of conversation among the people. The cause of possessing the two paving stones on the "crown" of the bridge became an obsession. The victors became heroes, and the vanquished were lost in shame. The winning parishes would light great bonfires in their *campi*, and arrange impromptu dances. The best fighters became famous all over the city, with their portraits hanging in the houses of their parish. They were given honorifics such as "Ditch Jumper" and "Eats the Dead" and "Destroyer of Boldness." They considered themselves to be "soldiers," although of course Venetians were never soldiers in a military sense. That may be one of the explanations for their pugnacity at home.

The first record of such fighting is found in 1369, but the first battle upon a bridge seems to have been staged in 1421. The roots of the contest are much older, of course, dating from the first period of exile when the groups from various cities made their homes upon separate islands in the lagoon. There were then real wars for mastery, of which the battle of the fists was a token. On the islands that eventually comprised Venice itself, it was said that there was a "landward" people looking towards the mainland and a "seaward" people looking towards the other islands. The canals were at one time real boundaries, the water between the small plots of land or parishes, which would suffer more than ritual transgression.

Many factions still clashed in fifteenth- and sixteenth-century Venice. The denizens of one parish might gather on a bridge and shout insults at the people of the rival parish; the youth of a parish might even initiate rapid "raids" on the camp of a rival, and throw sticks or stones at the natives. The experience of living in such crowded conditions fostered an intense spirit of territorial loyalty; it was said, for example, that the most partisan supporters of *la guerra dei pugni* were those who lived at or near the boundaries of their parish. The battles were also a way of celebrating the role of bridges themselves in Venetian communal life. They were the very axis around which the city turned. The city has always been an emblem of intense struggle, of the battle for life, and in *The City in History* Lewis Mumford alludes to "a bloody ritual fight with clubs between the forces of Light and Darkness held within an Egyptian temple precinct." Civilisation always retains elements of barbarism. That is how it survives. The essence of the city itself lies in competition and aggression.

27

A Divine Art

There is an anecdote concerning Tintoretto. In the spring of 1564 one of the Venetian guilds, the Scuola of S. Rocco, ran a competition for the painting of their hall. Tintoretto and Veronese were two of the contestants. It was agreed that each artist should submit a design for the central ceiling panel of the room. The artists went away and began work, but Tintoretto had no intention of sketching a design. He obtained the measurements of the panel and began work at once upon a large canvas. The artists gathered one morning, with their designs ready for scrutiny, but Tintoretto had forestalled them. He had brought the completed canvas to the hall a day or two before, and by secret means had it fixed upon the ceiling where it was to be displayed. He merely pointed upwards when asked for his design. When the masters of the guild remonstrated with him, he replied that the only way he could "design" an image was by painting it. He added, according to Vasari, that "designs and models should always be after that fashion, so as to deceive no one, and that, finally, if they would not pay him for the work and his labour, he would make them a present of it." Vasari concluded that the words of Tintoretto had "many contradictions" but nevertheless "the work is still in the same place." The painting, "San Rocco in Glory," is on the ceiling still. The comments of his thwarted competitors are not reported, although they are not likely to have been complimentary. He had in essence played a trick on them.

The stories of Vasari are not necessarily to be trusted, but there is some documentary evidence to support this particular anecdote. The records of the guild reveal that a competition between "three or four of the most excellent painters in Venice" was announced on 31 May 1564, but it was abandoned four weeks later when the guild accepted the finished painting of Tintoretto. He had completed this mighty canvas within a matter of days. Vasari was no doubt eager to reveal the somewhat devious tactics of Tintoretto in obtaining the commission, although it might be said that the artist was behaving in a manner perfectly understandable to any Venetian merchant or shopkeeper. He may have been prompted, too, by political machinations within the guild; intrigue is always in the Venetian air. Throughout his life Tintoretto would be an adept and wily bargainer, cutting his prices and changing his terms whenever the occasion demanded. Vasari was also intent upon disclosing the lack of diligence and of preparation on the artist's part. How could he possibly take up his brush without first preparing a design? Yet the anecdote also reveals the full force of Tintoretto's personality; it reveals his restless and headlong resort to paint as the medium in which he revelled. His figures sport like dolphins on the canvas, a reflection of his own mastery and exuberance.

He was a controversial figure from his earliest youth. Another story places Tintoretto in confrontation with Titian. Tintoretto was for a short time apprentice to the older painter; it is said, according to family legend, that Titian came upon some figures drawn by him. Observing at once their facility, and fearing for his own reputation, Titian ordered the young man to leave his studio. It is an improbable account of jealousy, but one of Tintoretto's sons spread it abroad after the death of his father. It may reflect the essential tension between Titian's utterly expensive art, created largely for foreign patrons, and Tintoretto's more local and artisanal genius.

There is no doubt that the artist's talents became quickly known. He was born as Jacopo Robusti in the autumn of 1518, in Venice, and in that city he would live and die. It owned his being. He is a distinct example of the territorial imperative, whereby the ground itself helps to shape him. He is the most thoroughly Venetian of all painters. He was the son of a dyer of silks; hence the name he gave himself as an artist. He was happy to be known as "the little dyer" because it was a token of his relatively humble Venetian origins. He only left the city once in his life and then, on a journey to Mantua, he insisted that his wife accompany him. Like other Venetian artists, he was a fervent amateur musician. He painted stage sets and designed costumes for the theatres of the city. His art cannot be understood without Venice. His great works are still to be found in the city. His paintings were once to be seen in more than forty of the city's churches. Only in Venice can his fieriness and extravagance be properly realised. His art *is* Venice in its purest and most spiritual form.

One contemporary reported that "in his gestures, expression, movement of the eyes and in his words he is alert and quick in argument." So his art embodied his person. He had what Stendhal called "Venetian liveliness" to the utmost degree. Vasari called him "hot-headed." His speed of execution was known to everyone. He could complete a painting in the same time as another artist might finish a sketch. His was a vivacious and exuberant and impetuous art. He was filled with divine fury, with all the rage and energy of creation. He was the lightning flash. When some young Flemish artists came to his studio, they showed him certain drawings over which they had laboured for weeks. He took up his brush and with three strokes of black paint created a figure. He put in some white highlights, and turned to his guests. "This," he said, "is how we poor Venetians paint our pictures." It was the Venetian way, known throughout Europe as *prestezza*. The Venetian painters, too, were known for the art of improvisation. They were also known for their speed. Tiepolo said that he could finish a painting while other artists were still mixing their colours. Two centuries earlier Vasari remarked that a work by Tintoretto was finished before others thought it begun.

Yet his was not entirely an improvised art. He fashioned little models out of wax, and placed them in tiny houses made out of wood and cardboard; then he would suspend lights above and around them. Out of this toy theatre came his great creations filled with radiance and majesty. Saints hurtle through the air at enormous speed. Then they come to a halt, suspended a few feet above the ground. Vistas of figures stretch into eternity. Light floods the dwelling place of mortals. His figures are always in energetic movement, quick and furious; they whirl around some central pillar of light, their limbs and muscles transfigured in centrifugal flight. In his later work light does not follow structure; it supersedes structure; it becomes structure. The world is dissolved in radiance. Drama was an essential element of Venetian art. Canaletto was trained as a designer of theatrical sets. Tiepolo worked as a costume designer. Veronese built up his canvases on the model of the sixteenth-century stage.

Tintoretto himself worked instinctively and naturally, caught up in the rush of inspiration which seems never to have flagged. Some have sensed in his pictures a certain anxiety—an unease, an insecurity, in the perpetually whirling forms. It is of a piece with his endless activity and prolificity. He could never rest. If this is so, then it may coincide with the anxiety of Venice in the sea, and with its endless search for meaning in the wilderness of the world. Tintoretto once said that "the further you go in, the deeper is the sea." In the late spring of 1594, at the age of seventy-five, he died of a fever.

In 1581 a Venetian collector wrote that there were more paintings in Venice than in all the rest of Italy. Painting, Ruskin said, is the way that the Venetians write. Can a graphologist of art, therefore, identify some salient characteristics in the wealth of Venetian painting? Are there certain harmonies between one artist and another that can be plausibly credited to the nature and position of the city itself? The way in which painting replaced painting, in the ducal palace and in the churches of the city, suggests that the art of Venice was deemed by the authorities to possess an identifiable history and an independent unity. It was capable of endless renewal without compromising its essential identity. For Venetians themselves there was such a thing as Venetian art. It was not the invention of art historians. In the mosaics and in the sacred paintings of the fifteenth century, for example, there is a mingling of Byzantine, Gothic and Tuscan art that is uniquely Venetian; the city drew on the traditions from East and West. Throughout Venetian history various styles and stylistic traits were mingled. It was a port at which many called.

The art of Venice, in the thirteenth century, was Byzantine in inspiration. The images of Christ Pantocrator, of the Virgin, and of all the saints, were painted on wooden panels burnished with gold. At least one workshop in the city specialised in copying, or faking, early Byzantine originals. Thus by imitation Venetian art acquired an identity. It had no other past. The looting of Constantinople in 1204 created the conditions for a Byzantine "revival" in the chief city of the looters. In previous centuries the art of Venice had been provincial and stiffly medieval. There was in fact no really important Venetian work until the middle of the fifteenth century. Yet there were frequent Byzantine "revivals" in the city, most notably in the latter half of the fifteenth century when hostility to the cities of the mainland led to the rejection of the Classical and the Gothic. Venice wished to create an historical and cultural identity with the region of the upper Adriatic, where the Byzantines had once held dominion.

The Byzantine influence had emerged earlier, in the first mosaics for the basilica of Saint Mark's. The earliest of them, dated to the latter part of the eleventh century, were the work of Greek artists imported from Byzantium. By the beginning of the thirteenth century, however, there had emerged a distinctive Venetian school of mosaic art. The mosaic then became an essential element of Venetian cultural identity. It has been described as "painting for eternity"; the materials do not fade or decay in demonstrably historical time. Mosaics reflect the Venetians' passion for surface and decorative pattern, as elaborate as the lace of Burano. They embody their love for rich and hard material. The smallest pieces or *tesserae* are cubes of gold or enamelled glass. They possess the sensual pleasure of jewels and other glittering merchandise, so dear to the imagination of a trading city. Mosaics fulfil the Venetian desire for colour and detail. Even the later work in Saint Mark's betrays no interest in the linear perspective of fourteenth-century Italian art; perspective is a reminder of the fallen world. Pattern and colour are eternal. The lesson was not lost on Venetian painters, who seemed to compete with the mosaicists in creating a glowing and richly tinted world. The art of the mosaic was taught in Venice long after it had fallen into disuse in other Italian cities, and indeed a school or establishment of professional mosaicists was organised as late as 1520.

The shining glass and gold surfaces glow with the hieratic detail and brilliant colour of the icon, but they also set up a play of light and shadow that is intrinsic to the Venetian genius. The glass was to hand in Murano, where the workshops were well known for the *lucidezza* or lucidity of their product. When Commynes came to Venice in 1494 he noted on the walls of Saint Mark's "the curious work called Musaique or Marquetry; the art also whereof they vaunt themselves to be authors of. . . ." This typically Venetian "vaunt" was of course without foundation, but his comment suggests how odd and exotic the mosaic seemed to a foreign eye. When Thomas Coryat came to Venice in the early seventeenth century he remarked that "I never saw any of this picturing before I came to Venice." So Venice became associated with the art of mosaic.

The city was the focus. The city was the arena for competition and display. There is not a huge leap from the art of Tintoretto to the art of

Tiepolo, although they are separated by almost two centuries. They are both recognisably Venetian. The city absorbed them. The city gave them strength. Whereas the great artists of Florence—Donatello, Leonardo, Michelangelo—seem unyielding and separate from their home city, the artists of Venice are at home and at ease with their birthright. Giorgione, Titian, Tintoretto and Veronese were not attracted to the patronage of other cities or other courts; they rarely, if ever, left the city on the lagoon. Giovanni Bellini spent his entire life in the neighbourhood of Castello. Titian hated leaving Venice. They seemed to be family men, whereas the artists of Florence tended to be single and of homosexual persuasion.

But there was also a larger continuity. Bellini is to be seen in the context of the work of his father, Jacopo Bellini; in turn Giorgione learned from Bellini, and Titian learned from Giorgione. Tiepolo was called *Veronese redivivio*. It is perhaps a familiar pattern of influence and inheritance, but one that takes place more fully and intensely in the small and relatively isolated city of Venice. The conservative bias of the citizens, in all matters of social and political policy, must also have had its effect upon the local artists. The importance of tradition and authority was asserted on all occasions of public discourse. If the mosaics in Saint Mark's were faded, they were replaced by exact replicas. If the paintings in the ducal palace were damaged or destroyed, they were replaced with images of the same historical or mythological scene. All of the instincts of the Venetian painter were to maintain, or to learn from, the past.

Their methods of working were different from their respective contemporaries in other cities. In Venice artists were characteristically viewed as a particular kind of artisan. In a city noted for its pragmatic tendencies, theirs was a wholly practical training. They were concerned with craft skills. They were not considered heroic, with the possible exception of Titian; they were not filled with the divine afflatus. They were essentially servants of the state. The painters belonged to a guild that was supervised by three magistrates. Alongside Tintoretto and Titian were sign-painters and makers of playing cards. Painters were also expected to practise their expertise in other matters pertaining to the state; they were hired as cartographers or as designers of festive banners and of shields. They made their own tools, like any other craftsman. They considered their work in its material rather than its aesthetic guise. They looked at a canvas as a carpenter might look at a wooden chest or a cobbler look at a pair of shoes.

In Venice, too, there was much greater specialisation of trade than in other cities. That, again, is part of the inheritance of the Venetian merchant tradition. The carvers of frames had their own guild, while the gilders formed a "column" of the painters' guild. The goldsmiths often practised their art in consortium. There were painters of furniture panels, and painters of chests. There were the ivory carvers, their art first emanating from Byzantium. It was always a question of supply and demand. Painted organ shutters, for example, were a Venetian speciality. Painting, in any case, is bound to be different in a city so attentive to the appetite for luxury goods. Luxury represents the love of the material world. Is that not the quality present in the paintings of Bellini and of Titian?

The imperatives of trade are to be seen in the replacement of wood by canvas as the preferred support for oil painting. The supply of material was guaranteed by the presence of a thriving sail industry. In any case the sea air rotted wood. Canvas was also easier to transport in a city, and a lagoon, notoriously difficult to navigate. The line between aesthetic and economic preference is a fine one. In Venice, of all cities, it is hard to know which of them was predominant. It is also worth noticing that the painters of Venice turned to landscape at precisely the time of the city's colonisation of the mainland.

So the studio or workshop (known as *bottega*) of the Venetian painters was created in response to the trading practices of the city. Tintoretto had one of the most efficient studios, for example, based upon the Venetian instinct for familial ties. His two sons were his assistants, and they continued to turn out replicas of their father's work long after his death. In his will Tintoretto left all of his "property, as far as appertains to my profession" to the sons. His wife was responsible for the finances, and his daughter married a young man on the perfectly acceptable grounds that he had proved himself to be a good artist. As she explained in her will, "if the said Sebastian proved to be an able painter I should take him for my husband; in this way, by virtue of his talent, the Tintoretto name would be maintained." Indeed the Tintoretto business lasted for more than a century and involved three generations. In a city that was established upon the primacy of family, too, the artists followed precedent. The sons of Bellini were painters. The studios of Tiepolo and Bassano, Veronese and Zuccaro, were family businesses. They were clearly created on the pattern of the merchant families of the city, in which trade was passed from father to son. A man might become a painter for the simple reason that he was part of a painter's family.

Art was seen as a communal, rather than an individual, enterprise. Paintings were worked upon by many hands. A master like Bellini would provide drawings of heads as "patterns" that his apprentices could copy; the same was true, in other studios, of figure and gesture. In a city that had pioneered the model of the production line, in the shipyards of the Arsenal, such enterprise is hardly surprising. So it is that the workshops created the identity and unity of Venetian painting. From the fourteenth to the nineteenth centuries it was a distinct and distinctive Venetian phenomenon. There was nothing comparable in the other cities of Italy. Art was pre-eminently a trade, and a profitable one at that, which may explain why artistic change was always slow in Venice.

So by indirection we may be able to provide a rudimentary portrait of the Venetian artist. He or she (there were female artists in Venice) was hard-working and energetic, content to be a member of the larger community and happy to serve that community, concerned not with aesthetic theory but with trading practice, intent upon contracts and profits. It is significant that not one Venetian artist ever completed a treatise on painting. In Florence there were many such works.

It is not altogether surprising, perhaps, that the ordinary Venetian seemed to know nothing whatever about art. There was a great appetite for devotional pictures, of course, but little debate about the quality of such productions. Throughout the centuries there has been a general indifference to the more sublime work of the natives. As W.D. Howells put it in *Venetian Life*, published in the middle of the nineteenth century, "As to art the Venetians are insensible to it and ignorant of it . . . I would as soon think of asking a fish's opinion of water as of asking a Venetian's notion of architecture or painting." In the modern age of the Biennale, the same judgement may apply.

From the latter part of the fourteenth century to the end of the eighteenth century, there were two dominant schools in the city. One emphasised sensuous and decorative effects while the other relied upon narrative exposition. The former encompassed the Venetian love for opulent surface and gorgeous texture. The latter served the Venetian passion for scenic display. Yet through them both can be traced the same instinct for rhythmic grace, the same flowing line. When the Venetian patrician, Pietro Bembo, described the Venetian dialect as "softer, more imaginative, more rapid and more alive" than any other variant of Italian, he might have been referring to the brushwork of the Venetian painters. There is a sense of movement and of rhythmic display. There has always been a certain sensuousness and voluptuousness in Venetian art, most clearly seen in the female nudes of Titian. Planes and lines are supplanted by curves. When Manet travelled to Venice, he had decided to paint the scene of the annual regatta on the Grand Canal. While sitting in a Venetian café he told a friend and compatriot, Charles Toche, that "there can be no sharp definition, no linear structure in something that is all movement; only tonal values which, if correctly observed, will constitute its true volume, its essential underlying design." This is also an interesting observation on the nature of Venetian painting itself.

The instinct for narrative is in part the instinct for drama. The Venetian stage was well known for its machines and spectacles. The public spaces of Venice were the home for elaborate processions. The earliest mosaics in the basilica of Saint Mark's are driven by narrative, and the first great narrative painting was executed by the school of Paolo Veneziano in the spring of 1345. In these early works, human existence is seen as a series of communal events. In that sense it is a public art. In the narrative paintings there are always groups and crowds of people. That would have been the experience of Venice itself. Such art lends coherence and impressiveness to the public record. It imparts significance to the diurnal life of the city. When Carpaccio, for example, depicted the occurrence of miracles in the streets and canals of the city his works were taken as proof positive that such events had in fact occurred.

The artists of the city were concerned with the glory of the city. They were attuned to social, rather than individual, reality. It is instructive that they did not suggest the content of the narrative cycles themselves, but were content to fulfil the demands of the state. If the state was not the patron, then the commissions came from the many social and religious institutions of the city. The patrician statesmen, also, wished to commemorate the role of their families in the increasing glory of the entire polity. So there is not much self-communing in the art of Venice. This may help to explain the intense conservatism, or rather the reliance on tradition, in that art.

Art was also a form of political life. Everything in Venice has to do with politics, and is enmeshed in the intricate network of power relations that linked state with guild and church. Public art, for example, can be an example of social control. This is as true of sixteenth-century Venice as of the twentieth-century Soviet Union. In Venice the essential notion is one of the underlying unity of the city, in its customs and in its traditions. The death of a doge made no difference to any of the artistic commissions then being completed. The death of a prince in Milan, or the death of a pope in Rome, would have meant absolute rupture.

The paintings of the doges arrayed in solemn lines on the walls of the great council hall are themselves designed to represent calm continuity, one to another, and loyal impersonality. They are images of stability. They bear themselves, and their robes of state, well. Their lucid gaze is not troubled by hesitation or inward meditation. Venice was the first city to preserve images of its rulers, not as individuals but as guardians and representatives of the city. The painter of these state portraits was himself known as *pittore di stato* or state painter; he also restored the paintings in the state collections, designed the banners and stage machinery for the pageants, and designed the mosaics for the basilica. Collectors often bequeathed their acquisitions to the city for the sake of *la patria*.

After two great fires in the 1570s had partially destroyed the ducal palace, a new programme of public art was instituted. So complex was the symbolism, and so significant the interpretation, that in 1587 a book was published under the title of a *Declaration of All the Histories Contained in the Paintings recently Placed in the Halls of the Scrutinio and Great Council of the Ducal Palace*; the long title concludes with an adumbration of the *Most Famous Victories Won over Various Nations of the World by the Venetians*. If history is seen in sacred terms, then historical paintings can become objects of devotion no less than the icon or the triptych. They pre-empt critical enquiry. In funerary monuments, and in sacred paintings, the doge is to be seen in the company of saints—

even in the presence of the Virgin and the crucified Christ. Thus the city is blessed by divine favour and protection.

The "myth of Venice" was therefore, in pictorial terms, endlessly being patched and redesigned. In the work of Giovanni Bellini the image of the Madonna and Child in the landscape was in part a sacred representation of the domination of Venice over the mainland. More than a century later, in the work of Veronese, the Queen of the Adriatic becomes the Queen of Heaven. Almost two centuries after that, Giambattista Tiepolo was depicting the homage of Neptune to Venetia. These images are all part of the same enterprise, a social and political project deeply imbued in the work of the Venetian artists.

We may seize upon the vigour and brilliance of Venetian colour as a token of cultural splendour. Volumes have been written on the subject. The painters of Venice laid one colour over another. They experimented with tonal harmonies, lending the world of the painting vibrancy and movement. It was an intuition about the nature of life. It was also a form of thought. When scarlet and green are joined, then power is created in the world. The words used to describe it are "rich," "sumptuous," "glowing," "radiant." That is why, from the mid-1470s, the Venetians became pioneers and innovators in the use of oil paint. The idea may have come from Flanders, but it reached its apotheosis in Venice. The Venetian artists worked from light to dark colour, building up layers of oil in which forms shimmered and dissolved. With oils there came light. The colours were said to "participate" one in another, and to produce the effect of harmony. The same might be said of the governance of Venice itself.

Vasari disapproved of the colorism of Venice. He noted that the artists worked immediately on canvas "without making a drawing"; he elucidated the general Venetian rule that "painting only with the colours themselves without any other work of drawing on paper was the best and true method." Giorgione never drew at all. It was, in abstract terms, the difference between *disegno* or drawing and *colorito* or colouring. Vasari considered *disegno* to be the "father" of art, architecture and sculpture; the Venetians believed *colorito* to be the mother of painting. They enjoyed the bliss of its warm and capacious embrace. Colour was soft and intimate and harmonious. That is why Venetian painting has often been associated with the depiction of the female nude. The naked woman can be said to be the invention of the Venetian artists of the sixteenth century. Willem de Kooning once remarked that "flesh was the reason that oil painting was invented." It may not be accurate, but it is suggestive. Where design was the product of intelligence and discipline, colour was the token of emotion and sensory pleasure. That is the setting in which English artists like William Blake and Joshua Reynolds expressed their disapproval of Venetian painting; they couched their criticisms in moral rather than aesthetic terms.

There are certain consequences of this method. It has been suggested that, as a result, the artists of Venice were less concerned with the "inner meaning" of the world than with the variety of surfaces and textures. There was no evident concern for ideality or profundity. But what do these resonant terms mean in the context of paint and canvas? As Wilde said, and Pater intimated, only superficial people do not judge by appearances. Venetian art is never learned, or even historically accurate, but instead elusive and evocative. The emotion and passion of the Venetian painters are to be found precisely in the revelation of the surface. Their profundity lies in the relationship between colours and tones. Are not colour, and light, and shade, the happenstance of the eye? As Aretino said of Titian, "he has the sense of things in his brush." There is optimism, and exuberance, in the air. There is a lightness of being manifest, for example, in the aerial figures of Tiepolo who skim the empyrean, uplifted by a wind of light. It might be depicted as Venetian gaiety, with the knowledge that eternity is in love with the productions of time. The constant refrain in Vasari's account of Titian is that the Venetian's work seems "alive"; it captures the movement and the appearance of life. It captures the effect of the transient moment. It is ardent. It has no sense of calculation or theory. It irradiates and envelops the spectator, so that it seems to acquire more than planar dimensions. It becomes part of the world.

There may on occasions be a certain straining after effect. That is the less pleasing aspect of the theatrical genius. There seems, in Venetian art, to be a taste for the extraordinary. Veronese and Tiepolo were condemned by some for creating vast and exuberant stage sets. There were also less than flattering comments upon the apparent gaudiness and over-elaboration of Venetian art. It was noted that Venetian painters liked to present what were almost inventories of goods, of fabrics, of ceramics, of furnishings, even of the latest fashions in dress. They had a tradesman's eye. They display tapestries and cloths and hangings like a hawker in a market. We may speak in almost a literal sense of the richness of the surface. Even the beggars of Tiepolo are sumptuously clothed. Joshua Reynolds concluded that "a mere elegance is their principal object, as they seem more willing to dazzle than to affect," with many Venetian works "painted with no other purpose than to be admired for their skill and expertness in the making of painting, and to make a parade of that art." Yet what is Venice but an endless parade?

28

The Eternal Feminine

Who is the woman on the balcony? It is a familiar Venetian motif. In the paintings of the public ceremonies of Venice, the women are to be seen looking down at the processions from a myriad of balconies and terraces. It is a sign, not of their presence, but of their seclusion. They are in the prison of the home. Yet in this ambiguous territory of the open balcony, half public and half sheltered, there are other possibilities. Byron wrote in *Beppo*:

> I said that like a picture by Giorgione
> Venetian women were, and so they *are*,
> Particularly seen from a balcony
> (For beauty's sometimes best set off afar).

The women are perhaps available; therefore they are all the more alluring. Turner painted many Venetian windows and balconies. His "Jessica," derived from *The Merchant of Venice*, is seen at an open window; the painting is accompanied by Turner's version of Shakespeare's text, "Jessica, shut the window, I say." The window is an opportunity for sexual display. It is a way of showing off the goods. The gaze is intrinsic to Venice. In Marco Polo's account of social life in China he congratulates the young ladies of that country for their modesty. "They do not," he wrote, "hang out at the windows scanning the faces of the passers-by or exhibiting their own faces to them." It is not hard to see the allusion here to his native city.

Venice has been called a feminine city. Henry James noted that "it is by living there from day to day that you feel the fullness of her charm; that you invite her exquisite influence to sink into your spirit. The creature varies like a nervous woman . . ." He then expatiates on the various "moods" of the city before reflecting on the fact that "you desire to embrace it, to caress it, to possess it." This, from a man who is never likely to have possessed any real woman, suggests the amount of displacement that Venice can provoke. It was considered to be licentious in action and attitude. It was, after all, the city of touch, the city of sight, the city of texture. It spoke openly to the senses. It revealed itself. The presence of water is also believed to encourage sensuality. Luxury, the stock in trade of the city, represents the apotheosis of sensuous pleasure. The lovers of the world came, and still come, here. It was known to be the capital of unlimited desire and unbridled indulgence; this was considered to be an expression, like its trade and its art, of its power. Venetian conversation was known for its lubriciousness and its vulgarity. The French poet, Guillaume Apollinaire, called Venice *"le sexe même de l'Europe."*

In poetry, and drama, Venice was often portrayed as the beloved woman, all the more charming for being constantly in peril. It could be said in Jungian terms that when the masculine identity of the city was lost at the time of its surrender to Bonaparte in 1797, it became wholly the feminine city enjoyed by exiles and tourists from the nineteenth century onwards. The journalism and literature of the last two centuries, for example, has included many representations of Venice as a "faded beauty." It has been celebrated for its power to seduce the visitor, to lure him or her into its uterine embrace. The narrow and tortuous streets themselves conjured up images of erotic chase and surprise. The city was invariably represented as a female symbol, whether as the Virgin in majesty or as Venus rising from the sea. It was stated in legend that Venice was founded on 25 March 421, the feast of the Annunciation, and on that same day Venus was in the ascendant. The city was doubly blessed. How could it not be invincible?

So Venice was the city of Venus. The goddess was born from the sea. She was intimately associated with the sea. It was said that she was created by the white spume that Neptune cast on the islands where the city arose, implying the deep sexuality of the city within the lagoon. For the traveller crossing the water from Marco Polo Airport the city does seem to rise up miraculously from the waves. It is one of the primal sights of the world. The word Venice conjures up Venus within its syllables. The naked Venus was represented by the city without walls. *"Venus* and *Venice* are Great Queens," James Howell wrote in his *Survey of the Signorie of Venice*, with a further pun on "quean" or

Giovanni Bellini's portrait of the early-sixteenth-century doge, Leonardo Loredan.
Note the sumptuousness of the dress and the strict serenity and reticence of his gaze.
This severity was part of the official imagery of the Venetian state.

A seventeenth-century painting, attributed to Joseph Heintz, depicting an audience with the doge in one of the chambers of the ducal palace. The government of Venice had perfected the art of self-presentation. Every political act had its own ceremonial. All the actions and decisions of the state were hallowed by tradition and sanctioned by divine authority.

Three eighteenth-century Venetian lawyers, depicted by Pietro Uberti. They were dressed for the part, and indeed every Venetian was clothed according to rank and status. The lawyers had an especial place in Venetian life, where it was believed that the people were more fond of talking than of doing. There was a saying to the effect that a Venetian law only lasted for seven days before being forgotten.

early-fifteenth-century tempera by
bello del Fiore depicting justice and the
hangels. The justice of Venice became
of the myths of Venice. It was deemed
be ancient. It was deemed to be divinely
ired. It was related, in ultimate form,
he judicial salvation of humankind.

A photograph of the lion's mouth in the
ducal palace, where evidence of scandal or
wrongdoing was posted. It was one of the
many mouths that became a post-box for
accusations against any Venetian. The lion's
mouth was of course a Venetian invention.
vas the mouth of the city, a capacious orifice
of whispers and rumours. It meant that there
was a general atmosphere of surveillance,
even in the most private quarters of the city.

DE NONTIE SECRETE
CONTRO CHI OCCVLTERA
GRATIE ET OFFICII,
Ô COLLVDERÀ PER
NASCONDER LA VERA
RENDITA D̄ ESSI

An eighteenth-century
engraving of Pozzi
Prison of Venice. The
"pozzi" were the wells of
Venice and this under-
ground dungeon, close
to the waters, was named
after them. It had a
reputation for noisome-
ness, with the suggestion
that it were better to be
entombed alive than to
be lowered into the hole.

Dream of Saint Ursula, painted by Vittore Carpaccio in 1495. The sacred interior is directly modelled upon Venetian interiors. Here are two double-arched windows, and two white Greek vases with a plant in each. The lower walls are covered with green cloth. There is a reading-table covered by a red cloth, and a very small three-legged stool covered with crimson cloth. On the table are a book and an hourglass.

Tailor by Pietro Longhi. This eighteenth-
century painting portrays one of the most
important figures in Venetian patrician society.
The Venetians had a keen eye for fashion and
striking colour. They manifested an almost
childlike delight in dressing up. The patrician
women of Venice, like the lady in the
painting, in particular loved sumptuous attire.

The Geography Lesson by Pietro
Longhi. The Venetians were expert,
and famous, cartographers. They
were looking for fixity and certainty,
in their watery world. They were
guided by the twin imperatives of
trade and of travel, both of them
embodied in the figure of Marco
Polo. In this painting a fashionable
patrician lady consults a globe with
a pair of compasses in her right
hand; an open atlas lies at her feet.

The Perfume Seller by Pietro Longhi.
Perfume was one of the many
luxuries in which Venice traded.
It might be expected, in a most
unnatural city, that everything
was scented—hats, shirts, socks,
handkerchiefs. Even the money
was scented. Note the ladies in
Carnival costume, a mantle of silk
or velvet that covered the head and
shoulders known as the *bauta*.

A wooden image of the Madonna of Mer[cy] carved and painted in the sixteenth centu[ry]. Images of the Virgin were displayed everyw[here] in Venice. Hers was a popular devotion. Th[ere] were many shrines on the corners of the [streets] with a votive lamp burning before the Vir[gin]. There was not a Venetian home, however humble, without its picture of the Virgin.

Madonna and Child Enthroned with Two Devout People, painted in the fourteenth century by Paolo Veneziano. This painting has the form and quality of an icon, and indeed images of the Madonna were venerated in Venice as the workers of miracles. The Virgin was also the archetypal "mother," in whose capacious embrace the sons and daughters of Venice could rest.

The Coronation of the Virgin by Giovanni Battista. The cult of Mary penetrated every aspect of Venetian society. There were more than three hundred altars, in the fifteenth century, devoted to the worship of the Virgin. Venice was the Virgin, too, because she had never been assaulted. She was inviolate and immaculate, protected by the waves of the sea like a precious girdle. Mary is peace. Peace is stability.

The Tempest painted by Giorgio da Castelfranco, otherwise known as Giorgione, in the early fifteenth century. In his study of this quintessentially Venetian artist the English critic, Walter Pater, declared that "all art constantly aspires towards the condition of music." In Venice oil paint can be liquid music.

Young Woman at Her Toilet by Giovanni Bellini. This painting of 1515 is evidence that the Venetians believed colour or *colorito* to be the mother of painting. They enjoyed the bliss of its warm and capacious embrace. Colour was soft and intimate and harmonious. That is why Venetian painting has often been associated with the depiction of the female nude. The naked woman can be said to be the invention of the Venetian artists of the sixteenth century.

Venus of Urbino by Titian (detail). The sensuousness and voluptuousness of Venetian art are most clearly seen in the female nudes of Titian. Planes and lines are supplanted by curves. His art is alive. It captures the movement and the appearance of life. It captures the effect of the transient moment. It is ardent. It has no sense of calculation or theory.

prostitute. Venus was queen of Love, and Venice was queen of Policy. Thus in the *Dunciad* Alexander Pope apostrophises the city:

> But chief her shrine where naked Venus keeps,
> And cupids ride the Lyon of the Deeps;
> Where, eased of Fleets, the Adriatic main
> Wafts the smooth Eunuch and enamour'd swain.

★

But Venice was also the city of the Virgin. Images of the Annunciation are to be found on the Rialto bridge, on the façade of Saint Mark's, and on the walls of the ducal palace, as well as diverse other places in the city. The worship of the Virgin entailed, even demanded, the glorification of the state. The endurance of the republic was another proof of its divine origin. Like the Virgin herself, it had been taken out of time. That is perhaps still its condition. In the paintings of Mary swooning before Gabriel, executed by Tintoretto and Titian as well as by a host of lesser Venetian artists, the Virgin is portrayed as a Venetian maiden in a typically Venetian house.

The cult of Mary penetrated every aspect of Venetian society. The doge attended mass at Saint Mark's, according to a sixteenth-century chronicler, "on all the days of Our Lady." There were processions and festivals, like that of the "Twelve Marys" which culminated in the ritual journey of twelve statues along the Grand Canal; the celebrations lasted for eight days. There were more than three hundred altars, in the fifteenth century, devoted to the worship of the Virgin. In the church of S. Maria Gloriosa there were no less than eight separate altars dedicated to her. The famous *nikopeia*, a Byzantine icon of the Virgin supposed to have been painted by Saint Luke himself, was carried in state around Saint Mark's Square on the feast of the Assumption; this relic became the palladium of the republic, its safeguard and defence, and is still to be found in the basilica of Saint Mark's. It was also a source of prophesying. It was said that if anyone wanted to know if a friend was alive or dead it was only necessary to place a lighted candle before the image; if the friend was alive the candle could not be put out by any wind but, if the friend was dead, its flame would be extinguished by the merest breath or sigh.

Venice was the Virgin, too, because she had never been assaulted.

She was inviolate and immaculate, protected by the waves of the sea like a precious girdle. Mary is peace. Peace is stability. James Howell, in his *Instructions and Directions for Forren Travell*, declared of Venice that "this beautious Maid hath bin often attempted to be vitiated, som have *courted* her, som *brib'd* her, som would have *forc'd* her, yet she hath still preserv'd her chastity intire." No other city had remained so pure for so long. The coronation of the Virgin in heaven by Christ was then employed, in painting and poetry, as the victorious image of Venice. The Queen of Heaven is also the Queen of the Sea, "like the dawn, fair as the moon, bright as the sun, terrible as an army with banners." As late as 1746, fifty-one years before the republic was destroyed, a Venetian friar, Fra Francesco, could utter a prayer to the divine protrectress. "O great Virgin, look down upon this City which you have elected here on Earth as the principal object of your Maternal Love."

Hers was a popular devotion. There were many shrines on the corners of the *calli*, with a votive lamp burning before the Virgin; these were maintained by the people of the immediate neighbourhood. There was not a Venetian home, however humble, without its picture of the Virgin. There were artists who did nothing else but execute cheap images of the Madonna known disparagingly as *madonnieri*. They were, however, only following in the tradition of Bellini. When the bells rang for the enunciation of the prayer "Ave Maria," the Venetians would fall down on their knees in the streets and squares.

Images of the Madonna were venerated as the workers of miracles; one icon in a niche on the exterior of an old house in the parish of S. Marina was believed to possess powers of healing. Votive lamps, candles and flowers were piled before it in ever greater profusion, and the crush of worshippers in the narrow street became so great that the statue had to be removed to an inner courtyard. On the site was erected the splendid jewel box of a church named S. Maria dei Miracoli. One evangelical Englishman of the early seventeenth century, William Bedell, wrote of the "multitude of idolatrous statues, pictures, reliquies in every corner, not of their churches onely, but houses, chambers, shoppes, yea the very streets . . . the sea it self is not free; they are in the shipps, boates and watermarks."

The Virgin was also the archetypal "mother," in whose capacious embrace the sons and daughters of Venice could rest. In Venetian folk songs the city is depicted as the mother. The mother is such a formidable figure in the Venetian imagination that there may be other and more remote forces at work. Is it possible that the Venetians yearned for the mother because their city was not built on the soil? Mother Earth did not bear it or rear it. In Jungian theory the mother represents the place of origin. But in a sense Venice had no place of origin. The mother also represents aspects of life and consciousness for which the Venetians longed, materiality and sensuousness among them. Could the art and culture of the city therefore be a form of recompense for a motherless state?

And then, as living proof of the efficacy of virgin love, there emerged in the sixteenth century a mysterious woman who became known in fact and legend as the Virgin of Venice. She appeared from nowhere. She began cooking for hundreds of homeless people, every day, in one of the public squares; she begged from the rich to feed the poor, and such was the force of her example that a permanent institution was found for the dispossessed named the *Ospedaletto dei Derelitti*. She uttered prophecies concerning Venice, the first of which began with the declaration that "The beginning of the Reformation of the world will take place in Venice." She called both herself and the city *Jerusalema Ponentina*, and as a result in sixteenth-century literature Venice became known as the New Jerusalem. The artificial city was also the archetypal city.

Michael Kelly, an Irish tenor who lived in Venice a century earlier than Henry James, declared that the city was "the paradise of women, and the Venetian woman worthy of a paradise." Note that for him it is a paradise of, rather than for, women. Mrs. Thrale, in the same century, remarked more astringently of the Venetian woman that "the government knows every pin she wears and where to find her at any moment of the day or night." This sense of watchfulness, and of close scrutiny, is part of the truth. The patrician women stayed out of sight; they appeared in public only on ritual occasions, and if they ever did stray from home they were accompanied by servants. They always wore veils. Theirs was an almost eastern seclusion.

The women of the middle and lower classes possessed considerably more freedom of movement. Peasant women brought their produce to market, and the "middling sort" (to use an ancient phrase) often worked in their husbands' shops or studios. Women are listed in the public records as linen-makers, bakers, spice-sellers and cobblers. It was often said that Venetian females were stronger, and hardier, than the males.

A Venetian wife was not considered legally to be part of her husband's family; she remained within the family of her father. Marriages were arranged between families rather than between individuals. In public documents the woman was known only in relation to her father or her husband. There were more severe restrictions. In a statute of the fifteenth century, adultery, on the woman's part, sometimes merited the death penalty.

Yet legal convention is not everything. It was widely reported that Venetian women commanded much authority at home. It is clear from testamentary bequests that, after the death of husbands or fathers, women of the upper and middle classes could often accumulate great wealth. There were also institutions, such as the singing schools, that consolidated the female presence in the city. The female servants or concubines of the Venetian priests often became the matriarchs of the local church, ministering to the community. There were also "wise women" and healers known in every neighbourhood. In such a superstitious place as Venice, they were fully employed.

There were many other social ties between women. The patrician females in one district, for example, might act as patrons to younger and poorer girls. The plays of Goldoni, and the memoirs of Venetian citizens, reveal a close-knit parish community of servants, neighbours and friends who would stand on the thresholds of their houses or cluster around the well-head to exchange news and gossip. There was not the sense of privacy that obtained in England or in northern Europe. If a husband was beating his wife unduly or unjustly, according to the standards of the time, he would become the target for abuse and even prosecution. In Venice it was the society that determined individual behaviour. The parish was essentially the female preserve in a male city; where the public areas were dominated by men, the private and domestic spaces were the realm of women. The parish was the place where they bartered, bought and sold, exchanged services. This arrangement satisfied all parties, and to a large extent maintained and consolidated the famous harmony of Venetian society.

Yet women had one crucial advantage. On marriage, they brought their dowries with them. There was always a dowry. It was the central feature of marital negotiation, in the marriages of the working people as well as of the nobles and merchants. One old Venetian song asks the question. "How many merchants got their start with dowries they were paid?" Yet although the dowries were in the control of the husband during his lifetime they were returned, at his death, to the wife to manage as she pleased. Most females became brides at the age of fourteen or fifteen; their spouses tended to be twenty-nine or thirty. Since the women were younger, they were likely to live longer. Some women became very rich. So even if they were invisible, they were still influential.

The more astute mothers used that wealth to increase the dowries of their own daughters, thus augmenting their eligibility. By the late fourteenth century, in fact, there was a phenomenon in Venice known as "dowry inflation"; the expenses, and the rewards, of a marriage were so great that only one girl in the family could be exchanged and only one male in the family could reap the rich harvest. As a result there was in the city a huge store of unmarried men and women; the men lived with their families, and the women characteristically were consigned to convents.

Herodotus wrote in the fifth century BC that the tribes of the Veneti were accustomed to sell their daughters at an open auction to the highest bidder. As late as the tenth century AD there are reports of annual matrimonial fairs in Venice itself, conducted on the feast day of Saint Mark (April 25) at S. Pietro di Castello, where the young girls came holding their dowries. It is an example of a persistent Venetian tradition, continued by other means. In a city of markets, unmarried women were the ultimate commodity. The merchandise of female flesh and money was exchanged for increase in nobility or political power. It was essentially a transfer from visible to invisible assets. When the newly married bride went in procession to her marital home, it was a way of making the exchange public and accountable. It represented the free circulation of capital through the body politic. Since the goods could be easily damaged, young girls were often placed in convents for a time; the nunneries were a kind of warehouse.

On the day for the signing of the marriage contract, in the families of the patricians, the bridegroom repaired to the house of his prospective father-in-law; when the groom and his friends were all gathered, the young girl, dressed according to convention in white gown and brilliant jewels, was paraded twice in a circle to the sound of fifes and trumpets. Then she proceeded into the courtyard, was greeted by all her female kin, and by means of a gondola was transported to all the convents where her relations were immured. The bride's gondoliers were obliged to wear scarlet stockings. Behind the walls of the convents the young girl was shown to the nuns, who may have had mixed feelings about the matter. On the dawn of the marriage day a small orchestra would play outside the bride's house as she prepared herself for the procession to the parish church. After the marriage ceremony itself there was a public feast, to which all the guests brought presents.

In the marriages of the other classes, there were customs no less rigorous. The aspiring groom would wear velvet or broadcloth; he would wear a dagger on his girdle, and he would be elaborately coiffed and perfumed. He first declared his love by singing under the window of the beloved. At a later date he would relay a formal request to the family. If he was judged suitable the two families would meet at dinner, and the two parties would exchange gifts of handkerchiefs and almond cakes. There was then a sequence of gifts, carefully regulated according to convention and superstition. At Christmas the man gave to the woman a *confettura* of fruit and a raw mustardseed, and on the feast-day of Saint Mark a button-hole of rosebuds; other gifts were given and received. There were prohibitions. No combs were to be exchanged, because they were the instruments of witches; scissors were also prohibited because they were a symbol of a cutting tongue. The pictures of saints, curiously enough, were forbidden; they were considered to be an evil augury.

The marriage day was always a Sunday, the other days deemed for a variety of reasons unfortunate. The bride's family was supposed to furnish the bedroom of the newly married couple; according to custom it had to contain a bed of walnut wood, six chairs, two chests of drawers and a looking glass. Walnut was the only permissible wood. It is an example of the stolid conservatism of the people. No race had a smaller propensity for social or political revolution. In this city, therefore, married life was not necessarily a pleasure; it was a solemn social and familial duty. Perhaps that is the source of the Venetian proverb that marriage comes from love in the way that vinegar comes from wine.

The relative anonymity of women in Venetian society is confirmed by the paucity of female portraiture. Tintoretto completed 139 portraits of men, and only 11 of women. There are 103 surviving portraits of men painted by Titian, with only 14 of women. Titian also left the women out of the family "group portraits" upon funerary monuments. This is not simply the consequence of a patriarchal society. There are plenty of examples of female portraiture in Florence, for example. This erasure of women from the public record is distinctively Venetian. It has to do with the authority invested in the state rather than in the individual. It has to do with the concept of restraint and control, characteristically seen as male virtues. That is why there are many female nudes, and far fewer women in full dress. The woman was considered to be the subject of sensuousness and delight rather than of serious attention. The women who do emerge on Venetian canvas are, in any case, almost always anonymous. They may not even be Venetian. So we have the paradox of the innumerable studies of the Virgin alongside the dearth of real women. And that may be the key. The image of the woman was idealised and sacred. It was not to be sullied by studies of the female in time.

When the wives of the merchants or richer shopkeepers did become visible, they were the subject of much comment. In the late fifteenth century Pietro Casola noted that "the women of Venice do their utmost, particularly the best-looking, to show their bosoms . . . when you view them, you become astonished that their clothes do not fall from their backs." He also observed the fact that "they neglect no artifice to improve their appearance." In 1597 Fynes Morrison described them as "tall with wood, fat with ragges, red with paint and white with chalke." The "wood" was that of large platform shoes. In an unnatural city, therefore, they were the image of unnaturalness. In the city of trade, fashion was a large element of consumption. In Venice female fashions changed faster than anywhere else in Italy.

For many travellers Venice was a vast open-air brothel, the "flesh shambles of Europe" as one visitor put it. Even Boccaccio, writing in the *Decameron*, which is not dainty, declared that the city was "the common receptacle for all sorts of wickedness." Roger Ascham, two centuries later, said that he saw in nine days "more libertie to sinne than I ever heard tell of in our noble Citie of London in nine yeare." It was remarked that the young men who went on the Grand Tour to Venice invariably returned with the present of syphilis to bequeath to future wives and children. Venice had no famous lovers, only famous roués and courtesans.

In the early seventeenth century Thomas Coryat estimated the number of prostitutes to be twenty thousand, "whereof many are esteemed so loose, that they are said to open their quivers to every arrow." It sounds like the overestimate of an outraged moralist, but the figure may not be so inflated. A century before, a Venetian chronicler, Marino Sanudo, estimated the number at 11,654. A great deal can happen in a hundred years, especially in a city that grew increasingly notorious for its incidence of lust and libertinism. Sanudo's figure is also to be placed in the context of a population in the early sixteenth century of one hundred thousand; on this evidence, approximately one in five Venetian women was a prostitute. It was reported that Venetian men preferred prostitutes to their wives. One explanation for their ubiquity may rest in the large proportion of unmarried patricians. Fornication, according to Fynes Morrison in the late sixteenth century, was "esteemed a small sinne and easily remitted by Confessors." Saint Nicholas was the patron saint both of sailors and of prostitutes, the two indispensable Venetian trades.

There were certain areas devoted to venality. There were brothels in certain favoured streets (some thirty or forty streets altogether) with a fair selection of them in the area of the city known as Castelletto. In one house thirteen prostitutes shared an apartment. The main centre was from the fifteenth century the Campo S. Cassiano, known as Carampane, close to the inns and hostels of the Rialto. Saint Mark's Square itself was used as a meat market by Venetian mothers—"every mother," a French traveller of the seventeenth century put it, "that is willing to be rid of her Daughter, carries her thither every Day as to a Market . . . nor are you oblig'd to buy a Pig in a Poke, for you may view and handle her as much as you will." In the memoirs of Casanova there is an account of just such a transaction. Casanova met a mother and daughter in a coffee house where, on understanding his intentions, the mother asked for money; her daughter was not to lose her virginity "without making a good profit out of it." Casanova offered ten sequins for her maidenhood, but wanted to assure himself first that he was not being swindled. And this, in his inimitable manner, he proceeded to do. This was an everyday story of Venetian folk.

The genteel courtesan, or "honest" courtesan, was a Venetian speciality. She was not to be confused with the common prostitute or *meretrice*. She was deemed to be a "free" woman, cultivated and refined. Coryat, who had become something of an expert in the flesh trade, described the courtesan as "decked with many chaines of gold and orient pearles like a second Cleopatra (but they are very little), divers gold rings beautified with diamonds and other costly stones, jewels in both her eares of great worth." He recommended that travellers carry with them a herb called "moly" or "Ulysses herb," a type of garlic, to ward off her attractions. But the merits of the courtesan were not merely carnal. She was disposed to intellectual conversation, to repartee and to poetry. She was considered to be the embodiment of the Renaissance ideal, of sensuality leading to the salon if not to sublimity. She also became the embodiment of a new type of woman, and a new form of female consciousness; the courtesans of Venice were significant figures, achieving a social and even intellectual dominance that other women could not equal. That is why they became notorious all over the European world. If Venice is indeed a female city, then it is best represented by the courtesan.

Sexuality also led to the painter's studio. The status of the unnamed women in Venetian paintings is not at all certain—although it must be the presumption, for example, that Titian's nudes were indeed courtesans. Images of the repentant whore, Mary Magdalen, may also have been based upon living originals. The ambassador of Ferrara in Venice revealed in a letter to his sovereign that "I suspect that the girls whom he often paints in different poses arouse his desires, which he then satisfies more than his limited strength permits."

The city was a market in most commodities, so why not in the human body? You had to be able to see what you were purchasing. "By the light of a candle," according to one Venetian proverb, "you do not judge women or paintings." A false mole placed by the nose indicated insatiability; in the cleft of the chin, it signified an adventuress.

The state itself condoned, and encouraged, these venereal practices. The prostitutes of the city had their own guild, and they traded under the auspices of the department of public health. The reasons for this toleration have more to do with money than with morals. The tax revenues from the earnings of prostitution were reputed to be worth twelve warships for the protection of the state. The prostitutes also encouraged what might be now called the tourist trade. The adult males would spend money on other commodities, thus increasing the general prosperity of the city. In the process the women helped to parade the famous "liberty" of Venice. They became part of the "myth of Venice." When Othello says to Desdemona, "I took you for that cunning whore of Venice," everyone in the audience would understand the allusion.

There were other social forces at work. It was argued that the presence of prostitutes meant that the more respectable women of the city were safer and purer. It was suggested, too, that the ready availability of women was a means of preserving order among the lower classes. They were also considered to be a guard against homosexuality. In the fifteenth century, in a period of sodomitical excess, the prostitutes of the city were ordered to bare their breasts as they leaned out of the windows. Some of them, however, decided to dress as young men.

The city was thereby also known as a centre of homosexuality and of homosexual prostitution. It was considered by many to be an "eastern" vice, and of course Venice was deeply indebted to eastern culture. It was believed that the men of Venice were, in the words of one eighteenth-century critic, "enervated and emasculated by the Softness of the Italian Musick." The tenderness and luxuriance of the city were considered to be corrupting. But there was also the ambiguous status of land and water, of frontier and mainland. Anyone of weak sensibility might thereby be aroused or stimulated into transgressing ordinary boundaries. The love of boys is reflected in Thomas Mann's *Death in Venice*, where the elderly Aschenbach is lured to his death by the sight of Tadzio. In the course of this novella Mann hits the perfect note to depict the sensuous genius of the city: "our adventurer felt his senses wooed by this voluptuousness of sight and sound, tasted his secret knowledge that the city sickened and hid its sickness for love of gain, and bent an ever more unbridled leer on the gondola that glided before him."

Venice appeals to those of ambiguous sexuality—Proust, James, "Baron" Corvo, Diaghilev, and many others. As the French writer, Paul Morand, put it in *Venises*, "in Venice homosexuality was nothing more than the most subtle of the fine arts." In the fourteenth and fifteenth centuries, however, it was the most feared and punished of all sex crimes. The shops of apothecaries, and pastry-makers, were denounced as centres of this criminal activity; the porticoes of certain churches, and the schools of gymnastics, were also considered to be dangerous. Venice was full of dark passage-ways, in any case, where Sodom might rise again. It was believed that homosexuality might "engulf" the city. It was believed that it was against nature and natural law, but then was not this also the case of Venice itself?

The city, in the eighteenth and nineteenth centuries, was being characterised as a whore. It was known for its apparent "decadence" and for its mercantile greed. The Queen of the Sea was transmogrified into "the whore of the Adriatic," just as Byzantium was once derided as "the whore of the Bosphorus." There seems to be something deeply troubling about cities of luxury and of sensation. In sixteenth-century London there was a brothel known simply as "Venice." The city was a decrepit courtesan, sporting its baubles of gold. The futurist, Marinetti, described it at the beginning of the twentieth century as "steeped in exotic lewdness." The English poet, Rupert Brooke, depicted it in a "tawdry and sensual middle-age." It was perhaps inevitable. A place that continually asserts that it is a sacred centre, a city of the Virgin Mary, will inevitably incur disgrace and disillusion. That reputation has since changed for the better. Is it a matter of degradation that Venice has become a museum city? There is no reason to believe so.

The pervasiveness, or at least the acceptance, of prostitution may have led to a change in public morals. By the late sixteenth and early seventeenth centuries, at least, there was a perceptibly more indulgent culture. When the women of Venice wore their dresses so low that their breasts were exposed, they may have been copying the example of their frailer sisters. The discipline of Venice, essential to its early survival, had relaxed.

In particular the presence of the confidant or lover, the *cicisbeo*, became noticeable in patrician circles. He became the intimate partner of the married woman; he, rather than her husband, escorted her to festivities or sat with her in the opera box. He dined with her, and travelled with her. He became her devoted servant. There was no remonstrance from the patrician husband. In fact the husband encouraged such a liaison; a wife without a gallant would lose prestige. Certain marriage contracts stipulated their presence in the household. The relationship may not have been a sexual one. It is possible that many of the *cicisbei* were in fact homosexual. But it was a sign that the desires of women were not altogether ignored.

The sensuousness of the women of Venice was the stuff of travellers' tales. "The women *kiss* better than those of any other nation," Byron wrote, "which is notorious, and is attributed to the worship of images, and the early habit of osculation induced thereby." So Romanist piety is associated with profligacy. This was nowhere more evident than in the reputation of Venetian nuns.

In 1581, there were two and a half thousand nuns in Venice; that figure rose or fell a little over the centuries, but it is good as an approximation. A century later, for example, there were three thousand nuns scattered across thirty-three convents in the city and seventeen in the lagoon. One of the reasons for these cowled and huddled women was the tendency of patrician families to place their unmarried daughters in captivity. Over 50 per cent of the patrician women of Venice ended in a convent. In theory they represented the purity and inviolability of the ruling class, but the outward appearance was deceptive. One seventeenth-century Venetian nun, Arcangela Tarabotti, wrote that nuns were created for "Reason of State"; too many dowries, in other words, would impoverish the ruling class. The young women were sacrificed for money. Their enforced seclusion also enhanced the financial status of the marriageable females. The cult of the Virgin sanctified what was essentially a commercial exchange assuring the exclusivity of the ruling class. Religion was a good investment. At the beginning of 1580 the senate declared that the nuns of the republic were "collected and preserved in those sacred sites as in a safe-deposit."

There is in any case something typically Venetian in the creation of these little prisons or little islands of unmarried females within the city. The ideal life, in the city of the lagoon, was one of enforced community. Convent life was itself modelled upon the constitution of the state, with a mixture of ruling powers including the abbess and a group of elders or "mothers of advice." Abbesses, like doges, were elected. Age, and money, were venerated. On the wall of one convent is inscribed the homily: "Hope and love keep us in this pleasant prison." It might have been the motto of the Venetian citizens.

The lives of the more saintly nuns were recorded in the annals of the city. In contemporary testimonies collected in such pious volumes as *The Necrology of Corpus Domini* there are many references to holy lives and deaths; there are references to "pure virgins" and the "purest virgins" whose demise is accompanied by visions and miracles. Virginity was a Venetian obsession. One of the enduring laments of the nuns on their deathbeds was the wish to be "released" from "this prison"; the prison is of course the prison of this life, but the wish is all the more heartfelt for issuing from the city of Venice.

For other nuns, the aura of pure virginity had evaporated long since. Some in fact earned a secondary living as prostitutes or courtesans. One English traveller, of the mid-eighteenth century, reported of the nuns that "their convents are light; the parlours of more extent and more open; the ladies have a gay air, fresher complexions, and a great deal of freedom in their behaviour and manner of talking . . . I need not add what is said of some greater liberties of the Venetian nuns." When officers were despatched to close down the convent of S. Zaccaria, in the summer of 1514, the nuns stoned them from the walls until they were forced to retreat. There were reports of fist fights between the sisters. An abbess and a sister duelled with daggers over the sexual favours of one gentleman. At times of Carnival the nuns dressed up as men. One of them was known for having ten lovers. On receipt of an expensive papal dispensation, the more fortunate among them were allowed to go "on leave" for weeks or even months at a time. Placards were put outside the gates of the convent, forbidding "all games, noises, tumults, speaking obscene words, committing improper acts, fouling the ground." Yet what was to be expected, in a society where most of the nuns were confined against their will? They were filled with resentment and with jealousy. Arcangela Tarabotti claimed that Venetian convents "represent a theatre where the darkest tragedies are performed . . . everything is vanity, perspective and shadow deceiving the eye." It is remarkable how all forms of Venetian life were, at one time or another, denounced or celebrated as "theatre."

A diarist of the first years of the sixteenth century, Girolamo Priuli, castigated the nuns as "public prostitutes" and the convents as "public whorehouses." Fifteen or more were nothing less than "bordellos." It was a common theme. A Franciscan preaching in the basilica of Saint Mark's, in 1497, declared that "whenever a foreign gentleman comes to this city, they show him the nunneries, scarcely nunneries at all in fact but brothels and public bordellos." To announce this fact from the pulpit suggests that it was recognised very widely indeed. The nuns of the Convertite convent, in the middle of the sixteenth century, were receiving gentlemen behind the walls; their father confessor was also their pimp. The male customers often dressed as nuns in order to escape detection. In his memoirs Casanova reports that he was offered the abbess of the Convent of the Virgins for one hundred sequins.

There seems to have been some deep consonance, in the public imagination, between the nun and the prostitute. Certain brothels were organised on the model of the convent. The madam was known as the "abbess" and the women were called "sisters," their behaviour just as severely restricted as any female taking the veil. Prostitutes were known to frequent convents and discourse with the nuns very freely. There was a camaraderie between them, established perhaps on their curious status within the Venetian community. Both nuns and prostitutes were "unkept," without spouses or families. They might merit the description of temple prostitutes, well known in the ancient world. In the modern world, Venice was their proper home.

29

What to Eat?

It is a truth universally stated that the food of Venice was, and is, not of the highest Italian quality. "The Venetians are wretched cooks," an Englishwoman wrote in 1771. Jan Morris, one of the most perceptive observers of Venetian life, remarked two centuries later that "Venetian cooking is undistinguished." The cuisine is, to say the least, limited. Yet this may be the fate of all small islands. The food of Corsica and Malta, for example, is well known for its poverty.

There can be no doubt about the quantity, if not the quality, of food in the city. Travellers noted the abundance of bread, of fruit, of vegetables, and of fish. Thomas Coryat, in the early seventeenth century, remarked upon "the marveilous affluence and exuberancy of all things tending to the sustenation of mans life" in Venice. He went on to describe "the Grapes, Peares, Apples, Plummes, Apricockes, Figges most excellent of three or foure sorts." The banqueting scenes of Venetian painting, particularly in the work of Veronese and Tintoretto, are well known for their munificence. There are endless Last Suppers in the Venetian canon. Tintoretto himself painted six of them. Here, at least in idealised form, is the epitome of what Coryat called "sustenation." The triumph of food represents the triumph of trade and of commerce. It can also be construed as the triumph of empire, with the colonies of Venice being obliged to provide comestibles to their "mother." In a city obsessed by show and the lure of the market, the colour of food was also important. Oysters were gilded. Saffron was indispensable in the kitchen as well as in the painter's studio.

Yet all was not as it seemed. One fifteenth-century observer, Canon Casola, remarked that although there was much fish in Venice he never saw a fine one nor ate a good one. There were fish everywhere, of course. But the fish in the canals were never eaten. It would be like eating rats.

The Venetians were in any case considered to be an abstemious people, easily pleased with plain fare. There was in the nineteenth century a typical Venetian invitation to dinner, *"venga a mangiar quattro risi con me,"* come and eat four grains of rice with me. They never gorged. They were rarely, if ever, incapacitated by drink. There was also a social as well as a dietary principle at work in Venetian temperance. To be drunk was to embarrass the whole city. Whereas in Paris or in London drunkenness was considered to be a necessary fact of life, reaping no dishonour, the tight community of Venice exacted its own particular control over the appetites of its citizens.

The patrician diet, through the centuries, was solid and unadventurous consisting of meat and vegetables such as cabbage and turnip, as well as fruit and cheese. The patricians had a fondness, however, for chocolate and ices; these may be classed as luxury items in a city of luxury goods. There were other forms of culinary display. The patricians of Venice were the first people in the world to use forks and glassware. Sauces were often sweet and cloying; but there was also a propensity for vinegar and other sharp ingredients. It is pertinent that the Venetians had a monopoly on the salt and sugar trades throughout Europe.

The people had their circuses, but they also needed their bread. It was one way of forestalling civic unrest for, in the words of one Venetian saying, "if your mouth is full, you can't say no." Many households possessed bread ovens. The government kept large stocks of millet in case of scarcity, but it was not much liked; its only virtue was its capacity for long storage. Maize was introduced, on *terra firma*, in 1539. It was a success. The Venetians, according to Fynes Morrison, "spend much on bread and oyle, and the very porters feede on most pure white bread . . . I never remember to have seen brown bread." Bread, and wine, were the only items about which the Venetians could be considered connoisseurs. White bread was a necessity of life.

There was also the food of the poor, the ubiquitous *polenta* consisting of white cornmeal mixed with water. It was, and is still, a dull and unappetising meal. Rice was introduced in the 1470s, thus creating the first dish of *risotto*. When the bell rang to summon workers to their midday meal, the general fare was fish, bread and fruit, with the occasional helping of pork or poultry. Pumpkin and melon were sold by the slice. The labouring people were inclined towards raw fruit and vegetables, disdained by the more refined elements of the population; raw food was considered to be bad for the health. On the Venetian mainland, beans and rye were the typical foodstuffs of the poor. It is claimed that such a diet kept the peasants weak and compliant.

The Venetians had a proverb to the effect that God would take water away from the man who did not like wine. There was a large variety of wines in Venice throughout its history, although by the sixteenth century much of it came from the Venetian colonies of Crete and Cyprus. Yet foreign observers tended to be dismissive of the quality of Venetian wine in general, one of them comparing it to vinegar and water. That cannot be said of the champagne of Venice, known as *prosecco*, from a white grape grown in the Veneto region. Venetians were, and still are, generally content with a small glass of white or red wine, known as *ombra*, taken with modest quantities of cheese or green olives. It is an ancient drink, its name meaning "shade." It refers to a custom of the late fourteenth century, when wine-sellers of Saint Mark's Square moved their stalls out of the sun into the shadow of the campanile. It was a way of attracting custom.

Venice has always been more famous for its cafés than for its restaurants. In the eighteenth century they were calculated to number two hundred, with thirty-five in Saint Mark's Square itself. Venice was in fact one of the first cities in Europe to favour coffee, which was borrowed from the Turks of Constantinople. Patrician ladies had a favourite café, as did their husbands; government secretaries frequented another establishment and, as in London, there were coffee shops for all the various occupations of the city. The most celebrated of them, Florian's, opened its doors in 1720 under the name of "Venice Triumphant" and has been doing business ever since. The Venetians seemed to favour entertaining out of doors, with cups of coffee and cups of chocolate, with glasses of lemonade and syrup. The people could also sit and drink in the barber's shop or the bookshop; the shops of apothecaries, or pharmacists, were also popular for the exchange of gossip and news. The city was constantly watching, and talking about, itself.

There were taverns and wine-shops or *malvasie* for nobles and merchants, gondoliers and workmen. In the morning they were the haunts of those coming for a small glass of wine; in the evening they became the eating places of the poorer people. They could also act as pawn-dealerships and gambling dens. The government was always suspicious of even moderate gatherings of people, fearing subversion of the state, and spies were employed in the more famous taverns and hotels such as the Black Eagle and the White Lion. The senate also legislated to reduce the size of such places. As a result there were many that could only hold five or six customers at any one time. The casks of wine were stacked at the back while, above them, was placed an image of the Virgin with its ever-renewed light.

IX

Sacred City

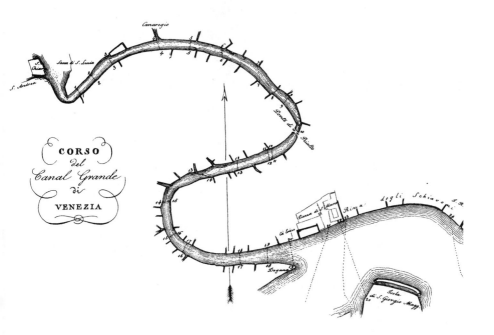

CORSO
del
Canal Grande
di
VENEZIA

30

Divine and Infernal

Venice was the gate of heaven. At a time of religious crisis, in the middle of the sixteenth century, a cleric wrote that Christ was about to return to Italy and "I believe Venice will be the door." The ranks of the rulers and the judges of Venice were compared to the numbers and dominions of angels and archangels; it was the nature of the city to inspire its citizens with the *aeterna beatitudo, quae in visione Dei consistit*, the eternal happiness which lies in the vision of the godhead. This is the context for Tintoretto's great vision of paradise in the ducal palace. It was proclaimed, if not believed, that the constitution and laws of the city had been "sent by God"; the success and expansion of the Venetian Empire were then seen as the working-out of divine providence in the world of time. The very survival of a city upon the waters was a miracle. The Venetians themselves referred to their home as "our holy earth" or as "the holy city."

In 1581 the Venetian writer Francesco Sansovino declared that Venice was "revered by everyone as a sacred thing on earth to be worshipped, were this possible." It was not permissible of course; it might have provoked comparison with the Israelites worshipping the Golden Calf (one of the favourite subjects of Venetian painting). Yet it was not altogether a novel doctrine. In the ancient religion of Mesopotamia, for example, the city was considered to be the essence of the divine. It need hardly be added that such worship encourages despotism and authoritarianism on a very grand scale. That is why the identity of church and state in Venice was so powerful. It allowed the governors of Venice to maintain their distance from the jurisdiction of Rome and the Roman pontiff. The doge was the pope of Venice, and the senators his cardinals. On Palm Sunday the doge released white doves from the doorway of Saint Mark's in commemoration of the Ark's coming to rest after the Flood. It was an invocation of the city's own rescue from the waves. But was it a religious, rather than a political, ritual? The distinction, in Venetian culture, did not apply.

It was an accident of geography, perhaps, that this was the city from which the pilgrims sailed to the Holy Land. The pilgrims came to Venice to purchase supplies and provisions for the long voyage, and slowly the city itself was seen to be an integral part of their holy journey. They participated in all the sacred rituals of the Venetian Church. They worshipped at the same oratories and chapels. They venerated the same icons. The shrine of Saint Mark attracted many thousands, and hundreds of thousands, of foreign visitors. The tomb smelled of spices, the Venetian trade. The intimate association between Venice and the East also helped to convey the image of the city as part of the Holy Land, an intimation or glimpse of the divine, worthy of pilgrimage in its own right.

The city was a sacred space containing many intimations of the spiritual world. There were innumerable images of the saints, as well as the Virgin, in its dark passage-ways. The candles or lamps in front of them created a luminous area, banishing vice and crime. There were more than five hundred street shrines, or *capitelli*; but their purpose was political as well as religious. They were a means of curbing disorder among the people. The Virgin would not look kindly down upon civic unrest. The archangel Michael guards the south-west corner of the ducal palace with his drawn sword. The landscape of the city is dominated by bell towers ringing out "Holy! Holy! Holy!" The churches of Venice, like the convents and monasteries, were all carefully sited. The church of S. Maria dei Miracoli, for example, is placed on the frontiers of the two northern districts of Cannaregio and Castello. One of the oldest churches in Venice, that of S. Giacomo, is situated at the very centre of the Rialto market. It was here that commercial contracts were signed. Machiavelli wrote that "we Italians are corrupt and irreligious beyond all others." That was not true of the Venetians. They were corrupt and religious.

Where there is the divine, there is always the infernal. One cannot exist without the other. There were many folk stories of the devil walking confidently over the bridges and along the *calli* of the city. He was reported to have taunted the mason working on the Rialto bridge, for example, with the claim that no one could build so wide an arch of stone. He offered to perform the work in exchange for the soul of the first person who crossed the bridge. It turned out to be the mason's infant son.

Venice was a sacred text to be read and meditated. In the fourteenth and fifteenth centuries the city was first seen as a totality, to be carefully structured. It had survived, by the exercise of the divine will, and now had to be sculptured. The body of Saint Mark, supposedly preserved in the basilica, was the central point of the configuration between the ducal palace, the market and the Arsenal. This was the sacred geometry of Venetian power.

It is noticeable, in Venetian painting, that the miracles of the Scriptures often take place in a Venetian setting. For Tintoretto the events of the New Testament were seen as an aspect of familiar Venetian life. In a manual of devotion written for young Venetian girls, the *Garden of Prayer*, the author instructs his readers to "take a city that is well known to you . . . hold in your mind the principal places where the episodes of the Passion would have taken place." So the agonies of Christ were to be pictured along the *calli* and within the *campi* of *la Serenissima*.

It was itself a city of miracles. No city in Europe, with the possible exception of Rome, has witnessed so many. Every parish had its own sacred events. The compiler of the *Cronica Venetiarum*, writing in the middle of the fourteenth century, describes miracles and portents in the same spirit of verisimilitude as more mundane events and actions. Miracles were announced with impressive frequency by the authorities of the city. It was another way of reaffirming its sacred destiny. An angel rescued a workman falling from the scaffolding around the basilica of Saint Mark's. A holy virgin walked across the water of the Grand Canal. A slave was rescued from condign punishment in Saint Mark's Square by Saint Mark himself. The same saint, together with his brothers in Christ Nicholas and George, exorcised demons threatening the city with flood. Miraculous events became particularly common in the 1480s, just after the end of the Turkish wars in which Venice lost its domination of the Mediterranean. In these miracles the Virgin became the agent of divine intervention, thus in theory restoring the status of Venice as "Queen of the Sea."

Carpaccio painted "Miracle of the Relic of the True Cross on the Rialto Bridge" when a lunatic was healed by the presence of the relic. There was the miracle at S. Lio in the early years of the fifteenth century, when in the parish of that name a holy relic would not be associated with the funeral of a wicked man. It grew so heavy that it could not be carried over the threshold of the church. Giovanni Mansueti completed a painting of the event in 1494. It is still possible to recognise the site, and certain of the larger houses, in 2009. That is another Venetian miracle.

The sacred sites of Venice can be enumerated. The first of them, by common consent, must be the basilica. It is the umbilicus, the central point, the core. It is the place where the divine and human meet. In the beginning there had been another church on this site dedicated to Saint Theodore but, when the supposed body of Saint Mark arrived in the lagoons, everything changed. As soon as the relics arrived in 829, a church with a wooden roof or dome was raised on the model of the church of the Holy Apostles in Constantinople. The church was largely destroyed by fire in 976, but was subsequently restored. The final reconstruction, vaulted and built in brick, assuming the shape of the basilica still before us, was undertaken in the second half of the eleventh century. The fact that it was based upon a model already five hundred years old was a material blessing. It emphasised the supposed antiquity of the Venetian religious tradition. The city had no true religious history of its own; so it borrowed or adapted what it saw. The undulating pavement of the basilica, for example, was not an accident or a mistake. It was deliberately modelled on the floor of the church of S. Giovanni Evangelista in Ravenna, built in the fifth century. The pavement was to rise and fall "as if agitated by winds and to present the likeness of a storm." It was supposed to invoke the position of Venice upon perilous waters.

   In the thirteenth century a programme of mosaics was formally introduced, taking their example from the church of the Holy Apostles but introducing specifically Venetian motifs. These in turn were erased, restored only in the seventeenth century. In the fourteenth century the façade of the basilica was partially transformed in Gothic style. So the church arose by a process of accretion and accommodation, encrusted and adapted over the centuries. Marbles and statues—bought or stolen, it made no difference—were attached to it in almost haphazard fashion.

   The basilica is unique. To some it has a Moorish air; to others it appears to be a relic of Byzantium; others admire the window traceries and the great screen as miracles of the Gothic style. The derivations do not matter. It is possibly the most beautiful building in the world. It rises from the square like an apparition wreathed in clouds of jasper and porphyry, of opal and of gold. As a piece of chromatic decoration, it is unsurpassed. The pillars and porches and domes rise one above the other, ornamented with mosaics and sculptures that tell stories from the divine and human worlds. The play of light and dark across the façade is increased by the deployment of closely ranged columns. It exudes a kind of barbaric splendour.

Upon entering the interior, the visitor is lost in twilight. It is like some great cavern beneath the sea filled with sunken treasure. It has been shaped in the form of a cross, but there are shadowy aisles and alcoves lit by the flame of a candle or the gleaming of an icon. There are five hundred columns of porphyry, serpentine and alabaster. The roof is a sea of gold. The mosaic work, covering forty thousand square feet (3,700 sq. m), is a skein of iridescence thrown across the walls and arches. Divine light was more significant than natural light. The interior is filled with silks and enamels, gold and rock crystal, as if it were itself a bejewelled reliquary. It is a church of merchants suffering from what one English traveller described as "religious horror," in the sense of awe and dread. It is a church of material wealth and costly display. It is also a church of rare commodities. Here is the icon of the Virgin painted by Saint Luke. Here is the stone of granite from Mount Tabor, on which Christ preached to the people. Here is the executioner's block, stained with the blood of Saint John the Baptist. Here are marble columns from the Temple of Solomon. Here, in the chapel of Saint Isidore, lies Saint Mark. It is the perfect stage setting for ritual devotion.

In its present form the campanile or bell tower of the basilica was erected at the very beginning of the sixteenth century, taking the place of an old watchtower that had stood on the site for seven hundred years. There had been an attempt to build a new bell tower in 1008, but the structure had sunk into the ground. The present campanile was used as a vantage point from which to view the city, and a defensive station from which to scan the sea. It was continually being struck by lightning until the introduction of a lightning rod, but there was no disaster worse than that of Bastille Day, 1902, when it buckled and folded upon itself, neatly imploding into a large pile of rubble. It fell, as the Venetians said at the time, "like a gentleman." There were no fatalities, except that of the caretaker's cat. The largest of the bells, "La Marangona," fell two hundred feet (60 m) without incurring any damage. It was then determined to rebuild the tower *dov'era, com'era*— where it is and how it is. Ten years later the campanile rose again, indistinguishable in its outward appearance from its predecessor. That was the Venetian way. It is said that if the visitor arrives in Venice to the sound of "La Marangona," then that visitor has the soul of some dead Venetian being welcomed back to the city.

The palace of the doge, beside the basilica itself, is the other sacred site of the city. Proust's grandmother journeyed to Venice, when she was dying, simply in order to visit this place. Proust wrote that "she would not have attached so much importance to that joy she got from the ducal palace if she had not felt it to be one of those joys which, in a way we imperfectly understand, outlive the act of dying, and appeal to some portion of us which is not, at the least, under the dominion of death."

The original palace was erected at the beginning of the ninth century, but was destroyed in 976 during one of the few civil riots in Venetian history. It was continually enlarged and adapted; wings were pulled down and constructed; halls and passages and galleries were introduced. In the early fourteenth century, according to the narrative of Ruskin's *Stones of Venice*, the original "Byzantine Palace" was supplanted by a "Gothic Palace," the latter coinciding with the final triumph of the aristocratic polity. This is the building that faces the *bacino* or pool. It became the home of government. Architecture has always been a statement of power. This Gothic palace itself grew and grew, with new halls and saloons to accommodate the increased complexity of the government apparatus. Ruskin compared it to a "serpent" that eventually bites its own tail.

The apartments of the doge were still within what was known as "the old palace" or, in other words, the decayed Byzantine original. In 1422 it was decreed that it should be pulled down and what Ruskin called the "Renaissance Palace" erected in its place. Ruskin believed that the demolition of the Byzantine structure was an act of vandalism, dating from its removal "the knell of the architecture of Venice, and of Venice itself." His eschatological tendencies may not now find favour.

Yet by degrees the whole complex took the form that can still be seen. It was gutted by fires, endlessly restored and adapted; but it survived. The ducal palace, as it is now, took its final shape in the middle of the sixteenth century. Like the city and the government, the development of the palace was gradual and pragmatic.

It was not the home of the doge only. It was the site of government, with chambers for the great council and the senate and the multi-tudinous committees that made up the Venetian state. It housed the prisons and the stables. What is most remarkable, however, is what is *not* there. It is not defended. There are no walls or barbicans. A wall was thrown around it at the beginning of the tenth century, in response to the threat of Hungarian invasion, but that was demolished two centuries later. The government was considered secure, both from internal and external enemies.

The palace is, or seems to be, a miracle of lightness. The European observer is accustomed to heaviness of foundation and lightness of summit. In the ducal palace the expectation is disappointed. The long double-storeyed arcade, at ground level, creates the illusion of space and airiness. The deep shadows within the arcade act as a metaphor for the foundation. The darkness has the illusion of volume. The upper part of the façade is made up of tiny marble pieces of pink and white and grey, in the pattern of damask, shimmering in the light of the lagoon. The whole structure has the exact proportions of a cube, but it is a cube of light. The palace might be said to float like the city itself. It is not, in Proust's phrase, under the dominion of death.

Two great fires, of 1574 and 1577, enveloped the halls of the senate and great council. The works of Bellini, Titian, Tintoretto, and others, were destroyed. Yet their destruction provided, as it were, a blank canvas on which the late sixteenth-century myth-makers of Venice could work their wonders. A new sequence of paintings was com-missioned. The official artists of the time (among them Veronese and the now elderly Tintoretto) did not invent any of the artistic programmes. They submitted to the wishes of their political masters. They were ordered to re-create the ideology of the ruling class in triumphal terms. This they proceeded to do. They invented a completely imaginary history of the city. They defined its power. They celebrated its virtues. They deliberately copied the Venetian art of preceding centuries in order to project the idea of enduring identity;

lost images were restored, old symbols reaffirmed. It is the essence of the conservatism of Venice. The artists depicted the battles won by Venice. They painted votive images of deceased doges. They proclaimed Venice as *Justitia* and *Liberator*. The works were not considered as individual masterpieces, but as parts of a coherent whole. The paintings in the palace represented the ethos of the Venetian community in a more embracing sense. The project lasted for twenty years. It was an allegory of the state itself.

Before the palace lies Saint Mark's Square, perhaps more properly known as the Piazza. It is the only true square in Venice. It was once the site of two islands, facing the Bacino di S. Marco, separated by a narrow canal. Much of the present square was a grass field on an island named "Il Morso" for its hard and tenacious soil. This was the site of the first ducal palace and the ducal chapel. On the same island were two churches, and a hospice for pilgrims travelling to the Holy Land. They were the nucleus from which the present square grew. It was decided that a place of assembly should be erected for the Venetian commune. It was necessary to build courts also for the administration of justice. So power, and authority, gradually accrued to the site.

In the twelfth century the Square was enlarged approximately to its present size. The trees and vines were cleared, and the new site was paved with bright brick of herringbone pattern. The new pavement covered the old canal that had once divided the two small islands. (Its waters still run beneath the present square.) Now all was a coherent whole. Covered walks were built around three sides of the square, against which houses were constructed, leaving the basilica clear to sight. The effect, according to Marino Sanudo, was "as if one were at a theatre." The effect had not been planned by one architect or designer; it was a miracle of collective will.

The importance of the Square was sealed when two great columns, brought from Constantinople in 1171, were placed on the edge of the *bacino*. There was a third, but it fell into the lagoon. The remaining two have stood there ever since, surmounted by a lion and an image of Saint Theodore. The columns and the basilica, however, are the only surviving remnants of the medieval arena—with the possible exception of the pigeons, or doves as some prefer to call them. The birds have haunted the Square since its beginnings.

Shops appeared under the newly built arcades, in the twelfth century, and in Venetian fashion proceeded to monopolise the territory. The square became a place of trade. Sheds and stalls of every description, selling food and merchandise, littered the site. The stalls of money-changers were set up beneath the campanile; a meat market conducted its business beneath the windows of the ducal palace. Rows of shops selling cheese and salami and fruit once stood where now the tourists line up for the *vaporetti*, the buses that run upon the water. Where the famous Library now stands, there were bakeries. In the piazzetta, the smaller part of the Square facing the lagoon, five hostelries competed for custom. The pillars of the ducal palace were used as public latrines, and it was noticed that the patricians would lift their gowns and paddle through the pools of urine without complaint. In fact it was observed that the Venetians relieved themselves wherever and whenever they wished.

And of course beggars congregated beneath the arcades, displaying their wounds and diseases. It was the space for the great religious and civic ceremonies of the city; it also was the arena for bull-fights and horse races. It was the place of punishment. Prisoners were hung in cages from the campanile, and beheadings were carried out between the two monumental pillars. In the summer of 1505 the gibbet was removed from the Square, and three flagpoles put in its place before the basilica. That was the final touch for the official canonisation of the space. Between the ducal palace and the basilica stood the stone of proclamation, a truncated pillar of porphyry from which the doge pronounced judicial sentence. It was like any large medieval town, in other words, except for the overwhelming majesty of the site itself. This order and this disorder, this beauty and this squalor, are the key to any understanding of fourteenth- and fifteenth-century Venice.

In the 1530s one architect above all others modelled the Square as it now appears. Jacopo Sansovino was charged with the task of creating a classical space out of the medieval confusion. He built the church of S. Geminiano, on the opposite side of the Square from the basilica, demolished later on the orders of Napoleon. He constructed the great Library and the Mint that faces the bacino; he also re-created the loggetta at the base of the campanile. He found a square of brick and turned it into marble. The Square was, for Thomas Coryat, "of that admirable and incomparable beauty, that I thinke no place whatsoever may compare with it."

It was the central point of the city, the place to which all of the tourists were directed or towards which they drifted. An Englishman of the eighteenth century noted "a mixed multitude of Jews, Turks, and Christians; lawyers, knaves, and pickpockets; mountebanks, old women and physicians . . . people of every character and condition." After his victory in 1797 Bonaparte razed the church of S. Geminiano in order to build a third range of stately apartments; this completed the trilateral shape of the Square in triumphant form. He also removed the bronze horses and dispatched them to Paris. They were returned in 1815.

Throughout the centuries of turmoil it remained the place of meeting and assignation. Ruskin's wife, Effie, described it as a "vast drawing room lighted enough by the gas from the arcades all around the Square" where wandered "a dense crowd in the centre of men, women, children, soldiers." Effie Ruskin's husband saw it in more apocalyptic terms. He described it as "filled with the madness of the whole earth," filled with "idle Venetians of the middle classes" and military bands; in the recesses of the arcades lay "men of the lowest classes, unemployed and listless" while around them begged the urchins of the city "full of desperation and stony depravity." And this is what aroused his anger—not one Venetian ever glanced at the wonderful basilica. "You will not see an eye lifted to it, nor a countenance brightened by it." It is still one of the paradoxes of the city. It has been often said that, if you sit at a table in Florian's or Quadri's for long enough, everyone you have known in your life will eventually pass by. If it were once the case for the middle-class Englishman or German, it is not the case now. You will see only knots of tourists from every country under the sun.

31

Of Belief

Pope Gregory XIII once confessed that "I am pope everywhere except in Venice." A Venetian historian, in 1483, reminded the cardinals of his city that "Venice was their true parent, and the Church only a step-mother." That is why Venetian cardinals in Rome were often considered by the papal authorities to be little better than spies. Because the bones of Saint Mark were preserved in the heart of Venice, the city claimed an apostolic status equal to that of Rome. Its power and authority effectively meant that it had inherited the mantle of the Holy Christian Empire.

So it was a very Venetian church, overwhelmingly subject to state control. The doge was considered to be a sacred no less than a secular figure. When the bishops of Venetian colonies on the *terra firma* received instructions directly from the pope, they relayed them to the council of ten for approval. Members of the clergy were forbidden entry into any of the state archives, and those patrician families who held ecclesiastical benefices were prohibited from involvement in ecclesiastical affairs. It was believed and widely stated that the supposed divine origins of the city meant that it had received its powers directly from God, and was simply retaining the traditional authority of state over church.

The state supervised all matters pertaining to the Church, including the content of sermons and the administration of the mass. Bishops were appointed by the senate. The bishops themselves never questioned the process, in any case, since all of them came from patrician families. No churches could be erected without the permission of the government. In the official documents of every period there are references to "*our* see of Grado" or "*our* bishops of Olivolo." There was also such a thing as state theology. It was painted on the walls of the ducal palace. The state had its own liturgy, quite different from that in use elsewhere, with texts that included homage to Mark above all other saints. Heresy, therefore, was principally a crime against the state. It has been suggested that the Venetian Church was inspired by the Byzantine state Church, in which religion was seen as an aspect of proper governance, but it was also directly rooted in the experience and situation of the city. It was not part of the Italian mainland. It had created its institutions *ab novo*. It refused to submit to any external authority.

So Venetian religion was a very potent and efficient mingling of superstition with practicality and good sense. When an Italian movement of fervent proselytisers, known as the Bianchi for the white robes that they wore, came to Venice in 1399 they were forbidden to process or preach in public; they were spreading an apocalyptic message on the eve of a new century. When one group did try to file into the Square before the church of S. Zanipolo, the leaders of the council of ten were waiting for them. They wrenched the crucifix from the hand of the principal worshipper, tore off its arms and threw the pieces of the cross at the others. The procession was then broken up, according to a chronicle, "with many insults and injuries." That is how the Venetian authorities dealt with any threatening minority. They could not endure dissent or disorder, however pious in origin.

Venice, however, did tolerate those who posed no threat. At the time of religious innovation in the sixteenth century, the authorities were not opposed to the presence of Protestant students at the University of Padua. Venice became known as a haven for European reformers who had fled the more orthodox kingdoms of the north. The city had always been open to travellers and merchants from the rest of the world. So it had no problem with foreign faiths. It had important trade relations with heretical nations such as England and the Netherlands. Commerce came first. Venice had to remain an open port. The German merchants, lodged in the centre of the city, were Lutherans. It made no difference. The English ambassador to Venice at the time of James I, Henry Wotton, believed that the city might in fact join the reforming nations. That was wishful thinking. Venice may have distrusted the papacy but it would never cease to believe in the Virgin and the intercession of the saints. It was unthinkable. They would have liked to reform the Catholic Church, of course. They would have liked to reform the pope out of existence.

The people were in any case excessively devout. They evinced what

Defoe called "prodigious stupid Bigotry." In a more kindly tone Philippe de Commynes wrote that "I believe God blesses them for the reverence they show in the service of the Church." There were more than a hundred churches from which to choose. There were statues and pictures at every corner. The aisles were filled with worshippers. There were endless processions, each with its own particular form of ritual—the procession of Corpus Christi, when a senator and a poor person walked side by side ahead of the others and rose petals were strewn across the route; the procession of Good Friday, when lamps and torches and candles were placed in front of the great houses; the ceremony of Palm Sunday, when a myriad of pigeons was set free in front of the basilica; the procession of the doge to the convent of S. Zaccaria on Easter Day. Each ceremony had its own social, as well as religious, purpose. A culture of public processions is very common within authoritarian societies.

Effie Ruskin remarked of the ordinary Venetians that "they don't seem to believe anything particularly, but are superstitious by habit." That is possibly the best definition of Venetian piety. When an Englishman, visiting a Venetian church, did not kneel at the elevation of the host he was taken to task by a Venetian senator. The Englishman said that he did not subscribe to the doctrine of the real presence, to which the Venetian replied, "No more do I. But kneel as I do, or else leave the church." The devotion of the people was also the greatest possible bulwark for the state itself.

The use of icons and relics meant that such devotion knitted all of the people together in a bond of piety. The body of Saint Mark guarded all of the citizens. But there were many other saints to be touched and seen. There were, at the last count, more than fifty dead saints in defensive formation. They were considered, in a city without walls, to be essential. One monastery possessed the relics of twelve separate saints. It is surprising that there were enough saints to go round. In November 1981 two gunmen rushed into the church of S. Geremia, ordering the priest and congregation to lie on the floor. They then seized the mummified skeleton of Saint Lucy and stuffed it into a sack. The head of the saint was broken off, unfortunately, and rolled into the aisle. The silver death mask of Lucy was also left behind. A month later the poor saint was found discarded in a hunting lodge near Venice.

The Venetians greatly preferred what might be called "full body" relics. They needed the whole body because insecurity in the spirit demands completeness. Yet in exceptional circumstances an arm or a leg would do. The head of Saint George was lodged in the Benedictine monastery on the island of S. Giorgio Maggiore. His arm had arrived some decades before. There were pieces of Saints Peter, Matthew, Bartholomew and John the Evangelist, scattered through the various shrines of the city. The head of the prophet Jonah, saved from the belly of the whale, had also somehow made its way to the city of the lagoon. The body of Saint Tarasius was doubly celebrated because it had miraculously escaped fragmentation; two robbers from another city had tried to remove his teeth, but the saint refused to yield them up. The whole thing came to the city. When a Dutch traveller of the seventeenth century went to gaze upon one piece of sacred flesh, he found it "whole and undamaged, with her breasts and her carnal appearance looking as though it was smoke-dried meat, feet and hands, since this holy body had been in the fire." Or, perhaps, some enterprising merchant had burnt another body so that it might pass as the genuine article.

Saint Isidore of Chios was buried in the doges' chapel. The head and the body of Saint Barbara, unfortunately separated, were stolen from their shrine in Constantinople and transported to the lagoon. When the Venetians were forced out of Crete by the Turks, they took the body of Saint Titus with them. Two Venetian merchants smuggled the body of Saint Simeon the Prophet from a church near Saint Sophia; it was reported that they had encountered "some difficulty."

It was said that whenever a Venetian entered a famous shrine the first question would always be "What can we steal for Saint Mark's?" Monks of foreign monasteries were bribed to give up their honoured dead. Other saints were simply pillaged. So the basilica itself was compared to the house of a pirate retired from business. Of course the thefts were excused under the guise of piety. It was said that these translations—we may call them borrowings—succeeded because the saints themselves wished to be enthroned in Venice. They wished to receive more prayers and more veneration. Otherwise they would have refused to leave their original shrines. Saints can be very stubborn. So the arrival of a purloined relic in the city was yet another sign of God's grace. It was a very convenient argument.

The relic-hunters were merchants under another name. The relics were in a sense also merchandise. They were collectable. They were a source of revenue from the religious tourists coming to the city. They were in themselves valuable—the crown of thorns that had once rested on Christ's head was valued at the sum of seventy thousand ducats.

In the basilica of Saint Mark's was a vessel containing drops of the blood that Christ shed while enduring the agony in the garden of Gethsemane. There were thorns from the crown, fragments of the true cross, and a portion of the flagellation pillar on which the Saviour had been bound. Here also are to be found portions of the hair, and a sample of the milk, of the Holy Virgin. The basilica is an enormous reliquary. In this way the Venetian Church could be associated in spirit with the heroes and heroines of early Christianity. By forging relics, as often happened, the Venetian authorities were inventing a religious history for themselves. But they could not supply the native saints to close the deal. There were more Venetian artists than Venetian saints.

There were a few native saints but, typically enough, they were all in some sense connected with the political status of the republic. Saint Pietro Orseolo had been a doge of the tenth century before retiring to a monastery. Saint Marina recovered Padua for the republic. Saint Lorenzo Giustiniani was a favoured son of the city who was intimately involved in the struggle to re-establish the doctrine of the Immaculate Conception. The holiness of the Virgin surrounds him.

It has been observed with some surprise that, in the absence of candidates from home, the Venetian authorities named many of their churches after Old Testament prophets. There are in fact forty Old Testament figures in the Venetian calendar of saints. That is not a feature of western Christianity. But it is an integral aspect of the eastern Church, from which Venice borrowed so many details of its devotion. There were churches for Saint Moses, Saint Job, Saint Daniel, Saint Samuel and Saint Jeremiah. The Venetians identified themselves with the chosen race that had similarly wandered over the wilderness in search of a divinely ordained homeland.

There were some visiting saints. Venice was, after all, the city of tourism from earliest times. The most famous of these divine travellers must be Saint Francis who, after attempting to convert the sultan, arrived in the city at some point in the 1220s. He stayed in Venice itself, and soon became aware of some birds singing on certain trees among the marshes. He rowed to that spot with a companion and, when they alighted on the marshy ground, Saint Francis began to pray aloud. But the birds kept on singing. The saint then commanded them to be silent. They obeyed, and would not depart until he gave them approval. On this site, then, there rose a church and a monastery of Franciscans.

The Venetians themselves had no particular fondness for the pope or for the Catholic faith beyond Venetian territory. The Jesuits, considered to be the agents of the papacy, were unpopular in Venice; it was the practice of children to follow them, crying out "Go away, go away, take nothing with you and never come back." Pius II called the Venetians "traders" and "barbarians" and "hypocrites." He declared that they "never think of God and, except for the state, which they regard as a deity, they hold nothing sacred, nothing holy." The Venetians in turn regarded the papacy as an enemy, a ruler of Italian lands rather than a representative of God. The city was an arena for pope-baiting. There was a famous story of a Venetian prisoner who, on hearing the news of the accession of Sixtus V, clapped his hands. "I will be free now," he said, "for he buggered me when I was a boy." That was the kind of story Venetians enjoyed. They were delighted to hear, from one of their ambassadors to England in the sixteenth century, that there were prints in London of the pope shitting out medals and mitres and beads.

So the powers of the Inquisition were, in Venice, restrained and restricted. There was no Spanish or Roman fervour. The Venetians insisted that, on the tribunal, three secular judges should act as a balance against three ecclesiastics. It was established in the city in 1547 but typically, in a city known for its superstition, the principal objects of its enquiries were women accused of witchcraft. The testimonials of these trials reveal an informal, and almost relaxed, mode of interrogation. The Venetian authorities had a tendency to record the most trivial details. So we can hear the people again—"and as she said these things, she was crying . . ." "Oh, he said, there's one thing I've forgotten to say . . ." "As he did not know how to reply, he kept silence for the length of one miserere."

It cannot be assumed that the Venetians were necessarily genial judges. It is simply evidence of the fact there was already in the city a well-attested culture of civic denunciation. Venetian citizens were used to being accused by one another. But harsh punishment was rare. There were few executions for heresy, in comparison with other

Catholic states, and there was little use of torture. Those women who were convicted of witchcraft were commonly sentenced to a period in the pillory.

The Venetian Church was capable of independent power because its authority was firmly based upon the will of the people. The priests were elected by the property owners of each of the seventy parishes. It was a relatively democratic system that demonstrates how indissolubly religion and society were mingled, reminiscent of the procedures of the early Christians. It has been estimated that one quarter of the priests of Venice were of patrician status, but this must mean that the overwhelming majority of the approximately six hundred clergy were ordinary citizens or even perhaps from the *popolani*. The word for parish priest in Venetian dialect, *pievano*, is derived from the Latin word *plebs*. So the unique role of the priest in the parish may ultimately spring from the earliest democratic societies of those who came first to the lagoon. It certainly helps to explain the rootedness and strength of Venetian popular devotion. The priests acted at every level of the parish. They took on the role of notaries, drawing up wills and marriage contracts; they were financiers, arranging the wages and costs of their churches; they were arbiters in social disputes. The priest could also act as a lawyer, or as an accountant.

Their parishioners were undoubtedly the most superstitious in Italy. The transcripts of the witch trials themselves reveal the intense credulity of the people. It was a city of omens and of prophecies. In 1499 the senate consulted an oracle known as "the spirit of Ferrara," asking such questions as "Are we to have war or peace with Milan?" and "Shall we lose Pisa?" In 1506 the doge and the council of ten were informed of the birth of a winged and hairy monster. In 1513 the council of ten deliberated on the warnings of an astrologer. There were many superstitions and superstitious practices. It was good to die on a Saturday. If it rained on the bier of the departed, the soul would be saved. It was unwise to walk between the two columns in the piazzetta; misfortune would surely follow you. A guest who crumples a napkin at dinner will never come to that table again. If the clock strikes the hour when you are asking the time, you have heard the knell of your own death. The first person whom you meet on New Year's Day holds the clue to your fortunes; a humpback is a sign of good fortune, a lame person is an omen of bad luck. These superstitions, and many others like them, were still current in the nineteenth and twentieth centuries.

The witchcraft of Venice was different from that of the mainland. It was the witchcraft of a tightly knit urban and mercantile society open to all the superstitions of the East as well as of the West. It was said that it was the delight of witches to unchain the gondolas, by night, and set sail to Alexandria. When the hair of children was cut, their mothers used carefully to gather it up in case it fell into the hands of the hags. You could recognise those who had been cursed by witch or demon. Their faces had the colour of green fruit, and their eyes were narrowed. Those who fell under a curse experienced a range of unpleasant symptoms: some felt as if dogs were devouring their flesh, or that a mouthful of food had stuck in the throat, or that their bodies were invaded by a freezing wind. Storms at sea were blamed upon the agency of fiends, which is why Saint Mark, and the other saints, stood guard by the side of the lagoon.

Yet the witches were also part of the religious culture of the city. They invoked the Virgin and the saints. One notorious witch, known as Apollonia, told the Inquisition that she prayed "in the name of God and the Virgin Mary, who puts her hands before mine." To stop a bleeding nose it was necessary to recite a ritual formula—"Blood stay strong, as Messer [Lord] Jesus Christ stayed strong in his death. Blood stay in your vein, as Messer Jesus stayed in his passion." One of Casanova's earliest memories concerned a nosebleed. His grandmother immediately took him in a gondola to a witch on the island of Murano, where he was promptly cured. It is an indication of Catholic folk culture with very ancient roots. It survived in Venice.

The key to Venetian witchery, however, lies in the acquisition of money. It was a culture in which scholarly necromancy was used to find hidden treasure. The discovery of treasure was a Venetian preoccupation. The pursuit of magical gold recurs again and again in the records of the Inquisition. One patrician had secretly imparted to friends that he knew of a huge mass of gold, guarded by spirits, in a deep cavern. It is as good as a fairy tale, suited to Venetian ingenuity and credulity. Alchemists were always welcomed in Venice; the prospect of turning base metals into gold was too alluring to resist. At the end of the sixteenth century there was a famous Venetian alchemist, Giambattista Angello, living in London.

And of course the spirit of commerce was also present in dealings with the supernatural powers. The devil had always to be paid for his services, for example, with salt or with a coin. The transaction had to be seen to be fair on both sides. Magic could be used for political purposes. There were many cases when the devil was summoned to reveal the names of those who would be successful in the election to the great council. Gamblers used spells and symbols. It was a culture, also, in which love potions flourished. One such potion was sage mingled with menstrual blood; when it was mixed with the food and drink of a male, he became irresistibly attracted to the woman who had dispensed it to him. Where people are packed so closely together, the passions may run high.

More than any other place in Italy, Venice was a harbour for ghosts. There are few other Italian cities where ghost stories are part of cultural tradition. Yet by the eighteenth century the city had become the setting for wraiths and phantoms, continued in a book such as Alberto Toso Fei's *Venetian Legends and Ghost Stories* published in 2004. In a real sense Venice was haunted by its past. It wanted to keep hold of its past. What better way to express it than to see ghosts in the corners? It was said that, on the vigil of All Souls, the dead left their resting places on the cemetery island of S. Michele and crossed the lagoon into the city. Each spirit visitant then returned to his or her home, and sat invisible by the kitchen fire. How did you see a ghost? Only those whose baptismal rites had been interrupted, or improperly conducted, possessed that ability. The lure of money, to the Venetians, was also to be found in the spirit world. The most frequent type of ghost was one who had concealed its treasure before death.

Some of the grander houses were reputed to be haunted. Certain passages of water were avoided. There are stories of shrieking skulls, of statues coming alive, of strange creatures of the deep. The Venetians have always loved the bizarre and the fantastic. Living on water opens the mind to the supernatural and to unconscious association. From this watery and uterine landscape, strange shapes will emerge representing the dreams or nightmares of humankind. Hence in Venice the intense fear of magic.

X

The Shadows of History

32

Decline and Fall?

At the beginning of the seventeenth century the city was no longer building enough ships; its share of the import trade from the Near East was shrinking; the merchants of Holland and England exploited the recently discovered Cape route to trade with the Indies; the German market collapsed, in part as a result of the Thirty Years War. There were only three Venetian merchants in Constantinople. The depredations of sea pirates meant, also, that the mercantile routes were under constant threat.

The Venetian government, in the face of economic competition from other European states, decided that its pre-eminent duty was to maintain standards of production; costs, therefore, remained high. In the face of challenge and competition the city reverted to its innate traditionalism. It retained all the institutional rigour of its existing guilds; the work practices of the manufacturers were unchanged. Laws were passed that gave priority to Venetian shipping in Venetian ports; goods destined for Venice could only be carried in Venetian-owned ships. Its conservatism and its new protectionism meant that it could not effectively confront the quickly changing mercantile world of the 1630s and 1640s. Cheaper manufactures undercut the Venetian markets in such areas as dyeing and printing. Venice retained its hold in the trade of luxury goods; in all other items, it fell behind. The annals are dominated by the melancholy, long, withdrawing roar of a once great economic and imperial power.

In the first decade of the seventeenth century Venice was placed under solemn interdict by the pope, thus effectively being excommunicated. The interdict failed of its effect, largely as a result of the indifference of the Venetian people to papal disapproval. When a member of the government told a prominent ecclesiastic that no papal bull was to be opened or read in the territories of the republic he replied, "I shall proceed as the Holy Spirit inspires me." The Venetian official told him that "the Holy Spirit has already inspired the council of ten to hang all disobedient subjects." When a priest conformed to the papal edict and closed down his church, a gallows was erected outside the porch on the following morning. "These leaders of your senate," one pope had told a Venetian ambassador fifty years before, "are tough fellows and need a lot of cooking." The successful rebuff to the pope materially hindered papal ambitions in the rest of Italy, but the threat of excommunication added to the impression that the independence of the city could never be taken for granted.

The sense of threat was given dramatic expression in the discovery of, and almost hysterical reaction to, what became known as "the Spanish plot." It is said that in 1618 a mercenary from Normandy approached the Spanish government, and its representatives in Italy, with a plan to destroy the city of the lagoon. On a certain day his agents would set fire to the Arsenal, the Mint and the ducal palace; at the same time all of the Venetian nobles would be massacred, and the Spanish fleet would take charge of all the passages into the city. Venice would fall to Spain. Such was the plan. According to report, it was enthusiastically received by the Spanish ambassador in Venice, the marquis of Bedmar, and by the French authorities. The duke of Osuna, the Spanish viceroy of Naples, was deeply complicit.

Yet, as so often happened in Venice, the conspirators were betrayed by secret informants. The scheme was revealed to the council of ten, who took prompt measures on 17 May 1618. By chance it happened to be the day when a new doge was to be elected. So the city was filled with travellers and interested observers.

On the morning of 18 May the people of Venice woke to find the bodies of two men suspended from a gibbet between the two columns of the piazzetta. The celebrations for the election of the new doge took place, over the next three days, with the bodies of the condemned in full view. Nothing was said about them by the authorities. It became known that they were Frenchmen. Some of the inns, populated by Frenchmen, suddenly found that they had vacant rooms. It was said that five hundred other conspirators had been drowned on that night in the canals. Bedmar was forced to flee. The French ambassador, also under suspicion, took the opportunity to make a pilgrimage to Loreto.

The silence of the authorities might be construed as embarrassment. It seems very likely that there was no real conspiracy at all, and that the council of ten acted in panic on the basis of false information. Their reaction suggests, however, that the leaders of the city considered Venice to be in imminent danger of destruction.

In historical literature "the Spanish plot" has taken its place with the "gunpowder plot" and the "massacre of Saint Bartholomew's" as an emblematic event. It was, according to Sir Henry Wotton, "the foulest and fearfullest thing that hath come to light since the foundation of the city." There were various explanations and interpretations of the conspiracy, none of them entirely convincing. It has, for example, been claimed that the Venetian authorities were in league with Osuna, to bring Naples under Venetian domination, but on fear of discovery of the plot they had covered up the evidence by killing all of Osuna's emissaries in the city. There may have been a conspiracy, and a conspiracy within a conspiracy, with all the machinations of a convoluted plot utterly suited to a suspicious and theatrical city. It became the subject of plays, and pamphlets, of the most melodramatic nature. It inspired Otway's greatest play, *Venice Preserv'd*. Venice has always been preserved. It always will be. One Venetian proverb, *sempre crolla ma non cade*, tells the story. It is always collapsing but it never falls down.

There was a further and major blow to civic harmony twelve years later; in the course of the great plague of 1630 almost fifty thousand residents of the city died. The government undertook a major effort in health care and sanitation; at all costs, at a time of weakness, civic panic or disorder had to be avoided. Yet the population dipped to 102,000, and never properly recovered in the following centuries. This was not necessarily a matter of lasting regret to the authorities. There was of course a fall in tax revenues, but the relative depopulation meant that there were more jobs available for those who remained and that wages increased exponentially. Incomes rose, and prices fell. At times of emergency, too, the city could prove its self-sufficiency.

How in any case can we speak of failure and decline in the context of a city that still survives intact? By the end of the seventeenth century Venice had a working polity. The English ambassador had in 1612 described the senators as "growne fractious, vindictive, loose, and unthriftie"; yet they had held together. In fact Venice experienced a commercial resurgence by the end of the century. Trade with Germany and the Turks of Constantinople enjoyed a revival. The revenues from taxes on shipping increased by some 70 per cent in the last three decades of the seventeenth century. The standard of living in the city had not fallen at all. It may have been no longer an international market, but it became a vital regional port serving the territories of the Po valley. A great scheme of public works was instituted to increase the traffic along the Adige river. New roads were built along the skirts of the lagoon. Projects were formed for legal, educational and technological reform. The functions of the city had changed. It had adapted and survived. It became in every sense a local, rather than a western, power.

By the eighteenth century, at the very latest, the city lost any illusion about its status as an imperial force. It held only Dalmatia, and some of the Ionian islands. But this was not necessarily a matter for regret. It was said of England in the twentieth century that it had lost an empire and had not yet found a new role. This was not the case with Venice. The city acted as the entrepôt for goods destined for western Europe in general and for the North Sea shores in particular. Thirty English, and fifteen Dutch, merchantmen visited the port each year. Trade in the latter half of the eighteenth century was in no way inferior to that of the fifteenth century. Canals were being deepened to accommodate the larger sailing vessels, and new canals were being dug on the mainland to divert the waters of the rivers threatening the levels of the lagoon. In regional matters Venice adopted a stance of studied neutrality, having realised that wars and rumours of wars were not good for business on the Italian mainland. The city, perhaps unwisely in the light of subsequent developments, became accustomed to peace. Yet its removal from battle also helped its reputation as a wise arbiter and a standard of good governance. The constitution was in no way adapted or amended.

In the eighteenth century Venice, as we have already observed, set itself the task of becoming the city of art and the city of pleasure. It redefined itself as the most seductive haven for foreign visitors. The public buildings were renovated, and the churches were restored. New theatres, and new hospitals, were erected. This was the age of Canaletto, whose views of the city have created a perfect myth of graceful urbanism. But this was also the century of Giambattista Tiepolo, born in 1696 and dead by 1770. He inherited all the liveliness and energy of his Venetian forebears, and thus is an apt token of the fact that the spirit and greatness of the city did not die. They revived, and flourished, under new circumstances. The first half of the eighteenth century, too, witnessed the music of Vivaldi. Is there not something more glorious about making music than making war? This was not a dying city. It was a city more vibrant than ever before.

That happy state would not last for ever. Quick bright things often end in confusion. By the end of the eighteenth century Venice had lost its freedom. It did not lose its fabric, or its inheritance, but it lost its status as a republic. Twenty years before the catastrophe, there was already nervous fever in the air. When Carlo Contarini addressed the great council in 1779, he declared that "all is in confusion, in disorder. Our commerce is languishing; bankruptcies continually prove it. Food is extraordinarily dear. That which sufficed to maintain our families and left a margin to help the State, is now insufficient to keep us alive." In the following year the doge, Paolo Renier, conveyed approximately the same sentiment, "We have no forces," he told the great council, "neither on land nor on sea; we have no alliances. We live by luck, by accident, and solely dependent upon the conception of Venetian prudence which others entertain about us." In 1784 the patrician, Andrea Tron, completed the litany of complaint. "The old enduring maxims and laws that created and could still create a great state have been forgotten . . ." The trade of Venice was now confined to "comforts, excessive luxuries, vain shows, alleged amusements and vices."

The three men were in their different ways intuiting what could otherwise not have been foreseen. Who could have predicted the rise of the Napoleonic Empire in Europe and the submission of Venice to one man's will? Yet of course it is not the consequence of one man. In *War and Peace* Tolstoy enquired, in relation to the phenomenon of Napoleon, "Why do wars or revolutions happen? We do not know. We only know that to produce the one or the other men form themselves into a certain combination in which all take part; and we say that this is the nature of men, that this is a law."

The "fall" of Venice was just a change in its historical identity. We cannot say that it was a disgrace or a triumph, because we do not know who in the end is triumphant and who is disgraced. That is the flaw in all moralistic interpretations of historical events. We must discount the possibility of ever discerning a purpose in human affairs, except that of blind instinct reaching its fulfilment, and we must admit that any ultimate purpose will be for ever beyond our understanding. Why did Venice "fall"? We may return to *War and Peace* to understand that an answer is not possible. "Why does an apple fall when it is ripe? Is it brought down by the force of gravity? Is it because its stalk withers? Because it is dried by the sun, because it grows too heavy, or the wind shakes it, or because the boy standing under the tree wants to eat it?"

The end came quickly. Ludovico Manin was elected the doge of Venice in 1789; it was by far the most expensive election in Venetian history, costing half as much again as the previous ducal election of 1779. The cost was hardly worth it. Manin, the 120th doge continuing an unbroken line of rulers since AD 697, was the last doge in Venetian history. Eight years after his accession the city of patrician government was shaken and destroyed by the conqueror still riding on the back of popular revolution. Bonaparte, twenty-six years old, was annoyed by Venice. He was annoyed that some of its mainland territories had become the centre of French émigré activity, and that the Venetian authorities had allowed the Austrian enemy to pass through its territories. When he arrived in the Po region he sent his agents into the city with the message of "liberation." The forces of Napoleon were not to be considered as blood-thirsty plebeian revolutionaries, but as a dedicated army ready to remove the injustice and ineptitude of an antique and discredited regime. There were indeed some Venetians who would have welcomed him.

When he crossed the River Po, the end was close. A new guardian of Venetian territories, a *provveditore*, was appointed with the official purpose of "preserving intact the tranquillity of the republic, and of administering comfort and consolation to its subjects." It is a most inexpedient turn of phrase, suggesting the onset of panic. When Napoleon occupied Verona, the *provveditore* and his staff entered negotiations with him; he was apparently affable, and even amicable, but no concessions were drawn from him. It was reported that he threatened, in the friendliest possible terms, to demand a ransom of six million francs for the safety of the city. The Venetians had no troops, and only the remnants of a navy. They were, to all intents and purposes, defenceless. Napoleon, meanwhile, continued his campaign of occupation throughout the Venetian territories.

The stated policy of Venetian neutrality, between France and

Austria, now turned back and bit the city. The French accused the senate of aiding the Austrians, and of course in turn the Austrian government denounced the Venetians for assisting Bonaparte. The doge and the senate did nothing. It was as if they were speechless with fear. A Paduan writer, Ippolito Nievo, said of this period that the Venetian nobility was a corpse that could not be revived.

When a truce was declared between France and Austria, Bonaparte waited for Venice to fall into his hands. He tested its responses. He sent a ship into the harbour of the Lido, on 20 April 1797, and a Venetian galley attacked it. That was enough to signal war. The senate met in permanent session. Napoleon instigated popular risings against Venetian rule in the cities of the mainland. Two Venetian nobles were sent to Bonaparte on 25 April. He was magnificent in his assumed wrath. He blamed the Venetians for atrocities against his soldiers. "I will have no Inquisition, no antique barbarities." He ended by saying that "I will be an Attila to the Venetian state." He knew something of Venetian history. Then over dinner he asked for reparations to the amount of twenty-two million francs from the Venetian treasury.

On 29 April the French soldiers occupied the Venetian frontiers. As the guardians of the city anxiously convened on the following day, the sound of the French artillery could clearly be heard. The doge walked up and down the hall of his private apartments, where they had gathered for safety, and told them that "tonight we are not even safe in our beds." The procurator then rose to his feet. "I see that it is all over with my country," he said. "I can certainly be of no assistance. To an honest man, every place is his country; one may easily occupy oneself in Switzerland." He was persuaded to stay for the time being, and comforted himself with snuff. The nobles then agreed that they would introduce any democratic changes that Bonaparte required of them, in the hope that this would forestall an invasion.

The great council met on the following day, 1 May, when the doge addressed them. He told them that it was necessary to make peace at any price, and that they must resort to prayer. So matters stayed for the next few days, with Venetian envoys going to and from the camp of Napoleon. They capitulated on every point. The great council met on 12 May to ratify their proceedings. Those present did not meet the required quorum of six hundred members, but they decided to go ahead anyway. They had just got to the point of debating the measure to accept "the proposed provisional representative government," a French government, when the sound of musketry was heard. It was in fact the parting salute of some sailors leaving the Lido, but the patricians believed it to be the noise of an invading army. They fell into a panic. The doge called out "Divide! Divide!," to conclude the vote. They did so, and promptly left the council hall never to return. Ippolito Nievo recorded that

> after sixty years I still see some of those frightened, dejected, alarmed faces. I visualise the deathly pallor of some, the discomposed almost drunken aspect of others, the nervous hurry of the majority, who seemed as though they would gladly have jumped out of the windows to escape this scene of infamy.

It is reported in the histories of the period that the doge returned to his apartment, and gave his ducal bonnet to his manservant. "Take it," he said. "I shall not be needing it again." So ended the republic of Venice. The last Carnival before the end was supposed to have been the most magnificent, and the most expensive, in the entire history of the city.

The French army occupied the city on 15 May. An official report to Bonaparte, on this occasion, reported that the ordinary people of Venice "retired in silence to their homes, exclaiming with tears— Venice is no more! Saint Mark is fallen!" The lion of Saint Mark was indeed toppled from its column, and a "tree of liberty" erected in the square. The ducal insignia, and the "Golden Book" of patrician membership, were ritually burned. The former doge, and members of the great council, joined in the dancing around the tree. Thus ended a polity that had endured for more than a thousand years. The most ancient government in the whole of Europe was another indirect casualty of the French Revolution.

Napoleon also plundered the art and treasures of the city, just as Venice had plundered Constantinople and the dominions of its empire. There is something apposite about the transference of the four bronze horses to Paris; they had been snatched by Venetians from Constantinople six hundred years before. They were always the spoils of victory. Then Napoleon bartered Venice itself. In the autumn of 1797 he handed it to the Austrians as part of the Treaty of Campo Formio. Eight years later, having defeated the Austrians, he took it back. In 1805 it became part of his unified kingdom of Italy. For Venice, accustomed to stand apart from the mainland, this was a further humiliation. It had never played any part in the burgeoning national consciousness of the Italians, and only reluctantly accepted its status as a peripheral part of a nation. In 1814 the city again returned to the control of Austria. It suffered these changes of regime with docility. It bowed its head. It was now a spectator of its own fate.

At the beginning of the nineteenth century Napoleon had instituted a policy of public works. A new royal palace was erected at the west end of Saint Mark's Square. Churches and monasteries were pulled down to create public gardens just beyond the Arsenal. A new road, the Via Eugenia, now known as the Via Garibaldi, was built along the waterfront towards the gardens. The public works continued under Austrian occupation. The lagoon was fortified. The Accademia bridge, only the second bridge across the Grand Canal, was erected in 1854. Yet the most radical change of all consisted in the building of a railway bridge that connected Venice to the mainland; the city was no longer an island, and it lost its hallowed status as a refuge from the world. This meant, too, that the prime significance of the water had gone for ever. It became a city of mechanical, rather than of natural, time. It had, perhaps, been prophesied. In the early 1500s the doge, Andrea Gritti, consulted the Delphic oracle. He had been assailed by rumours concerning the imminent collapse of Venice. There appeared to him, beside the statue of Apollo, a panorama showing Venice surrounded by green fields rather than by the sea. The priest told him that this signified one thing: the republic would die when Venice became part of the mainland.

Throughout this period, in fact, there was an accelerating economic slump from which the city scarcely recovered in the twentieth century. The patrician class was emasculated, and one family in three simply died out. Some of the remaining nobles were awarded honorary titles by the Austrian government. But these were empty forms. They fooled nobody except their holders. The general population diminished, too, as a result of epidemic sickness and migration. There had always been beggars in Venice, but by the beginning of the nineteenth century the poverty and mendicancy became the most obvious aspect of city life. It was estimated that a third of the population depended on charity. This was precisely the time when the

English Romantics became interested in Venice. They were drawn to decay and desuetude.

In some ways it was the most interesting period in the history of the city. The grass and weeds had sprung up in the *campi,* and the various *palazzi* had been converted into ruined tenements for the poor. The stone steps and bridges were covered with green algae, and the wood of the mooring posts was rotting away. The houses crumbled. "Venice indeed appears to be at her last gasp," an Englishman wrote in the winter of 1816, "and if something is not done to relieve and support her, she must be soon buried again in the marshes from whence she originally sprang. Every trace of her former magnificence which still exists only serves to illustrate her present decay."

A generation later, however, some of the prosperity of the city was recovered. It reverted to type. It became once more the haven for travellers and tourists; eleven large hotels, and innumerable smaller hostelries, were opened to serve them. Gas lighting was introduced to increase the romantic charm of the nocturnal city. This was the Venice that Turner depicted. The population began to rise. The merchants, and the glass-makers, and the gondoliers were prosperous. By the 1850s there were no less than eighty-two shoe-shops and one hundred retailers of silk. Yet the city was still part of the Hapsburg dominion, with the principal social and economic decisions being taken far away in Vienna. Venice had become only one distant and subsidiary limb of a large empire. Of course the Venetians resented their loss of status. There were complaints concerning high taxes, and oppressive censorship. The Austrian soldiers, in particular, were not liked. They were even compared unfavourably to their French predecessors. "There is hardly a Venetian house to which an Austrian is admitted," the English consul general wrote. "Persons supposed to have a leaning towards the government are held up to public execration and their names are written upon the walls as traitors to the country."

Shelley believed that the Venetian people themselves had forfeited their identity under the occupation of the French and the Austrian armies. "I had no conception," he wrote, "of the excess to which avarice, cowardice, superstition, ignorance, passionless lust, & all the inexpressible brutalities to which human nature could be carried, until I had lived a few days among the Venetians."

Yet it would be quite wrong to say that the Venetians had entirely lost their spirit or their energy. These human characteristics are stubborn and persistent. When the test came, in a few months of 1848, they rose to the challenge. This was the time of the siege of Venice.

It began in "the year of revolutions," 1848, when the dynasty of the House of Orleans fell and the second republic was instituted in France. The contagion of liberty spread all over Europe. Most significantly there was great unrest at the heart of the Austrian Empire, Vienna, and the emperor was forced to grant a new constitution to his entire dominions. On receipt of this news, brought by a postal steamer from Trieste, the Venetian people rose up against the Austrian army of occupation. They congregated in Saint Mark's Square and demanded the release of a Jewish lawyer, Daniele Manin, who had been imprisoned for uttering patriotic Venetian sentiments. The Arsenal was captured by the local people. In the face of general insurrection, with which they could not adequately deal, the Austrian army agreed to withdraw from Venice and retired by sea to Trieste. On 22 March Manin was declared to be president of a newly formed republic. When he was told that the people were idle and self-indulgent he replied that "Neither you nor anyone else knows the people of Venice. They have always been misunderstood. My boast is that I know them better. It is my only merit." It seemed at the time that Venice had once more risen from the depths. An editorial in the *Gazzetta di Venezia* announced that "We Are Free!" It took up the ancient cry of "Viva San Marco!"

But there can be no certainty in human affairs; all is miscalculation, error and confusion. What is predicted does not take place; the unforeseen, and the unexpected, make up the life of the world. In 1849 the Austrians defeated the nationalist forces on the Italian mainland, and reoccupied the Veneto. Venice once more stood alone against a threatening world. It was the crisis that throughout their history the Venetians had always most feared. Their fears then took material shape. The Austrian army laid siege to the city. It lasted for seventeen months.

Yet popular feeling demanded resistance at all costs. It was the ancient spirit of independence reasserting itself in a city that had for two centuries been dismissed as effete and inglorious. The Venetian people were ready to risk everything in order to defend themselves from foreign oppression. They gladly gave up their plate and jewellery to help in the noble cause of saving Venice; even the poorest of them donated their thin bracelets and silver hairpins. The workers of the Arsenal laboured through the night to produce more vessels of war. There were rumours at one stage that the city was about to be bombed from the air, by means of balloons, but the threat was lampooned mercilessly in cartoons and street placards. Some air balloons were released on 12 July, but they lived up to comic expectations; they fell into the lagoon or drifted back to the Austrian side.

At the end of July, however, began a serious bombardment that continued for twenty-four days. All of the palaces along the Grand Canal were struck. Most of the Austrian bombs fell in the northern Cannaregio district, but the fire and smoke dominated the entire city. Many citizens built towers or turrets on the roofs of their houses, so that they could eat or rest at the same time as they enjoyed the spectacle. The Venetians had always enjoyed fireworks. The spirit of the Venetian people, like that of Londoners during the "blitz" of 1940, remained cheerful and steadfast. They would hold out, it was said, "until the last slice of polenta." The children chased the Austrian cannon balls, as they landed, and then brought them to be used in the Venetian batteries.

The horrors of this period are well documented. In the face of famine and an epidemic of Asiatic cholera the Venetian people refused to surrender, consoling themselves with the chant of "Viva San Marco!"; but, in the end, resistance became impossible. On 24 August Manin signed the articles of surrender. The Austrian army returned to the ravaged city, and Manin was arrested. He was despatched as an exile to Paris. His dream of republican independence, based upon the remote history of the city, had come to nothing. Yet for a time Venice had once again become the emblem of republican liberty, and was admired by all those who despised Hapsburg imperialism. That support was short of material benefits, of course, and was not enough to save the city. Yet the bravery and endurance of the Venetian people were enough to dispel for ever the belief that they were spineless and spiritless.

In retaliation for the rebellion the Austrians removed the status of Venice as a free port. It was the final phase in the maritime life of the city. The occupation of the Austrians, after the siege, lasted for seventeen years. It was essentially a city in mourning. "There is no greater social dullness and sadness," the American consul wrote in 1865, "on land or sea, than in contemporary Venice." It was the home of "despondency"; it resembled "a sepulchre of the living." In early photographs the city has a slum-like appearance, the women in shawls and the men in battered hats.

Then the events of the outer world, to which the Venetians had become largely indifferent, cast a new light upon the city. In 1866 the Austrian troops withdrew, and the province of Lombardy-Venetia became part of the new kingdom of Italy. The air of gloom and abandonment that had hovered over Venice began to lift. The success of the Lido as a pleasure resort, from the 1880s into the twentieth century, opened up new vistas of trade and prosperity for the lagoon. Two luxury hotels were built on the island. Venice had once more become a pleasure ground for the rich and for the famous. There were any number of dethroned members of royal families, dukes and duchesses, popular singers, film stars, and what were once called "playboys." The Astors and the Desboroughs came. The middle class followed. In 1895 the first International Exhibition was organised. This soon became known as the Biennale, inaugurating what has become a thoroughly Venetian tradition of art, money and celebrity.

From this time forward it became clear to everyone that the only future for the city lay in tourism. The creation of the industrial zone on the mainland at Mestre and Marghera in the early decades of the twentieth century, just within the purview of Venice, only served to reinforce the belief that the developments of contemporary life were somehow to be kept in the margins. It was only the latest manifestation of the ancient instinct of the city to banish its industries to the borders. Venice had come to rely upon its history, real or imagined. The actual past was not specified. The city simply encouraged a sense of "pastness."

The decayed fabric of the thirteenth-century palace, known as the Fondaco dei Turchi, was purchased by the municipality (as it now was) and restored to a symmetrical elegance it never actually possessed. It was, in the language of architectural historians, "hypervenetianised." In 1907 the new fish market was built on the Rialto in the style of the fifteenth century. There was a "Gothic" revival, and a "Byzantine" revival. New hotels were built in "classical" or "Renaissance" style. New palaces rose up along the Grand Canal that, to all outward appearances, might have been designed and erected in the twelfth or thirteenth centuries.

During the First World War Venice's old masters, the Austrians, came dangerously close to the city when its army moved ever nearer to the borders of the lagoon; barrage balloons could be seen from the campanile, and the port was closed for fear of enemy attack. But the city did not fall. In fact it emerged almost intact from the ravages of both world wars; there was very little bomb damage, and through all the years of hostilities there were only two hundred fatalities—most of whom had fallen into the canals during the hours of "black-out."

But there were other victims. The Jews of Venice were destined to suffer on the orders of Mussolini and of Hitler. The city had been quick to embrace fascism in the 1920s, and organised groups of Mussolini's supporters were soon a powerful force in the city. The racial laws of 1938, and the active persecution of the Jews from 1943 to 1945, opened a wide wound in Venetian Jewry. Jews were dismissed from their jobs and were not allowed to use the beaches of the Lido. In public buildings there were signs stating "Dogs and Jews prohibited." The historical tolerance of the Venetian people had come to an end.

When the German army took over the city in 1943, approximately two hundred Jews were rounded up and deported to the concentration camps of the mainland. Some were sent on to Auschwitz. The mentally ill were taken from the hospital islands and despatched to their death. The world beyond Venice, the real world, had taken over.

The last half of the twentieth century was marked by the exodus of Venetians to the mainland, where industrial expansion promised better paid jobs and less expensive housing. The industrial activity of Mestre and Marghera has also helped to poison the waters of the lagoon, emphasising the vulnerability of the environment of the city.

Yet the city continued, and continues, to be beset by bureaucratic timidity and ineptitude. Gianfranco Pertot's study of modern Venice, *Venice: Extraordinary Maintenance* (2004), chronicles the "non-fulfilment of obligations, the failure to programme or to plan, and consequently to act" on the part of the Venetian authorities for many years. It is part of the "inertia, this *immobilismo*" of the city, allowing and even encouraging "scandalous exploitation, speculation, destruction and decay." Bribery and general corruption are said to be rife throughout the city. Yet what community has not been invaded by corruption? It is the human condition. And it has been the condition of Venice itself for many centuries.

For centuries, also, it was almost impossible to locate the source or centre of power, which was always distributed among overlapping governmental bodies. Was it the doge or the senate? Did it reside in the council of ten or in the great council? The present bureaucratic arrangements of the city have inherited that complexity and that obliquity. To quote from Pertot once more: "Who is in charge in Venice is a question that has still not been settled." It was always thus. In the fifteenth and sixteenth centuries new laws accrued upon old laws. This history is still repeating itself. In the late twentieth century "special law" followed "special law" concerning the preservation of the city. There were delays and obfuscations in every part of the administrative machinery. There is still no general agreement, among all the interested parties, about the future of Venice. Should it be a museum city and research centre? Should it be simply a tourist haven and stage set for the various international exhibitions that have gravitated to the lagoon? Or should it attempt to restore its past as a living city of residents?

It is perhaps too late for the last proposal. That great migration of the Venetian population to Mestre began in the 1950s and has continued ever since. By the early twenty-first century the inhabitants of Venice had the lowest incomes in the whole of the Veneto region. One third of the population was over the age of sixty. The death rate had overtaken the birth rate by a factor of four. That is why, at night, Venice now seems so empty. It *is* empty. It is hard to imagine a time when it was a city full of local people. Of course, in the day, it is full of tourists. But paradoxically tourists empty a place by their presence. They turn it into a spectacle without depth. There are now approximately sixty thousand residents within the city, and demographic experts have suggested that the last Venetian will leave in or about 2030.

Most young Venetians have migrated to the mainland, where there are jobs other than those within the "service sector." Venice has become too expensive for them. Foreigners have been buying, or renting, the houses and apartments. So affordable housing is scarce. Many houses have been turned into *pensions* or hotels. Many of the local shops have become little more than souvenir kiosks for tourists. Butchers and bakers have gone, while ice-cream shops have multiplied. Contemporary Venetians are under siege in another sense.

Away from the main tourist routes, however, the fabric of the city seems neglected. The stock of private housing has been deteriorating under the twin threats of subsidence and water seepage. The pollution from the chemical plants and petroleum refineries of Marghera, on the mainland, has also taken its toll on the brick and stone. Fissures appear; walls shift and crack; stonework falls off the buildings. The plaster peels in an air laden with salt. One recent study of Venice by John Berendt is entitled *The City of Falling Angels*, derived from a sign posted outside the church of S. Maria della Salute. In more general terms, it is hard not to detect a mood of cynicism among the remaining inhabitants of the city.

The great flood of 1966, when the afternoon tide rose more than six feet (1.8 m) higher than its average, reminded Venetians that their city was still precarious. The world shared the general sense of anxiety, and organisations such as "Venice In Peril" were established to raise funds for the restoration of Venice. As the city gradually subsides, the incidences of flooding increase. It has been estimated that Saint Mark's Square is flooded on fifty occasions each year.

The sea is still rising; the silt continually piling upon the floor of the lagoon, and the extraction of methane gas from the Adriatic, have combined with the more general threat of "global warming." The sea is returning to its old domain, unless it is prevented by assiduous and energetic human enterprise. A scheme is now under way, for example, to erect seventy-nine barriers at the tidal inlets where the sea and the lagoon meet; these would be raised, by means of compressed air, at the time of dangerously high tides. The proposal is controversial, however, and is opposed by many Venetians who claim that a tideless lagoon would be in danger of becoming a stagnant pond. It has also been argued that so much money has been expended on this project that the needs of the city itself have largely been ignored. But Venice is now, for better or worse, part of Italy. When it lost its autonomy, it forfeited its authority. It cannot control its own destiny. And, when it lost its uniqueness, did it also lose its energy? Peggy Guggenheim once said that "when Venice is flooded, it is even more truly beloved." Like Ophelia it seems to float expiring on the water, all that is hopeless and all that is hoped for.

Yet we have seen throughout this book that Venice has always been in peril, its existence most fragile. It is a man-made structure relying on the vicissitudes of the natural world. Yet it has endured. Its survival is exemplary. Let us hope that its will to survive will remain a potent source of energy.

Here ends the history lesson.

33

Death in Venice

At the foot of the baroque campanile of the church of S. Maria Formosa there is sculpted over the doorway a hideous mask of decay and suffering. Ruskin believed that "it is well that we should see and feel the full horror of it in this spot and know what pestilence it was that came and breathed upon her beauty until it melted away." For him the deformed visage was an image of the decline of Venice from the time of the Renaissance. In fact the stone mask is more interesting than that. It is an exact representation of the face of one suffering from neuro-fibromatosis or von Recklinghausen's disease.

Venice is associated with death. It is in large part a dilapidated city, the water lapping against crumbling brick and plaster. John Addington Symonds, in *A Venetian Medley*, recounts that "the blackness of the water whispers in our ears a tale of death." It is a city of shadows. The city is linked with pestilence, too, and with the hidden knife of the assassin. There is still a Rio Terra degli Assassini. The most famous narrative to have emerged from the city is still Thomas Mann's *Death in Venice*. Threnody suits the city well. Venice is doomed. That is the tale the waters tell. In the city of faded stone Byron meditated on decay. "Oh Venice!" he wrote:

> Venice! When thy marble walls
> Are level with the waters, there shall be
> A cry of nations o'er thy sunken halls . . .

It was a place of slime and ooze and mould. Marinetti described it as a "putrefying" city, a "magnificent sore from the past." For Ruskin it was already a ghost floating upon the sea. Its silence was forbidding. Its ruins were somehow more death-like than elsewhere, because there was no touch of nature about them with the promise of regeneration. These ruins of stone are final. No moss, or grass, will cover them. They are what Shelley described as "a windowless, deformed and dreary pile." In *The Last Man* Mary Shelley depicted a similar scene of desolation as "the tide ebbed sullenly from out the broken portals and violated halls of Venice." In a city that seemed to have deserted the changing world of time, the only fate awaiting it is apocalypse. It will be submerged. It will descend into the water silently and permanently. It is the image of the city as the final end of all human achievement and aspiration. Wordsworth wrote a sonnet on Venice that ended:

> Men are we, and must grieve when even the Shade
> Of that which once was great, is passed away.

"I do not *feel* any romance in Venice," Ruskin told his father. "It is simply a heap of ruins." In more remote ages, too, the Venetian chronicles are filled with accounts of churches or bridges or houses suddenly disintegrating and collapsing in piles of dust and broken stone. In the eighteenth century the city became part of the cult of picturesque ruins. There were ruins even in the fourteenth century. Many houses were left in a decayed state and never restored. There are of course no ruins of the classical past—almost alone among Italian cities, Venice has no such relics—but rather the slow and continuing decay of a still to be apprehended beauty. The city does not have the security of great and primordial ancestors. That is why decay and dissolution in Venice are somehow more beautiful than the most splendid edifices elsewhere. They are part of its unique enchantment. They are part of the sweet melancholy of transience. They are reminiscent of the human frame as it moves towards the tomb.

It was for Henry James the most beautiful sepulchre in the world, where the past "has been laid to rest with such tenderness, such a sadness of resignation." The churches are filled with graves. There was once a Campiello dei Morti, but the name has been changed to Campiello Nuovo. There was a Bridge of the Dead, but it is now called the Bridge of the Tailors. There is still a Calle della Morte. Yet the cemetery may also become a metaphor. In the eighteenth century Venice was described as "a tomb of noblemen in which healthy people are locked up."

There is now an island of the dead close to the city. S. Michele once sustained a monastery devoted to learning but in the nineteenth century a cemetery was constructed here, so that the cadavers would no longer be close to the living population of Venice. The bodies are placed in little marble drawers like an enormous sideboard of mortality. The church of S. Michele, built some four centuries earlier, is like a whitened sepulchre guarding the site. Its recumbent corpses outnumber by many times the inhabitants of the city. After a certain number of years the dead are taken up, their skeletons removed to an island of bones known as S. Ariano. Is this not the real *laguna morte*, the dead lagoon? Among the skulls and bones slink rats and reptiles; bony plants spring up amid the decay.

There is a cult of death in Venice. The Futurist movement of Italy believed that it was the temple of the cult of *l'adorazione della morte*, the worship of which was the foundation and being of the city. In its manifesto the movement declared that it was time "to fill the stinking little canals with the rubble of the tottering infected old palaces. Let us burn the gondolas, rocking chairs for idiots"; the entire city was a "great sewer of traditionalism."

The funerals were once very magnificent. Even in the beginning the rites of the dead in Venice resembled those of Egypt and of Assyria rather than of any Italian city. The corpse was laid on a floor that had been covered in ashes. The bereaved were obliged to enter all the paroxysms of grief, howling and moaning, and it became a custom for the relict to lie across the threshold of the house to prevent the corpse of the loved one from being removed; he or she was then ritually dragged away. The corpse was generally carried through the streets with its face and feet bare. The funeral processions were accompanied by banners, torches and flambeaux, while the rooms of the house of the departed were draped in black velvet. The family of the dear departed were then expected to cry and scream throughout the entire funeral service. It is another example of the eastern affiliations of the city. Anyone who died a virgin, male or female, was buried with a green garland around the head.

Anyone who has seen the film *Don't Look Now* will recall the hearse being carried across the water in a dark gondola. When the cemetery island was first in use there grew up a tradition of almost triumphal processions to the centre of the dead; there were funereal gondolas, designed for that purpose, with five gondoliers in gilded uniforms. One of them stood at the front of the hearse and coffin with a staff of office, while at the prow and stern were the sculpted images of saints and prophets. Even for the more modest funerals the gondoliers wore scarves and sashes of black, while the hearse and coffin were heaped with bright flowers.

There is a genuine morbidity in the folk tales and superstitions of the city. Louis XII of France said that the Venetians were too afraid of death to succeed in war; they had a merchant fear of violence and insecurity. The city is surrounded by islands to which the mad and the dangerous have always been expelled. In *Venice* Jan Morris wrote that "Venetians are fascinated by dead things, horrors, prisons, freaks and malformations." That is perhaps because the city itself is a freak and a prison. There is also a suspicion abroad that it is already a dead city.

There are people who seem physically to feel the onset of disease on their arrival in Venice. The French writer, Maurice Barrès, declared that as soon as he had stepped out of the railway station and walked to the gondola stand—feeling the wind of the lagoon upon his face—he knew that "I have taken quinine in vain to protect me. I believe that I can feel within me the re-emergence of millions of bacteria . . . One sees everywhere in Venice the conquests of death." Wagner glimpsed this, too, when he stepped into a gondola.

Wagner died in Venice. Browning died here, too. Diaghilev died here. There are some who expire here by proxy; Dante died in Ravenna from a fever he contracted in Venice. Byron had decided to end his days in the city, but events elsewhere overtook him. It is presumably a matter of statistical probability that a certain amount of artists would die in this most artistic of cities, but the truth is that many people come to Venice precisely in order to die. Henry James intuited the fatal appeal of the city in the character of the suffering Milly Theale in *The Wings of the Dove*. "I think I should like," she said, "to die here." There is something consoling about death near water, in a city that is itself in the throes of decay. To die in a grand Venetian house, as did Wagner and Browning, is to inhabit a vast funerary monument without the expense of building one. The perpetual sound of bells is a rehearsal for death.

It can be a melancholy and enervating place. It is not a city for the old, or for the ill, or for the mournful. The atmosphere can induce lassitude and depression. When the French painter Léopold Robert committed suicide in Venice his compatriot, George Sand, blamed it on the atmosphere. On hearing the music and the singing, during a Venetian evening, Anton Chekhov wished to weep. It has been a city of tears. Wagner was thrown into a mood of "extreme melancholy" when he first arrived in Venice. When the Irish balladeer, Tom Moore, visited Byron he instantly hated the city and declared it to be a "sad place." That is the reaction of many travellers who become afflicted by a strange and sudden gloom. Even in the carnival air of the eighteenth century the underlying mood was declared to be one of melancholy. Why else would you want to make so much show of gaiety? In the nineteenth century the English residents of Venice warned their compatriots, on their arrival, not to spend too much time in the city. It was supposed that a long residence would lead to a morbid depression of spirits. There is a cultural, as well as a psychological, explanation for this mournfulness. The English travellers believed at the time that the whole history of Venice was one of loss and decay—that the city had lost its purpose, had become hopeless and aimless. It was a way, perhaps, of anticipating the decline of England and of the British Empire.

There is melancholy, too, induced by the presence of water. Water represents memory and passing time. Water is an emblem of oblivion. So it attracts those who wish to hide from the world. It attracts those who wish to forget and be forgotten. There is something about the broken state of Venice that acts as a refuge and consolation for those who have failed in the struggle for life. The vast and often silent lagoon still broods over the city. For those departing for the East, merchant or pilgrim, this place was the last port on the western shore. All those farewells, perhaps, have left a tangible sense of nostalgia in the air. Those of an atavistic turn of mind may even regret the loss of the life of the past, so painfully apparent in the sometimes garish streets of contemporary Venice.

Cocteau described it as a sick and fevered city, floating on stagnant waters, discharging miasmal vapours. It was believed that the mixture of salt water and fresh water, at the edges of the lagoon, created noxious air and actively propagated malaria through the agency of the mosquito. In the early centuries, too, the use of fish traps and wooden piles meant that the water could no longer flow freely. Other once flourishing towns and islands were soon surrounded by pestiferous marshes. The mosquitoes of Venice, in the summer months, can still wreak havoc.

The correspondence of Sir Henry Wotton is filled with allusions to what he considered to be the unhealthy air. He was "much weakened by sweats, which are cheap in this air"; his chest pains were "more increased by this vaporous air." He felt himself prone to hypochondria "by the very inclination of this watery seat." Venice also induced in him "my infirmity of the spleen."

The stench of Venice, especially in the summer months, was remarkable. In the eighteenth century the city was known for its filthy state; the rubbish was heaped up in corners, by the bridges, while the canals were the receptacle of human waste of every description. Some of the smaller canals were little better than rivulets of ordure. Throughout the centuries the rubbish was discharged into the canals, in defiance of all the sanitary legislation of the city, on the under-standing that the tide would scour them clean. This laxity spread, so that housewives would simply throw their rubbish into the streets.

Hester Thrale, in the 1780s, remarked that "disgust gets the better of every other sensation." The basilica was filthy and malodorous. All the incense from all the altars could not disguise the rank smell. The prison reformer John Howard, in the same period as Hester Thrale, described the city as a "stinkpot charged with the very virus of hell." Goethe noticed that on days of rain a "disgusting sludge," made up of mud and excrement, collected underfoot. The Venetians themselves were considered to be dirty and unhygienic. This was a time when smell was itself considered to be the token of the presence of disease. It filled Gibbon with "satiety and disgust." It is not perhaps surprising that most of these reports come from the eighteenth century. Venice had not suddenly become noisome—it always was, and in some respects still is, a malodorous city—but it was only in the eighteenth century that travellers began to comment upon such matters. Before that date stench, human or otherwise, was a matter of course.

It was not until the end of the nineteenth century that the association between smell and disease was plausibly denied. One doctor, writing in 1899, remarked that the "many odours" of Venice were harmless, "being caused by the decomposition by drainage of the sulphates of the salt water into sulphides, than which there are no worse-smelling gasses." It was one explanation, but it was not necessarily reassuring. Ralph Waldo Emerson in the nineteenth century noticed a smell as of bilge-water and in the late twentieth century Donna Leon, the author of crime novels set in Venice, described in *The Anonymous Venetian* "the penetrating stench of corruption that always lurked beneath the surface." This may be taken in a metaphorical, as well as literal, sense. In the same period another crime writer, Michael Dibdin, wrote in *Dead Lagoon* of a canal where the "fetid odour of the disturbed mud hung heavy in the air, a noxious miasma so strong that it was almost tangible." The writers of crime are drawn to this noxious city where fugitive odours can be sensed beneath the beauties of the surface.

At times of famine and dearth, particularly in the early decades of the sixteenth century, the poor were struck with fever before they suffered from malnutrition. Fever was in the air. There were other diseases. Gastroenteritis, typhus and influenza came and went with the various seasons. Diarrhoea, and weakness of the eyes, were considered to be endemic. A sixteenth-century physician blamed the ailments of Venice on sexual excess and gluttony. Then in 1588 a previously unknown disorder, known as grippe, laid low the whole of Venice. The great council was for the first time in its history empty. Grippe seems to have covered a multitude of symptoms but the available evidence suggests that it was a virulent form of influenza.

And then of course there was the disease known colloquially as "the death." It is reported that the plague came first to Venice, of all European cities. When a Venetian galley returned to its home port in the autumn of 1347, after a trading voyage to Caffa on the Black Sea, it carried within its hold certain black rats troubled by a flea known as *Yersinia pestis*. The market of trade between East and West became the entrepôt of death. Venice exported the epidemic, too. (It is said that the Great Plague of London, more than three centuries later, began when two Venetians expired in a tenement house in the north of Drury Lane.) So the "black death" of Europe began. By the spring of 1348 the Venetian authorities, appalled at the massacre of its citizens, appointed a board of three men "to consider diligently all possible ways to preserve the health of the city and avoid the corruption of the air." This is the first recorded instance of public health administration and legislation in Europe.

From an early date, too, a network of public hospitals was

established in the city. There were many pious and charitable institutions catering for poor women, for infants, for orphans, and for the dangerously ill. By 1735, for example, special wards had been set up for patients suffering from tuberculosis. These were the first in the world to be so determined. There was already a guild of doctors and apothecaries by 1258, and fifty years later the state was paying an annual salary to twelve doctor-surgeons. In 1368 an Academy of Medicine was established. In that century doctors were treated very well. They were lightly taxed, and were permitted to dress in any fashion they wished. So they wore white silk stockings and coats of lace. They were also allowed to sport as many rings on their fingers as they desired. They were under strict instruction to supervise the work of pharmacists and apothecaries, but on no account to share in their profits. The pharmacy was of ancient date in Venice, sustained in part by the flow of remedies from trading ports such as Cairo and Byzantium. From the East came that most magical of cures known as *triacle*, a potent mixture of amber and Oriental spices that was supposed to treat all ills from plague to snake bite. From this came the English word treacle.

The economic and social consequences of the first onset of the plague were profound; but there was a difference in the city of the lagoons. The Black Death indirectly triggered the revolt of the Jacquerie in France and the Peasants' Revolt in England, but there was no such insurrection or rebellion in Venice. The people remained quiescent. Nevertheless the shortage of workers was so severe that in October 1348 the Venetian government announced that it would grant citizenship to anyone who settled in the city within the next year. It was an unparalleled, and unrepeated, offer.

In the annals of the city there are recorded no less than seventy visitations of "the death." A plague of 1527 took off one fifth of the population, and Venetian diarists noted that the afflicted were dying on the streets and that their bodies were floating on the canals. But the worst distemper of all occurred in 1575 and 1576, when it is estimated that a third of the population was lost; from July 1575 to February 1577, 46,721 people died in Venice. For fear of contagion wives abandoned husbands, and sons left behind mothers. Titian, who had in the course of his long life never suffered from any dangerous sickness, was one of the victims. The nearby islands of Lazzaretto Nuovo and Lazzaretto

Vecchio, previously the home of lepers, were given over to the victims of the plague. Those who were healthy but suspect, such as travellers who had just returned from foreign cities, were confined to Nuovo for twenty-two days. Those caught flouting the restriction were banished from the city for several years. Those already suffering from the sickness were despatched to Vecchio, where the conditions were predictably fearful. The dormitories were filled with screaming; some of the sick threw themselves into the surrounding water; clouds hung over the little island from the burning of the dead.

The city itself was plunged into one of those fits of self-hatred that were the dark side of its belief in its sacred destiny; the undefiled virgin had suddenly become, in the eyes of one Venetian poet, *orrido mostro* or fearful monster. The vice and luxury of the citizens had called down the vengeance of God. Yet the status of Venice as the ultimate model of the city was also held against it. All cities are meant to be sick. All cities are supposed to harbour death and disease. So in myth and story Venice itself had to be an actively unhealthy place.

The distemper repeated its visits. From July 1630 to October 1631, 46,490 people expired; in the summer of that first year, 24,000 people fled from the city in order to escape the peculiar cloying and oppressive heat that is itself an inducement to fever. At the time of plague a range of saints was invoked, to provide divine protection, but the saints were of no great assistance. The doctors of Venice clothed themselves in black robes, coated with wax and aromatic oils; they wore a hood and cowl over their head, large glasses to protect their eyes, and a long beak-like nose with a filter at its end. They looked themselves like ghouls. But by a curious act of transference this sinister outfit became a popular costume of the Venetian Carnival. It was a *memento mori*, so natural to the carnivalesque, but it was also a manner of laughing at death.

Yet, in general, those who mastered the climate of Venice enjoyed extraordinarily good health. The patrician population of Venice, at least, characteristically lived to a great age. The mildness of the climate was supposed to lead to lassitude and sensuality; in appearance the Venetians of the seventeenth and eighteenth centuries (and perhaps beyond) were characterised by softness of flesh and roundness of form. Their skin was considered to be of a velvety whiteness. Yet appearances can sometimes be deceptive. The chroniclers of the city remarked upon the vivacity of spirit and the impulsive nervous energy of the citizens. Just as the Venetians had formed a city out of adverse circumstances, so they had formed a firm character out of the constant need to defend and maintain it. Life, as was claimed in the nineteenth century, is sustained by excitation.

Many of the doges of Venice were elected when they had reached their nineties. The city was the nurse of old men, and has rightly been considered to be in essence a gerontocracy. "I never in any place observed," Fynes Morisson wrote in the early years of the seventeenth century, "more old men, or so many senators venerable for their grey haires and aged gravity." There is a report in the Venetian archives of the abbess of a convent delivering a complaint to the reigning doge in the summer of 1521; the abbess was 106 years old. Titian died at the age of ninety-one, while Tintoretto was seventy-six and Bellini eighty-six; Guardi was eighty-one and Longhi eighty-three. These were great ages in their respective epochs. Their age is a measure of their endless activity, that elasticity and energy that are the hallmarks of the Venetian genius.

It was said, in general, that Venetians lived longer than other men. The citizens and the poorer population, according to Machiavelli, kept illness at bay through their continual industry. The expenditure of energy in the business of life might withstand the assaults of sickness. The absence of transport, in the modern era, means that it is necessary to walk through the streets and over the bridges. So contemporary Venetians suffer from relatively less high blood pressure and heart disease; the damp air, however, makes them more liable to rheumatoid afflictions.

It was a city of death in quite another sense. Its judicial murders were renowned throughout Europe for their secrecy and swiftness. Those who had offended the state were despatched with efficiency. On a March morning in 1498 the Venetian diarist, Marino Sanudo, heard mutterings on the street to the effect that justice had been done. When he passed through Saint Mark's Square he saw a high government official hanging between the two columns of the piazzetta. The official, accused of treason, had been hanged in the night without notice given to the populace. He had been dressed up in his uniform, with great billowing sleeves. Almost three hundred years later the English artist, James Northcote, was shocked to discover a body suspended between the columns bearing a notice "For treason against the State." It was reported that, if the supply of the condemned grew low, the authorities would borrow corpses from the hospitals and string them up in order to overawe the populace. This is very doubtful.

The ceremonies of public execution were designed to emphasise the fact that the state itself took on a quasi-religious role as avenger of evil. The condemned was accompanied to the block or gallows by the members of a Venetian guild of death wearing black hoods. He or she then turned to an image of Venice, and intoned the *Salve Regina* before the last act. The doge was present, wearing his richest and most elaborate clothes. The people stood in silent order, as if they were members of a congregation. It was a sacred ceremony, designed to purify the collective state of an errant individual. These public executions had nothing of the disorder or gaiety of Tyburn, where individual felons were cheered and applauded as they made their path to the gallows. In Venice they were solemn communal rites.

Many internal enemies of the city were strangled in the cells of the ducal palace, however, their bodies secretly consigned to the waters of the lagoon. When a nephew of the doge was in 1650 seen in a gondola with a Spanish diplomat, he was taken to the cells of his uncle's palace and swiftly despatched. Behind the island of S. Giorgio Maggiore was a deep channel known as the Canale Orfano, where the bodies were released into the sea. One general, a mercenary lured by vast pay to the Venetian side, was suspected of dealing with the enemy. He was recalled in great state to the ducal palace, on the pretence of consultation, and on arrival was directed towards a secret door. "That is not the way," he said. "Yes, yes," he was told. "It is perfectly so." The corridor took him to the prison cell. "I am lost," he is supposed to have said. There was an old Venetian saying, "A dead man makes no war." There was no mercy, either, for any Venetian admiral or commander who failed the state.

The sentences were often very severe. In the fourteenth and fifteenth centuries, false coiners were burned alive. The sons of two senators, convicted of singing blasphemous songs, had their tongues ripped from their throats and their hands cut off. A friar convicted of impregnating no less than fifteen nuns was burned at the stake. Two priests accused of treason were buried alive, face down, on top of one another. The cruelty is somehow reminiscent of eastern practice. There was a novel method of death by starvation. The condemned man was placed in a wooden cage with iron bars, which was then suspended from a pole above the campanile in Saint Mark's Square. He was fed on diminishing amounts of bread and water, conveyed to him by a cord, until he expired from thirst or hunger or exposure in full view of the crowds that thronged the area.

The Venetians were also well known for their methods of secret assassination. In 1421 the council of ten decided to poison the duke of Milan, and agreed to test the liquid on two pigs; the results are not recorded. In 1649 a Venetian doctor concocted the "quintessence" of plague to use against the Turkish enemy; it is the first instance in recorded history of an attempt at biological warfare. It was in fact popularly supposed, in the capitals of Europe, that Venice employed a trained band of assassins ready to strike at their enemies wherever they could. The story was not true, but it represented the deep suspicion that Venice aroused in other states. As the power and wealth of the city began to disappear, the hostility also abated. It was said, in the eighteenth century, that the poison used by the officials of Venice had congealed and that the recipe for its manufacture had been mislaid.

If the reports of state violence were ever true, do they reflect a state of violence also? The nature of the violence is in itself important. It was identified by the authorities as that which abrogated the peace and honour of the society. The rights of the victims, to use a contemporary expression, were seldom invoked. Crimes against the state, such as treason, were treated with swift and brutal punishment. Lesser crimes against the state were treated with no less severity. Some of the most telling punishments, for example, were reserved for those who insulted the city. A Genoese sailor, on arrival, was heard declaring that he would like nothing better than to wash his hands in Venetian blood. He was immediately seized and hanged, the soles of his feet cut off so that his own blood might be sacrificed to the stones of Venice. When in 1329 a Venetian, Marco Rizo, declared that he wished to throw the nobles or "dogs" into prison, he was arrested and his tongue was cut out before he was banished from the city for ever.

Crimes against property were considered more important than crimes of passion. Torture was regularly used in cases of theft, for example, but not in cases of murder. Anyone convicted of robbery more than once was automatically hanged. It seems likely that rape was relatively common, particularly the rape of working-class women by patrician men. But the crime merited only the mild punishment of eight days' imprisonment, the rapist being freed when he had forfeited a sum equivalent to the woman's dowry. It was not considered to be important. The court records show that women under attack would often call "Fire!" rather than "Rape!" because the threat provoked more interest.

The patricians were often the most violent class of Venetian society, although their peers were inclined to moderate any punishment against them if their crimes did not threaten the status quo. The young patricians, in particular, could be ferocious. Casanova always carried a knife with him that, as he said, "all honest men in Venice carry to defend their lives." The citizens, and the people, were more docile. There was a large police force, and the *popolani* were themselves vigilant and fierce in protecting public safety. In a heavily populated mercantile city, it was in everyone's best interest to maintain order. There was room for party faction, but not for gangs. The individual criminal was not fêted, as, for example, Jack Sheppard was in London. In any case, in a city ringed with water, where was the criminal to flee?

Is it surprising, therefore, that many people go mad in Venice? This author has heard howling, as if from the damned, coming from the tiny tenement houses of the district of Castello. Madness afflicts islanders more insidiously than others. There has never been a madhouse in the city itself; that might be considered to be too provocative. The insane were instead incarcerated on the various islands of the lagoon. The female mad, for example, were from the eighteenth century locked up on the island of S. Clemente where for various transgressions they could be suspended in cages above the water. The male asylum on the island of S. Servolo was immortalised by Shelley:

> "What we behold
> Shall be the madhouse and its belfry tower,"
> Said Maddalo, "and even at this hour
> Those who may cross the water hear that bell
> Which calls the maniacs, each one from his cell
> To vespers."

The detail of Christ and the musicians from *The Marriage Feast at Cana* by Paolo Veronese. In sixteenth-century Venice, art and music were closely associated. Here a quartet is shown playing to the invited guests; the members of that musical group have been identified as Titian, Tintoretto, Bassano and Veronese himself.

An eighteenth-century painting by Gabriele Bella showing a concert given by the girls of the hospital music societies in Venice. The orphan girls in the charitable institutions of the state were given an extensive and elaborate musical training, so that their concerts became the wonder of the age. "I cannot imagine anything," Rousseau wrote, "so voluptuous, so touching as this music."

The Parlour of the San Zaccaria Convent in Venice. This painting by Francesco Guardi reveals the refined and luxurious atmosphere of the eighteenth-century convents of Venice. They were essentially homes for unmarried patrician women, accustomed to the comforts of the outer world. The convents of Venice became a form of theatre, with the nuns sitting behind gratings watching the rest of Venice cavort before them.

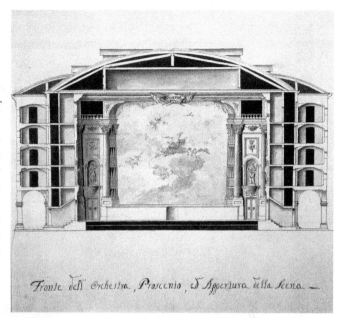

en and ink drawing of 1787
wing a cross-section view of
theatre on the Grand Canal.
The theatre was intrinsic to
etian life, and Venetians were
own throughout Europe for
their love of drama. It was a
sion that touched all classes,
from the gondolier to the
patrician. Venetian stagecraft
was also renowned for its
subtlety and elaboration.

Fronte dell' Orchestra, Proscenio, ed Apperiura della scena —

A portrait of the Venetian dramatist, Carlo
Goldoni, by Alessandro Longhi. Goldoni was
the greatest of all the city's playwrights. His
was the comedy of Venetian social life. He held
a mirror up to Venetian nature. He captivated
the eighteenth-century public with portraits
of gondoliers and of servants, of shop-keepers
and housewives.

n eighteenth-century watercolour of a
Venetian nobleman patronising a café.
ce has always been more famous for its
cafés than for its restaurants. In the
teenth century they were calculated to
mber two hundred, with thirty-five in
int Mark's Square itself. The customers
yed cups of coffee and cups of chocolate, or glasses of lemonade and syrup.

A fresco painted by Giandomenico Tiepolo, at the end of the eighteenth century, showing Pulcinella disporting with acrobats. Pulcinella was a character from *commedia dell'arte*, the characteristic Venetian entertainment that first emerged in the sixteenth century, growing eve wilder and more obscene over the centuries. He wore a white costume and a black mask, and was well known for his long nose.
In England he became known as Punch.

A pen and ink sketch, from the eighteenth century, showing three masked figures in Carnival costume. The Carnival was instituted at the end of the eleventh century, and has continued without interruption for almost seven hundred years. By the eighteenth century, at the very latest, the masks had become indispensable. Even the beggars wore masks.

Canaletto's painting *A Regatta on the Grand Canal*. The regatta was an annual event, at the tim the Carnival, watched eagerly by all Venetians; it was formally instituted in the fourteent century, and has continued ever since. This painting shows the one-oared light gondola ra

...ainting of a masked ball taking place in Saint Mark's Square during the Carnival. John ...n, the seventeenth-century English diarist, described such events as part of the "universal ...dnesse" with "the Women, Men & persons of all Conditions disguising themselves in antique dresses & extravagant Musique & a thousand gambols."

A painting by Gabriele Bella showing a battle with sticks on a Venetian bridge. It was know[n] *guerra dei pugni* or the war of the fists, fought between the inhabitants of the various territori[es or] neighbourhoods. A team from each of these territories met for battle on a chosen bridge, [while] thousands of spectators lined the streets and houses beside the canal. It was a glorified fist [fight] in which the object was to hurl opponents into the water and to gain possession of the b[ridge].

A game of bowls in the Camp[o] dei Gesuiti, painted by Gabrie[le] Bella in the eighteenth centur[y]. The square or campo was at t[he] heart of the neighbourhood. I[t] spread before the parish chur[ch and] was once its burial ground. It [was a] self-contained entity, marked [by] its well and carved well-head [where] the women of the parish cam[e to] gossip. It was a Venice in mini[ature].

An etching of the Bridge of Sighs, that led from the ducal palace to the ducal prisons. It was named after the laments of those about to be gaoled, and is the most picturesque of all penitential emblems. It was not in fact given that name until the nineteenth century; yet it serves the purpose, and the image, of Venice very well.

...he front cover of *Casanova* by ...é Jeanne, published in 1927. ...Jacques Casanova is the most ...of all Venice's favourite sons. ...is the quintessential Venetian, ...his memoirs demonstrate the ...ty with which life in the city ...be turned into self-conscious ...elf-serving drama. "The chief ...ss of my life has always been ...ndulge my senses," he wrote. ...ver knew anything of greater ...rtance." This might be justifi- ...ly described as a main article ...of the Venetian creed.

Chemin de Fer de L'EST

DE PARIS À VENISE
par BELFORT BÂLE, LUCERNE et le St. GOTHARD

A poster advertising the Eastern Railway travelling from Paris to Venice at the end of the nineteenth century. The Grand Tour had given way to upper-middle-class travel with Venice as the most desirable destination of all. By the 1840s tourist guides to the city were being written; the first "Cook's tour" of Venice was arranged in 1864. "The Venice of today," Henry James wrote, "is a vast museum where the little wicket that admits you is perpetually turning and creaking…"

From the grated windows of their cells the mad used to call out to the passing gondolas.

The city itself can be said to exhibit certain psychopathic tendencies. It has always been a city in a state of high anxiety. Ever since its difficult and dangerous origin in the waters it has felt itself to be besieged by all the forces of the world. It was once literally isolated, and it has always suffered from great ontological uncertainty. It is not difficult to understand the reasons for this; if you can imagine New York, or Paris, suspended upon water you may be able to understand the deep fear engendered by the position. Water is unstable. Water is unpredictable. That is why Venice has always emphasised its stability and permanence.

Throughout its history it has considered itself to be under threat. It conveys images of fragility and vulnerability, and thus insistently elicits responses of caring and nurturing. In the twelfth century a number of earth tremors sent the citizens into a panic. In 1105 the island of Malamocco was overwhelmed by water, and it was believed that the city of Venice would suffer the same fate. In the thirteenth century the danger of fire was almost hysterically emphasised; it was considered to be the enemy within, smouldering in concealment, ready to break out in the shadows of the night. In the fifteenth century the city was considered to be in great danger from the silting of the lagoon and the drying of the canals. It was said that it became more fragile with every passing year. In the latter half of the century it was believed that Venice was in imminent peril because of its sinfulness; the judgement of God would not be long delayed. There was a terror of total submersion as a sign of divine anger.

There has never been a time when Venice was not in peril. In every century it was concluded that the city could not survive. Deep and endemic anxiety is perhaps the key to all of the city's actions—its absorption of the mainland and its acquisition of an empire were attempts to reduce uncertainty. The slow grave government of the patricians was in effect a defence mechanism. The Venetians hated unpredictability. There was a genuine fear of the future. The acquisitiveness of the city, the lust after gold and other riches, can perhaps be explained as the miser Scrooge of *A Christmas Carol* was explained—"You fear the world too much." Yet its great triumph, the essential source of its civic pride in the seventeenth and eighteenth centuries, its claim to enduring fame, lay in one simple fact—it had placed itself in a vulnerable position, and yet it had remained inviolate. What other nation on earth could claim as much?

It has always been a self-conscious, indeed a self-obsessed, city. It has also been a self-deluded city. It has lied about itself. It has woven myths of itself. It has fabricated a history utterly at odds with the true one. It was at the mercy of conflicting impulses; it preached civic liberty, for example, at the same time as it demanded total control over its population. It could give all the appearance of festive gaiety, but at the centre of its polity was commercial calculation. There was self-hatred, too, in the numerous calls for the people of Venice to eschew the temptations of luxury and sensuality and prodigality. The message was that "we must be pure." We must ourselves be inviolate like the city. We must be above reproach. That is why any threat of disorder or danger was expelled to the margins. The fluctuations in the public mood were severe. Any sudden reversal or unexpected defeat threw the people into despair. The sixteenth-century diarist, Marino Sanudo, often used the refrain that "the whole city was mightily downcast." There was always the fear of conspiracy. In a human being, this would be considered a dangerous symptom of psychic disorder.

Yet Venice can be said to represent all cities. It embodied the anxieties that afflict cities—the fear of disease, the fear of contamination, the fear of being for ever cut off from the natural world. It represents, too, the anxieties concerning cities—their luxury, their power, their aggression. It is a fearful place.

XI

City of Myth

34

The Map Unrolls

There are many maps of Venice, not all of them very reliable. It must be one of the most mapped cities in the world, and yet in a sense it is unmappable. The *calli* are too labyrinthine, the connections are too circuitous. There are just too many alleys and passage-ways to be set down on paper. The city does not in any case exist on one level, but on the canals, along the bridges, beside the first-floor windows. An all too familiar sight is that of tourists brandishing maps and looking up vainly at the names of streets and bridges. They may find themselves somewhere that is "not there." It is impossible for the stranger not to get lost in Venice. Cities of the mind, in any case, cannot be found on any map.

The first surviving map of Venice, where the eventual shape of the city can clearly be seen, was produced in the early twelfth century. The most famous map, however, remains Jacopo de' Barbari's "bird's-eye view" of 1500. This was the map that created the image of Venice as significant form. Its detail was unparalleled, its execution unrivalled. Yet it was a symbolic, rather than naturalistic, representation. It imparted a form of sacred geometry and in the process emphasised the role of artifice in the creation of the city. Mercury, sitting on a cloud above the city with the axis of the Rialto market and the basilica of Saint Mark directly beneath him, announces that "I Mercury shine favourably upon this above all other markets." Neptune gazes at him from the waters of the lagoon, declaring that "I Neptune reside here, smoothing the waters of this port." The city itself takes the form of a dolphin disporting on the waves. It is also deserted, lending credence to the belief that Venice was more important than any of its passing inhabitants. They were merely the shadows upon its walls. The map was of course useless for any practical purpose. As another fifteenth-century Venetian cartographer, Fra Mauro, put it, "my map . . . was only one version of reality. It would only be of any use if it were employed as an instrument of the imagination. It occurred to me that the world itself should be seen as an elaborate artifice, and the expression of a will without end."

Many Venetian maps were also an expression of the city's mercantile interests. They were designed not simply to outline the trading routes to Cathay or Trebizond, but to facilitate the passage of trade in places where no one from the city had ever traded before. There was much competition, for example, to find a sea route to the spices of the Indies. On the back wall of the loggia beside the Rialto market were frescoes composing a *mappamundi*; in the loggia itself was kept a copy of *The Travels of Marco Polo*.

The Venetians were expert, and famous, cartographers. They were looking for fixity, and certainty, in their watery world. It is easy to understand their obsession in a city where map and reality rarely meet. Map-making represents the desire for order and control. It is another aspect of the all-observing government. The Venetian authorities, for example, commissioned many detailed maps on all aspects of the provinces on the mainland under their dominion. It was perhaps in this spirit of conquest that a Venetian cartographer wrote the first essay on landscape painting. There were no landscapes in Venice. Landscapes could only be created out of colonised territory. In 1448 another Venetian map-maker, Andrea Bianco, first intimated the existence of the Americas by drawing an "island" in the approximate position of Brazil. A Venetian, Giovanni Contarini, executed the first accurate map of Africa at the beginning of the sixteenth century.

Maps of the world covered the walls of the houses of the prominent merchants and patricians. The apartments of the ducal palace were decorated with maps that outlined the trading routes of Venice across the known world. In a painting of the mid-eighteenth century by Pietro Longhi, "The Geography Lesson," a fashionable patrician lady consults a globe with a pair of compasses in her right hand; an open atlas lies at her feet. Fra Mauro himself, a Benedictine monk from Murano, created a famous *mappamundi* complete with symbolic detail and scriptural reference. He declared that he had created it "for the meditation of the illustrious rulers" of the city. By the middle of the fifteenth century there was a workshop in Venice devoted wholly to the production of maps. The Venetian map-makers were particularly renowned for their portolano charts, maps of coastlines designed specifically for the use of sailors. In 1648 there was established in Venice an Academy of the Argonauts that specialised in the publication of maps and globes.

It is no wonder, therefore, that a copy of *The Travels of Marco Polo* was kept in the Rialto. Polo is the most famous of all Venetians, with the possible exception of Casanova, and he is the most famous of all travellers. His was in one sense a typical Venetian business story. He was part of a trading family. There were once two brothers, born in the Venetian parish of S. Giovanni Grisostomo, who were at the head of a mercantile house in Constantinople; it was a branch of their family business. They were patricians but, in Venice, patricians thrived on trade.

In 1260 Niccolò and Matteo Polo, at a time of great turmoil in the Byzantine city, decided to travel east in order to find new markets. They took with them a stock of jewels, well hidden in their clothes, and began a long journey into Central Asia. They made their way to the city of Bukhara, in the region now known as Uzbekistan, where wars and rumours of war delayed their progress for almost three years. It was their good fortune, however, to become acquainted with some envoys on their way to the court of the Great Khan, "the lord of all the Tartars in the world." It was not an opportunity to be missed. So they travelled to the city of Kublai Khan. The emperor was courteous and inquisitive; he questioned them closely about the laws and customs of their society. At the end of their stay in Peking, he entrusted them with a message for the pope and requested them to return to him with oil taken from the lamps that burned before the sepulchre of Christ in Jerusalem.

It took them another three and a half years to make their way back to Venice. They had not seen their city for fifteen years and, on their return, Niccolò Polo found in the household a son who was now sixteen. He had been named after the guardian saint of Venice. Eventually they received letters of papal blessing and privilege from the new pope, Gregory X, and were able to take a phial of the precious oil. Then they returned to the court of Kublai Khan, with young Marco Polo as part of their company. Once more their journey lasted for three and a half years. Yet the most intriguing part is yet to tell. Twenty-four years later, three strangers arrived in the parish of S. Giovanni Grisostomo. They wore coats of coarse wool like Tartar warriors. They had long hair and long beards, their skin harshly burned with long exposure. Marco Polo, together with his father and uncle, had finally returned home.

They were not recognised as members of the Ca' Polo. They spoke a barbarous Venetian. They would very likely have been removed from the parish as imposters. Then Marco put the matter to the proof. He took the three coats of homespun wool, and ripped them open. Sewn within them were multitudes of precious jewels—rubies, sapphires, diamonds, emeralds—that they had acquired through the generosity of the Great Khan. The Venetians were of course instantly convinced by this lavish display of wealth and, according to the chronicler, received the travellers "with the greatest honour and reverence." Marco Polo became known as Marco Millione, and the courtyard of his house became known as the Corte Millione. Recent excavations on the site of his family house have revealed the laying of new foundations that date from the time of Polo's return; his money did not remain in jewels.

The world knows that the story does not stop there. Marco was a great patriot and at his own expense fitted out a galley for the war against the Genoese. At the battle of Curzola, in September 1298, Polo was captured and taken. He was incarcerated in a Genoese gaol, where he lay for about a year. During that time he became known for his fabulous stories of distant lands. And he found an amanuensis. An old man from Pisa, known as Rusticiano, took down his narrative in a curious antique French borrowed from the romances. The written account has all the marks of verbal delivery—"this is enough upon that matter, now I will tell you of something else," "now let us leave the nation of Mosul and I will tell you about the great city of Baldoc," "but first I must tell you. . . ."

The manuscript was copied. It began to spread. But after his imprisonment Marco Polo returned to a quiet and obscure life in his native city, engaged in nothing more than the usual commercial routine. He presented one copy of his book to a visiting French knight, but there is no record of any other connection with the work that has made him immortal. He died in 1323, at the age of sixty-nine. On his deathbed he declared that he had not told half of the things that he had seen. It was once believed that his stories were just that—stories—but in recent years it has become more and more evident that he was in fact giving a true record of the nations and cities through which he travelled. He was practical and prudent, clear-headed and with an eye for detail. He also has an almost child-like energy and curiosity that permitted him to survive many years of wandering among bewilderingly strange peoples. He was very much a Venetian. We might almost deem him to be a Venetian hero, except that the city detested heroic individuals as a threat to the well-being of the state.

From the narrative of his travels it is clear that Polo journeyed across the whole longitude of Asia on behalf of Kublai Khan, eager to know the details of his empire. Only a Venetian, perhaps, could have carried out such a mission. He was the first traveller to reveal the wealth and greatness of China, to describe the steppes of Mongolia and the fastness of Tibet; he wrote of Burma and of Siam, of Java and of India; he expatiates on the sorcerers of Pashai and the idolaters of Kashmir; he narrates the battle between Genghis Khan and Prester John.

His was in many respects a miraculous journey, but Polo was really following a Venetian tradition. Diplomats and other officials were required to give detailed written reports or *relazioni* of the foreign cities they had visited. Polo's book was in part intended to provide the Venetians with an object lesson in good governance. It could be said in fact that, a few years after the traveller's return, the Venetian government did introduce some of the principles if not the details of the Mongol system. They were following the precepts of the Great Khan, the Great Lord of Lords, whom Polo describes as "the most potent man, as regards forces and lands and treasure, that exists in the world, or ever has existed from the time of our first father Adam until this day."

The merchants of Venice, too, needed precise relation of the conditions of local societies and local economies. What were their needs? What could they sell? Just as they were trained to appraise goods with an objective eye, so they were keenly observant of local conditions. They needed, above all else, information. It is appropriate, then, that Polo particularly observed the trade in all the cities that he visited. Of the city of Kubenan, in Persia, he wrote that "there is much iron and steel and *ondanique*, and they make steel mirrors of great size and beauty." Once he had described how people earn their livings he would often add that "there is nothing else worth mentioning."

The Venetian patricians were professional travellers, predominantly in their role as merchants. Unlike their contemporaries in Florence or in Hamburg, they could not survive without accurate knowledge of the coasts and seas. So the spirit of travel was always part of Venetian consciousness. How could it not be, when the city faced outwards to the Adriatic and the Mediterranean? By the ninth century Venetian traders had visited Egypt, the Euxine region and the sea of Azov. In the early fifteenth century there was a Venetian serving as a knight in Denmark. A century later a Venetian shipbuilder was prospering in the yards of Elefante in India.

There are travellers' tales of Greenland and of Tartary. Pietro Querini sailed into the Arctic Ocean in 1432; forty years later, Giosafatte Barbaro touched the shores of the Caspian Sea. When John Cabot (a citizen of Venice by choice and state decree) made landfall in the New World, he planted the flag of Saint Mark beside the English standard. It is worth mentioning, perhaps, that Sebastian Cabot was born in Venice; he went on to discover Labrador in 1498, and was to be found in the lower reaches of the Rio della Plata in 1526. In the middle of the fifteenth century a young Venetian patrician, Alvise da Mosto, travelled to Senegal and discovered the Cape Verde islands. He wrote down the details of his journeys, in true Venetian fashion, since he was "the first that from the most noble city of Venice have set forth to sail the Ocean beyond the straits of Gibraltar towards the south, to the land of the Negroes. . . ." He was first and foremost a trader, however, exchanging horses and wool and silk for slaves and parrots.

The object of the Venetian travellers was to achieve both profit and honour; social authority and esteem were derived from commercial wealth, and these journeys of discovery were designed to acquire all of them. That is why many merchants kept journals of their progress. It was a way of confirming their exploits, and their diaries acted as memorials for the family business. The first travellers' accounts were published at Venice in the fifteenth century. In 1543 was issued an anthology of travel writing entitled *Journeys from Venice to Tana, Persia, India and Constantinople*. The first steps were taken from the city of the lagoon.

Maps transcribe frontiers. Venice was always a frontier. It was called "the hinge of Europe." It has the essence of a boundary—a liminal space—in all of its dealings. It is a perpetual threshold. It is half land and half sea. It is the middle place between the ancient imperial cities of

Rome and Byzantium. It was the place where Italy mingled with the Orient, and where in more general terms Europe mingled with Africa. It was the place to take ship for the Levant and leave behind the world of Christendom. That is why some considered it to be the sacred mission of Venice to unite western Christendom to the rest of the world—to the Greek Christians of the Bosphorus as well as to the adherents of Islam and Hinduism.

Goethe described it as "the market-place of the Morning and Evening lands" by which he meant that the city, poised between west and east, is the median point of the rising and the setting suns. When the empire was divided in the time of Charlemagne the lagoons of Venice were ascribed neither to the west nor to the east; according to the Venetian historian, Bernardo Giustiniani, they were left "inviolate and intact almost as certain holy places." He went on to say that "these places were left as kinds of boundaries between both emperors." In the medieval period the postal service provided by Venetian galleys was the only means of communication between the courts of Germany and of Constantinople. The first images of the Muslim world came from Venice.

It was a frontier, too, between the sacred and the profane. The public spaces of the city were liminal areas between piety and patriotism. The boundaries between past and present were ill-defined, just as the boundaries between private and public were endlessly transgressed. This was the place where Catholics and Protestants, Jews and Christians, Turks and Europeans, Roman and Orthodox, all met and mingled. All the civilisations that made up the Mediterranean—Graeco-Roman, Muslim, Judaic and Christian—found a focus in Venice. It was said of Venetian painters of the fifteenth century that they had effected a synthesis between the Tuscan and Flemish styles of art. The city was the doorway between the cold north and the warm south, first fashioned for trade but then a means of access for the general business of life that flowed across Europe.

Venice in every sense represented cultural and social heterogeneity. By some it was considered to be Oriental, with the basilica of Saint Mark as the very model of a mosque and the Rialto as a souk. That was why the city was so distrusted by other European nations. It contained within itself intimations of "the Other." It is pertinent and suggestive that the Arabic words that penetrated the Venetian dialect are largely concerned with trade—so we have *zecca* (mint) and *doana* (customs house) and *tariffa*—or concerned with luxuries such as "sofa" and "divan" and "caravanserai." "Alas Venetian race," Pius II wrote in 1458, "how much of your ancient character have you lost! Too much intercourse with the Turks has made you the friend of the Mohammedans." The façade of the ducal palace, facing the lagoon, is Muslim in inspiration. There are in fact borrowings and adaptations—of Islamic architecture and Islamic art—throughout the city. Even the Venetian colours, ultramarine blue and gold, are derived from the Middle East. The trade routes, the organised seagoing caravans, even the craft guilds, of Venice were Muslim in origin. There was a genuine sympathy with, and admiration for, Islamic civilisation that was not unconnected with distaste for papal pomp. In the paintings of Carpaccio, for example, Venetian interiors are shown to be decorated with objects of eastern provenance; the throne of the Virgin in Gentile Bellini's "Virgin and Child Enthroned" is placed carefully on a Turkish carpet or prayer rug.

Venice was in many respects akin to Byzantium. It borrowed both concepts and practices from the ancient city, to the rule of which it had once submitted. It was even known as the second Constantinople. It was a hierarchical, rather than a feudal, society. The influence of Byzantine civilisation was noticeable in the way that the young girls of Venice were kept secluded, and in the custom of separating men and women at church services; it can be seen, too, in the stiffness and pomp of the religious ceremonies where the rituals and relics of the Byzantine Church are to be found in abundance. There is something Oriental, too, about the stateliness and symbolism of Venetian political life with its elaborate bureaucratic machinery and its solemn practices of election. Was the doge not also a form of emperor? He could be seen in a similarly sacred light. In Holy Week the doge impersonated the last days of Christ. This was also the role of the Byzantine emperor.

The basilica of Saint Mark was based upon the model of the Apostoleion in Constantinople. The chroniclers of Venice also report that the church was the work of an architect from that city, but the claim is disputed. There seems to be no doubt, however, that there were Muslim artisans resident at the time. The religious polity of Venice, with its notion of a state Church, is based upon Byzantine example; the head of that Church was known as the patriarch, as at Constantinople.

There are many other derivations. The notion of the Arsenal, an arms manufactory funded by the government, is taken from Byzantine practice. The long black cloak, worn by the male patricians of the city, is taken from the model of the Byzantine kaftan. The ritual scattering of coins to the people, on the occasion of the election of the doge, is a practice borrowed from the eastern emperors. The art of keeping detailed records is surely derived from the early experience of Byzantine bureaucracy. The word itself—"Byzantine"—has become a synonym for excessive detail. In Venice, too, everything was committed to writing. When Venetian males grew beards, at times of national or personal sorrow, they were following their eastern contemporaries. The love of puppets and of puppet theatre has an ancient ancestry. Of course Italians in general have long maintained a tradition of puppetry and mask theatre, but Venetians acquired their love of puppets from the more spectral tradition of Byzantium that emphasises the melancholy aspect of the inanimate doll until human desire gives it breath.

35

The Huddled Family

Until very recent times there was always a sense of brotherhood among the people of Venice. It was the merest cliché to state that they all represented one family. Everyone noticed it. It manifested itself in an air of sociability. The *popolani* were the "children" of the republic, and the male patricians were their fathers; Goethe described the doge as "the grandfather of the race." The provision of public health care, and the foundation of orphanages for fatherless children, testify to the fact that the state considered itself to be in essence one extended family. The governors of these institutions strove to create little families within the larger family. This was the Venetian way.

The degree of harmony can be overstated; there were the usual disputes and enmities that occur in any enclosed community. The Venetians were not saints. But there was none of that raucous disharmony or that partisan rancour that affected cities such as Genoa and Florence. The affections and attitudes of the people were confined within a small and insular space; it was natural and inevitable that social life would take a familial tone. The topography of the city was seen as an immense family house. James described it as a collective apartment, and remarked upon "the splendid common domicile, familiar, domestic and resonant." It is said that Napoleon coined the description of Saint Mark's Square as the finest drawing room in Europe. This was a family, however, that could never leave the house.

The family was itself the defining social force of Venetian society. Political and commercial alliances were built upon the foundation of family life. The phrase, *l'honorevolezza della casa*, the honour of the house, was often used and quoted. The success or failure of a political career depended in large part upon the influence of the patrician's family. The same names—Vendramin, Barbo, Zen, Foscari, and Dandolo among them—appear through centuries of Venetian history. They are far more enduring than the Bacons or the Cecils. The great council was essentially a meeting of families, tied together by sets of obligations and responsibilities; it was temperamentally a place of accommodation and compromise, therefore, rather than a partisan assembly. It was not an arena for the display of principle or ideology. Individual families were not able to form factions, or excessively influence the results of elections; they survived on the foundation of mutual dependence.

In law the Venetian authorities considered the entire family to be responsible for the misdeeds of an individual member of the household. The anonymous compiler of the *Cronica Venetiarum*, in the middle of the fourteenth century, described particular families just as if they were individuals with certain habits and characteristics; the Dandolos were "audacious," whereas the Barberini were "senseless . . . sporting themselves throughout the world." It was said that there never had been a rich Barbo, a poor Mocenigo, or a compassionate Erizzo. The same surname will occur among lists of the senate, of the episcopal authorities, of the great traders. There was an obsession in Venice with genealogy, and in the fifteenth century *Libri d'Oro* or Golden Books were instituted to record patrician marriages and births.

The major agent of business in the city was the *fraterna* or family collective. Its ledgers would comprise household accounts and business accounts as part of the same equation. Brothers who lived together were treated as business partners unless they formally dissolved their association; family businesses were considered to be more efficient and more responsive. Fathers and sons, according to one patrician, worked for each other "with more love, more honour, more profit and less expense." Certainly the "overheads" could be cut. There were many more bachelors in Venetian society than anywhere else in Italy. In the fifteenth century, for example, more than half the adult male patricians of the city remained single. When they died they left their property to the married brother's children, thus keeping the business in the immediate family.

The household itself was considered to be an image of the state. It was an institution in which the individual will was obliged to submit itself to the collective decision. The husband held an impersonal authority; the wife was meant simply to breed; the children were ordained to silence and obedience. Masters and servants were bound together in a tight context of control. Without the family, there would be no state; without the state, there would be no family. The ideal of familial harmony was, therefore, very strong. The statutes of the building commissioners of Venice invoked "love and fruitful happiness between . . . good neighbours and dear friends." The members of the confraternity of S. Giovanni Evangelista desired grace "through love of brotherhood," while the stonecutters worked for "the good and welfare of all."

We may compare the people of Venice, therefore, to the bees working together in their hives of gold. Bees are obedient to the general purpose of the hive. They compete, but they do not struggle. They are tireless in their work, but there is no obvious coercion exercised upon them other than the search for the common good. There are no civil wars. In *The Feminine Monarchy or the History of the Bees*, published in 1609, Charles Butler named certain characteristics of the bees; they were profitable, laborious, loyal, swift, nimble, bold, and cunning. All of those qualities have also been ascribed to the Venetian people. Pliny the Elder remarked that bees are bee-like because "they recognise only what is in the common interest." That is also the key to the understanding of Venetian society. We may also adduce the nature of Venice from Bee Wilson's *The Hive*, in which she states that the bee-hive "is a place where the world of nature and the world of artifice collapse into each other, which is why it is so mysterious." This is also the mystery of the city.

What is that common good for which the people of Venice strive? It might be called the necessity of survival itself, the continuation of being. There need be no other goal than the maintenance and preservation of life itself. It is primordial, manifest in the cry of a child and the gasp of a dying man. "On one point alone is there agreement," the Spanish ambassador wrote of Venetian government in the early seventeenth century, "and that is the perpetuation of ruling." All the other motives for human action—wealth, power, glory—are subordinate to this central need. It is a principle of interrelation or interaction, based upon organic force rather than mechanical power. It is the flow of connected purposive activities that is the history of Venice. In history of course we trace separate events, and attempt to designate "causes" to them. But the central cause is beyond reach. It is part of the inner being of things. Instead we may glimpse only a network of relations, more important and more fundamental than the events or objects that are related.

The common good embodied the communal will and the communal sensitivity. Every individual was supposed to subordinate his or her interests to those of the state. If it is possible for proto-capitalism also to be a form of proto-communism, then Venice represents that condition. But these terms may be anachronistic. It may be better to subsume them within the context of the medieval collective, and with the notion of the city as a human organism created in the image of God. "Capitalism" and "communism" then become instruments of the instinctive need to battle and to survive. It was said that in a republic such as Venice, unlike a dukedom or kingdom, the common good took precedence over the role and will of individuals. The nature of the republic lies in a legal and institutional process, not in power or in personality. There was no single focus of power in Venice. It was a pluralistic force. There were no despots in the whole course of Venetian history. The city itself was always pre-eminent.

The idea of the family manifests itself in four different instincts or beliefs. The territory of the city is deemed to be a common heritage; the government of the city represents a sacred covenant; the origin of the city is to be found in family or clan; the piety of the city lies in the respect for forefathers. The citizens of Venice were born into a setting of human interdependence and natural need. This is perhaps the condition of life itself. Social life is man's state of nature. There is no need to posit some Rousseau-esque social contract. This was also the insight vouchsafed to George Eliot who, on observing sunset in the Venetian lagoon, remarked that "it is the sort of scene in which I could most readily forget my own existence, and feel melted into the general life."

The goals were unanimity and solidarity. The major projects of Venetian trade, for example, were collective endeavours whereby groups of merchants bound themselves together in formal treaty for the carriage of goods. The government itself took responsibility for the largest galleys. The people of Venice found their meaning in the network of guilds and parishes and *scuole* that formed the social life of the city. There were endless committees and councils and boards of control.

The equality of the Venetian people themselves is a matter of argument. The division of the populace into patricians, citizens and *popolani* might suggest that there was indeed a hierarchy of social position and social responsibility. But there is also no doubt that there were levelling tendencies at work within the Venetian polity. As early as the sixth century Cassiodorus, the Ostrogothic leader, remarked to the Venetians that "among you there is no difference between rich and poor; your food is the same, your houses are all alike." According to tradition all the houses in the city had once been of the same height. When in the eleventh century two or three old families tried to create ruling dynasties they were rebuffed by the patriciate who said that "we did not come here to live under a lord."

There is in fact a broad equality among merchants. Money knows no class or barrier. So Thomas Coryat noted that "their Gentlemen and greatest Senators, a man worth perhaps two millions of duckats, will come into the market, and buy their flesh, fruites, and such other things as are necessary for the maintenance of their families." The streets of the city, and the narrowness of its bounds, meant that there was a constant mixing and mingling of classes. As merchants, too, the patricians could not divorce themselves from the common life. That is why the lowest floors of the grander houses were often let out for shops and warehouses. The laws of Venice prohibited displays of ostentatious extravagance. But frugality, or what was known as *mediocritas*, was in any case a Venetian instinct; many wills stipulate that the person is to be buried "with as little pomp as possible." And then there is the natural environment. Water is a great leveller. It has been remarked, for example, that the River Thames is a great haven of social equality. On water all are at an equal level.

So there was a pronounced cordiality among all the people of Venice. An English aristocrat of the eighteenth century observed that "there is a universal politeness here in every rank; the people expect a civil deportment from their nobles towards them; and they return it with much respect and veneration; but should a noble assume an insolent arrogant manner towards his inferior, it would not be borne with." They were all in it together. In the comedies of Goldoni servants often lose their tempers with masters. And masters never, ever, strike their servants. There were some who deplored this freedom of manners. In a dialogue entitled *Discorsi Morali*, of the late sixteenth century, a speaker remarked that in Venice "servants are licentious, dissolute, vicious and disrespectful" whereas those who attended princely courts were "good, loyal, sincere and well-mannered."

There was a stated belief, then, in the concept of "freedom," manifested in the original notion of a state that was not the servant of princes. The myth of communalism, when in reality the refugees had fled under the leadership of bishops or local lords, was very strong. For the government, freedom did not consist of private liberty, but of freedom from interference by other states.

From at least the fourteenth century, Venice offered visitors and strangers the luxury of liberty of belief. That is why it was seen as an open city, accommodating Calvinists and Anabaptists as well as Greek Orthodox and Muslims and Jews. Bigotry does not consort easily with free trade. "Because I am a man born in a free city," one senator told his colleagues, "I will freely express my feelings." It is not a sentence that could have been uttered in many places at the beginning of the sixteenth century. At the end of the seventeenth century, too, a French chronicler wrote that "The Liberty of *Venice* makes every thing Authentick, for whatsoever the Life is, or Religion one Professes, provided you do not Talk, or Attempt anything against the State, or the Nobility, one may be sure to Live unmolested, for no Body will go about to Censure their Conduct, or to oppose the Disorders of their Neighbours."

That is the reason why this freedom of conscience migrated into freedom of behaviour. It has always been a feature of the city, and in the fourteenth century Petrarch had condemned the "foul language and excessive licence" of the Venetians. But it became the defining feature of the city in the seventeenth and eighteenth centuries. Venice became known for what would now be called "permissiveness," and it was soon remarked that personal liberty was not incompatible with ordered government. This was a revelation to the rest of the world. English tourists often contrasted the atmosphere of Venice with that of London, in which city the major occupation consisted in censuring the behaviour of other people. Nothing of the kind ever happened in the city of the lagoon. There was method, however, behind the emollient atmosphere. Freedom prompted visitors into spending more and more money. There was another kind of liberty. In Venice you could leave your past and acquire a new identity.

It has often been remarked that there are very few biographies or autobiographies in Venetian literature. The individual is indeed absent in Venetian life. The children of the patrician class were taught at an early age that they must not strive to stand above their fellows. It was said that the Venetians never forgave failure by their admirals or commanders but, similarly, they never forgave success. Individual glory might imperil that of the city.

The predominant mode of portraiture in Venice was group portraiture; it has in fact been suggested that the collective portrait first emerged in the city. The great nineteenth-century historian of Venice, Pompeo Molmenti, remarked that "in Venetian painting the individual is lost in the joyous throng." Tintoretto, for example, was fascinated by the movement and orchestration of crowds; he was rarely interested in the depiction of individual human beings, who are subordinate to the overall rhythm and unity of the composition in much the same way as the Venetian people are part of the rhythm of the state. In the paintings of Carpaccio there are always groups of people exchanging pleasantries and engaging in gossip. They are never arguing. There is never a sense that they could change anything about their lives. That is the nature of Venetian society. Venice was always a place for crowds rather than for solitary wanderers; the most common sight, in the twenty-first century, is of groups of tourists. If the individual is depicted by the Venetian portraitist he (and it is almost always he) is shown in his social and political role. There is no trace of the inner life and no attempt at psychological revelation. There is instead a careful anonymity. The expression is character-istically remote or aloof. The note is one of reserve and decorum, what was known in Venice as *decoro*. The individual is less important than the rank or class of that individual; the sitter is seen to be absorbed by his role in the state. It is almost invariably the case that the hands are concealed.

It is hard, therefore, to praise the famous men and women of Venice. There were great artists, but there were no great individuals such as Lorenzo de' Medici or Pope Julius II. In literature, as well as history, Venetians were not individualised. They were not well known for their eccentricities or for their triumphs. The comedies of Goldoni are the comedies of ordinary life; they are filled with the poetry of domestic fact and local intrigue, not the exploits or adventures or sensibilities of outstanding individuals or aberrant types. They reflect a benign social order. The people of Venice were always known for their docility. They might have been easily aroused to private passion, but they were always respectful to the authorities.

Burckhardt could never have written of Venice, as he once wrote of Florence, that "the individual was led to make the utmost of the exercise and enjoyment of power" and that the leaders of the people "acquired so marked a personal character." None of the doges or governors of Venice ever had a "personal character." The city had never been and could never have been a feudal state; feudalism was a system that sanctioned and maintained individual lordship. Machiavelli observed that the security and happiness of the city derived from the fact that, unlike any other state, its gentlemen did not have castles, or private armies, or retainers. Venice was "a great reputable work of joint human endeavour," Goethe wrote, "a splendid monument, not of a master, but of a people."

This was a matter of congratulation to the people themselves. Gasparo Contarini, in his book on the state and government of Venice published in 1547, remarked that "our ancestors, from whom we received so prosperous a commonwealth, all came together to maintain, honour and increase their country without any thought of personal glory or advantage." They remained anonymous in life and in death; their only memorial was the state itself. "Though these Venetian gentlemen are extraordinary wise when they are *conjunct*," James Howell wrote in the seventeenth century, "take them single they are but as other Men." The secret lay in their cohesiveness, one to another. Outside this context, these patricians had no identity; their private selves were taken up by their political selves. They were nothing without the state. With no "great men" Venice represents Tolstoy's dictum that human history is governed by a million different chances and interests, bound together by what can only be called a communal instinct. Each period is an unveiling of that instinct. The author is truly overwhelmed by the complexity of this process.

36

Moon and Night

The night and silence of Venice are profound. Moonlight can flood Saint Mark's Square. Venice is most characteristic at night. It has a quality of stillness that suits the mood of time preserved. Then it is haunted by what it loves—itself. The doorways seem darker than in any other city, lapped as they are by the black water. The little lamps still flicker before the statues of the Virgin on the corners of the *calli*. There are many kinds of night in Venice—the capacious blue of the summer night, and the fierce blackness of the winter night. The modern Venetians rarely seem to go out at night. There are no drunkards roaming through the street in the hours of the early morning. There are no raucous shouts. One contemporary acoustics engineer has measured the level of nocturnal sound in Venice at thirty-two decibels; the night of other cities is approximately thirteen decibels louder. There is no "background" noise.

In the second half of the thirteenth century a government agency was established known as the *signori di notte* or lords of the night who were obliged to safeguard public order under cover of darkness. The Venetian night seems to have been an object of suspicion. It contained the horror of unseen water, deep and dark, and of winding labyrinthine alleys. It is the time of assault and of subversion. The night was the time for the spy or the assassin. Night was the opportunity for secret groups, or even for the writing of graffiti on the walls of the city against the lawful government. For a city that prided itself upon its rational order and control, the night was an especial enemy. In decrees it was announced that there were many *pericula* or dangers in the night; there was always the risk of *"disordines et tumultationes"* or disorder and riot. Night was chaos. Night was threat. The night of Venice seemed to invoke the original blackness and silence of the lagoon, from which the city rose; the night was the memory of origin.

Yet the ubiquity of the Carnival in later centuries literally lightened the mood. In the eighteenth century the memoirs of Goldoni reveal a little world of night. The shops remained open until ten o'clock in the evening, many of them not finally closing their doors until midnight; at midnight, too, "all the taverns are open, and suppers are in preparation in every inn and hotel."

What, then, are the sounds of the night? The sound of the footfall echoes through this city of stone. Venice is a good acoustic instrument. There is the occasional chime. There is the sound of water lapping and slapping against stone as part of its everlasting movement. There may be a call upon the water, pure and resonant; still water carries the voice very far. The narrow streets can also act as funnels of sound. Then there is the scarcely discernible sound of the gondola. In the nineteenth century the more romantic travellers noted that there were times when music crept over the waters. Liszt, more perceptively, invoked the "silent noises" of the city; the murmur of the boat floating across the water is one of them.

There are always moments when silence seems to descend upon Venice. "Everywhere," Dickens wrote in *Pictures from Italy*, "the same extraordinary silence." For him it was the enforced silencing of modern life—no carriages, no wheels, no machinery. For many Victorian travellers the charm of Venice lay in its distance from modern industrialised civilisation. Two centuries before, John Evelyn had described Venice as "almost as silent as the middle of a field, there being neither rattling of coaches nor trampling of horses." Nor noise of cars. You may turn a corner, and come upon an area without sound. No other city still has so many pockets of silence. In Michael Dibdin's *Dead Lagoon*, the narrator declares that "such absolute, unqualified silence was troubling, as though some vital life function had ceased."

There was a dark side of Venice, a side that the night conceals. There were many poor, and many outcasts. Beggars have always been an aspect of Venetian life. In the late fifteenth century the senate discussed the problem of old men, and others, who lay each night in the precincts of the ducal palace. A "home" and a hospital were constructed. But they were not enough. At times of famine, as in the winter of 1527, the poor died against the pillars. Children stood in the market of the Rialto, or in the Square, crying out "I am dying of hunger! I am dying of hunger and cold!" One contemporary recorded that "the city stank with their odour." This is a measure of the intense confinement of urban living. And of course Venice could produce no food of its own.

In the early seventeenth century a new institution, the Ospedale dei Mendicanti, was erected to clear the streets and squares of the countless vagrants. All beggars in Venice were obliged to obtain a licence, and to lodge at the hospital; unlicensed beggars were expelled, and those who were reported to be too successful in their trade were consigned to the galleys. The owner of an unofficial beggars' lodging house was whipped all the way from Saint Mark's Square to the Rialto bridge.

Not all of them, however, found their way into the public haven. Effie Ruskin noted that in the evening "we see them all lying packed together at the edges of bridges, wrapped in their immense brown cloaks and large hoods." One Venetian patrician, Gasparo Contarini, was not sure if they were citizens of the Venetian republic or stray animals. Some families lived on rickety boats beside the quays. In the nineteenth century the palaces along the canal were converted into tenements, where the poor huddled. No pictorial view of Venice in that century was complete without the appearance of a picturesque vagrant, preferably young and female and pretty.

In the middle of the sixteenth century there were estimated to be six thousand beggars in the city. By the end of the eighteenth century that number had risen to twenty-two thousand. This was perhaps partly a reflection of the reputation of Venice as a centre for travellers; it has always been the case that beggars are more likely to find succour from foreigners. Mrs. Thrale described them as "saucy and airy and odd in their manners." She also noticed that they were treated by the Venetian people themselves with great softness and courtesy. An account of the Venetian beggars of the sixteenth century records their words. "I made the people think I was a madman." "I dressed up as a pilgrim and with an image of Saint James in my hand, I covered my face. I made piteous signs and gestures and the rich gave me money." They showed their wounds, their cancers and their ulcers in the public squares. There were familiar calls for succour. "Pity! Pity!" "I will pray for your life if you throw me a coin." "Give money for the blessed Virgin." The beggars came to Venice from many other cities. A list, dating from the summer of 1539, registers them from Milan, Sicily, Pisa and even France. In the twenty-first century, for example, old women and young men are to be found lying bowed on the bridges with their hands outstretched. Venice has been known as the haven for the outcast and the exile in every sense. Why should it not extend that courtesy to the genuinely dispossessed?

There is no dawn chorus of small birds in Venice. Yet as day breaks, the life of the city wakes from its silent slumber. Once more the traveller hears the rising voices, the whistles, the songs, the shouts, the pealing of bells. It is the morning of a human city. There is endless chatter in the air.

37

While the Music Lasts

Friedrich Nietzsche wrote, in *Ecce Homo*, that "when I seek another word for music, I always find only the word Venice." One evening in the city, in the late nineteenth century, Richard Wagner was being carried home on a gondola across the dark waters; his gondolier plied the oar when suddenly "from his mighty breast came a mournful sound not unlike the howl of an animal, swelling up from a deep, low note, and after a long-sustained 'Oh!' it culminated in the simple musical phrase, 'Venezia' . . ." So Venice is the music, while the music lasts.

In a guidebook to Venice, published in 1581, the city is celebrated as the seat of music, *la sede di musica*. It was the harmonious community, with an unrivalled tradition of sacred and secular music. The ducal orchestra played every day for an hour in Saint Mark's Square; throughout the centuries, that central space has always been filled with music. There were other street bands, as well as concert halls and choirs. All of the *sestieri* echoed with the sound of voices and of instruments. On Good Friday the members of each parish—the wine-sellers, the fishermen, the gondoliers—would sing out the long chant of the Twenty-Four Hours. This was nothing to do with church observance. It was the choice of the people themselves. Each guild had its own songs and melodies. There were popular choral societies. There were many *accademie*, or private societies, where amateur musicians performed. The inventories of middle-class Venetian households reveal the presence of string or keyboard instruments in most of them.

All the public festivities of the city were conducted to the sound of music. There were concert barges, moored in the Grand Canal and elsewhere, performing for the Venetian public and for visitors. An engraving of 1609 shows a host of musical entertainments upon the canal. Concerts were also given by virtuosi in private houses. Musicians were even employed in the gambling houses of the city. And there were always comic ballets at the time of the Carnival. One English traveller noted, in 1770, that "the people are so musical here, that all day long the houses send forth the most melodious sounds, which die off charmingly along the water." The presence of water invites song and music; there is something about its flow, and the sound of its flow, that elicits other melodies. So we read of "the solemn flow" of Venetian church music.

In the late eighteenth century Charles Burney remarked that the Venetian people seemed to converse in song. The gondoliers were notorious, if that is the word, for singing recitatives taken from the sixteenth-century poetry of Torquato Tasso. Yet these were laments, because the sadness of Venice entered its songs. Goethe has described how the women of the other islands of the lagoon, sitting on the seashore, would sing Tasso to their husbands fishing in the waters; the men would then reply in song, setting up a domestic conversation in music. Tasso was one of Venice's favourite sons, having lived in the city during his early youth; his father was a member of the Aldine circle.

There were also popular songs, known as *vilote*, sung by the women as they sat sewing or preparing food. These were often laments of love, concerning hopes and dreams and desires. The *vilote* were also danced out in the *campi* to the music of harpsichords. And of course there were the famous Venetian serenades, sung beneath the ubiquitous balconies to the accompaniment of the mandolin or the guitar. It could be said that the Venetians were infatuated with music. They loved love and they loved melody. It is reported that when the Byzantine exarch, Longinus, visited the city of the lagoons in 567 he was almost deafened by the sound of bells and musical instruments waiting to greet him.

So there are records of Venetian music from the earliest periods of its history. In 815 "Priest Giorgio of Venice" became so expert in the art of organ-building that he was said to be guided by *"mirifica arte."* Subsequently the organ-builders of Venice became famous throughout Europe. There are records of a singers' guild in the basilica of Saint Mark's from the beginning of the fourteenth century. A singing school for males was established there in 1403. Yet essentially the beginning of the sixteenth century initiated the long period when Venetian music took the palm. After the great expansion of its empire had ended, it aspired to other forms of supremacy. Venice was the home of the madrigal, invented in the city. It was the centre of church music. It was the capital of opera. There was scarcely a European composer of note who did not make his way to Venice—Scarlatti, Gluck, Mozart, Wagner, Handel, Mendelssohn, Monteverdi, Stravinsky, all visited the most serene city. Wagner and Monteverdi died there.

The masses in the churches, sustained by music and choir, lasted for many hours. Some passages of that sacred rite, particularly at the gradual and at the elevation of the host, were sustained by instrumental music so that people attended church as if they were visiting the concert hall. Instrumental music was also employed to suggest wordless prayer. What might be private, and intimate, becomes in Venice public and theatrical. The words of the songs for the heroes and heroines of the opera were altered to celebrate the male and female saints of the day; arias could be transformed into oratorios. Churches were in fact designed to be zones of sound. The church of the Incurabili, for example, was constructed as an oval space.

On one occasion in the 1750s five orchestras were deployed in the basilica of Saint Mark's under the direction of Baldassare Galuppi. In that church, too, there was a tradition of polyphony taken up by two or more choirs singing antiphonally or simultaneously to the accompaniment (if they were needed) of four organs. It was a divine machinery of sound, amplified by the labyrinthine acoustics of the space. It is not at all extraordinary that musical events were held there, on the afternoons of Sundays and of holidays. The nature of these "polychoral" events, in which opposing forces eventually achieve harmony, was uniquely suited to the bias of the Venetian state. The "echo" effects of polychoral music were not inimical, either, to a city of reflections upon water.

The orphan girls in the charitable institutions of the state were given an extensive and elaborate musical training, so that their concerts became the wonder of the age. These institutions, known as *ospedali*, became in essence musical conservatories where young girls learned how to sing, to play, and to compose new works. They also attracted the maestri of Venice as their instructors. Antonio Vivaldi, for example, was for four decades the musical master of the Ospedale della Pietà. The girls were situated in singing galleries, enclosed by wrought-iron grilles so that their voices and melodies might have come from unseen angelic powers. Charles Burney reported, in the summer of

1770, that "the girls played a thousand tricks in singing, particularly in the duets, where there was a trial of skill and natural powers, as to who could go highest, lowest, swell a note the longest, or run divisions with the greatest rapidity." Individual girls had their own cabals of admirers. The fact that they were orphaned only contributed to their power. But they were not nuns. Young men came to the *ospedali* with offers of marriage to those whose voices pleased them best. There was no sound of applause, in the churches of these institutions, but instead the audiences wept and prayed. There are reports of men and women fainting at the intensity of sound. Gondolas were moored in the adjacent canal, or *rio*, with their passengers straining to hear the sounds from within. Diverse observers, Rousseau and Goethe among them, have testified that these girls ravished and stupefied the senses. "I cannot imagine anything," Rousseau wrote, "so voluptuous, so touching as this music." This sensuousness strikes the right Venetian note.

The harmonies of Venice had another aspect. The ancients believed music to be the token of the ordered cosmos. Since Venice was the pre-eminent exponent of ordered governance in the world, it was only natural that music should emanate from it. It contained the music of the spheres. It partook of heaven and of earth. The gates of paradise had opened in the city. All the various forms of constitution—monarchy, oligarchy and republic—were moulded and mingled together. These were celestial harmonies, imparted by God. Even the merchants of Venice were educated in the rules of proportion, in mercantile textbooks such as *The Rule of Three* also known as *The Golden Rule* or *The Merchants' Key*. Pythagorean mathematics was an important feature of commerce. The architecture, or architexture, of the city was conceived harmoniously. If it is indeed true that buildings have been raised by the power of music, then the churches and noble houses of Venice have assuredly embodied the melody of the world. The architects of the day studied theories of harmony. In foreign policy the doge and senate strove to maintain a "balance" of powers; they strove for peace, it was said, because peace reflected harmony in every sense.

Just as in a sonata or concerto no one instrument must dominate the others, so in the Venetian state no one interest or authority could be allowed to influence the rest; all was of a piece. No one may rise too high, or fall too low. Nothing was out of proportion. The aim was perfect order. And that, to a large extent, and to the amazement of the rest of the world, was achieved. When the figure of Apollo was carved in a niche of the loggetta at the base of the campanile of Saint Mark's its sculptor, Jacopo Sansovino, declared that "it is known that this nation takes natural delight in music, and therefore Apollo is represented to signify music . . . extraordinary harmony perpetuates this admirable government."

The dances of the city, therefore, have some significance. The diaries of Venetians suggest that there was almost uninterrupted public dancing in the squares and courtyards of the city. In the noble houses, dancing in the ballroom was a favoured means of expression. There were "dances for women," events in which more than a hundred females might participate. There were scores of dancing schools, teaching "the Hat dance," "the Torch dance" and "the Hunt." Dances were performed on barges. They were an important aspect of the ubiquitous street theatre. So the movement of the spheres was reproduced in the streets of the city. In one painting by Gabriele Bella, "Festo dà Soldo in Campiello," a group of Venetians, male and female, are to be seen dancing in formal measures to the accompaniment of two violins and a cello. Their fellow citizens watch from the balconies, or from the neighbouring tavern, as the women twirl their aprons and the men raise their arms in the air. And of course the popular performances of the *commedia dell'arte* had their own frenzied dances, together with a litany of vulgar and satirical songs.

And then there is the nature of music as an expression of political life. Thus we may say that humankind comes into the world to maintain and to celebrate the structure into which it is born; there is a joy in formal order and display. There is a joy in the endless echoes and repetitions, so much like the governance of Venice. There is deep solace to be found in the experience of harmony where is heard the voice of tens of thousands rather than that of one. The music of Saint Mark's was under the direct control of the state procurators, an expression of the evident fact that Roman Catholicism had been transformed into a state Church. There was, or was supposed to be, a profound concord between faith and the city and the harmony of song. To put it more crudely, music became a form of political propaganda. The paintings and engravings of the various civic processions always depict the drums, the cymbals and the silver trumpets. Music then became a method of maintaining social order. Many Venetian operas used allegory to comment upon contemporary events, with Venice as the heroine of all encounters. Venice then became Venetia, the unassailable virgin holding sword and scales—"*ecco Venezia bella*"! In one production, *Il Bellerofonte*, an exact and elaborate model of the city arose from the sea to the accompaniment of music.

The painters of Venice were also devotees of music. Vasari seems to consider Tintoretto's musical skills, for example, as more worthy of praise than his painterly achievement. Veronese's "Wedding at Cana" shows a quartet playing to the invited guests; the members of that musical group have been identified as Titian, Tintoretto, Bassano and Veronese himself. Thus when Walter Pater, in his study of the Venetian artist Giorgione, suggested that "all art constantly aspires towards the condition of music" he was identifying one of the central tendencies of Venetian art. Pater adds that in the Venetian school following Giorgione "the perfect moments of music itself, the making or hearing of music, song or its accompaniment, are themselves prominent as subjects." Oil paint can be liquid music. So we read of Titian's "tonic harmonies" and "rhythmic movements," and of the "eager, quick tempo" of Lorenzo Lotto. The language of Tintoretto's composition seems invariably to be also the language of music. When we gaze upon the architectonic harmonies of Tiepolo, we hear the music of Vivaldi's violins energetic and triumphant. On the other side, there are references to Vivaldi's "delight in orchestral colour." In the language of the Venetian arts, music and painting seem to be twinned. In his painting known as "The Vision of Saint Augustine" Vittore Carpaccio, the great designator of Venetian scenes, depicts the saint in a musical universe; Augustine has written on sheets of music the notes for tenor and contralto, while at his feet lie works of music sacred and secular. The vision, then, is one of transcendent harmony.

The painting of music is a thoroughly Venetian art. There are many hundreds of paintings that show men and women holding musical instruments. The angels of Venetian religious painting are generally musicians; angel choruses are replaced by angel orchestras, but no other artistic tradition places so much emphasis on these images of celestial harmony. There are drawings of girls and boys singing; there are paintings of music being played by pools and by wells, as if the Venetian consonance between music and water was being endlessly celebrated. Titian was entranced by the spectacle of music-making and of concert scenes. Heard melodies are sweet, but those unheard are sweeter. Yet the music of Venice is the music of performance and of display. It is never the music of meditation or of sorrowful intro-spection. It relies upon improvisation and dramatic interpretation. Once more it is the love of surface, and the rich deployment of the effects of the surface, that define the Venetian sensibility. It is what is known as *coloratura*.

Yet Venice would not be Venice without the smell of trade as well as the sound of music. The city became the capital of music-publishing, and of instrument-making. There were many collections of instruments, designed for investment as much as display. The great Venetian composers can in another light be seen as very successful men of business. We may take the case of that quintessentially Venetian artist and violinist, Antonio Vivaldi. No one was more eager for commission and more avaricious for gain. He had the trading instinct in his blood. At one point he called himself *"un franco intraprenditore"* or candid businessman.

He was born a Venetian in 1678, and baptised at the parish church of S. Giovanni in Bragora. His father, Giambattista Vivaldi, was a musician in the basilica of Saint Mark's. It was here that Vivaldi himself began his training as a violinist. His father taught him the rudiments of the family profession. This was the Venetian tradition. At the age of fifteen he was received into the minor orders of the Church, and ten years later he was ordained as a priest. He became known as the *prete rosso* or red-haired priest, the red hair perhaps being an expression or indication of his fiery temperament. He had a prominent arched nose, pointed chin and large expressive eyes.

Vivaldi had a congenitally weak constitution, having been close to death as a premature baby, and he always needed assistants to help him travel. As he explained in a letter, written towards the end of his life:

> When I had just been ordained a priest, I still said mass for rather more than a year and then gave it up, because three times I was forced to leave the altar without finishing mass on account of my illness. For this reason I spend my life almost entirely at home, leaving my house only in a gondola or carriage, because with my chest complaint, known as heart seizure, I cannot walk. No nobleman invites me to his house, not even

our doge, because they all know of my ailment. I can usually leave the house immediately after breakfast but never on foot.

Yet this was the man who plunged himself into a relentless round of composition, administration and direction. He was quixotic and impulsive, by all accounts surrendering himself to the moods of the moment. Like his music he seems to have acquired some extraordinary internal energy from an unknown source of power. He was said by one English musician of the time, William Hayes, to have "too much mercury in his disposition"—which meant that he was impulsive and quixotic. He was, perhaps, a little eccentric. In 1704, at the age of twenty-six, he was appointed to the music school of the orphanage, the Ospedale della Pietà, and was music master there for most of his life. When he joined that institution he became a thorough master of all its music. He became teacher, director, and player. Nine years later he was appointed as the official composer of the *ospedale*. During those years his fame as a composer had increased, and spread throughout Europe. The king of Denmark, Frederick IV, made an especial visit to the *ospedale* to hear one of Vivaldi's oratorios.

Yet already his energy and determination were driving him in another direction. In the same year that he was appointed official composer, his first opera was staged in the city of Vicenza on the mainland of the Veneto. This was a prelude to the performance of his operas in Venice itself, where he quickly earned both popularity and income. For the rest of his life he divided his compositions between operatic and sacred work. The pursuit of profit was part of his purpose. He was in the habit of offering his works to foreign musicians, demanding very high prices. He marketed Venetian music in the same way that his contemporary, Canaletto, marketed Venetian views on commission to visiting tourists. He haggled over prices and costs. He decided not to publish his works, on the supposition that he could earn more money by selling the manuscripts. He discussed his finances with an English traveller, Edward Holdsworth, who reported that "he finds a good market because he expects a guinea for every piece."

In his operatic works he was an entrepreneur as well as a musician. He rented the theatre. He engaged the singers and the musicians. He chose the libretti. He conducted the orchestra and provided solo accompaniments on the violin. He had to respond to the demands of the public. If an opera were unsuccessful he found a replacement within a matter of days. Yet this supreme impresario was also a man of the cloth. The Venetian dramatist, Goldoni, recorded a visit to Vivaldi. "I found him surrounded by scores," he wrote, "his breviary in his hand. He rose, made the sign of the cross with broad gestures, put his breviary down . . ." This conflation of piety and business, of the sacred and the secular, seems so thoroughly Venetian as to need no further comment.

Yet all things in Venice were dependent upon fashion. A close friend of Vivaldi, Charles de Brosses, wrote in 1740 that "to my great surprise I found that he is not so highly regarded as he deserves to be in this country, where everything follows the trend of the moment." It was for this, and other reasons, that Vivaldi looked for patrons abroad. He journeyed to Vienna, and was about to travel on to Dresden when in 1741, at the age of sixty-three, he died. It was reported that after a life of excessive prodigality he died a pauper. Yet this may be the usual pious epilogue for a career of extravagant genius.

In his rapidity of execution, Vivaldi is thoroughly Venetian. He wrote more than five hundred instrumental works, and almost one hundred operas. He boasted that he could compose a concerto with all its parts "faster than a copyist could copy it." His playing, too, had the fire and energy of lightning. The German scholar, Zacharias von Uffenbach, attending one of Vivaldi's concerts, noted that he "quite confounded me, for such playing has not been heard before and can never be equalled. He placed his finger but a hair's breadth from the bridge so that there was hardly room for the bow. He played thus on all four strings, with imitations, and at an unbelievable speed." Von Uffenbach then commissioned Vivaldi to write for him some *concerti grossi*. Three days later, Vivaldi delivered ten of them. On the manuscript score of his opera, *Tito Manlio*, there is the inscription *"Musica del Vivaldi fatta in 5 giorni"*—music by Vivaldi, completed in five days.

In his manuscripts there is evidence of a tremendous force of conception and execution outstripping the ability of the hand to register it. There is such animation and rhythmic drive that the momentum is irresistible. The coloristic effects, the vivid impressionism, the shimmering harmonies, the fantastic ingenuity of Venetian music find their acme in Vivaldi. Any imitated pattern creates excitement.

Agitation creates excitement. Vivaldi is vivacity. Speed, of composition and of execution, is the key. The words used by his contemporaries were *"fierezza,"* fiery energy, and *"prestezza"* or rapidity. The melodic force is overwhelming. The impression is one of inexhaustibility.

He was also a man of the theatre, creating an environment of insistent and unrelenting sound for the expression of extravagant and violent feeling. His most famous work, *The Four Seasons*, is intensely expressive. It was a way of translating a pictorial and operatic genre into music. There is in fact in his art a thoroughly Venetian tendency to combine display with melody, so that he introduces operatic effects within his instrumental music and sustains his operas with the techniques of his *concerti*. The first page of the solo violin part of the "Spring" concerto resembles a composition by Mondrian; the notes seem to dance together. They arch and leap and soar in serried ranks. On his scores Vivaldi will scrawl down hurriedly *"spiritoso"* or *"allegro."*

Sometimes he will continue the notation for three or four pages; then pause; then cross it all out; then with the same vigour and rapidity begin all over again from the first notes. On occasions he would write out two movements for the same place, and then leave it to the interpreter or musicians to make their preference. He worked some-times so quickly that he forgot his original key. His writing became more abrupt and elliptical in the course of composition.

The same rush of genius, the same facility and prolixity, are evident through the history of Venetian culture. Tintoretto was well known for the ferocious energy of his artistic practice. He could paint the walls of a church, or the hall of a guild, within a week. In a later century Tiepolo was known for being able to finish a large canvas in ten hours. So in the music of Vivaldi there is a tremendous quickness and pressure, guided by a driving force and rhythmic impulse that astonished his contemporaries. It is as inexorable as fate. It rushes forward like the tides of the lagoon. What is the secret of this exuberance in the artists of Venice? It is joy. Joy in creation. It has to do with the fact of living in an harmonious city. Yet it is also the joy of living in unity with the culture and society that surrounded them. They were at home. The ground of their being was Venice itself.

Is it then possible to interpret the nature of Venetian music as an organic whole? It is marked by exuberance and spontaneity, a ferocious gaiety that is manifest in other forms of Venetian art. The most used and favoured word is brilliance. It has associations with the glitter of Venetian glass, and the glittering light upon the water. Yet Venetian music also has associations with the richness of colour and texture in Venetian art. We read of the brilliant "tone colours" and "chromatic phrases" associated with the musicians of Venice, as opposed to those of Naples or of Florence. The Venetian manuals of music written in the sixteenth and seventeenth centuries, rely largely upon expounding the arts of improvisation and ornamentation. Venetian music, therefore, is predominantly expressive. The temperamental affinities, to put it perhaps too crudely, are with show over substance. One German musicologist of the eighteenth century, contrasting Venetian melodies with Roman harmonies, remarked that "the Venetian makes its way to the ear more quickly, but its spell continues for a shorter time." The art of echo, already noticed in sacred polychoral music, was also an aspect of secular music. The Venetian sonata, for example, has been noticed for its marked contrapuntal effects.

The music of Venice has a certain sweetness. It was often light and clear. In that sense it could be suggested that it contains little interior life. There could be no Beethoven in Venice. It has an irresistible flow. It has the rhythm of the sea, not of the wheel. It provokes astonishment and admiration rather than contemplation. Yet it could also be unruly and abrupt, with sudden and unexpected turns both in melody and in harmony. It is often eccentric or extravagant. It sometimes relishes strangeness, or what were known as *bizzarria*. It has an eastern flavour. It can even be claimed that, through the agency of Venice, the music of the East entered the classical European tradition. Venetian music is sustained by constant and subtle variation. It favours contrast and intricacy; it can be fast, and florid. It perfectly suits the genius of the virtuoso. It has been suggested that the solo concerto was first heard in Venice. It may be possible, then, to define the nature of this music as an expression of the Venetian temperament; Stendhal remarked that "the glittering reflection of the Venetian character falls across the texture of Venetian music." The process of transmission and inheritance has never properly been understood, except in the evident relish of a language that describes art and character in identical terms. And so we have the words—vivacity, gaiety, radiance, extravagance, energy, buoyancy, spontaneity, urgency, facility, exuberance, impetuosity. Oh! Venezia!

A Venetian Chronology

FOURTH, FIFTH AND SIXTH CENTURIES AD

The Veneti tribe leave the Italian mainland for the islands to escape successive waves of barbarian invaders. The islands form part of the Byzantine Empire.

421: The legendary founding of Venice. The real date of the city's foundation is probably over a century later.

446: The Veneti meet at Grado and establish the rule of a tribune.

568: Torcello founded.

SEVENTH CENTURY

Early: The basilica of S. Maria Assunta is built at Torcello.

697: The first doge of Venice, Paoluccio Anafesto, is elected by the people.

EIGHTH CENTURY

Byzantine domination of northern Italy is ended by barbarian invasions.

NINTH CENTURY

Beginning: The original palace of the doge is constructed in the area now known as Saint Mark's Square.

810: Pepin unsuccessfully attempts to claim the islands for the Frankish empire.

825: The area of Saint Mark's Square is completed.

828: The body of Saint Mark is brought from Alexandria to Venice. Saint Mark replaces Saint Theodore as patron of the city.

TENTH CENTURY

900: The lagoons are fortified.

928: The first mention of a Venetian glass-maker.

ELEVENTH CENTURY

End: Venice establishes itself as an autonomous state and a maritime republic. It develops into a strong naval power and builds an empire in the East, seizing the eastern shores of the Adriatic before 1200, and capturing many of the islands in the Aegean, including Cyprus and Crete.

The Venetian Carnival is instituted.

TWELFTH CENTURY

1100: Venice participates in the First Crusade.

Early: The Arsenal is constructed.

1167: The first public loans are issued in Venice.

1171: Two great columns, one surmounted by Saint Theodore and the other by a lion, are erected in Saint Mark's Square.

1178: Venice takes control of the Brenner Pass from Verona, and establishes an extensive empire on the Italian mainland or *terra firma* over the next four centuries.

Late: The earliest surviving mention of a gondola.

The great council, comprised exclusively of aristocratic families, is established. It elects the doge and the senate.

THIRTEENTH CENTURY

1203–4: Venice plays a major role in the assault and sacking of Constantinople. It brings home the four horses of the triumphal Quadriga. Venice dominates trade throughout the Byzantine Empire.

1229: Venetian laws are codified.

1242: The first jousts are recorded in Saint Mark's Square.

1270: The earliest reference to private banks.

1284–5: The first gold ducat is issued; the Mint is founded.

1298: The imprisoned Marco Polo narrates his voyages in foreign lands to an amanuensis.

FOURTEENTH CENTURY

1310: The judicial committee known as the council of ten is created. It is elected by the senate, and made permanent in 1335.

1348: Plague in the city.

1380: The long war between Venice and Genoa, which had continued intermittently for a century, ends with a Venetian victory.

FOURTEENTH TO FIFTEENTH CENTURIES
Venice is at the height of its military and naval power.

FIFTEENTH CENTURY
1421: The construction of the Ca d'Oro begins.
1422: The old palace of the doge is replaced by a Renaissance palace in Saint Mark's Square.
1462: War breaks out between the Venetian and Turkish empires; it ends in 1479 when the Venetians sue for peace. This signals the beginning of the end of Venetian power in the East. Gradually Venice ceases to dominate trade in the area.
1495: The publisher Aldus Manutius establishes a workshop in Venice for the production of texts in Greek, Latin and Hebrew.

SIXTEENTH CENTURY
1516: The Jewish ghetto is established in Canareggio.
1519: The birth of Tintoretto.
1527: After the sack of Rome by barbarian invaders, Venice offers a haven to countless Roman artists and intellectuals.
1527: Jacopo Sansovino, a refugee from Rome, is appointed public architect. He designs the Mint, the Library, the loggia of the campanile, and part of the Rialto market. He also transforms Saint Mark's Square into a classical piazza.
1565: The first European theatre, built specifically for the production of plays, is constructed in Venice.
1570: Venice loses Cyprus to the Turks.
1585: Beginning of the construction of the Rialto bridge.

SEVENTEENTH CENTURY
1618: The failure of the "Spanish Plot" to destroy many important political buildings in the city.
1637: The world's first public opera house is created in Venice.
1669: Venice loses Crete to the Turks.
1678: Vivaldi is born.
1696: Tiepolo is born.

EIGHTEENTH CENTURY

Venice becomes the city of art and pleasure.

1725: Casanova is born.

1774: The greatest Venetian gambling house is closed by public order.

1797: Venice falls to Napoleon, who hands the city over to the Austrians. The doge is deposed and the Venetian republic ceases to exist.

NINETEENTH CENTURY

1805: Napoleon defeats the Austrians and reclaims the city.

1814: The Austrians reclaim Venice.

1848: The Venetians oust the Austrians from the city and re-establish the republic of Venice.

1849: The Austrians reoccupy the city and the republic falls.

1854: The Accademia Bridge is constructed.

1866: The Austrians withdraw from Venice and the city becomes part of the newly established kingdom of Italy.

End: The Lido becomes a popular beach resort.

1895: The first international exhibition is organised. It soon becomes known as the "Biennale."

TWENTIETH CENTURY

1902: The campanile of Saint Mark's Square falls.

1917: Venice, as part of the Italian alliance with Britain and Russia in the First World War, is once again menaced by Austrian forces.

1943: German forces take over the city.

1966: The year of the great flood.

1996: Venice's most famous opera house, La Fenice, burns down.

Bibliography

Appadurai, Arjun: *The Social Life of Things* (Cambridge, 1986).

Arslan, Edoardo: *Gothic Architecture in Venice* (London, 1972).

Baldauf-Berdes, Jane L.: *Women Musicians of Venice* (Oxford, 1993).

Barbaro, Paolo: *Venice Revealed* (London, 2002).

Baron, Hans: *Humanistic and Political Literature in Florence and Venice* (Cambridge, 1955).

—— *The Crisis of the Early Italian Renaissance* (Princeton, 1966).

Bassnett, Susan (trans.): *The Flame of Gabriele D'Annunzio* (London, 1991).

Berendt, John: *The City of Falling Angels* (London, 2005).

Berenson, Bernard: *The Venetian Painters of the Renaissance* (New York, 1901).

—— *Lorenzo Lotto* (London, 1956).

Berkeley, G.F.H.: *Italy in the Making*, 2 volumes (Cambridge, 1940).

Bolt, Rodney: *Lorenzo Da Ponte* (London, 2006).

Bouwsma, William J.: *Venice and the Defence of Republican Liberty* (London, 1968).

Braudel, Fernand: *Civilisation and Capitalism*, 3 volumes (London, 1984).

Brion, Marcel: *Venice* (London, 1962).

Brown, Horatio F.: *Venice, An Historical Sketch* (London, 1893).

—— *Studies in the History of Venice* (London, 1907).

—— *Life in the Lagoons* (London, 1909).

Brown, Patricia Fortini: *Venetian Narrative Painting in the Age of Carpaccio* (New Haven, 1988).

—— *Venice and Antiquity* (New Haven, 1996).

Bull, George: *Venice* (London, 1980).

Burckhardt, Jacob: *The Civilisation of the Renaissance in Italy* (Oxford, 1945).

Burke, Peter: *Venice and Amsterdam* (London, 1974).

Cairns, Christopher: *Domenico Bollani* (Nieuwkoop, 1976).

—— *Pietro Aretino and the Republic of Venice* (Florence, 1985).

Calimani, Riccardo: *The Ghetto of Venice* (New York, 1987).

—— *Storie di Marrani a Venezia* (Milan, 1991).

Chambers, D.S.: *The Imperial Age of Venice* (London, 1970).

Chambers, David and Pullan, Brian (eds): *Venice, A Documentary History* (Oxford, 1992).

Chojnacka, Monica: *Working Women of Early Modern Venice* (Baltimore, 2001).

Chojnacki, Stanley: *Women and Men in Renaissance Venice* (Baltimore, 2000).

Cole, Bruce: *The Renaissance Artist At Work* (London, 1983).

Concina, Ennio: *A History of Venetian Architecture* (Cambridge, 1998).

Crawford, F. Marion: *Gleanings from Venetian History*, 2 volumes (London, 1905).

Crouzet-Pavan, Elisabeth: *Venice Triumphant* (Baltimore, 2002).

Da Mosto, Francesco: *Francesco's Venice* (London, 2004).

Datta, Satya: *Women and Men in Early Modern Venice* (Aldershot, 2003).

Davia, James C.: *A Venetian Family and Its Fortune* (Philadelphia, 1975).

Davis, Robert C.: *The War of the Fists* (New York, 1994).

Davis, Robert C. and Marvin, Garry M.: *Venice, The Tourist Maze* (Berkeley, 2004).

Demus, Otto: *Studies in Byzantium, Venice and the West*, 2 volumes (London, 1998).

Dotson, John E. (ed.): *Merchant Culture in Fourteenth-Century Venice* (New York, 1994).

Douglas, Mary and Isherwood, Baron: *The World of Goods* (London, 1979).

Eisler, Benita: *Byron* (New York, 1999).

Eisler, Colin: *The Genius of Jacopo Bellini* (London, 1988).

Fehl, Philipp P.: *Decorum and Wit: The Poetry of Venetian Painting* (Vienna, 1992).

Fei, Alberto Toso: *Venetian Legends and Ghost Stories* (Treviso, 2004).

Feldman, Martha: *City Culture and the Madrigal at Venice* (Berkeley, 1995).

Fenlon, Iain (ed.): *The Renaissance* (London, 1989).

Ferraro, Joanne M.: *Family and Public Life in Brescia* (Cambridge, 1993).

—— *Marriage Wars in Late Renaissance Venice* (Oxford, 2001).

Finlay, Robert: *Politics in Renaissance Venice* (London, 1980).

Flagg, Edmund: *Venice, City of the Sea*, 2 volumes (London, 1853).

Fletcher, Caroline and Da Mosto, Jane: *The Science of Saving Venice* (Turin, 2004).

Geanakoplos, Deno John: *Greek Scholars in Venice* (Cambridge, 1962).

Georgopoulou, Maria: *Venice's Mediterranean Colonies* (Cambridge, 2001).

Gilbert, Felix: *The Pope, His Banker, and Venice* (London, 1980).

Gleason, Elizabeth G.: *Gasparo Contarini* (Berkeley, 1993).

Glixon, Jonathan: *Honouring God and the City* (Oxford, 2003).

Goffen, Rona: *Piety and Patronage in Renaissance Venice* (New Haven, 1986).

—— *Titian's Women* (New Haven, 1997).

Goldthwaite, Richard A.: *Wealth and the Demand for Art in Italy* (Baltimore, 1993).

Goy, Richard: *Venice, The City and Its Architecture* (London, undated).

—— *Venetian Vernacular Architecture* (Cambridge, 1989).

Grundy, Milton: *Venice* (London, 1980).

Guiton, Shirley: *No Magic Eden* (London, 1972).

—— *A World By Itself* (London, 1977).

Hale, J.R. (ed.): *Renaissance Venice* (London, 1973).

Halsby, Julian: *Venice, The Artist's Vision* (London, 1990).

Hart, Henry H.: *Venetian Adventurer, Marco Polo* (New York, 1947).

Hazlitt, W. Carew: *The Venetian Republic*, 2 volumes (London, 1900).

Heller, Karl: *Anthony Vivaldi* (Portland, 1991).

Hewison, Robert: *Ruskin in Venice* (Venice, 1983).

Hibbert, Christopher: *Venice* (London, 1988).

Hills, Paul: *Venetian Colour* (New Haven, 1999).

Hodgson, F.C.: *The Early History of Venice* (London, 1901).

—— *Venice in the Thirteenth and Fourteenth Centuries* (London, 1910).

Howard, Deborah: *Venice and the East* (New Haven, 2000).

—— *Jacopo Sansovino* (New Haven, 1987).

Howells, W.D.: *Venetian Life* (New York, 1866).

Humfrey, Peter: *Painting in Renaissance Venice* (New Haven, 1995).

Huse, Norbert and Wolters, Wolfgang: *The Art of Renaissance Venice* (Chicago, 1990).

Hutton, Edward: *Venice and Venetia* (London, 1911).

Jardine, Lisa: *Worldly Goods* (London, 1996).

Jepson, Tim: *Explorer Venice* (London, 2001).

Keahey, John: *Venice Against the Sea* (New York, 2002).

Keates, Jonathan: *The Siege of Venice* (London, 2005).

Kedar, Benjamin Z.: *Merchants in Crisis* (New Haven, 1976).

Kendall, Alan: *Vivaldi* (London, 1978).

Kittell, Ellen E. and Madden, Thomas F. (eds): *Medieval and Renaissance Venice* (Chicago, 1999).

Kolneder, Walter: *Antonio Vivaldi* (London, 1970).

Lane, Frederic Chapin: *Andrea Barbarigo* (New York, 1967).

—— *Venice, A Maritime Republic* (Baltimore, 1973).

—— *Venetian Ships and Shipbuilders* (Baltimore, 1992).

Larner, John: *Italy, 1290–1420* (London, 1971).

Lauritzen, Peter: *Venice* (London, 1978).

Laven, David: *Venice and Venetia under the Habsburgs* (London, 2002).

Laven, Mary: *Virgins of Venice* (London, 2002).

Lepschy, Anna Laura: *Tintoretto Observed* (Ravenna, 1983).

Levey, Michael: *Painting in Eighteenth-Century Venice* (London, 1959).

Lieberman, Ralph: *Renaissance Architecture in Venice* (London, 1982).

Links, J.G.: *Venice for Pleasure* (London, 1966).

Littlewood, Ian: *A Literary Companion to Venice* (London, 1991).

Logan, Oliver: *Culture and Society in Venice* (London, 1972).

Longworth, Philip: *The Rise and Fall of Venice* (London, 1974).

Lorenzetti, Giulio: *Venice and Its Lagoon* (Trieste, 1975).

Lovell, Margaretta M.: *A Visitable Past* (Chicago, 1989).

Lowry, Martin: *The World of Aldus Manutius* (Oxford, 1979).

Lowe, Alfonso: *La Serenissima* (London, 1974).

Macadam, Alta: *City Guide to Venice* (London, 2001).

Machen, Arthur (trans.): *The Memoirs of Jacques Casanova*, 2 volumes (New York, undated).

Mackenney, Richard: *Tradesmen and Traders* (New York, 1987).

—— *Renaissances* (London, 2005).

Martin, John Jeffries: *Venice's Hidden Enemies* (Baltimore, 2003).

Martin, John and Romano, Dennis (eds): *Venice Reconsidered* (Baltimore, 2000).

Martineau, Jane and Hope, Charles (eds): *The Genius of Venice, 1500–1600* (London, 1983).

McAndrew, John: *Venetian Architecture of the Early Renaissance* (London, 1980).

McCarthy, Mary: *Venice Observed* (London, 1961).

McNeil, William H.: *Venice, The Hinge of Europe* (Chicago, 1974).

McPherson, David C.: *Shakespeare, Jonson and the Myth of Venice* (London, 1990).

Miller, Daniel: *Material Culture and Mass Consumption* (Oxford, 1987).

Milliken, William Mathewson: *Unfamiliar Venice* (Cleveland, 1967).

Molmenti, Pompeo: *Venice*, 6 volumes (Bergamo, 1908).

Morand, Paul: *Venises* (Paris, 1971).

Morris, Jan: *Venice* (London, 1960).

—— *The Venetian Empire* (London, 1980).

—— *A Venetian Bestiary* (London, 1982).

Muir, Edward: *Civic Ritual in Renaissance Venice* (Princeton, 1981).

Mukerji, Chandra: *From Graven Images* (New York, 1983).

Mumford, Lewis: *The City in History* (London, 1961).

Musu, Ignazio (ed.): *Sustainable Venice* (Dordrecht, 2001).

Newton, Eric: *Tintoretto* (London, 1952).

Newton, Stella Mary: *The Dress of the Venetians, 1495–1525* (Aldershot, 1988).

Nichol, Tom: *Tintoretto* (London, 1999).

Nicol, Donald M.: *Byzantium and Venice* (Cambridge, 1988).

Norwich, John Julius: *Venice, the Greatness and the Fall* (London, 1981).
—— *Venice, Paradise of Cities* (London, 2004).
—— *The Middle Sea* (London, 2006).
Okey, Thomas: *The Story of Venice* (London, 1907).
—— *Old Venetian Palaces* (London, 1907).
Oliphant, Margaret: *The Makers of Venice* (London, 1905).
Oreglia, Giacomo: *The Commedia dell'Arte* (New York, 1968).
Pater, Walter: *The Renaissance* (London, 1873).
Pemble, John: *Venice Rediscovered* (London, 1995).
Pertot, Gianfranco: *Venice, Extraordinary Maintenance* (London, 2004).
Pfister, Manfred and Schaff, Manfred (eds): *Venetian Views, Venetian Blinds* (Amsterdam, 1999).
Pike, Ruth: *Enterprise and Adventure* (New York, 1966).
Pincherle, Marc: *Vivaldi* (London, 1958).
Pirrotta, Nino: *Music and Culture in Italy* (Cambridge, 1984).
Plant, Margaret: *Venice, Fragile City* (New Haven, 2002).
Pullan, Brian: *Rich and Poor in Renaissance Venice* (London, 1971).
—— *A History of Early Renaissance Italy* (London, 1973).
—— *The Jews of Europe and the Inquisition of Venice* (London, 1983).
—— *Poverty and Charity* (Aldershot, 1994).
Putnam, Samuel (ed.): *The Works of Aretino* (New York, undated).
Queller, Donald E.: *The Venetian Patriciate* (Illinois, 1986).
Quill, Sarah: *Ruskin's Venice* (Aldershot, 2000).
Rapp, Richard Tilden: *Industry and Economic Decline in Seventeenth Century Venice* (London, 1976).
Redford, Bruce: *Venice and the Grand Tour* (New Haven, 1996).
Robertson, Alexander: *Venetian Sermons* (London, 1905).
Robbins, H.C. and Norwich, John Julius: *Five Centuries of Music in Venice* (London, 1991).
Romano, Dennis: *Patricians and Popolani* (Baltimore, 1987).
—— *Housecraft and Statecraft* (Baltimore, 1996).
Rosand, David: *Painting in Sixteenth-Century Venice* (Cambridge, 1997).
—— *Myths of Venice* (London, 2001).
Rosenthal, Margaret F.: *The Honest Courtesan* (Chicago, 1992).
Roth, Cecil: *Venice* (Philadelphia, 1930).
Rowdon, Maurice: *The Silver Age of Venice* (New York, 1970).
—— *The Fall of Venice* (London, 1970).
Ruggiero, Guido: *Violence in Early Renaissance Venice* (New Brunswick, 1980).
—— *The Boundaries of Eros* (New York, 1985).
—— *Binding Passions* (Oxford, 1993).

Runciman, Steven: *Byzantine Civilisation* (London, 1933).

—— *Byzantine Style and Civilisation* (London, 1975).

Ruskin, John: *The Stones of Venice* (London, 1851–3).

Schulz, Juergen: *The New Palaces of Medieval Venice* (University Park, Pennsylvania, 2004).

Schutte, Anne Jacobson: *Aspiring Saints* (Baltimore, 2001).

Sekora, John: *Luxury* (Baltimore, 1977).

Selfridge-Field, Eleanor: *Venetian Instrumental Music* (London, 1994).

Smith, Logan Pearsall (ed.): *The Life and Letters of Sir Henry Wotton*, 2 volumes (Oxford, 1907).

Smith, Pamela H. and Findlen, Paula (eds): *Merchants and Marvels* (New York, 2002).

Sombart, Werner: *Luxury and Capitalism* (Michigan, 1967).

Sperling, Jutta Gisela: *Convents and the Body Politic in Late Renaissance Venice* (Chicago, 1999).

Steer, John: *A Concise History of Venetian Painting* (London, 1970).

Stokes, Adrian: *Stones of Rimini* (London, 1934).

—— *Venice, An Aspect of Art* (London, 1945).

Symonds, Margaret: *Days Spent on a Doge's Farm* (London, 1908).

Tafuri, Manfredo: *Venice and the Renaissance* (Cambridge, 1995).

Talbot, Michael: *Vivaldi* (London, 1979).

Tanner, Tony: *Venice Desired* (Cambridge, 1992).

Thayer, William Roscoe: *A Short History of Venice* (Boston, 1908).

White, Jonathan: *Italy, The Enduring Culture* (London, 2000).

Wiel, Alethea: *Venice* (London, 1894).

Wilde, Johannes: *Venetian Art from Bellini to Titian* (Oxford, 1974).

Wills, Garry: *Venice, Lion City* (New York, 2001).

Wilson, Bee: *The Hive* (London, 2004).

Wind, Edgar: *Bellini's Feast of the Gods* (Cambridge, 1948).

Worsthorne, Simon Towneley: *Venetian Opera in the Sixteenth Century* (Oxford, 1954).

Zucconi, Guido: *Venice, An Architectural Guide* (Verona, 1993).

Index

Acknowledgements

I would like to thank my two research assistants, Thomas Wright and Murrough O'Brien, for their invaluable work on this project. I would also like to extend my thanks to my editor, Jenny Uglow, and my copy-editor, Jenny Overton.